Imperial Metropolis

The David J. Weber Series in the New Borderlands History

Andrew R. Graybill and Benjamin H. Johnson, *editors*

EDITORIAL BOARD
Juliana Barr
Sarah Carter
Kelly Lytle Hernández
Cynthia Radding
Samuel Truett

The study of borderlands—places where different peoples meet and no one polity reigns supreme—is undergoing a renaissance. The David J. Weber Series in the New Borderlands History publishes works from both established and emerging scholars that examine borderlands from the precontact era to the present. The series explores contested boundaries and the intercultural dynamics surrounding them and includes projects covering a wide range of time and space within North America and beyond, including both Atlantic and Pacific worlds.

Published with support provided by the William P. Clements Center for Southwest Studies at Southern Methodist University in Dallas, Texas.

Imperial Metropolis
Los Angeles, Mexico, and the Borderlands of American Empire, 1865–1941

....

JESSICA M. KIM

The University of North Carolina Press Chapel Hill

© 2019 The University of North Carolina Press
All rights reserved
Set in Charis and Lato by Westchester Publishing Services

The University of North Carolina Press has been a member of the Green Press Initiative since 2003.

Library of Congress Cataloging-in-Publication Data
Names: Kim, Jessica, author.
Title: Imperial metropolis : Los Angeles, Mexico, and the borderlands of American empire, 1865–1941 / Jessica Kim.
Other titles: David J. Weber series in the new borderlands history.
Description: Chapel Hill : University of North Carolina Press, [2019] | Series: The David J. Weber series in the new borderlands history | Includes bibliographical references and index.
Identifiers: LCCN 2018052925 | ISBN 9781469651347 (cloth : alk. paper) | ISBN 9781469666242 (pbk. : alk. paper) | ISBN 9781469651354 (ebook)
Subjects: LCSH: Los Angeles (Calif.)—Economic conditions—19th century. | Los Angeles (Calif.)—Economic conditions—20th century. | Los Angeles (Calif.)—Relations—Mexico. | Mexico—Relations—California—Los Angeles. | Mexico—History—Revolution, 1910–1920—Economic aspects. | United States—Territorial expansion—Economic aspects.
Classification: LCC HC108.L55 K56 2019 | DDC 330.9794/9405—dc23
LC record available at https://lccn.loc.gov/2018052925

Cover illustrations: Front, detail of photo of Automobile Club staff and board members meeting with Mexican official in Los Angeles, 1930 (courtesy of Huntington Library, San Marino, © Automobile Club of Southern California Archives); back, detail of photo of mill construction at the Bradbury mine in Sinaloa, 1908 (courtesy of Special Collections, UC Davis Library, Bradbury Family Papers D-449).

Chapter six was previously published in a different form as "Destiny of the West: The International Pacific Highway and the Pacific Borderlands, 1929–1957," *Western Historical Quarterly* 46, no. 3 (Autumn 2015): 311–34.

For my parents, Nancy and Wonil

Contents

Acknowledgments, xi

Introduction, 1
City-Empire

1 Pueblo, City, Empire, 21

2 Organizing Capital and Controlling Race and Labor, 48

3 Revolution around the Corner and across the Border, 77

4 Like Cuba and the Philippines, 111

5 Against Capital and Foreigners, 142

6 Highway for the Hemisphere, 176

Epilogue, 205
Global City

Appendix. List of Companies Incorporated in Los Angeles County to Conduct Business in Mexico, 1886–1931, 215

Notes, 225

Bibliography, 255

Index, 269

Illustrations, Map, Table

Illustrations

Interior of the Bradbury Building, 2

Mill construction at the Bradbury mine in Mexico, 3

Griffith Park and Observatory, 4

Bankers and railroad executives in front of a special train chartered from Los Angeles to Calexico, 22

Harrison Gray Otis on a hunting trip in Mexico, 55

Los Angeles bankers and railroad men in the Imperial Valley, 59

Doheny greenhouse, 72

Quimichis Colony investors and managers at lunch, 78

Quimichis workers, 88

The Lopez family, 163

Harry Chandler and President Álvaro Obregón in Baja California, 165

Route of the International Pacific Highway, 177

International Pacific Highway outdoor luncheon, 187

International Pacific Highway promoters, 193

Map

Los Angeles–based investments in Mexico, 1865–1941, xvi

Table

Los Angeles population, 1850–1930, 29

Acknowledgments

Writing a book often feels solitary, but it is a family and community endeavor. A network of supportive colleagues and mentors and loving family members made thousands of hours of research and writing possible. I am so happy to finally be able to thank them all for over ten years of sage advice and steadfast encouragement.

I want to start by thanking William Deverell for his kind and consistent guidance and enthusiastic support of this project, even in its earliest iterations. He saw something promising in a very shy graduate student with an unconventional academic background, and I am eternally grateful for it. Bill embodies what it means to be a generous scholar and thoughtful mentor, and it continues to be a great pleasure to work with him. His intellectual imprint is also deeply woven into this project. The Huntington-USC Institute on California and the West also shaped this project in innumerable positive ways, including funding a very memorable summer of research in Mexico City and a year of postdoctoral study. Other faculty and mentors while I was at the University of Southern California also provided invaluable mentorship and shaped this project in important ways, especially María Elena Martínez, Laura Pulido, and George Sánchez. María Elena's presence in this world is deeply missed, and I thought of her often as I grappled with revisions and the meaning of the Mexican Revolution. Additional faculty and staff at USC also provided invaluable support over the course of my graduate career, including Richard Fox, Peter Mancall, Terry Seip, Sandra Hopwood, Laverne Hughes, and Lori Rogers. Two additional historians were instrumental in getting me to graduate school in the first place. Cheryl Koos probably did not realize she was signing up for a lifelong job as a mentor when she first encountered me as an undergraduate in 1996. For over twenty years she has taught me through example and kind words how to be a historian, a teacher, and a mentor. The work of someone we both loved very much, Clark Davis, also inspired this project. I miss his brilliant mind and gentle spirit and hope that this book reflects, in some small way, that his legacy continues through his students.

When I made the transition from graduate student to academic colleague, I was lucky to find a home in the History Department at California State University, Northridge. Colleagues in this department are full of warmth, good humor, and a healthy skepticism of academic bureaucracy. The mentorship and friendship of many, including Thomas Devine, Susan Fitzpatrick-Behrens, Richard Horowitz, Patricia Juarez-Dappe, Merry Ovnick, and Josh Sides, make life at CSUN rewarding and fun. I want to thank Josh in particular, for often lending a supportive ear and for reading and giving feedback on the manuscript in its entirety. I also want to thank the other "junior" faculty who helped me navigate the early years of an academic career—John Paul Nuño and Jeffrey Kaja. Nothing, and I mean nothing, is possible without outstanding administrative staff. Susan Mueller, Pepper Starobin, and Kelly Winkleblack-Shea are the finest. Finally, a number of research grants from the university and the College of Social and Behavioral Sciences allowed me to carve out the time to finish this book.

Other colleagues in academia supported this project in many ways. I want to give a very special thanks to the members of my writing group—Genevieve Carpio, Sara Fingal, and Priscilla Leiva. They read every chapter of this book multiple times and gave good counsel on history, writing, and living life gracefully as academics. Dear friends in the profession, from graduate school and beyond, also contributed to this project and to making life in academia a more welcoming place. Many thanks to Verónica Castillo-Muñoz, Sarah Keyes, Elizabeth Logan, Andie Reid, and Raphaelle Steinzig. Marc Rodriguez helps to demystify academia and provided valuable feedback on portions of this book. I would also like to thank my former student and research assistant, David Vázquez. David provided invaluable help in tracking down sources in Mexico and is a scholar with his own exciting project on labor in the U.S.-Mexico borderlands.

Other historians, colleagues, and institutions gave generously to this project. The smart and funny editor of this series, Benjamin Johnson, helped me better understand borderlands and saw potential in my research and writing, even in their roughest form. His enthusiasm for this project came at a crucial moment and helped me see it through to completion. I also appreciate the very thoughtful editors and staff at the University of North Carolina Press, including Andrew Graybill, Chuck Grench, Cate Hodorowicz, and Dylan White. The anonymous readers also made substantive and constructive suggestions that made this a much stronger book. I appreciate the time and thought they put into considering its arguments and merit. A number of archivists were also instrumental in this project, including Peter Blodgett, Matt Roth, Jill Thrasher, and Paul Wormser. Funding from the Huntington Library, the National Endowment for the Humanities, the Society for Historians of American Foreign Relations, and the University of Southern California also supported research and writing for this project.

Dear friends sprinkled across greater Los Angeles nurtured me through graduate school and continue to make this city my favorite place in the world. An Le and Vy Nguyen are some of the kindest people I know, and I so admire their decades of work to make Los Angeles more livable for all. Patricia Hanson, my partner in so many eclectic Los Angeles adventures, makes living and teaching here an exciting journey. Jazmín Ochoa can make me laugh like no one else and generously edited every chapter of this book. My roommate through all of graduate school, Pablo Morgana, knows firsthand what a blindingly stressful experience it was and was always incredibly supportive. Gabriela Martinez has been my intellectual and political soul mate since college and inspires me to think harder and more critically. Bich Tram has been part of this journey since high school and is the most caring person I know. She knows what you need before you realize it yourself.

My family deserves the greatest thanks. My parents-in-law, Steve and Karen Cottingham, have given warm and generous support over the past nine years. My talented sister, Johanna, read and edited many a funding proposal and chapter, always with good humor. My brother, Elliott, reminds me through his own work that social justice is not just about the past but also about the present and the future. Throughout the course of my life my wonderful parents, Nancy and Wonil, have taught me through example how to engage the world with curiosity, humility, and compassion. The quiet pride on their faces when I accomplish something, no matter how small, makes the hard work feel worthwhile. From the moment we met, my husband and partner, Joshua Cottingham, has believed in me more than I believe in myself. His enthusiasm for everything I do is an unparalleled gift. The other great gift in my life we enjoy together—Leon Belafonte—who daily lights up our lives with his pure and unencumbered toddler joy.

Imperial Metropolis

Locations of Los Angeles–based investments in Mexico, 1865–1941 (drawn by David Deis). Source: Data from incorporation records of approximately 150 companies incorporated in Los Angeles County to do business in Mexico between 1886 and 1931. Seaver Center for Western History Research, Natural History Museum of Los Angeles County.

Introduction
City-Empire

· ·

At the diminutive population of 50,000 people, Los Angeles in 1890 had more in common with Des Moines or Saginaw than with New York or Chicago. A dozen blocks bustled with commercial activity before giving way to a number of residential streets and wood-framed homes. Beyond that, a small river, farmland, and open space. The famous Bradbury Building, inspired by Edward Bellamy's renowned novel *Looking Backward* and its utopian vision for the future, may have seemed incongruous in this small-city landscape. Though the building was not very tall—just four stories—its interior stunned everyone. Famed chronicler of California history Kevin Starr observed that the Bradbury Building, "in an architecture of steel and glass, marble, tile and movement envisioned and presented the material dream of Southern California as a technology flooded by sunlight . . . This orchestration of steel and light announced the city that was to be."[1] Even for twenty-first-century tourists and visitors who tiptoe into the building's lobby to catch a glimpse of one of the city's most famous landmarks, the Bradbury Building is breathtaking. Light filters down from a ceiling composed entirely of a skylight, then illuminates elaborate French wrought iron balustrades and pillars, exposed birdcage elevators, and pink Italian marble staircases. Like buildings and monuments in imperial capitals such as London, Paris, and Madrid, the Bradbury also served in its early years as a paean to empire.[2] Encaustic tile, shipped north from Mexico, covers the floors, a cool and silent reminder of the source of wealth that paid for one of Los Angeles's iconic edifices.

Lewis Bradbury, an investor and emissary of American commercial empire in Mexico, and the millionaire who commissioned the building, suffered from asthma his entire life—and those wheezy lungs may have brought him west in search of warm, dry weather. Originally from Maine, Bradbury began his professional life as a sailor, eventually commanding several ships. Sailing brought him to Mexico, where he decided to settle in Rosario, Sinaloa, along Mexico's west coast. While in Sinaloa, he invested in mining enterprises, including the legendary Tajo silver mine, from which

Interior of the Bradbury Building, undated. Security Pacific National Bank Collection, Los Angeles Public Library.

he extracted a fortune. At the time of his death in 1892, Bradbury had amassed more than $15 million in wealth wrought from Mexico, approximately $442 million today in today's dollars.³ Bradbury reinvested his Mexican millions in Los Angeles. In addition to the Bradbury Building, he owned one of the most extravagant homes in the city, a fifty-room mansion on the corner of Court and Hill Streets. He developed a full block of commercial buildings on Broadway in the heart of the city's business district. He also purchased the extensive Duarte rancho a few dozen miles east of downtown Los Angeles and made plans to develop it. Funded by a fortune drawn from veins deep in the Sinaloa mountains, Bradbury's Los Angeles infrastructure stood as a literal brick and mortar testament to the wealth

Workers constructing a mill at the Bradbury mine in Sinaloa, Mexico, 1908. Courtesy Special Collections, UC Davis Library, Bradbury Family Papers D-449.

that investors could extract from Mexico—a hinterland the city could extend across the border.[4]

At the dawn of the twentieth century, Bradbury was not the only Los Angeles capitalist busy building personal, civic, and imperial monuments in Los Angeles with dividends from Mexico investments. In the fall of 1896, Griffith J. Griffith donated 3,000 acres of land to the city of Los Angeles to create one of the nation's largest urban parks. When Griffith owned the property, he liked to ride his favorite horse through the manzanita and coastal sage scrub that clung to the park's rocky canyons to catch a glimpse

City-Empire 3

Griffith Park and Observatory shortly after the completion of the Observatory, 1935. Ernest Marquez Collection, Huntington Library, San Marino, California.

of the Pacific Ocean. Ever a Los Angeles booster, Griffith envisioned his donation as a great urban park for the city he was certain would grow up at its feet. He described the gift, located on a mountainous section of the former Los Feliz Spanish land grant just five miles north of the Bradbury Building, as a "Christmas present" to his "favorite city." Griffith also had grand visions for the ways Angelenos could enjoy the park's staggering mountaintop views of the Los Angeles basin, from downtown to the Pacific. Inspired by a glimpse through what was then the world's largest telescope at the research observatory atop neighboring Mount Wilson, Griffith vowed to bring views of the heavens to his fellow city dwellers. After consulting with renowned astronomer George Ellery Hale, he followed up his land donation with a cash gift to build the Griffith Observatory, a gleaming white Greek and Beaux-Arts–influenced edifice that now sits on a rugged hill in Griffith Park and overlooks greater Los Angeles.

Like Bradbury, Griffith funded this lavish gift of mountainous parkland to his beloved Los Angeles through a growing American investment empire and the extraction of resources from Mexican mountains. Born to a family of modest means in South Wales, Griffith made his way as a teenager first to the East Coast in 1866 and then to the booming city of San Francisco in 1873. In the mining boomtown, he found a job as a reporter covering the mining industry in the American West. Eager to apply his growing knowledge of mining and to extend his investments into new territories, Griffith traveled to northern Mexico, where in the state of Chihuahua he purchased interests in some Sierra Madre mines.[5] Wanting to be closer to these Mexican investments, Griffith relocated from San Francisco to Los Angeles in 1882. Although he was creating a personal fortune from Mexican resources, Griffith happily observed that Los Angeles was rapidly becoming less Mexican. He noted that he "was more favorably impressed with its qualities, because its white population had increased and it was beginning to show some enterprise."[6] For Griffith, Anglo domination of Mexican resources foretold a marvelous future for his adopted city; at the end of his life he reflected, "My faith in Los Angeles has never wavered; I have loved my city, and my confidence in her dominance has been ever constant. I place no limit upon her splendid tomorrows."[7] Although he became notorious as a violent alcoholic, Griffith's sentiments reflected a desire for growth and Anglo ascendancy that permeated the city's investor class. Los Angeles, Griffith was sure, would not just grow but control people, regions, and commercial orbits.

Following the American Civil War, Los Angeles boosters and capitalists like Bradbury and Griffith built what would become the American West's most important city—in part by tying their fate and that of their city to the exploitation of Mexican labor and Mexican natural resources. Los Angeles promoters took their cues from western cities such as Chicago and San Francisco where belief in growth and the control of hinterlands was as fervent as a religious revival. They followed a template often used by urban boosters, particularly in these western cities, who turned to the surrounding countryside with eager investment schemes and hungry expectations for high returns. In relationships often more parasitic than symbiotic, urban elites withdrew resources from surrounding environments to fuel personal fortunes and municipal growth. At the heart of these entwined geographies were cities or urban cores. The corpus that surrounded them was their hinterland, periphery, countryside, or territory.[8]

In Los Angeles, this gospel of growth and the familiar rhetoric of western urban boosterism also assumed imperial and transnational dimensions. Urban promoters in Los Angeles argued for "taking in" surrounding territories, both domestic and international. The *Los Angeles Times*, ever the voice of boosterism in the city and owned by Angelenos who would invest heavily in Mexico, declared, "If Los Angeles is to grow as it should grow our merchants and manufacturers and financiers must be broad-minded and enterprising, continually reaching out for new commercial worlds to conquer."[9] This was the contemporary language of empire, a perspective on urban growth that believed in the martial expansion of cities, or at least their economies, into "unconquered" commercial realms. Los Angeles boosters surveyed surrounding areas and took sweeping and incorporative views of the city's "tributary territories"—from Kern and Tulare counties to the Inland Empire, from Arizona to New Mexico, and from Baja California to Sonora. Indeed, as early as 1892 the *Los Angeles Times* trumpeted its hometown as an "embryo empire."[10]

Consequently, urban promoters in the borderland city not only sought to exploit the resources of their domestic environs but looked across the border for land, labor, and emerging markets to feed municipal growth. Situated at the U.S. periphery, Anglo Angelenos believed they could transcend certain unfortunate natural disadvantages, such as a parching lack of water or the absence of a natural deep-water seaport, by following an international plan for growth. The lynchpin in this plan was aggressively connecting a city short on resources to the assets in its Mexican hinterland. Oilmen such as Edward L. Doheny pursued fortunes in Mexico's petroleum regions. The interlocked Chandler and Otis families, who were owners of the *Los Angeles Times* and successful real estate developers and corporate ranchers, developed a million-acre cotton and cattle ranch in northern Mexico. The Los Angeles Chamber of Commerce organized investment excursions to introduce Angelenos to lucrative economic opportunities just across the border. Even "cactus rustlers" built profitable businesses transplanting specimens from Mexican deserts into the gardens of arriviste Angeleno horticulturalists. In fact, in an era that saw hundreds of millions of dollars invested south of the border, Angelenos invested more money per capita in Mexico than any other region of the United States.[11] Los Angeles investors sat at the western edge of the nation during a period when American economic opportunists believed they needed to reach beyond the bounds of the nation and into Latin America and the Pacific world. As a result, Mexico presented a particularly appealing emerging market. In Los Angeles, returns on investments in new markets south of the border helped fuel urban growth and spurred interest in further international ventures. In short, Mexican resources helped create the moment when the small town of Los Angeles transformed into a large city.

If investment in Mexico fueled urban growth in Los Angeles, its very development and progression as an extractive process created the conditions for revolution in Mexico—and Los Angeles investors in Mexico thereby generated their own undoing. Their withdrawal of resources yanked the borderlands into the Gilded Age economy, intensified inequality, and fomented populist revolt, which arrived in the form of the Mexican Revolution (1910–1920) and undermined the economic logic of Los Angeles as a city with a Mexican hinterland. Los Angeles capitalists such as Bradbury and Griffith may have celebrated their urban core while exploiting a Mexican periphery, but this formulation lasted only as long as Los Angeles, or indeed American, capitalism could advance without the coordinated or violent resistance of Mexicans. Fearful of revolution around the corner and across the border, Los Angeles capitalists anxious to protect their Mexican investments became the leading proponents of American political and military intervention in Mexico. However, the radical nature of the revolution and failures to secure the backing of the U.S. federal government ultimately undid the power of Los Angeles investors, disrupting speculative schemes and resource and labor exploitation that had controlled the borderlands for sixty years.

Close examination of the networks created between Los Angeles and Mexico by both capitalist investment and revolution refocuses the study of the southwestern borderlands around an urban core with a periphery that stretched across the U.S.-Mexico border. By investigating the doctrine of urban growth and the transnational investment strategies of wealthy white Angelenos, this book reveals the role of a borderlands city as a portal to the growth of American capitalism and empire building south of the border. It also uncovers the racial and economic ideology that drove expansionist city boosters who believed that an enterprising "white" city should control a nonwhite periphery. This group of ambitious investors and city boosters imagined Los Angeles's hinterland expanding out from a Southern California core into northern Mexico and afield, and Anglo Angelenos argued that Mexican natural resources could transform a small town into the capital of the western United States and the Pacific Rim. Moving south of the border, this study also traces the history of Mexicans who collaborated with and then challenged this vision, from the welcoming government officials under President Porfirio Díaz and the era known as the Porfiriato (1876–1911), who facilitated foreign investment, to the revolutionaries who demanded "Mexico for Mexicans."

In addition to reconfiguring borderlands around city and periphery, this study and the stories of Los Angeles and Mexico told here bring new geographic scales to histories of American capitalism and empire building during the late nineteenth and early twentieth centuries.[12] Urban growth and metropolitan elites often drove investment choices and patterns and the incorporation of new territories into national and global economies in the second half of the nineteenth century. This phenomenon overlapped with the growing international power of the United States during the Gilded Age and the nation's increasing political and commercial dominance around the world, particularly in Latin America. In the case of Los Angeles and Mexico, these two potent trends intersected. Not only did Los Angeles emerge as an American city with a phenomenal record of growth, but the city's elites also became leading proponents and practitioners of imperial strategies, from investment to military intervention to occupation. Situating Los Angeles at the forefront of American imperial expansion into the U.S.-Mexico borderlands illustrates both the intertwined dynamism of American cities and capitalism at the turn of the century and how American imperial growth unfolded at regional and local levels.[13]

Considering the growth of American capitalism and imperialism via Los Angeles and Mexico also reveals intersections between urban growth and the transnational nature of popular revolt against incorporation into the world economy. Just as farmers, workers, and Populists across the American West rejected the grossly unjust nature of their inclusion in American corporate capitalism, Mexican revolutionaries launched a similar critique against their own government and foreign investors, particularly Americans. Inspired by the writing and leadership of figures such as Enrique and Ricardo Flores Magón, Francisco "Pancho" Villa, and Emiliano Zapata, Mexicans increasingly called for "Mexico for Mexicans" and "tierra y libertad." Their rejection of absorption into a world of corporate capitalism dominated by an American investor class fueled the first social revolution of the twentieth century. This revolt and the backlash against capital's flow had urban, regional, and transnational dimensions. Los Angeles's proximity to the U.S.-Mexico border and borderlands, along with networks of capital and the flow of people between the city and Mexico, placed the city at the fulcrum of empire and revolt at the dawn of the twentieth century.[14]

Geographies of City-Empire, Border, and Revolution

In foregrounding international urban development in the West and the borderlands, the possibilities of which exerted such influence over Los Angeles investors, I argue for understanding Los Angeles as a city-empire. Similar to what geographers and urbanists describe as "global city-regions" in the twentieth and twenty-first centuries, Los Angeles in the late nineteenth century and at the dawn of the twentieth functioned as a node of concentrated wealth and power in the borderlands economy and operated at an alternative scale to the nation-state.[15] Looking hungrily across the border, wealthy Angelenos held that Los Angeles should be a city with international reach and should serve as the commercial portal to Mexico and Latin America. In other words, a city could function as the vanguard of an American commercial or "informal" empire.[16] This meant cultivating relationships between municipal leaders and a commercial elite in Los Angeles and elected officials at all levels in Mexico. These relationships opened opportunities for investment in properties and commercial ventures south of the border, promoted trade between Los Angeles and Mexico, and supported infrastructural links across the border and between the two regions. The city's imperial project also included creating a hierarchy between Los Angeles and Mexico, employers and laborers, white and nonwhite, core and periphery. Finally, when revolution threatened cross-border investments, the dense and diverse connections between Los Angeles and Mexico also led Angeleno elites to clamor for American armed invention in Mexico and protectionist state policies both north and south of the border.[17]

As historians of both capitalism and the American West have demonstrated in studies ranging from Boston and New York to Chicago and San Francisco, Americans often extended territorial control and empire in the West through the marriage of capitalism and the nineteenth-century city. As traced in this book, however, western cities also had an international financial dynamic and momentum of their own. Hinterlands were not always domestic, and, in this case, capital, resources, and people flowed across the border between Los Angeles and Mexico. The wealthy Angelenos who orchestrated their city's prodigious growth between 1865 and 1941 continued a long and imperial history of building cities to control resources in the American West and to incorporate vast swaths of new territory into the nation's rapidly growing capitalist economy. Boston Brahmins, for example, financed ventures such as railroads, stockyards, and mining from Kansas City to Denver. New Yorkers invested heavily in the American West (as well as the Caribbean and Mexico). Cities in the American West, notably Chicago and San Francisco, also organized extractive economies in surrounding hinterlands to exploit natural resources, which, in turn, fed urban growth. As historian Robert Self argues, cities were the "architects of the countryside" in the nineteenth- and twentieth-century West.[18] Thus, investment capital originating in both eastern and western cities was key to the exploitation of western resources and the economic incorporation of western territories into regional and national economies.[19]

This process of city building in the West and the borderlands was deeply embedded in the dynamics of American empire, as urban growth linked westward settlement and continental conquest on the one hand and overseas empire building on the other. Although these two impulses, which met and overlapped in Los Angeles at the end of the nineteenth century, are intimately related, historians often treat them as disconnected. As historian Kornel Chang observes, "The history of U.S. expansionism is often split into two, distinct phases: continental expansion, on the one hand, and overseas empire, on the other, with Western historians studying the former and diplomatic historians and scholars of international relations researching the latter."[20] Instead, and as the history of Los Angeles in Mexico proves, while American territorial expansion in North America may have halted formally at the end of the Mexican-American War, it continued in a more "informal" capacity, sometimes in the form of urban growth, well into the twentieth century.[21]

At the forefront of this imperial process in Los Angeles were city boosters and transnational investors, often the same people, who well understood the intersection between city building in the American West and global empire building.[22] Empire can take many forms, from formal annexation and political control to spheres of economic influence. At its very essence, however, empire is an economic endeavor that takes land and property and assembles them into a larger system of extraction and profit.[23] Thus, for Los Angeles boosters and investors, the expansion of their personal investments and their city's economy into Mexico often aligned in ways that made sense on the personal, civic, national, and international levels. For example, organizing investors in Southern California to purchase an agricultural property in rural Mexico represented not only a chance for private enrichment but also an opportunity for regional urban development and the advancement of American global power. In the minds and actions of Los Angeles investors, all of these impulses were not mutually exclusive but actually mutually beneficial and reinforcing. Thus regional boosters acted as part of the vanguard of American empire in the late nineteenth century.[24]

The urban growth of Los Angeles, then, offers a new geography for understanding this dynamic of commercial empire in Latin America. Historians of American empire have for more than half a century argued that an American empire cannot be understood simply as the formal acquisition of new territories by a nation-state. Instead, the United States, led by commercial interests, created a vast "informal" empire that has spanned the globe since the second half of the nineteenth century. Rather than continue territorial acquisitions as they did in the American West and through conquests such as the Mexican-American War, American nation builders and their close allies in business and commerce looked to expand American global power through economic influence.[25] The driving motivation: to make the globe safe for American capitalism. As geographer Neil Smith argues, this American empire was "built on a strategic recalibration of geography with economics, a new orchestration of world geography in the pursuit of economic accumulation."[26] Most studies of this recalibration focus on American commercial expansion and foreign policy generally or on corporate entities and their influence on American foreign policy specifically.[27] As I argue in *Imperial Metropolis*, however, part of this recalibration toward imperial expansion also took the form of designing regional economies that crossed borders while benefiting urban centers such as Los Angeles. At global and local levels, this new form of empire relied on the ostensibly benign practices of free trade, economic integration, and the expansion of markets, precisely the tools and goals of Los Angeles investors in Mexico. At the nexus between western conquest and the global expansion of an American empire, Los Angeles elites and boosters believed that an expanding urban economy benefited themselves and their city while contributing to global American commercial interests.[28]

The city boosters and builders of empire who believed that investment in Mexico could catapult their city to national and international prominence were predominantly part of an emerging, but generally understudied, upper class in nineteenth-century America. Although long ignored by social historians, urban elites played an outsized role in the development of nineteenth-century American cities and capitalism.[29] While the biographies of the architects of the Los Angeles city-empire are treated with more depth in subsequent chapters, as a group they deserve a brief introduction here. Most were transplants to Southern California from fairly modest economic backgrounds in the East, Midwest, and Europe. Some were Civil War veterans. Others needed the dry, warm air of Southern California to treat asthma or tuberculosis. Still others had tried to get rich in other parts of the West and kept attempting new schemes in new locales until they hit the Pacific. But almost all reached Los Angeles in search of Gilded Age West economic opportunities. They were not necessarily wealthy when they arrived, but most had become successful in some California industry—mining, oil drilling, trade, agriculture, real estate, newspapers, finance—before applying skills sharpened in Los Angeles to ventures in Mexico. Most also saw clear personal financial benefits in the growth and success of their adopted hometown and were not shy to announce their desire to see Los Angeles grow.[30] Almost all of the Los Angeles boosters and promoters of investment in Mexico also knew each other. After all, Los Angeles was a relatively small place when they arrived. They belonged to the same veterans' associations, social clubs, and commercial organizations, from the Grand Army of the Republic to the Jonathan Club to the chamber of commerce. Finally, the Los Angeles investors who promoted city growth via investment in Mexico were also part of a generation of American global empire builders. For example, Civil War veteran and Los Angeles rancher William Rosecrans became the leading proponent of American investment in Mexico in the 1860s. Similarly, *Los Angeles Times* publisher Harrison Gray Otis boisterously volunteered to serve in the Philippines during the Spanish-American War and declared that the archipelago "must remain absolutely under American control." In his opinion, Filipinos were "still in a state of savagery."[31] Like their American counterparts on banana plantations in Central America or sugar fields in Hawaii, these Angelenos believed in the commercial and martial expansion of American interests across borders and the racialized control of colonized peoples.

As with most imperial ventures, cultivating a city-empire required alliances with local elites and in national capitals, and Angelenos eagerly advanced pro–Los Angeles and pro-trade policies with regional and national Mexican leaders. South of the border and prior to the start of the Mexican Revolution in 1910, the policies of the Porfirian administration intersected neatly with these ambitions as well as with a growing American commercial empire. During his almost twenty-five years in office, Porfirio Díaz actively sought foreign investment, such as that originating in Los Angeles, to develop Mexico's economy; he offered tempting incentives to foreign investors. A proponent of Mexican modernization, Díaz believed that foreign investment could, more quickly than domestic investment, build up Mexico's communication networks, transportation lines, and participation in the world economy. As a result, he opened up railroad concessions, banking charters, mines, oil properties, and farmland to extensive foreign investment at the end of the nineteenth century. These policies had an expansive impact. By the end of his tenure, foreign investors owned 35 percent of Mexico's surface area; Americans alone controlled 27 percent of the nation's land. Many of these investment opportunities in Mexico presented Americans, often Angelenos, with the chance to expand across the border extractive and commercial enterprises, such as mining, railroads, and ranching, that they had already established in California and elsewhere in the American West.[32]

Angeleno investors also shared a perspective on the interconnectedness of personal, urban, and national fortunes. They thought they had a successful social, economic, and imperial blueprint in Southern California that could be easily replicated in Mexico. Organizations such as the Los Angeles Chamber of Commerce and the Merchants and Manufacturers Association, both founded at the end of the nineteenth century, pursued an aggressive agenda to develop the city's economy, enforce a racial hierarchy, and strictly limit the power of organized labor—an effort they termed "industrial freedom."[33] While this producer-centered philosophy was hardly unique to Los Angeles, the city's elite exported their worldview to Mexico alongside their investment dollars.[34] They believed that capital and labor each played a unique role in a global capitalist economy and that with proper management of the system by capital, both groups could reap the benefits of profits and steady wages.[35] During a period of intense national conflict between organized labor and capital, Los Angeles elites believed they had found an ideal solution to class strife—strictly ban labor organizing, provide an expanding economy to employ workers, maintain a stringent economic and racial hierarchy, and expand transnationally. Historian Emily Rosenberg terms this ideology "liberal developmentalism" and argues that it drove the expansion of the nation's influence around the globe. This system of beliefs included the idea that other nations should develop along a similar trajectory to the United States, that private enterprise and free trade would create development, and that government should protect private enterprise globally.[36]

Unsurprisingly, doctrines of urban growth and the geography of Los Angeles as core with Mexico as hinterland were racialized, and part of this study argues for understanding city building, like empire building, as a racial endeavor. Like Griffith and American empire builders more generally, Angeleno city builders believed that their urban core should be, and would be, dominated by whites. A Mexican underclass might linger, or even grow, but it would do so under the rule of a rapidly growing Anglo majority. This racial and class hierarchy would extend, in the minds and practices of city builders, into the imperial relationship between the city and its periphery. In this, Anglo Angelenos echoed the racial perspective of their counterparts entering into commercial and imperial relationships around the globe during the Gilded Age, from Cuba to the Philippines. Unique in the case of Los Angeles, however, was the added impetus of urban growth. Anglo elites coupled the particular racial makeup of Southern California, which included a sizable Mexican and Mexican American population, with the regimen of race and labor control they sought to perpetuate across the border. They believed that carefully controlled labor in Los Angeles and in Mexico would make them rich and grow their city.[37]

Elites and urban or national cores do not operate in the world unchallenged, however. Hinterlands shape urban cores. Colonies mold imperial capitals. Workers resist the conditions of their employment, and challenge, sometimes even topple, larger economic and political structures. Although this work pays significant attention to urban elites and investors in Los Angeles, I do not want to suggest that core and periphery were starkly divided. Instead, as evidenced by the Mexican Revolution and the Los Angeles response to it, the system of capital investment promoted by Los Angeles investors was profoundly connected to populist revolt south of the border.[38] The focus here, however, is to build on existing histories of the Mexican Revolution and rural Mexico, as well as histories of Mexican Los Angeles, through the lens of Los Angeles elites and their ambitious investment schemes.[39] Thus, part of the argument of this study of investment in the borderlands is to connect urban speculation schemes to the undoing of capitalist agency. That revolt erupted in Mexico during the same period that Angelenos invested heavily south of the border went well beyond coincident timing and proximity. Cause and effect were tied together in a series of tremendous economic and political transitions north and south of the border. In this way, the dynamic between an urban core and a borderlands periphery was never one-way or unilateral, and Mexicans profoundly shaped Los Angeles.

Beginning in 1910, revolution transformed this intertwining of an American city and the Mexican nation as well as the belief that white investors could easily control a nonwhite workforce. During the same decades that Los Angeles rose to national prominence, American investment dollars deluged Mexico, leading to the twentieth century's first social revolution. Nearly forty years of privatization and capitalist development under the welcoming Porfirian administration concentrated power and wealth in the hands of foreigners, many of them Americans, and a small Mexican elite. This process dispossessed Mexican indigenous populations and campesinos and shifted over 90 percent of communal lands from villages to private landowners. By 1910, when the Mexican Revolution began, Americans had invested over $1 billion in Mexican agriculture, railroads, telegraph systems, timber plantations, mines, and petroleum fields.[40] As historian Friedrich Katz notes, foreign investment pulled Mexico into the "frenetic development of world capitalism" in the final decades of the nineteenth century.[41] Much of this pull, at least in the U.S.-Mexico borderlands, originated in Los Angeles.

Finally, this book takes this history and geography of investment, empire, and revolution in Los Angeles and Mexico and overlays these across the borderlands and borderlands history. In doing so, it offers a new and broader model for understanding the history of the U.S.-Mexico borderlands. Some borderlands scholars critique the field, particularly studies of the twentieth-century borderlands, for being too narrowly defined by the border itself, sticking too close to the international boundary, and telling "small-scale tales."[42] As this book explores, however, if historians consider alternative geographies, they open opportunities to broaden the scope of borderlands studies without losing the field's analytical foci: namely, issues of territorial control and negotiation, the paradox of division and union, the rules of inclusion and exclusion, and the tensions between core and periphery.[43]

Exploring the relationship between Los Angeles and Mexico reveals a history of urban growth, capitalist expansion, imperial designs, and populist revolt as at once bisected and connected by the border between the United States and Mexico. Exploring the development of a city in relationship to a borderland allows historians to evaluate borderlands at a new scale, connecting the regional to the local and the national.[44] Taking up this challenge, this study looks at the unfolding history of the American West's most important city at multiple levels, from booster desires in Los Angeles, to on-the-ground labor and revolutionary conflict in Mexico, to negotiations between Angeleno investors and the U.S. and Mexican states. By pulling back from the "small-scale" narratives of communities immediately adjacent to the political border, additional borderlands actors and relationships come into relief and illustrate that borderland dynamics stretch far beyond the border in the core-hinterland configuration, in this case from Los Angeles to northern Mexico and beyond.

City to Empire to Revolution

My arguments about Los Angeles and Mexico and reconsidering geography in the context of cities, borders, capitalism, empire, and revolution follow a narrative arc that begins during a period of economic synergy between Los Angeles and Mexico during the Porfiriato under the administration of

President Díaz. We then trace Angeleno enterprises in Mexico through the violent years of the revolution, the unraveling of Angeleno power in a Mexican hinterland, and the subsequent expropriation of American-owned properties, which curtailed but did not eliminate investor power in the borderlands. Finally, the study examines the creation of a postrevolutionary affiliation between Los Angeles and Mexico based on a grudging respect for Mexican nationalism, a renewed enthusiasm for cross-border economic collaboration, and new imperial morphs. Through all of the chapters that follow, a history of real and imagined geographies of investment, race, empire, and revolt binds Los Angeles to Mexico.

The first chapter of *Imperial Metropolis* explores how early boosters and investors coupled the aggressive growth of urban capitalism in Los Angeles with commercial expansion and "informal" empire across the border. From the local to the international, Los Angeles boosters advocated harnessing city growth to borderlands enterprises. Keenly aware of their proximity to the borderlands, Los Angeles investors believed not in the expansion of formal territorial control but instead in the migration of American capital into global regions such as Mexico. Eager for far-flung tributary territories and with the aid of Mexican partners, Angeleno financiers invested heavily in Mexico and drew a wide swath of the borderlands and Mexico into the city's economic orbit. They advocated for regional development in Southern California while simultaneously purchasing properties, building trade networks, and fostering productive relationships with Porfiriato officials. The policies advanced by Los Angeles investors, coupled with their on-the-ground networks and investments, reveal how urban growth shaped borderlands relationships and advanced an American empire in Mexico.

As Los Angeles capitalists embarked on investment ventures and urban-imperial expansion across Mexico, they extended concepts of race and labor forged in Los Angeles to build networks for investment and to control their Mexican workforce. As explored in chapter 2, they channeled a history of working with California's Mexican American elite into productive partnerships with Porfirian elites. This proposition met a supportive executive in Díaz who believed that private and foreign capital investment would transform Mexico into a modern nation. Mimicking their designs for race and labor in Southern California, Anglo investors in Mexico also expected Mexicans to do the backbreaking manual labor required of the extractive industries that would make these investors rich. They also expanded Southern California definitions of working-class Mexican Americans as ideal workers to employees in Mexico. Ultimately, Los Angeles investors believed in a shared "identity of interest" between employers and workers that extended across racial, ethnic, and even national boundaries.[45] They combined the racialized system of labor from both sides of the border to build the machinery of capitalism and empire.[46]

This schematic, however, worked for only a limited period, and Los Angeles investors soon found they had cultivated a city with an imperial hinterland and a political economy with the seeds of its own destruction. The "frenetic pull of capitalism" fostered enough economic and political inequality and discontent in the borderlands and greater Mexico to ignite the twentieth century's first social revolution in 1910. Chapter 3 explores this phenomenon through revolutionary activities on properties owned by Angeleno capitalists and as rejections of the core-periphery economic model. The city's proximity to the border and borderlands, coupled with the thick network of financial relationships that linked Southern California investors to Mexico, meant that the Mexican Revolution shook the core of Los Angeles capitalism. Although "Los Angeles" may not have been on the tongues of Mexican revolutionaries, their actions represented a direct attack on the imperial structure cultivated between a city in California and a hinterland in Mexico. Although subject to much heated historiographic debate, the rhetoric and violence of the Mexican Revolution did target American investors as causal in the severe problems facing Mexico and its poorest citizens. Analyzing the fate of regional elites from Southern California, this study maintains that ordinary Mexicans understood the United States and its rapidly expanding capitalist economy as a direct cause of land loss and poor working conditions.[47]

Unable to protect investments south of the border, Angelenos proposed armed intervention in Mexico and a formalization of the imperial relationship between the United States and Mexico. Chapter 4 examines how Los Angeles urban elites, like imperial agents around the globe, tried to compel the power of the American state to intervene in Mexico on their behalf. Angelenos demanded that U.S. constitutional safeguards should extend south of the border to protect investments and guarantee systems of white ownership and nonwhite labor. Investors used urban imperialism and its racial components to appeal to the U.S. federal government for armed intervention in Mexico and to try to shape American foreign policy in the midst of revolution. In the context of the global expansion of American state power to protect private investments, from the Philippines to Haiti, the Angeleno expectation of state protection in transnational locales was not unfathomable. Efforts to control labor and property during the Mexican Revolution came in the form of an extraordinarily well-funded national public relations and lobbying campaign led by Los Angeles investors and directed at the U.S. federal government. Although they failed to win the decisive intervention they desired, the effort placed Angelenos at the forefront of shaping U.S. policy toward Mexico.

The failure of Angeleno investors to secure imperial intervention in Mexico during the revolution fundamentally shifted the power relationship between core and periphery. By the end of the Mexican Revolution, Los Angeles investors found themselves drawn inextricably into the conflict, rather than into the center of an urban empire. Chapter 5 explores this transformation of the city-hinterland formulation. On the ground and below the border, Mexicans and the Mexican revolutionary state claimed Los Angeles–owned properties, making the landscape of American investment ground zero for the implementation of revolutionary land policies. As a result, Mexican farmers and revolutionaries slashed the flow of investment returns from Mexico to Los Angeles and forced the expropriation or nationalization of American properties. The challenges represented by the Mexican Revolution, however, did not divorce Los Angeles from Mexico. Even while Mexican revolutionaries successfully stymied the flow of dividends from south to north across the border, a single-minded determination to maintain investment properties continued to link Los Angeles to Mexico. Anglo Angelenos refused to relinquish Mexican investments and instead clung tenaciously to ranches, mines, and oil wells while simultaneously demanding from the federal government protection for periphery properties.

As discussed in chapter 6, however, by the 1930s Angeleno investors and Mexican policymakers sutured back together the connective tissue between Los Angeles and Mexico by building cross-border infrastructure and rhetorically declaring hemispheric friendships. This unfolded, however, within a new imperial context as the U.S. state and American investors called for coerced increased global trade and removing barriers to the flow of capital. A highway project, promoted by a number of Los Angeles investors who had just lost private properties to expropriation in Mexico, reveals that Angelenos still wanted to take advantage of their geographic relationship to the borderlands. The revolution, however, had tempered their explicitly imperial aspirations. Instead, Los Angeles boosters built cooperative relationships with regional Mexican officials and elites to construct lateral geographic ties between Southern California and the west coast of Mexico and along the shores of the Pacific. Their efforts abandoned prerevolutionary strategies of resource extraction and reorganized the Los Angeles–Mexico relationship along a highway and the adjacent geography of the American and Mexican Pacific coast. While the political borderline running horizontally between the two countries became an increasingly rigid marker during this period, the construction of a transnational highway between Los Angeles and Mexico City reveals how regional elites hoped to strengthen ties through tourism and along an alternative and expansive geography of a lateral coastline, with Los Angeles at its center.[48] These efforts also intersected with and reflected the emergence of a pan-American and pan-Pacific ideology on both sides of the border as well as a new American imperial emphasis on free trade and globalization. As explored in this final chapter and the epilogue, empire and the inequities of globalization continued to haunt the relationship between Los Angeles and Mexico into the twenty-first century.

Imperial Metropolis

Although Mexico and Los Angeles were intimately linked, it is nearly impossible to quantify the amount of money and resources that flowed between them between 1865 and 1941. Based on the value of investments reported by Los Angeles investors during and after the Mexican Revolution, their property holdings totaled in the tens of millions of dollars. The primary investors in Mexico, many of whom make an appearance in this book, were certainly extraordinarily wealthy individuals despite losing investments due to the revolution. They owed their wealth to Mexican investments prior to expropriation as well as to the investments they were able to make in Los Angeles and the West as a result of wealth extracted in Mexico. As in the examples of the Bradbury Building and Griffith Park, part of this wealth transformed the Los Angeles landscape. Additionally, oil baron Edward Doheny built a gilded library on the University of Southern California campus with his Mexican petroleum wealth. He also donated hundreds of millions of dollars to the Archdiocese of Los Angeles and helped develop Beverly Hills.[49] Meanwhile, Harry Chandler continued the *Los Angeles Times* dynasty based in part on his California and Mexico real estate investments.[50] Thomas Bard, who owned a ranch in Nayarit, helped found and fund Occidental College;[51] Henry Workman Keller, who invested in a dude ranch in Baja California, led the Automobile Club of Southern California, which remains the nation's largest motoring organization. Overall, Los Angeles investors in Mexico left a clear institutional and infrastructural imprint on the city.

Perhaps more significant than the actual wealth wrought from Mexico was the global orientation generated by Los Angeles's proximity to the borderlands. Many of the Los Angeles boosters and capitalists who invested in Mexico were also desperate to surpass rival cities such as San Diego and San Francisco, fixated by what they envisioned as Los Angeles's destiny in the West, the borderlands, the Pacific, and the world.[52] Through personal investments coupled with persistent lobbying and support from state and federal entities, Los Angeles financiers and policymakers transformed a small town into an international hub for agriculture, transportation, oil, trade, and industrial production. It was not by chance but by design that Los Angeles eclipsed San Francisco as the West Coast's busiest seaport by the 1920s and became the nation's busiest port following World War II.[53] After the arrival of transformative railroad lines in the 1870s and 1880s, city boosters fiercely advocated for federal funding for the construction of the city's deep-water port in the 1890s. They also worked feverishly to promote ocean trade between Los Angeles and the Pacific after the port's completion and following the Spanish-American War when the United States gained a significant foothold in the Pacific world. Los Angeles also craved the trade that would result from the completion of the Panama Canal in 1914; this ultimately led to the proliferation of Los Angeles sea trade from the Americas and Asia. A focus on investment and trade in a Mexican periphery launched this global orientation.

In studying the roots of this global orientation, which grew out of the profound relationship between Los Angeles and Mexico in the late nineteenth and early twentieth centuries, this book reorganizes historical understandings of cities, empires, and borders. It also highlights how urban growth shaped the tumultuous world of borderlands capitalism and the growth of American empire. Urban boosterism united a generation of wealthy borderlands investors, systematizing and internationalizing their investment strategies, structuring their relationship with labor, arranging their conceptions of race, and configuring their connections with the state on both sides of the border. Revolution in Mexico reoriented these dynamics, forcing the Angeleno investor class to reconfigure their relationship with Mexican workers, policymakers, and the nation itself. Whether the relationships between Angeleno investors and their Mexican partners and workers were congenial or contentious between 1865 and 1941, Los Angeles and Mexico remained intertwined in the complex web of a city, its cross-border hinterland, and empire.

1   Pueblo, City, Empire

Between the 1880s and the height of the Mexican Revolution, a span of two and a half decades, over 150 businesses incorporated in Los Angeles County explicitly to do business in Mexico. Combined, the companies' initial stock offerings totaled over $70 million and involved the investments, large and small, of thousands of Angelenos. These business schemes included a dizzying array of industries in Mexico. Angelenos funneled money into the mining of gas, coal, silver, gold, copper, zinc, lead, borax, iron, gypsum, tin, salt, and marble. Extracting subsoil resources spawned secondary investments in mining supplies and general merchandising enterprises in Mexico. Ranching and irrigation of Mexican farmland also proved attractive to Angelenos who eagerly purchased agricultural land and began planting cash crops, many that had already proved extraordinarily lucrative in California, including grain, sugarcane, hardwood, corn, nuts, oranges, lemons, limes, pineapples, dates, figs, and cotton. Money invested in agriculture also led Angelenos to spend money on raising stock in Mexico, including cattle, pigs, chickens, and horses. Ownership of land also led to real estate speculation on the part of Angelenos, who developed Mexican subdivision, irrigation, and colonization schemes much as they had in the previous decade or so before in Southern California. The necessity of moving people to property and goods to market as well as the call of connecting periphery to core also resulted in investments in the technologies of travel and transportation, from railroad lines to roads, sailing vessels, wharves, piers, warehouses, steamship lines, and hotels.[1]

These significant investment ties between Los Angeles and Mexico did not come about by accident or happenstance. A zealous pro-growth press daily extolled the virtues of urban and commercial growth. Ever the mouthpiece of urban development, the *Los Angeles Times* beseeched city investors to connect to Mexico. Headlines read, "Commerce of Mexico and Our Interest Therein" and "How to Gain Mexican Trade" or "Mexico, a Country of Unsurpassed Fertility."[2] Institutions sprouted to put this type of growth into action, including the Los Angeles Chamber of Commerce and the city's Merchants and Manufacturers Association, both designed to promote

Bankers and railroad executives in front of a special train chartered to transport them from Los Angeles to investment properties on the California–Baja California border, early twentieth century. Colorado River Land Company Collection, Sherman Library.

regional economic growth. As a result, Angelenos hustled across the border in a fairly well coordinated campaign to construct not just a financial relationship between their city and a Mexican hinterland, but an imperial relationship, one that intersected with urban development in the West as well as emerging campaigns to advance America's place in the global economy.

The urban dimensions of empire and capitalism arose from deep imperial roots in Los Angeles. As explored in the first section of this chapter, Los Angeles was born of empire, first as a colonial outpost of the Spanish crown, then as a point of conflict between Mexicans and expansionistic Americans bent on continental domination, and finally as a nascent Anglo-American city built on the controlled labor of colonized Mexicans. The long history of overlapping empires and imperial expansion that overlay Los Angeles and the borderlands in the nineteenth century meant that the city and its residents were never far from ideas of expansionistic growth, international commerce, and transnational politics. As a result, when Anglo-Americans arrived in a trickle and then a torrent following the American Civil War, they already understood Los Angeles as situated at the intersection of the United States, Mexico, the rest of Latin America, and the Pacific world. Los Angeles was not just the remote edge of the United States. It was also the portal to empire and the hemisphere.

As a result, as Los Angeles became more and more Anglo-American from the 1860s through the 1890s, Angeleno investors began to couple urban growth with the spread of American empire in Mexico. They crossed the border with a set of imperial projects, ranging from international diplomacy to cross-border commerce, and prioritized urban growth with personal financial benefits. Connecting core to periphery took place at multiple scales—the international, the regional, and the local—and wrought an exchange in everything from borax to oranges to chickens to oil between Los Angeles and Mexico in the decades leading up to the Mexican Revolution. Several scales of empire building converged in the Los Angeles–Mexico borderlands precisely to "secure a share of the prize" and to transform Mexico, particularly the northern portion of the country, into Los Angeles's "tributary territory." Tracing the relationship between Los Angeles investors up, toward U.S. international policy, as well as down, to individual relationships between Los Angeles capitalists and Mexican officials, reveals an imperial and expansionist philosophy infused with ideas of an "informal" or commercial empire and operating at multiple levels but always emanating from Los Angeles and placing its growth and boosters first. Bridging recent studies of American empire that foreground the local, on-the-ground functioning of imperial exploits with the rich history of capitalist development in the U.S.-Mexico borderlands, this chapter explores the ways in which privileging urban growth shaped borderlands relationships between an urban core in Los Angeles and a periphery in Mexico.[3]

First, at the level of national diplomacy, Angelenos wanted the United States to have a rigorous trade relationship with Mexico without the formal ties of traditional imperial endeavors. Epitomized by the efforts of Civil War general and Los Angeles–based investor William Rosecrans, Los Angeles investment schemes were deeply embedded in the schema of American global expansion following the American Civil War. Los Angeles, long the outpost of several empires, was home to investors attuned to the growing role and power of capital in the American West, in the borderlands, and around the world. As explored through Rosecrans's role as ambassador to Mexico following the Civil War and his simultaneous investments in the Los Angeles–Mexico borderlands, Angeleno investors embarked on urban and imperial adventures at the same time investors and policymakers began articulating the formation of an American commercial empire. As famously expressed by Secretary of State William Seward, who purchased Alaska for the United States in 1867, "the flag would follow trade" in this philosophy of global capital connections. Racial philosophies colored this advance of American commercial interests around the globe; an aversion to absorbing nonwhite peoples into the American body politic sparked much heated political debate over American control over places such as Hawaii or the Philippines. On the edge of the American continental empire, Los Angeles investors, eager to expand the commercial reach of their city, regionalized this highly racialized approach to trade and empire building and hoped to expand commercial connections between Los Angeles and Mexico without formally annexing additional portions of Mexico or absorbing more of its nonwhite population.

At a more regional level, Los Angeles investors actively cultivated a dense set of relationships between commercial and civic leaders in Southern California and brokers, investors, and government officials in Mexico. Like agents of empire around the world, they believed that a network of relationships, as well as formalized commercial and governmental ties between Southern California and Mexico City, would expand Los Angeles's influence and economic supremacy. These relationships, both informal and formal, took the form of friendship between some of Los Angeles's most powerful investors and high-ranking Mexican officials such as Díaz. Others pursued close working relationships with Mexican American and Mexican investors and brokers such as Los Angeles lawyer Ignacio Sepúlveda and Mexican investor Guillermo Andrade to facilitate business dealings south of the border. These relationships culminated in a campaign to formalize a commercial relationship between an urban core in Southern California and a Mexican periphery. This came in the form of a Mexican consulate office located in Los Angeles primarily to attend to the economic relationship between Los Angeles and Mexico. While Angelenos did not want a formal imperial relationship between the United States and Mexico during this period (and actively reassured the Mexican government that annexation of Mexico was not their ultimate goal), they did want formalized commercial ties between city and hinterland and sought these in the establishment of an outpost of the Mexican government within the geographic bounds of the city. In this, Angeleno investors mirrored efforts of American capitalists, traders, exporters, and investors who looked to expand both private corporate and national power and informal or commercial imperial endeavors overseas following the American Civil War.[4]

Born of Empire

The philosophy of urban empire propagated by Los Angeles boosters emerged in a city long bound up in the building of empires. Founded in 1781, El Pueblo de Nuestra Señora La Reina de Los Angeles de Porciuncula began as an outpost of the Spanish crown. A motley group of settlers traversed the parched deserts of northern New Spain from Sonora and Sinaloa into Alta California to establish the pueblo. Once in the Los Angeles basin, the colonists set about the first project of most colonial endeavors—controlling and converting a region's native population, in this case, the Tongva people. While busy with the forceful control of indigenous populations at the local level, the pueblo's founders also found themselves swept into the global dimensions of empire. As historian Louise Pubols so succinctly argues, "Los Angeles was born a global city."[5] The very founding of the town came as a mandate from a Spanish crown that wanted to restructure its American empire to better defend it from European challengers. Between its founding in 1781 and the start of the Mexican-American War in 1846, Los Angeles's population remained relatively small but closely linked to global political and economic shifts. An international trade in the products of ranches and cattle made up an important portion of the pueblo's economy, and Angelenos, particularly those with political and economic power, Californios or *gente de razón*, participated in Mexico's movement for independence and its transition from colony to republic in the first decades of the nineteenth century.

The dynamics of a different empire overtook the city and the borderlands in the middle of the nineteenth century in the form of the Mexican-American War. Soaked in the ideology of Manifest Destiny, exuberant American expansionists believed it the providence of their nation to span the continent. This imperial impulse brought about the next dramatic shift in the history of Los Angeles. Manifest Destiny and its more profane counterparts—ideas of racial superiority, American settler colonialism, and military conquest—brought new territories into the American nation, including California and its southern outpost, Los Angeles. Again, broader continental and global forces aligned to transform a place far from traditional centers of power. Annexation to the United States brought waves of ambitious Anglo migrants and booster designs for conjuring cities out of manufactured real estate booms.[6]

On the ground in Los Angeles, the close of the Mexican-American War in 1848 brought with it tides of new Anglo settlers, awash in high economic expectations and a desire to connect Los Angeles to the greater United States and the Pacific world. As a result, these arrivals set the stage for further American military and economic forays into the borderlands and beyond. Pio Pico, California's last Mexican governor, lamented, "We find ourselves suddenly threatened by hordes of Yankee emigrants, who have already begun to flock into our country and whose progress we cannot arrest."[7] Anglo-Americans in the postwar period arrived anticipating open tracts of land ready for claim and ripe for development. Instead they found Californios, the Mexican American political and economic class who had long controlled Southern California property in the form of expansive ranchos and who rightly anticipated maintaining their property under the provisions of the Treaty of Guadalupe Hidalgo, which guaranteed citizenship and property rights to the territory's population. Taxes and prolonged legal proceedings to prove ownership under American law with Mexican documents proved disastrous for the Californios, who found themselves faced with the difficult challenge of protecting properties from an onslaught of aggressive American capitalism and a racialized American legal system. By the end of the nineteenth century, a few Anglo-American capitalists based in Los Angeles and San Francisco controlled most of Southern California's ranches. Given this wide-scale transfer of wealth and property in Southern California from Californios to Anglo-Americans between 1848 and the 1880s and the city's already established ties with international trade and Mexico, it is not difficult to understand why Los Angeles's Anglo-American settlers and boosters also looked to the U.S.-Mexico borderlands and beyond for financial opportunities to fuel urban growth. If Mexican property could become American wealth in Los Angeles, Anglo-Americans saw no reason to stop their acquisitions at the border.

Indeed, the violent imperial and expansionist impulse that drove events such as the Mexican-American War proved difficult to quell on the edges of American empire, particularly in California. As Anglo-Americans flooded the state, they carried out one of the bloodiest campaigns of extermination against native peoples in the nation's already bloody relationship with indigenous communities. They also launched vigilante campaigns against Mexican Americans and engaged in the less bloody but still troubling dispossession of both native and Mexican populations. Extralegal killings in Southern California during this period constituted what historian William Deverell describes as the "unending Mexican war." Los Angeles also served as the launching point for further violent forays into Latin America. In campaigns mirroring William Walker's failed attempt to extend American rule to Central America, Anglo-Americans utilized Los Angeles's position as the far outpost of empire to extend their country's reach. As Deverell chronicles, Henry A. Crabb led a small force of disgruntled ex–gold miners on an ambitious and ill-fated expedition to finish up what Crabb believed the U.S. government had left undone at the end of the Mexican-American War. In 1857 "All Mexico!" was his cry as he and his crew departed from Los Angeles and crossed the new international border into the deserts of Sonora. Crabb's expedition failed spectacularly. Mexican authorities ended his ambitious plan to redraw the border and take the rest of Mexico in front of a firing squad. According to Los Angeles folklore, they shipped his head back to Southern California, hastily preserved in a jar of vinegar—a grim reminder not to cross the border with expansionist fantasies.[8]

Crabb's efforts to expand American territorial rule south of the newly marked border ended in a gruesome footnote to Los Angeles history. His belief that biting off additional chunks of Mexico could prove beneficial to Los Angeles and the greater nation, however, had a longer life. Crabb's border transgressions represented the violent end on a spectrum of common thought—that Los Angeles deserved to grow beyond the bounds of the border established in 1848. Early Anglo-American arrivals in Los Angeles, such as Abel Stearns, who constructed and operated the city's first port, had already looked eagerly for ways to augment the town's limited natural resources, often through ambitious plans to link the small town to larger markets and the global economy. Arrivals in the city in the 1860s and 1870s followed suit, laying aspiring plans to connect Los Angeles to booming San Francisco, the long Pacific coast, and Mexico.

American empire building and urban development in Los Angeles at the turn of the century were also intricately bound up in the city's Mexican past, present, and future. In terms of sheer demographics, Mexicans and Mexican Americans continued to be a significant part of the city's population, often augmented by border crossings from the states of northern Mexico. The region's Californios even maintained their role as part of its ruling elite, while both Anglos and elite Mexicans relied on the labor of the city's mestizo and indigenous population. In 1850, just after the close of the Mexican-American War, Mexicans constituted more than 75 percent of the city's population. A decade later, despite the substantial influx of Anglo-Americans, Mexicans still represented about 50 percent of Angelenos. Even as Anglo settler colonialism transformed Los Angeles from a city with a hefty Mexican majority in the 1850s to a majority Anglo city by the 1870s, Mexicans remained key to the city's development as both civic and commercial leaders as well as the region's largest labor force. Los Angeles even experienced a period of governance shared between new Anglo-American arrivals and an older Mexican elite who brokered an intercultural system of civic control through the 1860s.[9]

The fate of Los Angeles shifted again, however, as the stream of Anglo-Americans became a deluge and transformed a once Mexican town into an American city. The completion of the city's first transcontinental railroad, which arrived in the form of a Southern Pacific trunk line from San Francisco in 1876, facilitated this process and thrust the region into the Gilded Age economy. Not coincidentally, the 1870s were also the decade when the Anglo population overtook the Mexican, transforming Los Angeles for the first time into a majority white city. A second transcontinental rail line completed in 1886, as well as a real estate boom that tripled property values and transactions, helped drive a population boom in the 1880s, a decade that witnessed the phenomenal growth of the city from just over 11,000 people to over 50,000. Fifty thousand would double to over 100,000 in the final decade of the nineteenth century. During these two decades of spectacular growth, the city also paved streets, hung telephone wires, laid cable car tracks, ran electricity lines, built its first university, held its first major art exhibition, and started a symphony and a museum.

Growth, however, did not diminish the city's relationship with Mexico, Mexicans, or its Mexican past. In fact, urban and regional growth depended on the labor of Mexican Americans and Mexican immigrants. And, as a number of Los Angeles historians observe, the newly Anglo city also laid claim to memories of Mexican Los Angeles during this period, refashioning a violent past into a palatable fantasy of "Spanish caballeros" and a tranquil Mediterranean lifestyle. The city's proximity to Mexico and Mexican history became transformed into a commodity marketed to American settlers and tourists.[10] Mexican American and Mexican labor laid the bricks and picked the fruit in these new enterprises.

Economic growth, dependent on national and global exchange networks, cross-border commerce, and the international migration of workers, accompanied railroad lines and flocks of tourists and population booms in Southern California. Commercial agriculture, rooted in nonwhite labor, became the region's gold. Southern California became wealthy based on labor-intensive crops such as citrus in hinterland regions including Ventura and Riverside, and then consolidation in centralized fruit markets in Los Angeles, and finally export to markets across the nation. Agriculture and a transnational workforce, particularly for the cultivation of citrus, powered the

Los Angeles population, 1850–1930

Year	Total	Mexican American
1850	1,610	1,213
1860	4,385	2,069
1870	5,728	2,160
1880	11,183	2,166
1890	50,395	3,000–5,000
1900	102,479	data not available
1910	319,000	5,632
1920	577,000	30,000
1930	1,200,000	97,000

Source: This data comes from a variety of sources. For the total population of Los Angeles during this period, see "Historical Census Statistics on Population Totals by Race, 1790 to 1990, for Large Cities and Other Urban Places in the United States," https://www.census.gov/library/working-papers/2005/demo/POP-twps0076.html. The U.S. Census counted Mexicans and Mexican Americans as white until 1930, when it included the category of "Mexican Race." This makes calculating the Mexican and Mexican American population of Los Angeles difficult between 1850 and 1930. Some historians have made calculations based on Spanish surname as well as the status of "foreign born" in Mexico. Estimates of the city's Mexican and Mexican American population from 1850 to 1880 are drawn from Richard Griswold del Castillo, *The Los Angeles Barrio, 1850–1890: A Social History* (Berkeley: University of California Press, 1979), 35; for the years between 1880 and 1920, see Molina, *Fit to Be Citizens?*, 7; for the year 1900 the number of Mexican residents is particularly unclear for reasons cited above; for the years 1920 and 1930, see Sánchez, *Becoming Mexican American*, 90.

relationship between an urban core in Los Angeles and a hinterland that extended deep into Southern California and beyond. This process of urban/hinterland development was part of a larger project of American empire building in the West. As white Americans expanded their imperial control into the West, they did so through the organization of towns and cities that connected agriculture and the extraction of natural resources with transportation lines and markets. The western relationship between cities and hinterlands was epitomized in Southern California's first major industry, which centralized the exchange of cash crops grown in a hinterland, most notably citrus, in downtown Los Angeles. It was in the financial and transportation hub of the city where crops became cash.[11]

As the city grew, boosters with international aspirations eagerly eyed a possible hinterland and commercial empire just across the U.S.-Mexico border. They pointed to a long and shared history between Los Angeles and Mexico as justification for the city's commercial expansion south of the international boundary. According to the *Times*, the links extended beyond history to race, language, and geography: "A history in common with that of Mexico, race affiliations, the prevalence of the Spanish language in Southern California and Mexico, geographical proximity, ship and railroad facilities and many other considerations,—all point to the unsurpassed advantages possessed by Los Angeles as the distributing point for a large portion of Mexico."[12] Even the phrase "race affiliations" likely referred to the imperial and racial arrangement of labor in both Los Angeles and Mexico that placed propertied whites in control of nonwhite workers. Echoing the discourse of American empire, Southern California investors argued that Mexico fell "naturally" into the orbit of a dynamic, aggressive, and expansionistic Los Angeles. This place, Los Angeles boosters insisted, was a city destined to have an empire, or at least an international hinterland.

At first glance, the investment strategies of Los Angeles–based financiers and shareholders may seem to simply reflect the larger growth of American global imperialism and capitalism in the U.S.-Mexico borderlands in the second half of the nineteenth century. They were certainly embedded in both American empire and borderlands capitalism. As a number of borderlands scholars have chronicled, the U.S.-Mexico border became the site for intense capitalist development at the end of the nineteenth century. Borderlands industries such as copper mining and ranching constituted an "industrial reorganization" of the region and bound people, businesses, towns, and infrastructure together across an international boundary.[13] In Los Angeles, however, urbanism colored cross-border imaginings and relationships. Urban growth shaped both the expansion of the city's economy and the relationship between its investor class and what they hoped would be the region's cross-border "tributary territory" or hinterland.

Not coincidentally, borderlands American capitalists and Anglo Angelenos extended investment in extractive industries that had been so successful in the West, such as agriculture, along with its racialized system of labor, into the borderlands and across the border. Angelenos invested most heavily in Mexico between 1870 and 1910 during a period of extraordinary growth in Southern California and, not coincidentally, foreign investment in Mexico. Industries developed and refined in Southern California transformed themselves into cross-border enterprises, including agriculture, mining, cattle ranching, oil drilling, manufacturing, and leisure and tourism. As exemplified in the histories of investors such as Lewis Bradbury and Griffith J. Griffith and as discussed throughout this study, much of their wealth circulated back across the border and became reinscribed in the Los

Angeles landscape in the concrete form of edifices like the Bradbury Building or urban oases such as Griffith Park. Mexican money, withdrawn from investments south of the border by Anglo-American venture capitalists reliant on Mexican labor, became reinvested in real estate and infrastructure in an emerging metropolis just north of the border.

All of this activity in Los Angeles and in the greater U.S.-Mexico borderlands relied on the cooperation of the Mexican executive and state. Díaz, assuming power in 1876, embarked on a strategy of state building and economic growth that prioritized foreign investment. In fact, Díaz eyed the successful economic development of the American West by Wall Street interests as a model for Mexico. Mexican elites generally supported this approach to national development and opened opportunities in the public and private sectors that allowed for the flow of investment dollars from north of the border into southern ventures. As Matías Romero, Díaz's minister to the United States, said to an audience of American investors, "Nature has made us neighbors." "There is no reason, therefore," he continued, "why we should not trade largely and to our mutual advantage."[14] Railroad companies and banking interests led the way in the 1860s, followed by mining ventures, agriculture, and manufacturing. This shakeup of the borderlands transformed natural landscapes into sites for capitalist extraction and profit.

Los Angeles and Commercial Empire

The growth of American investment and capitalism in Mexico and the borderlands provided the laboratory for the expansion of an American "informal" empire and the nation's rise to global power following the Civil War. After the close of the conflict, as the American economy grew at an astronomical rate, financiers and industrialists chased riches across the West and south of the border. They expanded many of the enterprises that worked so well in the incorporation of the West, such as mining, railroads, and banks, into Mexico. This expansion had one key difference, however. American investors and their politicians generally did not want to formally annex additional territories, particularly if they had nonwhite populations. Instead, American elites hoped to turn to places such as Latin America and Asia to source raw products and open markets. John Miller, a senator from California, argued in 1884, "New markets are necessary to be found in order to keep our factories running. Here lies to the south of us our India, and if we have the nerve, and the foresight, and the sagacity to utilize it by proper methods we shall have new markets for our products and for our manufactures which will keep every loom, and every anvil, and every manufactory of this country in motion."[15] It was in Mexico that Americans could test these approaches and stratagems of a commercial empire. Angelenos were at the center of this enterprise.[16]

The post–Civil War career of General William Starke Rosecrans demonstrates how this era of commercial empire intersected with the early expansion of Los Angeles investment into Mexico. For over thirty years, between the end of the Civil War and his death in 1898, Rosecrans's commercial and political projects promoted development in Los Angeles as well as the expansion of the nation's financial reach into Mexico. When he arrived in Los Angeles in 1868, Rosecrans was well known as a brilliant Union Army general and strategist who met an unfortunate and disastrous defeat at the Battle of Chickamauga in 1863. Luckily for him, he would prove more successful in both Southern California real estate development and American empire building south of the border. In fact, Rosecrans's commercial and diplomatic projects in Los Angeles and Mexico built a set of relationships between American investors and Mexican policymakers that would shape the connection between the two regions for half a century. At the scale of the national, the international, and the diplomatic, Rosecrans utilized an ambassadorial assignment in Mexico as well as his own investment dollars to spearhead a campaign to promote American investments in Mexico without a loss of Mexican sovereignty. Instead of advocating for official territorial control of Mexico, as had resulted from the Mexican-American War just a decade and a half before Rosecrans arrived in Mexico City and Los Angeles, the general argued that the United States and his newly adopted city could expand its economic reach and power through the migration of capital. In this, Rosecrans's career north and south of the border embodied the spread of American capitalism into the American West and from there to points south of the border and around the globe.

Rosecrans and his fellow Angeleno investors resided in a city recently acquired through the martial efforts of American empire builders. They also followed in the footsteps of their northern rival, San Francisco, where capitalists had begun pouring millions of dollars into mining enterprises in Sonora as early as 1863.[17] Desperate to eclipse their nemesis in the north, Los Angeles–based capitalists transformed economic enthusiasm for Mexico into a frenzied call for Los Angeles to get "its share" of transnational trade. From Los Angeles, they also led the nation in connecting two geographic scales in the expansion of American empire. They worked to link a particular geographic point in the United States—Los Angeles and its commercial ventures—to economic opportunities and "informal" imperial relationships outside of national borders. Rosecrans's career in particular offers a glimpse of some of the aspirations and efforts to connect Los Angeles to Mexico, as well as the growth of Los Angeles as an urban empire, in the first two decades following the American Civil War. Two points in Rosecrans's biography are particularly key to the history of Los Angeles and its aspirations in Mexico. First, Rosecrans served as the leading proponent of American investment in Mexico in the two decades following the Civil War. Second, he coordinated this call from his rancho in Los Angeles.

Like most Anglo-Americans arriving in the city following the American Civil War, Rosecrans hoped to make money and anticipated doing so in the greater American West. His plan was to develop land and extend American settler colonialism into Southern California in the form of small farms and urban subdivisions. He invested in an attractive and extensive piece of property located just southwest of Los Angeles's small downtown, Rancho Sausal Redondo. Like the rest of Southern California, the property was formerly a Mexican land grant and had originally been deeded to Antonio Ygnacio Avila by the Mexican government in 1822. Although Avila successfully defended his title to the rancho under the Land Claims Act of 1851, probate expenses forced his family to sell the property to pay the cost of settling his estate in 1868. While wrangling between Rosecrans and other Anglo-American speculators and squatters put the land in legal limbo for almost a decade, the general eventually secured title to the property. On the 14,000-acre Los Angeles ranch he built a rambling one-story ranch house with a wide front porch and surrounded it with pepper and eucalyptus trees. He planted the ranch with barley and wheat and began cultivating citrus, potatoes, and strawberries. He also began planning to divide up the valuable real estate to sell to eager Anglo-American buyers arriving in droves on the city's new rail line, which arrived in 1876.[18]

At precisely the same moment that Rosecrans was maneuvering to purchase a Mexican land grant in Los Angeles, he was also serving as the United States minister to Mexico and was the leading national proponent of American investment south of the border. In the elaborate diplomatic language of the nineteenth century, President Andrew Johnson's official appointment letter named Rosecrans the "Envoy Extraordinary and Minister Plenipotentiary" to the Republic of Mexico.[19] This tenure in Mexico initiated ties between American capitalists and the Mexican political class that would last well into the twentieth century. Although the appointment would last less than a year—a change in administrations put Rosecrans's political nemesis, Ulysses S. Grant, into power in 1869—Rosecrans's term as ambassador to Mexico convinced him that Americans could, and should, make fortunes south of the border. In fact, Rosecrans accepted the appointment in part because he represented the powerful Pennsylvania Railroad and hoped to spearhead the company's expansion into Mexico. Ultimately, he hoped to bind Mexico with iron tracks, from Tampico to the Pacific and from Mexico City to the U.S.-Mexico border, a lattice neatly sewing together a country and stitching its future to international and borderlands capitalism. Although the political appointment was short-lived, Rosecrans's time in Mexico was significant, both for U.S.-Mexico relations and for Los Angeles.[20]

Rosecrans arrived in Mexico on the eve of massive change in the country. Following decades marked by civil and foreign wars, European interventions, and the collapse of French imperial aspirations in Mexico, Liberal leader Benito Juárez won the presidency in 1867. He embarked on a period of national investment in infrastructure and education as well as the building of friendly diplomatic relations with European nations and the United States. Juárez also had a guarded interest in incorporating American financiers into his plans for modernizing Mexico. In a letter to Rosecrans in 1870, Juárez observed that he believed Rosecrans's efforts to move American investment capital south of the border would help his nation: "I will be greatly pleased if the venture capitalists you have referred to would come here and invest part of their wealth in industrial enterprise, extending by that means the bonds of fraternity between the two republics and linking their identities by means of the same democratic institutions."[21] This sentiment only intensified under the administration of Porfirio Díaz, who served as Mexico's president from 1876 to 1910. Díaz believed that foreign investment, particularly American investment, could modernize what he considered a backward nation. Under his leadership, the Mexican government granted concessions to or worked closely with American railroad companies, mining interests, banks, land developers, ranchers, and manufacturers. Transfers of land and resources were staggering and totaled in the millions of acres and dollars. By the time the Mexican Revolution forced Díaz to leave office, American investors alone owned 27 percent of Mexico's land.[22]

Within this context of growing American empire and budding foreign investment in Mexico, Rosecrans had a short career as a diplomat but a long life as an investor. He took ideas for transnational investment schemes back to Los Angeles in 1869 and implemented them on international, national, and local scales to ensure American and Angeleno commercial expansion south of the border. He developed his property in Southern California while simultaneously running a lobbying campaign to encourage American private and governmental investment in Mexico, particularly the country's railroad and banking systems. In these efforts, Rosecrans argued that investment in Mexico would lead to increased trade and economic benefits for the United States and would solidify the power of the United States in the hemisphere. Like many of his contemporaries, Rosecrans viewed Mexico as endowed with innumerable natural resources but lacking the enterprise or energy necessary to transform nature into capital. As a result, it was the duty of American citizens and even the U.S. government to lend a hand and make a fortune.[23] Commenting on Rosecrans's efforts, a contemporary ally observed that Mexico's inhabitants were "unequal to the task of redeeming it and General Rosecrans conceived the idea of invoking the aid and enterprise of his own people."[24] Investment in Mexico, Rosecrans maintained, would help the United States become in the Americas what England was in other parts of the globe—the center of an empire.

Again reflective of a new approach to American empire building, Rosecrans was careful to iterate that he was not the "great annexer," as some had dubbed him in Mexico. He fully intended for Mexico to maintain political autonomy while embracing American capital. In this, Rosecrans embodied the emerging new perspective on American expansion: rather than extending formal territorial control, the United States could grow its international power and influence through the spread of its investment dollars. Rosecrans cloaked his promotion of neocolonialism in the language of hemispheric fraternity as well as Manifest Destiny and the Monroe Doctrine. In other words, Rosecrans coupled the doctrine that the United States was ordained by God to be continental in scope with the political ideology that it should also control, or at least oversee, major political and economic development in the Western Hemisphere. While these ideologies certainly appeared threatening to Mexican sovereignty, Rosecrans's approach argued that in order to ensure hemispheric peace, the United States needed to simultaneously assure its Latin American neighbors that it would respect their sovereignty while also "safeguarding" economic growth and political stability. Within a widely circulated resolution he submitted to Congress, entitled "Manifest Destiny, the Monroe Doctrine, and Our Relations with Mexico; a Letter from Gen. Rosecrans to the People of the United States," Rosecrans argued that Americans could assure Mexico that they would not repeat the aggressive land grab of the Mexican-American War by instead letting investment dollars flow south of the border. Writing just twenty years after the conclusion of that predatory conflict, Rosecrans hoped that American investments would be taken as a positive sign of fraternity between the two neighboring nations. Manifest Destiny and the Monroe Doctrine, he maintained, gave the United States the responsibility to ensure the financial success of countries within the hemisphere while simultaneously respecting the sovereignty and independence of American nations. According to Rosecrans, the goal of Manifest Destiny and the Monroe Doctrine was the "complete political, commercial, and industrial fraternity among the Republics of the New World."[25]

Like many of his imperial compatriots, Rosecrans also articulated a racial argument about American commercial expansion south of the border that would not result in the formal political annexation of Mexico. In a slur disguised as a reassurance, Rosecrans announced to Juárez, "I frankly say to you that I am not in favor of annexation. I do not think our Government can take in so much untrained humanity and digest it without danger."[26] Mexico was safe from annexation by the United States, Rosecrans maintained, because Americans could not and did not want to include more nonwhite Mexicans in its body politic. As one newspaper reported, Rosecrans planned to "do something with American capital to furnish Mexico with currency, railroads, and the means of securing immigrants, but he does not look forward to annexation at present, and prefers to see the country governed by its own people."[27] This, of course, was race at work within an ideology of American empire. The United States could grow its interests and economy abroad without the messy absorption of nonwhite people by simply extending commercial control and leaving governance to a native political class.

It was in Los Angeles that Rosecrans's ideology for American commercial growth intersected with his individual investments in Mexico. On the ground, he worked to extend the reach of Los Angeles commerce and his own personal economy. He did not simply have the interest of the American economy or Mexican autonomy in mind as he crisscrossed both nations advocating American investment in Mexico and peppered American newspapers with his promotion of south-of-the-border business ventures. At precisely the moment that he submitted his resolution to Congress and issued his open letter to investors in the United States, Rosecrans continued to expand his Los Angeles, California, and Mexico investments. In particular, he invested heavily in Collis Huntington's Southern Pacific Railroad (SPRR), which had significant interests in expanding south of the border. Huntington had close political and economic ties to Mexican officials and often provided advice to policymakers in Mexico City. Traveling in the same circles as Mexican legislators and American railroaders, Rosecrans purchased 9 percent of SPRR stock in the 1870s, the period when Huntington and his compatriots in the Big Four were extending their system south to Los Angeles from San Francisco.[28] Notably, the Southern Pacific also had plans to extend its California and Arizona lines south across the border and along the west coast of Mexico.[29]

Rosecrans also partnered with Guillermo Andrade, who would later become the first Mexican consul in Los Angeles, to establish the Mexican Colonization and Industrial Company. The company received permission from the Mexican government to develop colonies in Sonora and Sinaloa as well as fishing rights for islands off Mexico's west coast.[30] Not one to limit his financial and corporate interests by geography, Rosecrans also partnered with Robert Symon, a leading force with the Santa Fe and Mexican Central Railroad, to buy property in Tuxpan in eastern Mexico and Mazatlán on the country's west coast. In Los Angeles, Rosecrans partnered with William Winder to buy a sizable property in Baja California. Finally, Rosecrans facilitated the expansion of Anglo-American settler colonialism in Southern California by subdividing and selling his extensive Los Angeles lands. By the 1880s, Rosecrans and his associates, many of them based in Southern California, owned property across Southern California and Mexico and had invested particularly heavily in states adjacent to the United States, including Durango, Sinaloa, Sonora, and Baja California.[31]

Rosecrans's career in both Los Angeles and Mexico embodies the spread of American capitalism and empire at multiple scales. His investments spanned the international, the national, and the local, from Los Angeles to Washington, D.C., to multiple locales south of the border. Seeking a fortune after the close of the Civil War, Rosecrans turned west and south. One of his first investments following the war, which he organized from his diplomatic position in Mexico City, was the purchase of a Mexican land grant in Los Angeles. For the next two decades, Rosecrans traveled among Mexico City, Washington, D.C., and Los Angeles in a variety of political and commercial capacities, promoting the settlement and growth of Los Angeles as well as American investment south of the border. His development of real estate in Southern California facilitated the Anglo-American settlement of what had only recently been Mexico. He paired his Los Angeles commercial ventures with various investment schemes in Mexico, hoping for personal fortune while he simultaneously became the leading proponent for a new kind of American empire—one that did not require the formal political control of Mexico or the possible absorption of nonwhite Mexicans into the United States. Instead, as Rosecrans insisted from his ranch in Los Angeles, and as his speculative dollars proved, Anglo-Americans could extend commercial and regional power south of the border through transnational investment schemes.

Commercial Networks and City-Empire

In Los Angeles and the borderlands, Rosecrans's compatriots took up his call for American commercial expansion in Mexico with exuberant energy. Beginning in the 1870s, they formed dozens of cross-border ties to facilitate commerce between the city and its international southern neighbor. By the 1880s and 1890s, Rosecrans's crusade and the obvious material success of Angelenos such as Bradbury and Griffith induced hundreds, if not thousands, more to invest south of the border. As in other imperial ventures, these investors and firms partnered with brokers and local elites to build commercial enterprises. In the case of Los Angeles, investors worked with Mexican and Mexican American agents such as Sepúlveda and Andrade to make transnational investment possible, relying heavily on their language skills, bureaucratic knowledge, and legal expertise to facilitate the southbound flow of capital. As trade and investments increased and Los Angeles commercial leaders envisioned even more, they would also seek a formalized relationship between the city and the Mexican government in the form of a consulate office to facilitate business ties between core and hinterland. It was this network of investors and brokers, many already with direct ties to Rosecrans, that would lobby the Mexican government to establish a consul in Los Angeles.[32]

In the two and a half decades between Rosecrans's purchase of Rancho Sausal Redondo and the city's campaign for a Mexican consulate, the Los Angeles business class carefully planned for and executed municipal and regional growth. Expansion was not left to the vagaries of chance. During this period, Los Angeles transformed from a small town of under 5,000 people to a growing western city that would reach a population of over 50,000 by 1890. Key to executing growth were the city's business organizations. The Los Angeles Board of Trade, founded in 1883, actively sought to elevate Los Angeles's regional and national significance through campaigns for improved federal facilities, including a major post office, veterans' home, and army headquarters. In 1888, commercial leaders also founded the Los Angeles Chamber of Commerce, which boasted over 1,000 members by 1899 and carefully nurtured the city's growth. The chamber lobbied the state and federal governments for infrastructural development in Los Angeles, including the improvement of the city's port, as well as coordinating and paying for nationwide advertising campaigns to promote economic and leisure opportunities in Southern California. Finally, the Merchants and Manufacturers Association, founded in 1896, coordinated both economic growth and the brutal suppression of union organizing in Southern California. Touting Los Angeles as an "open shop" town, Merchants and Manufacturers members proudly supported employers in labor disputes, imported strikebreakers, and won injunctions against forms of protest such as the picket line. While unions and union labor thrived in rival cities such as San Francisco, Los Angeles boasted that it was the friendliest place in the West for employers and capital.[33]

A fervent belief in growth characterized Los Angeles business associations and their membership, as well as their excitement about economic opportunities south of the border. Enthusiasm and urban boosterism animated turn-of-the-century evangelists of urban progress, and city boundaries or even international borders did not delineate the limits of advancement. Instead, as boosters did in many western cities, the Los Angeles business class looked to a far-flung hinterland to fuel urban growth. Situated in the U.S.-Mexico borderlands, a place alive with economic possibilities at the end of the nineteenth century, Los Angeles boosters turned aggressively south to fuel city development. As the *Los Angeles Times* reported in 1882, the city was the "natural distribution point for the Southwest and Northern Mexico . . . attracting the attention of outside capitalists," marking "a new era in the commercial importance of Los Angeles."[34] As the *Times* noted in the same article, however, growth required vigilance and constant campaigns to expand an urban empire.

Building on the imperialist logic of Rosecrans, now residing full-time on his ranch just southwest of Los Angeles's growing downtown, city businessmen looked for a strategy to officially link not just their commercial interests but also their city to Mexico and its government. Precisely because Los Angeles's elite had a vested interest in seeing their city boom, and perhaps because they had visible and tangible evidence of fortunes made in Mexico, Rosecrans's economic peers set about creating a dense network between their growing city and resources they were certain awaited them south of the boundary line between the United States and Mexico. Municipal growth required direct access to an expansive hinterland and, unwilling to accept simply Riverside or even Arizona as the city's tributary territory, Los Angeles elites looked beyond the border for resources that they could exploit, extract, and concentrate in their city north of the border. Taking up Rosecrans's twenty-year campaign to promote American investments in Mexico, elite Angelenos actively connected core to hinterland.

As in most imperial ventures, the growing network of business elites in Los Angeles and their commercial interests in Mexico relied on strategic partnerships with local and regional elites.[35] Mexican Americans and Mexicans were key in creating the dense network of business and political ties that linked city and hinterland. Take, for example, the life and work of Ignacio Sepúlveda. Sepúlveda was a fourth-generation Californian born into a Californio family in 1842, just a handful of years before the United States would declare war on Mexico to take California. Educated in a boarding school in Massachusetts in the 1850s, Sepúlveda developed the language skills and legal background necessary to navigate in a California that now belonged to the United States. In fact, these abilities allowed Sepúlveda to partner with American lawyers newly settled in Los Angeles and to build a thriving law firm that boasted a clientele of both Californios and wealthy migrant Anglo-Americans. A successful law practice also propelled Sepúlveda into civic life and leadership in 1860s Los Angeles, a period of shared political power between Mexican American elites and new white arrivals.[36]

Although his family had deep roots in Southern California, Sepúlveda also maintained strong ties to his Mexican identity and heritage. He traveled to Mexico City in 1865 to offer his services to the Mexican government under the rule of Maximilian I, the Austrian emperor installed by Napoleon II and a coterie of conservative Mexican elites. When Maximilian's rule came to an abrupt and violent end in 1867, Sepúlveda found himself a prisoner of republican forces in the state of Querétaro. Despite this precarious position in Mexico, Sepúlveda's ties to Los Angeles remained strong and saved him from a prison sentence. Phineas Banning, a prominent land developer and investor in Los Angeles as well as a California state senator, persuaded Secretary of State William H. Seward to intervene on Sepúlveda's behalf. The intervention worked, and republican forces released Sepúlveda if he promised to return to the United States. He promptly headed north to Baltimore and then Los Angeles, taking with him a sword and an oil painting of Maximilian as a memento of his exploits in Mexican politics.[37]

Back in Los Angeles, Sepúlveda continued to operate as a leading lawyer and political figure in both Anglo and Californio society. He married an Anglo-American woman, Ora Anderson, in 1868 and was elected to a powerful Los Angeles County judgeship in 1869. He won elections to a number of judicial seats between 1869 and the 1880s, and the Democratic Party even considered nominating him for the State Supreme Court. However, Los Angeles's swelling Anglo population diminished Sepúlveda's political appeal to an electorate that believed whites were superior to Mexicans and that nonwhites had no place in American political institutions. Sensing that he would not be able to continue to win elections to judicial positions, Sepúlveda instead harnessed his language skills and ethnic background to his connections with Angeleno investors interested in Mexico.[38]

Sepúlveda left Los Angeles for Mexico City, where he partnered with a Mexican lawyer to start a firm providing legal and business services for American interests in Mexico. As an "international power broker," Sepúlveda took on as his first client the San Francisco–based firm of Wells Fargo, which wanted to extend its operations south of the border.[39] Investors from Los Angeles and around the nation quickly followed. For example, Sepúlveda provided legal services to the California Development Company, an irrigation company operating at the border of California and Baja California with close ties to the Colorado River Land Company owned by Harrison Gray Otis and a number of other wealthy Los Angeles investors.[40] He also represented the San Isidro Ranch Company, a hunting club founded by Angelenos Henry Workman Keller and Harry Chandler and located in Baja California.[41] He also served as the lawyer for the Hearst family's extensive Mexican land investments and maintained a lifelong friendship with Phoebe Hearst and William Randolph Hearst (who would have significant publishing interests in Los Angeles by the turn of the century). His growing list of clients and promotion of American investments in Mexico brought him to the attention of Porfirio Díaz and into Díaz's circle of advisers. Sepúlveda also continued to grow his network of Anglo-American friends and investors, eventually becoming president of the American Club in Mexico City, an elite organization of American business interests in Mexico. As an American citizen with extensive knowledge of Mexico, Sepúlveda was also appointed secretary of the American legation in Mexico in 1896. Sepúlveda's life came full circle when he eventually sought refuge from the Mexican Revolution in Los Angeles in 1913. He maintained some of his Los Angeles–based clients and continued to serve as the legal advocate for American interests in Mexico, including the San Isidro Ranch.[42]

Sepúlveda's prodigious legal and business pursuits and his rotations in and out of Los Angeles and Mexico reflected the types of transborder networks so important to linking city and hinterland. His relationships with elites, investors, and political players on both sides of the border allowed him not only to succeed personally but to connect Americans, particularly Angelenos, to the levers of power in Mexico. He was able to channel his Mexican American identity, forged in Los Angeles as it transitioned from a Mexican to an American city, into a set of meaningful cross-border relationships that not only earned him a living but also connected eager core with periphery.

Cross-border relationships like the ones embodied by Sepúlveda and Los Angeles–Mexico networks grew into a campaign for a more direct commercial and diplomatic relationship between Los Angeles and Mexico in the 1890s. To this end, the city's energetic and vocal business alliances, including the Los Angeles Chamber of Commerce, the Merchants and Manufacturers Association, and the Los Angeles Board of Trade, embarked on a vigorous campaign to secure the city's first official tie to a foreign government—a Mexican consulate in Los Angeles. Otis, owner of the *Los Angeles Times*, vociferous empire builder, heavy investor in Mexico, raucous supporter of "free labor" in Los Angeles, and personal friend of President Porfirio Díaz, led the lobbying campaign for the Mexican federal government to appoint a consul to Los Angeles. While Washington, D.C., housed Mexico's ambassador, strategically placed consuls in other American cities facilitated commercial ventures between U.S. and Mexican citizens and worked to protect the rights of Mexicans and Mexican Americans residing in the United States. In the 1880s and 1890s, Los Angeles merchants likely felt a particular pressure to win a consulate office because other southwestern cities with sizable Mexican and Mexican American populations already had consuls, including San Diego. Securing a consul would signal the growing significance of Los Angeles both nationally and internationally.[43]

The Chamber of Commerce and its allies organized a variety of activities to demonstrate the economic dynamism that already existed between Los Angeles and Mexico and to support its call for a Mexican consular office. For example, they circulated a survey to their constituents requesting information about their business dealings with Mexico. The survey, sent to the city's most "prominent commercial and industrial firms," asked the following questions: "Do you do any considerable amount of business with citizens of Mexico? If so, in what lines? Have you any line which you believe could be introduced there to advantage if the commercial relations were made closer? Would the establishment of a Mexican Consulate in this city tend, in your opinion, to improve the condition of trade between the two countries?"[44] The responses provide a snapshot of business dealings between

Angelenos and Mexican firms at the close of the nineteenth century. Meatpackers, wholesale druggists, fruit merchants, wholesale grocers, machinery supply firms, harness and saddle manufacturers, wagon and carriage manufacturers, cracker and candle producers, a macaroni company, mining corporations, and magazine publishers all responded in the affirmative and noted with enthusiasm that they would like to see trade between the city and the Republic of Mexico grow. C. J. Shepherd, a fruit importer and exporter, replied, "I have exported oranges from Mexico, packing headquarters being at Hermosillo, State of Sonora, to various districts in the United States, and I know that our firm would be greatly benefited if closer relations existed, which would be done certainly by having a Mexican Consulate in this city."[45] Like Shepherd, other respondents were enthusiastic about the possibility of a Mexican consulate in Los Angeles. They believed that the presence of the consul would aid in their efforts to expand commercial enterprises with their southern neighbors. One respondent enthused:

> The establishment of a Mexican Consulate in this city would surely improve conditions of trade between the two countries. We have a large amount of Los Angeles capital invested in Mexico and more would go if there was a means of getting better data about the country. The growth of Mexico in the last three years has been so great and the inducements held out to miners and manufacturers has been so flattering, that we believe a large business could be built up between our coast and Mexico, especially the west coast of Mexico which is directly tributary to this coast.[46]

This quote, included in the chamber's official request to the Mexican secretary of foreign relations for a consulate in Los Angeles, reflects the relationship between city and hinterland as well as the imperial aspirations of the city and its business elite. A substantial amount of Los Angeles capital had already flowed south of the border. More would certainly go if Angeleno investors had more information about the recent growth in Mexican economic opportunities. Mexico, particularly the nation's western coast, was "tributary" to Los Angeles and therefore needed to be closely integrated into Southern California's economic development. Ultimately, the chamber argued, the Mexican government could facilitate this process by opening a consulate in Los Angeles.

In presenting its case to the Mexican government, the chamber also pointed to Los Angeles's regional significance. "Los Angeles," they noted, "is at the center of a rich and productive region."[47] In other words, Los

Angeles was the center of an expansive and rich region with a periphery that could more formally include Mexico if state officials were so inclined. The chamber also boasted about the city's two rail lines, arguing that the presence of two railroads meant competitive freight rates and a significant advantage over other regional commercial centers with only one line. In addition, the chamber enthused, the city desired to establish a steamship line between Los Angeles and the western coast of Mexico. The federal government had recently allocated several million dollars for the improvement of the port at San Pedro. All was ripe for a boom in Los Angeles, and the chamber hoped to convince Mexico's secretary of foreign relations that his country did not want to miss out on this opportunity to be closely tied to the American west coast's most important new city.

The chamber closed its case for a consulate to the Mexican government with these encouraging words: "From the information that has been furnished this body by commercial houses having business relations with Mexico, the sales to that country must be considerable and we have no doubt that they will increase rapidly if the relations between the two countries became closer. In view of all the facts as set forth above, we earnestly petition your Government to establish a Consulate at Los Angeles, in the State of California, U.S.A."[48] Representative of the interests of both the city and its elite class, the chamber argued to the Mexican government that assigning a consulate to Los Angeles would serve as an important link between two developing regions, albeit one a city and the other an entire nation.

The chamber's long entreaty to Mexico's secretary of foreign relations succeeded, in part because the Mexican federal government welcomed American investment at the end of the nineteenth century. In conducting his government's own reconnaissance on Los Angeles's economic significance, the secretary of foreign relations noted that there were over 2,000 businesses in Los Angeles—evidence that the city was an emerging commercial center. In June 1897, Mexican president Porfirio Díaz appointed General Guillermo Andrade, Rosecrans's old investment partner and close friend of Otis, as the first Mexican consul to Los Angeles to facilitate trade and investment between Southern California and northern Mexico. A borderlands capitalist in his own right, Andrade had moved to Los Angeles precisely to promote the type of American investment in Mexico that the chamber had envisioned the previous year.[49] A Mexican investor and landowner, Andrade had resided in California for thirty-two years, spoke English fluently, maintained an extensive network of commercial and political relationships that stretched from Mexico City to San Francisco, and owned a vast tract of prime agricultural land in Baja California that he hoped to sell.

From the perspective of Angeleno businessmen aching to link their city to Mexico, Andrade was an ideal appointee. His experience and relationships would significantly strengthen the city's relationship to Mexico. Los Angeles mayor Meredith Snyder boasted, "He will prove a valuable personage to Los Angeles."[50] The *Los Angeles Times* celebrated his arrival in the city, noisily emphasizing the importance of Andrade and the consulate position for Los Angeles: "He will work to stimulate trade between the two countries, and in every way endeavor to knit together the two republics in bonds of friendship and sound business relationship."[51] Andrade embodied those possibilities. As a Mexican citizen with an extensive business network in both California and Mexico, he acted as the conduit to coveted Mexican resources. In the case of Otis and his son-in-law Harry Chandler, investors in the Colorado River basin (discussed in more depth in the next chapter), Andrade's Mexican citizenship granted them access to an expansive tract of land, and his residency in Los Angeles resulted in the transfer of that property to an ambitious cohort of Angeleno businessmen. More broadly, Andrade's appointment and the opening of a consulate office strengthened the investment ties between Los Angeles and Mexico. The hubbub over Andrade's arrival reflected the intense hope on the part of the city's elite that Los Angeles and Mexico would share in a lucrative partnership.

As discussed earlier, Angeleno interest in Mexico intersected with Díaz's economic plans for his country and explains his administration's receptive response to Los Angeles's request for a consulate. When he assumed the presidency in 1876, Díaz already had extensive networks in the United States, particularly among those interested in foreign investment. He believed that modernization in Mexico would come as a result of foreign capital, and he enlisted American landholders, bankers, railroad executives, and congressmen as his allies.[52] As president, Díaz began granting huge concessions to American investors and corporations. For example, in exchange for developing railroad lines, he gave millions of acres of property to companies such as the Southern Pacific. He expanded the mining industry by rescinding a colonial law that made subsoil resources the property of the state and invited American corporations to develop silver and copper mines. In the agricultural sector, purchases of communally held lands by Americans allowed them to expel Mexican "squatters" and develop huge agricultural holdings across Mexico.[53] American financing applied to Mexican landholdings and natural resources would develop lucrative copper mines, railroad lines, oil fields, cattle ranches, sugar plantations, and communication systems across Mexico. Díaz believed these ventures could yield personal fortunes while simultaneously advancing Mexico's economy and developing its infrastructure.

Los Angeles capitalists believed that the success and future of their city lay in international commerce. Díaz believed that foreign investment would modernize and develop his nation. It was in this context that the city of Los Angeles embraced Andrade with a lavish banquet and thunderous applause in June 1897. Cheers resounded from a gaggle of elite Angelenos, including Otis and Chandler, the mayor, several California legislators, two Mexican senators, members of the Los Angeles Chamber of Commerce, representatives of the Merchants and Manufacturers Association, and most of the city's noted Anglo- and Mexican American citizens.

Speeches delivered at the welcome festivities touched upon what both Angelenos and Mexicans such as Andrade and Díaz hoped to build—a transnational commercial network that would link Los Angeles's capital to Mexico's raw natural resources.[54] As Snyder gushed, "Each year relations between the United States and Mexico are growing closer and closer and the coming of Gen. Andrade means to increase the good feeling and the commercial ties between Southern California and Mexico."[55] Andrade reciprocated the feelings of goodwill in Spanish, noting that "the attention of the world has been attracted to [Mexico's] vast resources," and that Los Angeles was "well-known for its active and enterprising businessmen."[56] He concluded that these two characteristics—the rich natural resources of Mexico and the vigorous commercial energy of Los Angeles capitalists—made for an ideal and mutually beneficial combination.

Cross-border networks between Los Angeles and Mexico, like those embodied in Sepúlveda, Andrade, the Chamber of Commerce, and the campaign for a consulate, helped to facilitate the flow of capital from Southern California and into Mexico. As noted at the beginning of this chapter, in the twenty years after the city secured a consulate office, over 150 businesses incorporated in Los Angeles specifically to do business in Mexico with stock offerings of over $70 million, approximately $1.33 billion to $38.6 billion in today's dollars.[57] Investment schemes covered a broad spectrum of turn-of-the-century economic endeavors, including mining, natural gas drilling, irrigation, ranching, farming, railroads, roads, hotels, electricity, pharmaceuticals, manufacturing, fisheries, and even the production of fire and burglar alarms.[58] Ultimately, the opening of the Mexican consulate in Los Angeles marked two things for the city's boosters and investor class. Symbolically, the city could now boast a direct and official link to Mexico's federal government in the form of the consulate office. Los Angeles had a hinterland that stretched to the seat of executive power in Mexico City. In addition, friendships with consular staff helped facilitate relationships with the Mexican officials who needed to sign off on investment schemes south of the border. On a very practical level, the consulate could open opportunities for investment dollars headed for Mexico. As Andrade stated, he would make it his mission to facilitate "large and profitable business transactions between these two bordering sections of the two sister republics."[59] Andrade's position and the opening of a consular office also reflected the larger agenda of Los Angeles boosters. The city could now boast that it had a direct tie to the Mexican national government and an international diplomatic and trade center within city limits. In the form of a consulate office, urban aspirations intersected with Mexican national interests to unite regional economies with international growth and expanding commercial empires.

Conclusion

Following Los Angeles's long imperial history and the blueprint for a new "informal" empire articulated by Rosecrans after his diplomatic tenure in Mexico, Angeleno investors ventured south of the border in search of a hinterland that would simultaneously enrich individuals and the urban core. Taken together, these histories illustrate how American empire building in the West and empire building globally met on the ground in Los Angeles and its Mexican investments. Angelenos were uninterested in formally adding more territories or peoples, particularly nonwhite peoples, to American control but intent on expanding personal and urban power over commercial orbits and "tributary territories." Instead of extending American sovereignty south of the border, Angeleno investors relied on the kinds of relationships that could be fostered through figures such as Sepúlveda or Andrade and a consular office in Los Angeles to build a commercial empire between an urban core in Southern California and a Mexican periphery. As one Los Angeles businessman with extensive mining interests in Mexico wrote to Mexico's secretary of the treasury at the dawn of the twentieth century, "Los Angeles is rapidly becoming the great financial center of the Southwest, and the commercial interests of the ports of Mexico and this city will grow closer as time goes on."[60]

2 Organizing Capital and Controlling Race and Labor

Connecting Los Angeles to Mexico did not rely just on consulates or chambers of commerce. Linking city to "hinterland" also required Mexican allies and Mexican labor. More so, it reinforced and expanded hierarchies of race and class unique to Los Angeles and the borderlands. Los Angeles elites developed an ideology of race and empire that argued that white investors should oversee the development of the city, its surrounding countryside, and the laborers therein. In their estimation, Anglos in Los Angeles resided at the center of a region with a population that was, while racially inferior, also an ideal labor force. Harry Chandler, son-in-law of Harrison Gray Otis and a longtime investor in Los Angeles and Mexico, may have best expressed this when he took the stand on a Friday afternoon in January 1930 to testify to the House of Representatives Committee on Immigration and Naturalization. Although his testimony came several decades after the period discussed in this chapter, Chandler reflected on his opinion of the value of Mexican migrants and labor in Southern California developed since his arrival in Southern California in the 1880s. His credentials on the subject included fifty years of conducting business in Los Angeles and a litany of financial successes in California and Mexico, vigilantly documented in the *Congressional Record*: publisher of the *Los Angeles Times*; owner of 862,000 acres of land in Baja California; president of the California-Mexico Land and Cattle Company; producer of $18 million worth of cotton in Mexico in a single year; owner of 47,000 acres of suburban tracts in Los Angeles; head of the Los Angeles Suburban Homes Company; head of the syndicate that owned the 281,000-acre Tejon Ranch; officer or director of twenty-five corporations in California.[1]

He was a financial titan, and he candidly admitted that over his five decades in Los Angeles, Mexican and Mexican American labor had created his wealth and the wealth of his city. He perceived this labor, which he utilized both north and south of the border, as reliable, pliant, and itinerant. From the stand he commented, "Mexican laborers are helpful to all of our industries . . . Mexicans never have created problems in Los Angeles . . . The peon who comes there is an innocent, friendly, kindly individual . . . They are not enterprising, of course, like other races, but they are more desirable from our standpoint than any other class of labor that comes, and they create fewer problems."[2]

Toward the end of his testimony, Chandler also made some telling observations on his relationships with Mexico's political and economic elites and his understanding of the racial composition of the nation. Asked about race south of the border, Chandler replied, "About 85 per cent of the population in Mexico are of Indian blood; and the other 15 per cent are the most cultured people on the continent, usually educated abroad, and as a rule they are the ruling class in Mexico, the greatest aristocrats in the world . . . These Spanish aristocrats are white."[3] Chandler's observations encapsulate the narrative and argumentative threads that move throughout this chapter. Namely, in the multiracial context of Los Angeles, white investors understood race as a continuum and assessed Mexican elites and Mexican workers on that scale to advance their economic agenda. In the context of transnational and borderlands enterprises, the Los Angeles investor class also worked to apply their constructions of race to similar systems of class and labor in Mexico. Chandler's comments on Mexican workers and Mexican "aristocrats," for example, reflect constructions of race, class, and labor rooted in many years of conducting business in Southern California and then Mexico.

This chapter explores how Los Angeles–based investors built systems of race and labor in Southern California and Mexico prior to the Mexican Revolution. Southern California systems were rooted in the Spanish and Mexican periods and then layered with Anglo-American racial ideologies. These ideologies also circulated across the border with investors as they tried to utilize similar systems of race and labor in Mexico. As historians of Los Angeles and California have documented, race and labor were constructed in the region, as in much of the greater American West, in ways that diverged from the black and white binary common in the rest of the nation. As Natalia Molina argues, "The black/white imagery that dominated conceptions of race elsewhere gave way in Los Angeles to a notion of race as a graded continuum shading from white, at the top, downward through various forms of 'nonwhite' . . . In Los Angeles, people 'saw' race differently."[4] For example, starting before the Mexican-American War and continuing through much of the nineteenth century, Anglo settlers in Los Angeles prioritized business partnerships and intermarriages with a Californio elite that superseded strict definitions of racial purity to facilitate access to land, citizenship, and economic privileges. Although Anglo migrants into Southern California did not necessarily consider Californios white under American

Organizing Capital and Controlling Race and Labor 49

conceptions of race, they recognized their strategic importance in the region's economic and political systems, partnered with them for economic gain, married into Californio families, and shared governance of the region through the 1870s.[5] To advance their own economic interests, Anglo migrants and settlers essentially stretched or ignored strict definitions of whiteness in economic and political dealings in Los Angeles. Chandler said as much during his congressional testimony. Reflecting on his relationships with Mexican Americans beginning in the 1880s, Chandler observed, "[Los Angeles's] traditions and background are mostly Mexican, and all of the old timers who came to the vicinity of Los Angeles and lived with the Mexicans and knew them, had a little different attitude toward them than the rest of the Americans would have naturally. A good many of my friends were Mexicans, and I worked with Mexicans."[6]

Anglo settlers in Los Angeles, as Spanish colonizers and Californios had for decades, also relied on indigenous and mestizo labor from the other end of the race and class continuum to build their city and profitable enterprises. Southern California's diverse late nineteenth-century workforce also included immigrant workers from China and Mexican workers who crossed the border to work in Los Angeles and environs. These workers provided the muscle required to build a city, construct the transportation systems that connected it to the nation and the world, and transform arid pastureland into productive agricultural hinterlands. Despite the indispensable labor of nonwhite and immigrant workers in Los Angeles and its Southern California hinterlands, to be nonwhite also consistently meant to be subjugated by a dominant Anglo class.[7] However, even while Anglo-Americans certainly believed Mexican workers to be well below them on a racial hierarchy, they also consistently defined Mexican migrants and Mexican Americans as ideal workers or as ideally suited to work for whites. In the estimation of Anglo Angelenos, Mexican workers were simultaneously inferior and ideal.[8]

As investors like Chandler expanded enterprises south of the border as early as the 1870s and accelerating through the end of the century, they adapted these understandings of race and class forged in the racial milieu of Los Angeles and rooted in the region's Mexican and Californio past. Los Angeles investors relied heavily on networks with Mexico's "white aristocrats" and channeled their experiences and alliances with Californios into productive partnerships with Mexican elites south of the border. White investors in Los Angeles expressed high praise for Mexican economic and political elites, no matter their racial or ethnic makeup, because they required their cooperation for economic success. Simultaneously, Anglo investors applied their Southern Californian definition of Mexican workers as controllable "peons" to their enterprises and employees in Mexico. Investing in a south-of-the-border hinterland felt familiar and secure precisely because investors believed they could successfully adapt definitions of race, class, and labor generated north of the border to enterprises south of the border. As Angeleno investors advanced across the U.S.-Mexico border, they also combined the racialized labor system of Southern California with the racialized labor schematics of Mexico to create the common mechanics of capitalism and empire—a nonwhite labor force that did the work of extracting resources and transforming them from crops or minerals into cash.

As discussed in the previous chapter, Los Angeles's borderlands growth also intersected with wider debates over American global and imperial expansion following the American Civil War. At a national level, these debates were highly racialized, with both expansionists and anti-imperialists deploying race to argue respectively for or against imperial expansion or the possible annexation of places from the Dominican Republic (1870) to the Philippines (1898). As explored in this chapter, the racial rhetoric of labor, investment, and civic growth in Los Angeles traversed this wider debate over race and empire with specific regional dialects and dimensions. Dating back to the Spanish period, Los Angeles shared with Mexico a history of imperial systems of race and labor. Anglo-American settlers and American annexation of the territory layered another set of racial practices and hierarchies atop, but did not upend, older practices and classifications. As Anglo Angelenos expanded investment schemes from Southern California into Mexico, they manipulated older systems of race and labor rooted in Spanish, Mexican, and American institutions to suit their needs north and south of the border. Investors such as Otis, for example, redefined whiteness and political power as they curried favor with mixed-race executive President Díaz. Los Angeles–based employers also sought to find or construct commonalities between Southern Californian and Mexican systems of race and labor in their management of investment properties in Mexico.[9]

Exploring the growth of Los Angeles investments in Mexico and the politics of race, investment, and labor, this chapter follows the exploits of a number of large Los Angeles–based commercial enterprises in Mexico. The dealings of Chandler, Otis, and their Colorado River Land Company (CRLC) with Porfirio Díaz provide insight into how Anglo Angelenos mirrored earlier alliances with Californios in their relationships with Mexican elites. This chapter also follows the Quimichis Colony and the Mexican Petroleum Company (MPC) as they sallied into Mexico with imperial notions of race and labor developed in the American West, sharpened in Los Angeles, and deployed and refashioned south of the border. These investors heaped praise on Mexico's economic and political elite, particularly Díaz, while simultaneously expecting Mexican workers to provide the same type of labor that nonwhite workers provided in the orange groves and lettuce fields of greater Los Angeles. As Los Angeles business ventures extended beyond the boundaries of the United States, white investors fully expected the support of elite Mexicans to grow their enterprises and the capitulation of nonwhite workers to organize their workforce.

Courting Mexican Aristocrats

As explored in the previous chapter, empires often control territories and investments through collaboration and negotiation with local elites, and the relationship between Los Angeles investors and Mexican officials followed this familiar imperial pattern. As historian Alan Knight once observed, "Informal control requires congenial collaborating elites."[10] In the nineteenth century the power of racial categories also profoundly shaped American imperial ventures and commercial partnerships. In the formal imperial control of the Philippines, for example, Americans controlled the territory through collaboration with Filipino elites and a racial formation that deemed Filipino collaborators "civilized" Christians and the Filipino resistance non-Christian and "savage."[11] In the imperial relationship between Los Angeles and Mexico, racial hierarchies, collaboration, and empire building followed a similar trajectory. The friendship between Harrison Gray Otis and President Porfirio Díaz best embodies the class and race alliances fostered between Los Angeles investors and Mexican officials, one that mirrored, in many ways, earlier alliances between Californios and Anglo migrants in Los Angeles. It is also significant that Otis enthusiastically volunteered to fight in the Philippines, reflecting his support of American empire globally and undoubtedly shaping his aspirations for Los Angeles empire building in Mexico.

Otis and a group of Los Angeles–based investors, including his son-in-law Harry Chandler, purchased the CRLC, a property of almost a million acres of agricultural land directly south of the California–Baja California border, in 1904. Many of these investors, including Otis and Chandler, had been instrumental in building the dense network of relationships between Los Angeles and Mexico as early as the 1880s. In fact, the key investors in the CRLC, one of the largest Los Angeles–based investment schemes south of the border, were the same individuals central to winning the campaign for a Mexican consulate in their city in 1894. And not coincidentally, they purchased the enormous tract of agricultural land from the prominent Mexican they helped secure the first consulate position in Los Angeles— Guillermo Andrade. Lacking the capital to develop the large piece of agricultural real estate in the Colorado River basin, Andrade sold the property to the group of investors he had met during his tenure in Los Angeles.[12]

The activities of CRLC investors, particularly Otis's relationship with Díaz, exemplified how Los Angeles–based investors understood and constructed race along the lines of class and access to political power and economic resources. This relationship reflected the types of relationships that Otis and his ilk had already developed with Californio partners such as Sepúlveda and Andrade north of the border. As Chandler described in his congressional testimony decades later, the city's investor class defined elite Mexicans, including Díaz, as racial equals due to their political and economic power.[13] Los Angeles financial elites recognized that they needed the collusion of the Porfiriato and set about demonstrating to themselves and their Mexican partners that they could operate as relative equals based on class status while largely ignoring issues of racial "purity." As CRLC investors cultivated close relationships with a Mexican political and economic elite to advance economic interests rooted in Southern California, they borrowed from a long history of fostering economic and familial alliances between white businessmen and Californios in California.

In turn-of-the-century Los Angeles, Otis and Chandler and their newspaper served as some of the staunchest and most vocal proponents of regional growth, north and south of the border. Otis, a Civil War veteran, arrived in Los Angeles from Ohio by way of Santa Barbara and Alaska. In search of economic opportunities in the publishing business, he purchased an interest in the *Los Angeles Daily Times* in 1882 and became the paper's sole owner and publisher by 1886. As he built his newspaper empire, Otis imagined a spectacular imperial future for Los Angeles: "a mightier Pacific empire, with a population numbering millions where now we see only thousands, and possessing a measure of wealth, civilization and power now inconceivable."[14] In keeping with this belief, Otis embraced American empire and its corollary racial hierarchy. He requested an army appointment immediately after the outbreak of the Spanish-American War in 1898 and won his military ranking of brigadier general during his tour in the Philippines, where he helped oversee a bloody repression of Philippine nationalists and vocally declared his distaste for the territory's nonwhite population.[15]

Bellicose editorials penned by Otis and his staff supported the expansion of American commercial interests and political control into Hawaii, Puerto Rico, Cuba, and Panama. He likely refrained from suggesting the same fate for Mexico because he subscribed to Rosecrans's philosophy of "informal" empire building south of the border and because he maintained a close friendship with the country's supportive executive and fellow general, Porfirio Díaz. A participant in both the racial debates around American empire and the racialization of Mexicans and Mexican Americans in the American West, Otis may also have understood that the majority of white Americans would never agree to the formal annexation of such a sizable neighbor with undisputed natural resources but also a sizable nonwhite population. While he did not advocate formal American control of Mexico, Otis did leverage his relationship with Díaz to promote personal and municipal interests from Los Angeles.

Otis's son-in-law and business partner shared his ardent aspirations to grow Los Angeles into a city with international reach. As evidenced in his congressional testimony, Harry Chandler also believed that Mexican labor represented a key component of city building and regional economic development, advocating for increased access to migrant Mexican labor as well as strict control over that labor. Chandler arrived in Los Angeles, like so many others, a sickly consumptive in search of warm, dry air for ailing lungs. Despite his illness, he worked agricultural jobs to survive, eventually moving on to a job in the *Times* circulation department in 1885. He moved up quickly, becoming chief of collections as well as the paper's chief distributor. In 1894, he married Otis's daughter, Marian Otis, and joined the *Times* family. In addition to his role in the *Times* company, Chandler also itched to own property, and acquired extensive real estate holdings across Southern California. By World War I, Chandler had pieced together the largest individually owned cache of land in California. In a profile of the newspaper and real estate titan, the *Saturday Evening Post* observed that he was involved in so many ventures that "nobody, with the possible exception of himself, has ever been able to count them."[16] Toward the end of his life, the *Times* estimated that he was the eleventh richest man in the world.[17] Mexico and the CRLC constituted a key part of Chandler's real estate and investment empire, and he would maintain financial interests south of the border for over forty years.

Chandler and Otis—and their associates—wielded an extraordinary amount of power and influence in Los Angeles. The success of their Mexican venture and the development of a Mexican hinterland for Los Angeles,

Harrison Gray Otis, left, on a hunting trip in Mexico, early twentieth century. Colorado River Land Company Collection, Sherman Library.

however, depended on an important variable—finding private Mexican citizens and public officials willing to collaborate in their cross-border regional ventures. They relied on both Mexican labor and willing Mexican officials to promote successful transnational investment ventures. Mexican citizens had relationships with Mexican federal officials, access to Mexican land grants, and knowledge of Mexican law. As Andrade had done with the tract of land purchased by the CRLC, Mexican citizens could file claims on *terrenos baldíos,* or "vacant" lands, and then partner with American capital to develop that land. They saw lucrative opportunities in coupling these assets with the capital of American financiers and served as brokers and intermediaries for Angeleno investors. Andrade and other elite Mexicans with links to Baja California and the Mexicali Valley had a particular interest in promoting congenial relationships with their powerful neighbors immediately to the north.

As Otis and CRLC investors worked closely with Mexican officials, including Andrade and Díaz, they also confronted a reality that Anglo settlers had encountered in Los Angeles several decades earlier—they were dealing

Organizing Capital and Controlling Race and Labor 55

with a Mexican elite that did not fit easily into Anglo-American conceptions of white racial purity. President Díaz, for example, was mestizo, the descendant of Spanish colonists and indigenous ancestors from Oaxaca. Given his position as the nation's chief executive and his welcoming stance on American investment dollars, however, Angeleno investors decided to consider his mixed lineage a strength, a combination of the best traits of his Spanish and Indian ancestry. For example, Charles Lummis, the legendary *Los Angeles Times* writer and Otis employee, commented specifically on Díaz's physiognomy and character: "[His] features and expressions are essentially of Spain; it is only in full repose that the face recalls that certain hauteur and inscrutableness of the first Americans . . . This man seems to have taken the best from both types."[18] As historian Jason Ruiz observes, white Americans "both admired and denied Díaz's *mestizaje* . . . [adjusting] the amount of 'Indian blood' contained in the president's veins in order to fit with their own agendas."[19] For Los Angeles investors, this meant ignoring strict definitions of whiteness in order to promote partnerships to expand the city's periphery south of the border.

Otis led the way in forging relationships with Mexico's top executive and promoting Los Angeles investment in Mexico. From almost the moment he arrived in Los Angeles, Otis carefully cultivated a close relationship with President Díaz. And he justified his respect for a not-entirely-white head of state based on their shared social distance from clearly nonwhite workers. For example, Otis was particularly generous in his praise of Díaz's treatment of Mexican workers in the pages of the *Los Angeles Times*. Otis's descriptions of Díaz, penned by himself or a commissioned staff writer like Lummis, commonly referred to Díaz in glowing terms, as a benevolent mentor to the lower classes: "He is an enlightened statesman of the broadest gauge and the ripest intelligence . . . Díaz has been a great educator and the Mexican people are just beginning to realize the true value of his teaching."[20] *Times* editorials even excused Díaz's thirty-year dictatorial rule over a "sister republic," arguing that although he was entering his eleventh term, he was the one Mexican leader equipped to lift his nation from "darkness and suffering up to light and power."[21] The *Times* also explained that ordinary Mexicans were in a formative stage, not yet ready for the full responsibilities of republican citizenship, and that Díaz had correctly evaluated just how much freedom his people could safely enjoy.[22] Otis's observations built on both the language of race that permeated Los Angeles's labor system and the rhetoric of race that undergirded the United States' global expansion in the late nineteenth and early twentieth centuries. According to Otis and his newspaper, Díaz himself utilized the language of civilization and racial uplift, and Angeleno investors could exploit this to promote their investments in Mexico.

Otis and the *Times* spoke with particular admiration of Díaz's ability to create order and stability, or racial and economic "civilization," in Mexico. This was precisely the type of labor and racial order that organizations such as the Merchants and Manufacturers Association sought to establish in Los Angeles. In an article commissioned by Otis, Lummis described Mexico in the early years of Díaz's rule as "unsettled by revolutions, moth-eaten with brigandage, Tweedian in local politics, remote, uneasy, ignorant, inaccessible, unsafe and beggared."[23] According to Lummis's observations, Díaz had created a safe, law-abiding, well-administered modern state that rivaled the United States. Other *Times* articles highlighted Díaz's especial respect for the rights of property owners. Do not be afraid to invest below the border, the *Times* argued; property in Mexico was as safe as property in the United States. After a trip to Mexico City and several meetings with Díaz in 1902, Otis reported that the political stability established by Díaz created an extraordinarily safe environment for investment. He also explicitly outlined his understanding of the benefits of capital investment for investors and workers, Americans and Mexicans alike: "Our investors do not, of course, pretend to come in the role of philanthropists; they are animated by an intelligent self-interest. But this, when directed upon a right plane, and within the limitations of the laws of the country, must result for the good of the whole republic, as well as of the investors themselves. What a great country such as this, with its vast and rich natural resources, needs more than anything else is development—the application of capital, skill and labor well directed."[24] Eyeing development on both sides of the border, Otis argued that Angeleno and Mexican financial and political elites could collaborate to extend the reach of Los Angeles as a city-empire and develop Mexico's resources, all within a system of strictly managed labor relationships.

Indeed, a well-directed system of labor and race was a key component of this worldview, shared between regional leaders in Los Angeles and a national executive south of the border. CRLC investors often defined themselves and Mexican elites such as Díaz as relative equals precisely because of their social and economic distance from nonwhite laborers.

In this line of reasoning, Otis and the *Times* particularly admired Díaz's control over organized labor in Mexico. In 1906, when hundreds of workers went on strike against the Mexican Central Railroad, the *Times* triumphantly announced, "Díaz Smashes Union Octopus," and gleefully reported, "He Makes Unionist Strikes Bend Knees for Mercy." At the same time, port workers in San Pedro, California, struck, and the paper editorialized that "it would be a lucky thing for everybody concerned if we could get President Díaz of Mexico up here for about fifteen minutes to settle the strike at San Pedro."[25] According to *Times* reports on the strike in Mexico, Díaz granted the striking workers a meeting, heard their demands, and then explained that capital's rights superseded workers' rights. The progress of the nation, Díaz explained, depended on "the introduction of capital, both domestic and foreign, and every imposition that is unjustly placed upon capital retards the forward movement of the country and its industrial development."[26] The newspaper applauded Díaz for commanding the railroad employees, most of them indigenous or mestizo, to return to work, comply with company policies, and respect the great industrial progress of the nation. Ardently anti-union, Otis delighted in this approach and rhetorically asked Díaz to come implement his stringent labor policies in Los Angeles.

Otis was also not shy to use his large newspaper and its circulation to strengthen ties between Los Angeles and Mexico and promote his relationship with Díaz. In addition to praising Díaz in the pages of the *Times*, Otis often used the paper to directly promote investment in Mexico by publishing favorable pieces on the material resources of the country and the Díaz regime. Ever an opportunist, Otis sent one such piece to Díaz with a personalized note reading, "I trust that we have not worked in vain in this direction and also that the [article] will stand the test, fairly well, of our critical judgment and your superior knowledge of your own country, of which I am a personal admirer, and to whose great hand I have the honor to renew my personal pledge of friendship and affection."[27] Otis even hoped that the *Times* might find a readership in Mexico and hired a special correspondent to cover Mexican news for a readership on both sides of the border. He also arranged to have the newspaper shipped to Sonora and then to Mexico City, including instructions to deliver a copy to the presidential palace.[28] The *Times* employed the correspondent for most of a decade, a bilingual American named E. C. Butler who estimated that his writing on Mexico and economic opportunities under Díaz reached a Mexican readership of over 250,000 with every publication.[29]

Otis's admiration of Díaz and knowledge of Mexican resources made the geographic expansion of his personal and urban economies all the more enticing. In partnership with other investors, Otis and Chandler used the

Los Angeles bankers and railroad executives on an investment excursion to the Imperial Valley and Mexicali, early twentieth century. Colorado River Land Company Collection, Sherman Library.

CRLC as their vehicle to drive investment south of the border into regions where they believed they could utilize or construct familiar racial hierarchies, labor regimes, and supportive state apparatuses. The company represented an extension of their regional strategies across greater Los Angeles, namely, developing "tributary territories" for the benefit of an urban core and with the labor of nonwhite workers. They planned to buy cheap land and increase its value by applying water and transportation. Thomas Gibbon, one of the CRLC's investors and the organization's attorney, described the group's activities across Southern California: "The largest stockholders of the company, myself included, have for years acted together in buying and improving lands by putting water on them, and subdividing and selling them."[30] Gibbon confessed that it was his "favorite method of trying to make money" because he felt a moral and philosophical satisfaction when creating fertile and productive properties out of borderlands "deserts."[31] Members of the syndicate also saw the CRLC property as firmly part of the commercial orbit of Los Angeles. While applying for financing for the endeavor, Chandler wrote, "Our property is in the region which makes it just as much tributary to the commercial and business interest of Los Angeles... Anything you can do to assist us in a financial way will be contributing to the development of the general business and industrial growth of Los Angeles... Los Angeles financiers, as a matter of good morals and good business policy, can afford to show a broad gauged and progressive spirit in their dealings with our close neighbors of the South."[32] According to Chandler's assessment, financial investment in the CRLC south of the border would prove beneficial to the city of Los Angeles as well as build productive relationships with neighbors below the border.

In this way, CRLC investment strategies, visions for urban and imperial growth, and conceptions of race hierarchies and controlled labor extended across the border to build a relationship with the Mexican government and promote regional growth between Los Angeles and Mexico. Otis, through the mouthpiece of his newspaper and columnists such as Lummis, welcomed Díaz into their conceptions of civility, extending to him many of the privileges of whiteness based on his support of American capital and his handling of a nonwhite labor force. This made both Díaz and Mexico safe for Los Angeles investors and for the orderly expansion of their city's commercial orbits and economy. If Mexico organized race and labor in systems familiar to Los Angeles investors and if the country's executive appeared to support the types of racial formations common in Southern California, they made investing south of the border both familiar and exciting. As we will explore in later chapters, however, these twined systems of investment, race, and labor were only possible for a confined period.

Controlling Race and Labor

As the architects of the Los Angeles city-empire embarked on investment ventures in Mexico, whether to irrigate desert farmland, mine for borax, or manufacture fire alarms, they based the growth of their metropolis on two important pillars of turn-of-the-century municipal growth. The first: a productive periphery. The second: a carefully controlled labor force. This was the machinery of empire at work on the ground. While political figures such as Rosecrans or investors such as Otis negotiated the policies of empire at the levels of the national and the urban, they also implemented the on-the-ground practices and policies that utilized labor to transform river deltas or mountain mineral lodes into profits. In the case of Los Angeles and Mexico, Angeleno investors capitalized on and extended the overlap between systems of race and labor that existed both north and south of the border.

In the Los Angeles hinterlands, whether irrigating and picking oranges in Riverside or digging an oil well in Veracruz, turning a profit required backbreaking work that an investor class was certainly not willing to do themselves. Empire builders in Los Angeles and beyond assigned the hard and sweat-inducing labor of capitalism and empire—digging, cutting, harvesting, constructing, weeding, and all of the other tough tasks of transforming natural resources into capital—to nonwhite workers. Historically, Native Americans, Mexican Americans, and Mexican immigrants, along with workers from China and Japan, filled the demand for labor on the gentleman farms, orchards, and vineyards of Los Angeles's domestic tributary territories. Consequently, Los Angeles investors in Mexico transported their system of racialized labor to their investment properties south of the border. This approach certainly mirrored the larger project of empire building that engaged the American state and American investors, in the American West and globally, from the end of the Civil War.

Within the California portion of this city-empire formulation, Los Angeles investors and boosters, farmers and citrus growers, city officials, and commercial organizations also created and maintained a strict open-shop labor system cast in the hues of white and brown skin. The open shop was one component of what Otis and his contemporaries in organizations such as the Merchants and Manufacturers Association termed "industrial freedom" or the right of employers to operate free of the limitations of organized labor or restrictive government policies. While workers did not have the right to organize under this schema, employers saw no hypocrisy in joining forces to control their workers. As noted in the previous chapter, two of the city's most powerful organizations, the Los Angeles Chamber of Commerce and the Merchants and Manufacturers Association, actively promoted city growth alongside an authoritarian and paternalistic governance of the region's labor force, predominantly nonwhite and immigrant. Growers and employers capitalized on this system, stringently controlling the economy and labor relations along a racial hierarchy that placed nonwhite workers at the bottom.[33]

Nonwhite labor laid track for railroads, tended orchards, picked fruit, transformed clay into brick, dug sewer lines, and paved roads, all under the watchful eyes of typically white foremen and almost invariably white investors and landowners. In fact, Southern California's unparalleled growth, particularly its staggering agricultural productivity between the 1890s and the 1920s, resulted from the bent backs of thousands of nonwhite workers, both native born and immigrant.[34] White employers so closely associated labor and class with race that, as described by Chandler at the beginning of this chapter, they argued that Mexican laborers were racially predisposed for the brutal work of planting, tending, and harvesting the region's agricultural gold. Armed with the power of this racialized system of labor and the support of state and local officials, the Los Angeles investor and landowning classes emerged as agricultural and labor "fascists."[35] They paired the power of the state with a racialized disdain for the laborers who made their comfortable lifestyles and economic and political power possible.

This labor ideology overlapped with a racialized system of labor that had developed in Mexico since its days as a Spanish colony. Of course, race and labor developed differently in English and Spanish colonies in North America and subsequently in the nations of the United States and Mexico. By the late nineteenth century and from the perspective of urban boosters and investors in Los Angeles, however, there was much overlap. Namely, a small population of property owners would control land and the labor of a nonwhite labor force. In Mexico, a pattern of rapid privatization of communal landholdings, initiated and accelerated during the presidency of Díaz, displaced millions of indigenous and mestizo communities who had traditionally held their village land communally. Foreign investors and wealthy Mexicans emerged as the beneficiaries of this massive shift in landownership. By 1910, the year that ignited the Mexican Revolution, a small oligarchy of Mexican and American elites controlled 85 percent of Mexico's surface area and tried to exert an equal amount of control over Mexico's agricultural and industrial labor force. As a result, as Angelenos crossed the border with investment dollars, they found familiar patterns of landownership, political power, and race and labor.

Consequently, while welcomed by the Porfiriato, the advance of American capital on the ground, particularly Angeleno capital, carried with it inherently racial undertones. While the CRLC carefully cultivated strategic relationships with a Mexican elite to expand the power of their investment dollars as well as a Los Angeles hinterland, other investors were busy transplanting their expertise in Southern California racial and labor systems to Mexican investment properties. The Quimichis Colony, founded in 1910, and the Mexican Petroleum Company, founded in 1901, both exemplify how Los Angeles–based investors arranged systems of labor that capitalized on and expanded Southern California's racial hierarchy as well as the racial ideologies of American empire building at the turn of the century. These arrangements of race and labor also functioned well under the policies of the Porfiriato south of the border. Thomas Bard, founder of the Quimichis Colony, and Edward Doheny, founder and head of the Mexican Petroleum Company, were both practiced in extracting natural resources to create personal fortunes in Los Angeles's tributary territories north of the border. As they expanded their Southern California–based enterprises into Mexico, they utilized a mostly nonwhite labor force to extract agricultural and mineral resources for their own benefit. In this process, both companies reflected not only the racial labor regime of Southern California but also its overlap with race and labor regimes in Mexico. The on-the-ground activities of Los Angeles–based companies such as Quimichis and the MPC reflect how arrangements of race and labor that existed in Southern California initially found easy replication in Mexico.

The Quimichis Colony

Long before he invested in Mexico, Thomas Bard built a fortune and adopted a highly racialized perspective on labor in California. In a description of Bard, one of his business partners admitted candidly, "Mr. Bard was a man of great wealth and influence. We regarded him as a multimillionaire, while the rest of us combined could not have approached a million at the time."[36] Notably, he also based his Southern California empire on a foundation laid by the region's population of Mexican descent and its history of American imperial expansion. Bard made his first fortune in oil and real estate speculation, both ventures built on the former properties of Californio landowners, in the West following the Civil War. He arrived in Los Angeles at the close of the war as an emissary of Thomas A. Scott, assistant secretary of war, to manage Scott's extensive properties in Southern California. Most of Scott's territories were located in and around Ventura, just north of Los Angeles County, including Rancho Simi and Rancho Santa Clara, both former Mexican land grants. Mirroring Rosecrans's purchase of Rancho San Pedro, Bard helped arrange for Scott's purchase of these lands from prominent but indebted Californios, the del Valle family, who sold off all of their sizable rancho with the exception of the land immediately surrounding their home.[37]

While in Santa Barbara County, Bard also befriended additional members of the region's Californio landowning class, including the del Valle and Camarillo families. Through them, he learned of opportunities to purchase additional swaths of land from cash-strapped Mexican Americans. He bought portions of several Californio ranchos and earned a considerable fortune through land speculation. Even during a sharp recession, he held enough cash in drought-parched and financially stymied California to buy 17,000 acres of Rancho Ojai from cash-strapped Juan Camarillo for just over $17,000, or about $1 per acre.[38] In addition, Bard prospected and drilled for oil in the region beginning in the 1860s. In 1867 he brought in California's first "gusher" on land owned by Scott and won the election for county supervisor, eclipsing his Californio rival and putting himself at the forefront of Ventura politics and its capitalist transformation. It is not a stretch to argue that Bard built his Southern California empire on Mexican roots—he acquired land from former Mexican citizens in a territory that had recently belonged to Mexico. He then relied on a Mexican labor force to provide the muscle that built his personal empire.

Bard also led a dramatic transformation of the Ventura County economy and racial hierarchy. Through his land purchases, he befriended Californios while also participating in their swift dispossession. Then he helped shift the region's economy from small-scale farming to the rise of intensive and industrial agricultural output and the "proletarianization" of Ventura's Mexican population in the 1880s. Many of the new agricultural ventures employed sharecropping and wage labor as a labor system, foreshadowing the labor regime that Bard and his associates would utilize in Mexico a few decades later. According to historian Albert Camarillo, the shift of the California economy from Mexican pastoral to Anglo capitalism displaced Mexican workers across the southern part of the state and pushed them into poorly paid exploitative, part-time, migratory, and seasonal work.[39] An active participant in this process, Bard advocated for the use of Mexican and Mexican American labor on properties being acquired by new Anglo-American settlers.

In Bard's estimation, this work suited Mexican workers, who he believed lacked the skills, ingenuity, and shrewdness necessary for participation in an aggressively capitalist economy as anything more than laborers. In a letter to his mother early in his tenure in California, Bard wrote: "That evening we made the acquaintance of the 'Americanos' of the place which number . . . 10 or 12 and out of these are about 5 who are respectable, the balance of the population consisting of greazers and Digger Indians . . . These Greazers are the laziest cusses you ever saw . . . They are idle and thriftless."[40] Clearly, Bard's ordering of racial and ethnic groups placed "greazers" firmly at the bottom—innately indolent, lethargic, and incapable of Yankee prudence and industriousness. While Bard's description of Mexican workers differed from Chandler's, his conception of a racial hierarchy and the utility of Mexican workers in Southern California's economy did not. Bard shared the mind-set of most of his Anglo compatriots in California: that they could make money and provide a service by hiring idle Mexican laborers on their ranches and farms.

While Bard left no record of his specific interests in expanding his financial empire into Mexico, he was part of the generation of Los Angeles venture capitalists that included Rosecrans, Chandler, and Otis, who saw ripe investment opportunities across the border. In fact, Bard and Otis built a political alliance that helped win Bard a Senate seat in 1900. In office, Bard chaired the Senate irrigation subcommittee and worked closely with Otis and the CRLC on irrigation issues in the Imperial and Mexicali valleys. This type of relationship with one of the largest Los Angeles–based investors in Mexico must certainly have left a lasting impression on Bard and influenced his decision to purchase his own investment property south of the border. In fact, Bard significantly widened the circle of investors in Mexico by recruiting middle-class shareholders in communities such as Pasadena. He also drew from a network of wealthy family members and friends to purchase a limited number of preferred stocks, holding the largest share for himself. The strategy reflected Bard's business acumen—he rarely leveraged too much of his own money in investment ventures, preferring to diminish risk by borrowing investment funds or inviting other investors to join him.[41] In the case of Quimichis, he made the dubiously ethical decision to turn to former constituents in Pasadena and the surrounding San Gabriel Valley to fund his Mexican enterprise.

Middle-class Americans from across the country enthusiastically entered the nation's booming capitalist economy and imperial expansion following the American Civil War and eagerly sent their dollars to (hopefully) multiply on Cuban sugar plantations or along Mexican rail lines. Pasadena investors hoped for no less as they pooled their money to send to Mexico. And most investors held no reservations about sinking savings into the city's Mexican periphery. Likely they were witnessing the Los Angeles region's spectacular growth and recognized the role of Mexican American and Mexican immigrant labor in making Los Angeles's regional economy boom. Logically, at least for white upper- and middle-class investors, the region's race and labor system could extend, along with investment dollars, into lucrative ventures in Mexico. Joseph Rawles, one of the Pasadena investors, noted excitedly, "Mexico is beginning to show up every day, better than ever, and we may be very glad that we have an interest down there which has so great a future in store for those fortunate enough to grasp the opportunity."[42] Enthusiasm like Rawles's characterized the purchase of stock in Quimichis Colony. For just ten dollars per share, a middle-class resident of Pasadena or Alhambra could own part of Mexico. Many expected that land and Mexican labor would return a three- or fourfold profit for every dollar they invested. And many were likely responding to the tremendous enthusiasm for investing in Mexico in the first decade of the twentieth century.

Like so many empire builders before them, the Los Angeles–based Quimichis investors saw personal fortunes in productive agricultural land and dense natural vegetation, as well as in the Mexican workers attached to the Quimichis property. American visitors to the ranch, located in the coastal territory of Nayarit, described it as one of the best agricultural properties in Mexico and enthusiastically compared its potential for agricultural production to California's phenomenal agricultural success. During his first trip to Quimichis, the company's ranch manager wrote to his wife that the cabbage seeds he planted one evening were peeking green shoots out of the rich soil within a mere thirty-six hours.[43] He also described Quimichis as a "second" and superior California. California agricultural land might be good, but Mexico's was better and would ensure that their investment paid off generously. One investor compared the property in Mexico to Ventura County farmland a generation earlier and to the "pioneering" work that Quimichis investors were engaged in south of the border.[44]

Much like early Anglo investors and settlers in the American West, and Southern California more specifically, Quimichis stockholders looked to indigenous and mestizo workers to convert investment dollars into profit. Approximately 6,000 people lived on Quimichis's 75,000 acres, with an additional 10,000 people in neighboring towns and villages. According to Quimichis officers, all of these families relied on agriculture to support themselves; they assured their investors that Quimichis residents would supply a stable labor force. Quimichis investors considered them the human instruments that would transform fertile land into dividends. Like the CRLC, Quimichis investors also expected to facilitate the orderly expansion of Los Angeles race and labor systems across the border and into Mexico. As they believed agricultural enterprises did in Southern California, investors claimed the ranch would provide food, shelter, regular employment, and wages for "reliable and energetic workmen" in Mexico.[45] One investor observed that ranch managers had "planted crops and kept the natives employed and fairly well satisfied."[46] Observing the ranch's American foreman, a man named William Windham, who had previously lived in Pasadena for many years, one investor wrote that the investment had "benefitted the people in that section" and that Windham "doctored and helped the people not only of the ranch but of that whole section."[47] They believed that successful business ventures in Southern California and the region's Mexican hinterlands created a prosperity that benefited all while also promoting a harmonious economic hierarchy. More importantly, Bard and his fellow investors claimed that the racialized system of labor that they had already successfully exploited in Southern California would provide healthy corporate profits while simultaneously "uplifting" Mexican workers. Capital investment and imperial control represented a form of racial and class uplift, transmuting uncivilized or childlike peons into industrious and obedient laborers. The "white man's burden" was alive and kicking in the minds of Quimichis capitalists and in the policies they implemented on their ranch.

As in other parts of rural Mexico, the Acaponeta Valley was in the midst of drastic economic restructuring, much of it facilitated by American investors like the Quimichis stockholders. Under the leadership of Díaz, shifts in Mexico's economy and system of landownership increasingly swept agricultural laborers onto large haciendas like Quimichis. As commonly held land disappeared under federal "settlement acts"—often seized violently from peasant villages and communities—entire village populations found themselves living and working on huge latifundia.[48] The country's growing railway network (often developed and owned by English and American companies) accelerated the commercialization of agriculture and rapidly integrated local economies into regional, national, and international markets.[49] As a result, large agricultural holdings could produce more, move goods to markets faster, and yield bigger profits.

This process of foreign investment and commercialization disrupted long-established customs of commonly held property and cooperative forms of labor. Porfirian economic policies concentrated the region's land in a few hands. Twelve elite Mexican families and American companies controlled 75 percent of Nayarit's land in 1910.[50] These families and companies dominated the political and economic landscape of Nayarit and kept firm control of the region's labor force. As wealthy landholders accumulated acres of agricultural land, they wanted to gain access to workers for "increased commercial productivity and profit-making 'money' crops."[51] Losing land under Porfiriato policies, peasants, mostly indigenous and mestizo, found themselves forced to seek work in the new hacienda system as permanent and temporary workers or as sharecroppers.

These conditions were not unfamiliar to Bard and his ilk, many of whom had led American imperial expansion into California. As discussed earlier, Bard had acquired his first properties in Southern California under very similar circumstances. Before American conquest in 1848, the Mexican government had redistributed California land, much of it held by the region's mission system, to individual Californio families in the form of land grants (where Californio families employed Indian and mestizo labor) as well as to the territory's remaining indigenous population. Anglo conquest began with the acquisition of these lands and accelerated after American annexation. Arriving in California in the 1860s, Bard benefited from an economic and legal system that facilitated the transfer of property from former Mexican citizens to Anglo-American speculators and investors. This process transformed Mexican workers into a racially marked proletariat in Southern California. By the turn of the century, Mexican workers were the majority of the agricultural labor force in Southern California counties.[52] Bard had not only witnessed this but had actively participated in the process of land dispossession and racialization of labor. As a result, both the acquisition of the Quimichis property and the system of labor in Mexico presented profitable parallels for the wealthy senator and his coterie of Angeleno investors.

The Mexican Petroleum Company

Race, labor, and urban capitalist expansion coalesced in similar ways in Mexico's oil region along the country's eastern coast. While the CRLC and Quimichis Colony busied themselves with courting Mexican elites, building an agricultural hinterland, staffing enterprises with workers of color, and expanding their city-empire, other Los Angeles–based investors ventured into even more profitable enterprises. In the case of Edward L. Doheny, this meant extracting the energy source that would fuel the twentieth century, first from beneath Los Angeles and then from beneath the eastern coast of Mexico. Although his medium for wealth differed from that of the likes of Otis, Chandler, and Bard, Doheny's strategy for extracting wealth from Mexico mimicked theirs. He honed a particular skill for prospecting and extracting oil in Los Angeles and then exported and transplanted that skill to the oil regions of Mexico. In doing so, Doheny also transferred his ideas about the intertwined systems of race, labor, civilization, and empire from his mansion in Southern California to his oil fields in the Huasteca region of eastern Mexico. In some ways, Doheny's exploitation of Mexican labor most resembled the racialized open shop of early twentieth-century Los Angeles. Doheny was explicit in his racial ideas of labor and uplift and translated this belief system into notoriously brutal working conditions. One Mexican historian nicknamed the infamous oilman "Doheny el Cruel."[53]

Doheny's diminutive stature and scholarly, bespectacled face belied his hardheaded business acuity and his single-minded determination to control an oil empire. Doheny self-identified as a quintessential westerner, pioneer, and frontiersman. He believed that dedication and commitment resulted in capitalist success and that personal fortunes also benefited the financial success of the nation. During his time in Mexico, he held that pulling the fuel of the modern era out of the earth was an endeavor that would propel Mexico toward modernity and civilization. As biographer Margaret Leslie Davis observed, Doheny arrived in Mexico "full of confidence, certain that he was bringing what Mexico needed, that he would be welcomed, and that he would make a fortune."[54] This attitude also reflected Doheny's perspective on American empire building. Like many American empire builders, he saw his investment in Mexico and his dealings with Mexican workers as both a civilizing force and a way to enrich himself. Doheny viewed the world through a racial and class hierarchy in which he, as a white American, had reached a pinnacle of civilized masculinity, self-evident in his wealth, power, and refined taste. His job, as he saw it, was to make a fortune while simultaneously "uplifting" the nonwhite workers he employed in Mexico.[55]

He was born and grew up in Wisconsin in a large Irish Catholic family. In 1872, at the age of sixteen, he left Wisconsin and landed in Los Angeles after several unsuccessful mining ventures in other parts of the West. He arrived in the city just at the moment when railroads were experimenting with petroleum as a feasible fuel source. In the fall of 1892, Doheny and his partner, Charles Canfield, leased a plot of land on State Street (in the heart of downtown Los Angeles) and dug their first oil well by hand. By 1894, Doheny controlled the largest portion of the city's emerging oil industry. Doheny also forged a partnership with the Santa Fe Railway and its subsidiaries and began supplying the company with oil for its locomotives. He tapped wells across Southern California and had become a millionaire by 1902. As an oilman, Doheny was also at the helm of Los Angeles's first important industry outside of agriculture. In the first two decades of the twentieth century, the Los Angeles region became one of the world's most important oil producers. Wells sprinkled across Southern California produced 20 percent of the world's supply by World War I.[56]

Eager to apply his petroleum knowledge in other locales and to reap further fortunes, Doheny looked eagerly to extend his personal empire beyond the environs of Southern California. In fact, it was Doheny who first exported the oil expertise developed in Southern California's oil industry to Mexico. In 1900, Doheny took his first trip to Mexico to prospect for oil near Tampico in the state of Tamaulipas on the Gulf of Mexico. His practiced eye identified opportunity along the humid east coast of Mexico. According to Doheny, "It is the belief . . . of many experienced oil men of California . . . that the Republic of Mexico is destined to become one of the greatest petroleum producing countries of the world."[57] In fact, Doheny identified Mexico in 1901 as the equivalent of California a few years prior—perched on the precipice of an enormous oil fortune. In a letter to José Yves Limantour, Mexico's minister of finance, Doheny wrote, "Mexico is today, in respect to fuel and petroleum products, situated very much as California was seven years ago."[58] This promise of wealth led Doheny, with Canfield, to found the Mexican Petroleum Company (MPC) of California in 1900 and to begin buying up properties around Tampico. Their investors included a long list of notable Angelenos.[59]

In his first decade in Mexico, Doheny produced 85 percent of the oil extracted in the country and emerged as the largest independent oil producer in the world.[60] These extraordinary production levels unfolded quickly after Doheny's first trip to the region. By the beginning of 1901, the MPC had purchased over 600,000 acres of land in Tamaulipas and had invested over a million dollars in the operation.[61] Doheny then expanded his drilling operations to Huasteca, near the borders of the states of Veracruz, Tamaulipas, and San Luis Potosí. In 1915, Doheny discovered the largest oil well in the world—Cerro Azul No. 4—which produced almost eleven million gallons a day. One of Doheny's foremen pointed out that this was more than was produced by the entire state of California, one of the world's most productive oil regions at the beginning of the twentieth century.[62]

Doheny brought the bulk of his fortune back to Los Angeles. Although not as overtly active in the city's boosterism as figures such as Otis and Chandler or even Bard, Doheny did become integral to Los Angeles's development. He almost single-handedly sparked the city's oil boom and helped establish one of the region's most lucrative industries. He helped to develop the city of Beverly Hills. He gave generously to the University of Southern California, located just a few blocks south of his lush complex of mansions at Chester Place, the city's first gated community. A devout Catholic, Doheny also gave millions of his oil dollars to various Catholic churches and causes in Southern California. One biographer estimates that Doheny gave the local Catholic church as much as $100 million over the course of his life in Los Angeles.⁶³ In Los Angeles, Doheny also surrounded himself with the gilded profits of his black tar empire. Life at his lavish home in Chester Place included a private bowling alley, a small private zoo, and an indoor pool large enough to float a canoe. The grounds included a greenhouse filled with Mexican plant specimens. The Spanish-language press in Los Angeles did not miss the fact that Mexican resources had transformed Doheny's life. In a scathing critique of Doheny published by *La Prensa*, an anonymous author observed: "Where did his colossal fortune come from? Simply from Mexico . . . The whole fortune accumulated by the 'parvenu' Doheny has come from Mexico without the least benefitting the country. On the contrary, every dollar coming from the Tampico Oil Fields is invested in the United States and especially in Los Angeles where he has a palatial mansion which attracts attention through a lavish display of oriental luxury."⁶⁴ Mexican Americans in Los Angeles were well aware that Doheny's exploitation of Mexican mineral resources and labor had translated into astonishing wealth north of the border.

Much like the CRLC, Doheny and his MPC developed class- and race-based alliances with a Mexican elite, all the while relying on an exploitative relationship with Mexico's laboring classes. With millions of dollars at stake in his Mexican oil investments, Doheny was careful to cultivate strong alliances with Mexican officials from President Díaz down. The Díaz administration believed that oil production in Mexico would provide a valuable fuel source to help propel Mexico into the twentieth century. Doheny would regularly reference his close relationship with Díaz to lobby other officials in the Mexican government to create public policy beneficial to the MPC. In a letter to a Mexican official in 1902, for example, Doheny argued against the possible imposition of a tax on crude oil by the Mexican government and suggested that such a tax would represent a policy entirely "to the contrary" of what President Díaz and his minister of finance, José Yves Limantour, had promised him and the MPC.⁶⁵ Doheny and the MPC also took pains to inform Díaz and his administration of the good they were doing in Mexico, reminding him in 1902 that their oil production in the Huasteca was geared toward domestic consumption by Mexican railroad lines such as the Ferrocarril Central Mexicano. Doheny also provided painfully detailed outlines of his expenditures in Mexico, seemingly to prove his commitment to Mexican infrastructure. In a 1902 letter to Díaz, Doheny listed all expenditures made by the MPC in its first year of operation,

The swimming pool and greenhouse at Edward Doheny's Los Angeles home, 1926. Doheny filled the greenhouse with plant specimens from Mexico. Security Pacific National Bank Collection, Los Angeles Public Library.

totaling almost $1 million. Doheny referred to the investment as "las grandes cantidades de dinero" that the company had invested in view of the very optimistic results of their preliminary prospecting. Mexico's "vast oceans" of petroleum, Doheny assured Díaz, would bring the country equally vast returns.[66]

Despite claims that the MPC was investing heavily in the development of the Huasteca oil region, much of the wealth created by Mexico's "oro negro" flowed into Los Angeles. Doheny's bank accounts overflowed by way of the dispossession of Mexican hacendados and indigenous communities. With parallels to the dispossession of California's native peoples and the Californios that Bard had helped to lead in Southern California, Doheny and his Mexican Petroleum Company took advantage of shifting patterns of landownership in the Huasteca to make money. Policies under the Porfiriato forced many indigenous communities in the oil region to divide up their *condueñazgos*, or community-held lands, into individual lots. This process left individual indigenous families with the option to sell small lots, which they often did, to a wealthier hacendado class. While hacendados accumulated land from their indigenous neighbors, they also found it difficult to turn dense jungle into productive ranches. When oil prospectors like Doheny and Canfield appeared on their doorsteps with cash in hand, many hacendados were eager to sell land that they had not yet been able to transform into farmland or cattle ranches. Doheny's offer of cash for land also interested indigenous landowners in the Huasteca, who often preferred to lease or sell to foreign interests rather than to the nearby hacendados, with whom they had a historically antagonistic relationship.[67]

In addition to the acquisition of indigenous land and displacement of indigenous peoples, an exploitative practice with historical parallels in California and imperial ventures globally, Doheny and his oil companies wrung wealth from the local Mexican workers they pressed into service. Their labor provided the human power necessary to extract oil riches from the Mexican jungle. While some volunteered, attracted by relatively good wages, others found themselves swept up by local officials or forcibly recruited by oil company foremen. These workers performed the most strenuous and dangerous oil work, including digging trenches, constructing moats, carving out roads, conducting controlled burns of dense jungle foliage, capping explosive wells, and fighting dangerous oil fires. At the peak of oil production in the Huasteca, oil companies employed approximately 40,000 Mexican men at their production sites.[68] In an effort to counter accusations of worker abuse, Doheny repeatedly told the Mexican government that the MPC provided amenities not normally accessible to Mexican laborers—electricity, distilled water, refrigeration, ice, newly constructed housing, and company schools.[69] Of course, what Doheny failed to mention was that these amenities often came at the cost of individual freedom on the part of his employees.

Doheny also imported American concepts, particularly Angeleno triangulations of race, labor, and land, to his Mexican enterprises. These practices overlapped with Mexican divisions of race and labor on large landholdings. He brought white foremen, craftsmen, and drillers to spearhead production. These workers enjoyed comfortable accommodations, excellent meals, access to the best transportation methods, and amenities such as radios and telephones. According to historian Myrna Santiago, the tangible benefits of light skin, or the "wages of whiteness," accompanied

American workers from the United States to the jungles of the Huasteca.⁷⁰ Santiago argues that white MPC overseers "never let Mexicans forget that they were fit only for 'low grade labor,' for work 'not fit for a white man.'"⁷¹

Doheny, then, capitalized on the intersections of the racial and labor hierarchy of his home city of Los Angeles in the petroleum jungle of Veracruz, Mexico. As he stated numerous times in company correspondence, he had successfully overseen the extraction of millions of dollars of oil from Los Angeles through a carefully managed labor system. This could be exported to the eastern edge of Mexico and yield similarly rich results. As the U.S. Department of State reported to the Mexican government, the MPC had "established a model camp, with the best of sanitary arrangements . . . It established schools, baths and hospitals, as well as training schools for Mexican boys, and on account of its proper housing arrangements, free lighting, homes rent-free, and considerate treatment of laborers, it has never had a strike or any unpleasantness."⁷² This description, written by an American official, hinted at the strict working and living conditions on Doheny's properties; according to Doheny's official line, wages were good, living conditions were excellent, and workers had no cause for complaint. Of course, authoritarian company oversight of workers' lives and activities, rather than Doheny's benevolence, created this "ideal" company town. The description also contained a lie, as Mexican oil workers repeatedly struck or engaged in labor stoppages to contest the conditions of their employment.

Angeleno concepts of race and labor also placed Mexican workers at the bottom of the industrial labor hierarchy and informed Doheny's approach to labor discipline. His companies maintained strict control of workday schedules and living conditions. They also enacted a color line in employment, delineating specific (skilled) jobs for white workers and less skilled work for Mexican laborers. The MPC prohibited the training of Mexican workers for the more skilled and more highly paid positions of white workers.⁷³ The disciplining of Mexican workers also included draconian methods not used on imported white workers. Hitting and kicking Mexican workers was not unusual. Neither was the use of company jails to detain workers deemed unruly. One worker recalled being imprisoned in an empty oil storage tank as punishment for trying to organize a union of petroleum workers.⁷⁴ Company control also extended to workers' personal and social lives through segregated company housing and carefully monitored company stores.

As alarming as these stories of the violent control of labor in Mexico's petroleum region are, they would not have been unfamiliar to laborers in

Los Angeles and greater Southern California. As the racial and class perspectives and practices of men such as Doheny as well as Otis and Bard suggest, white employers in Southern California had no qualms about brutally repressing labor organizing or segmenting labor along racial lines. And the violent subjugation of workers and their organizing efforts was as common north of the border as it was south of the international boundary. Of particular importance for this study are the ways in which conceptions of and practices around landownership, labor, and race met and overlapped in Los Angeles and Mexico. Although differences certainly existed between the racial hierarchies of the United States and Mexico, part of what made Mexico appealing for Angeleno investors was the ways in which they could export both their strategies for making money and their conceptions of race and labor across the border. Once in Mexico, they found a race and labor regime that similarly placed nonwhite workers at the bottom of an economic hierarchy that concentrated wealth and land at the (mostly) white top.

Conclusion

In the decades preceding the Mexican Revolution, Los Angeles investors hustled across the border with concurrent dreams of personal fortunes and civic empires. Their activities that tied Los Angeles to Mexico between the end of the American Civil War and the start of the Mexican Revolution echoed the imperial exploits of American capital and commercial empires in the West and around the world while simultaneously assuming specific regional dimensions. For example, Angeleno investors borrowed from the borderlands structures of race, class, and labor as the ingredients of expansion into Mexico.

In building this core-periphery relationship, Los Angeles investors relied on expanding Southern California's racialized economic structure, where they found that it overlapped with similar patterns in Mexico. The owners and supervisors of Los Angeles–based investment properties, including the Quimichis Colony, the Colorado River Land Company, and the Mexican Petroleum Company, all relied on the race and labor structures developed in Southern California in the second half of the nineteenth century. They exported overseers, racial ideologies, and business practices that placed Mexican workers at the bottom of a labor and class hierarchy designed to generate profits for the citizens and a city of another nation. This structure of race and labor also created alliances between Los Angeles–based investors and their compatriots in Mexico. From the executive office down, Mexican officials believed that strict control over a largely nonwhite indigenous or mestizo workforce would simultaneously uplift "uncivilized" workers while enriching foreign investors and the nation. Leveraging their shared class interests, Los Angeles investors united with a Mexican political and economic elite to facilitate the development of a city with an international periphery.

Investments, labor, and elite alliances all bound Los Angeles to Mexico as the twentieth century opened. As explored in the following chapter, however, the relationships that tied Los Angeles to its investments in Mexico could prove very tenuous. Beginning in 1910, workers on both the Mexican and American sides of the border began to challenge the economic structures of Los Angeles as a city with international reach and an American empire. From individual acts of resistance to more organized rebellions and even violence, the workforce that Los Angeles investors expected to quietly acquiesce to empire building exploded. While revolution shifted the relationship between Angeleno investors and their empire, it continued to bind the city and its hinterland in a combative grip.

3 Revolution around the Corner and across the Border

Dusk was falling across the lush Acaponeta Valley, where Mexico's rugged western cordillera softens and slopes toward the Pacific. William S. Windham, the manager of the Quimichis Colony, rested against a log in the dimming light, lost in thought and a headache. He may have been contemplating the warm weather and prospects for planting the new crop of corn. Or he might have been nervously calculating the profits on the sacks of harvested and shelled corn he had counted earlier in the day. His thoughts may have ambled as far as Berkeley, where his daughter Gladys was probably turning on a lamp to study classics in the twilight.

As his assistant, W. C. Dunn, walked toward him through the falling light, his thoughts may have returned abruptly to Mexico, to the routine and unexpected tasks of running an American-owned ranch in a country torn by the twentieth century's first social revolution. Perhaps Windham considered placing an order with the butcher that night so he could have bacon for breakfast tomorrow, or how best to catch a troublesome group of bandits and cattle thieves. As Dunn reached Windham's makeshift bench, the two men paused in conversation, reviewing their work for the following day, discussing schemes to prosecute the cattle rustlers and rid the ranch of anyone with revolutionary sympathies. After an hour or two of discussion, Windham evidently decided the problem of bandits and revolutionaries could be solved the following day and excused himself with the headache.[1]

Dunn and Windham left the log in opposite directions—Windham toward his bed in the nearby hacienda and Dunn to oversee crews of Quimichis residents and workers laboring through late-night double shifts to finish shelling the recent corn crop. A few dozen yards away, Dunn stopped abruptly, ordered to halt by a startling voice in the dark. Surprised, Dunn peered at the figure in front of him and then glanced back over his shoulder to the place where he had left his supervisor. No doubt, what he witnessed made his skin prickle with fear. Three men, wrapped in blankets, stood in the doorway to Windham's rooms. Windham "rassled" against them as they corralled him into the building with pointed guns. Glancing back

Quimichis Colony investors and managers having lunch on the ranch in Nayarit, early twentieth century. William Windham sits in the center right. Museum of Ventura County.

toward the voice, Dunn saw its owner retreating "as fast as he could go" into the night. Shots reverberated in Windham's room and jerked Dunn's attention back to the hacienda. Shots again. Unarmed and stunned, Dunn raced in the direction of his guns. As he ran, he heard more shots and Windham's anguished voice cry out, "Oh God! Gladys! Gladys! Gladys! Oh God!"[2] As rapid footsteps faded, quiet returned to the dark valley.

Windham's death at the hands of Mexican revolutionaries occurred in the fall of 1915 as Mexico was in the throes of the twentieth century's first social revolution, brought about in part by the rapid development of capitalism in Mexico as well as the voracious financial and imperial appetites of American investors. Mexican revolutionaries identified American investment as one of the causal factors in their mounting economic misfortunes. As a result, revolutionaries specifically targeted American investors and companies as they waged a civil war to topple and rebuild the country's political and economic systems along more egalitarian principles. While certainly not all Mexican revolutionaries were rebelling against Los Angeles per se, they were certainly challenging the larger system of imperialistic capitalism that linked the city to a hinterland south of the border. This aggressive capitalism had dug deep into the veins of their nation's natural and labor resources to siphon off wealth that ended up in financial capitals around the world, from London to New York City to Los Angeles.[3]

Revolutionary activity on properties owned by Los Angeles–based investors did constitute a critique of the tightly knit financial and political alliances that had developed between the city-empire of Los Angeles and Porfirio-era Mexico. As explored in the previous chapters, Angeleno investors successfully drew Mexico into their city's financial orbit. They did so by buying properties in Mexico, promoting trade with Mexico, fostering mutually beneficial relationships with Mexican officials, and pairing the repressive labor and racial regime of Southern California with that of nineteenth- and early twentieth-century Mexico. Beginning in 1910, however, revolutionary tides spread quickly from Mexican investment properties to Los Angeles and back again, rolling back and forth across the border in waves of expatriate political philosophers, disguised revolutionary generals, workers and rebels, destitute refugees, and frightened Americans. Revolution meant that what Los Angeles investors had envisioned and constructed as their city-empire's economic periphery—the place where they could extract great wealth for themselves and their metropolis—had revolted against the very economic structure that moved wealth from a colonial edge to a municipal core. Given Los Angeles's proximity to the border and to greater Mexico, as well as the dense grid of economic interests that bound Los Angeles investors to their investment properties, the Mexican Revolution shook the city's capitalist class, perched in the center of a transnational financial web. This web, however, proved difficult to sever, and Los Angeles investors continued their intimate involvement in Mexican affairs.

Although they believed they had built an orderly system of resource extraction, Los Angeles capitalists had also helped create the conditions of their own undoing. As in the case of all empires, imperial subjects, from workers to state officials, resisted and rejected imperial ventures. This was as true in the Los Angeles periphery as it was in other sites of commercial empire in Latin American and the Pacific—Cuba, Hawaii, the Dominican Republic, and the Philippines, to name but a few.[4] In Mexico, rejection of imperialism came in the form of a nationwide revolution. The workforce that had muscled natural resources into pesos and dollars on Los Angeles–owned properties rebelled not only against their own government but also against their immediate employers. Los Angeles–based investors believed they had built a successful periphery for their city by carefully cultivating a workforce that would serve their financial and municipal objectives. The greater extractive and agricultural empire of Los Angeles required the minds and labor of Mexican workers to dig oil wells or harvest rows of produce. The Mexican Revolution, however, meant that the workforce carefully cultivated and controlled by Los Angeles oligarchs no longer paid attention to the rules of empire, labor, or private property. In essence, capitalist investors could no longer control the world they had created.

This chapter explores how three different Los Angeles–based enterprises, all discussed previously, dealt with the revolt of Mexican working people against their own government as well as against foreign investors. The scale of various Los Angeles investments, their geographic locations, and their ability to forge protective relationships with local Mexican leaders all determined their varying levels of success during the violent decade of the Mexican Revolution (1910–1920). The smaller Quimichis Colony suffered the heaviest losses, primarily due to their inability to find a local Mexican official to protect their property from Mexican revolutionaries. In contrast, the larger investments of Otis and Chandler in the Colorado River Land Company (CRLC) and Doheny's Mexican Petroleum Company (MPC) remained productive, even profitable, during the decade of the revolution. Their location in regions relatively protected from the revolution, coupled with the emergence of regional leaders who kept revolutionary violence at bay, protected their properties and allowed them to continue to make money throughout the tumultuous decade of the 1910s. Nonetheless, investors in all three enterprises worried incessantly that the revolution would compromise their substantial investments in Mexico or, even more frighteningly, spill across the border and into Los Angeles. This fear increased the significance of Mexico to Los Angeles investors and caused them to tighten their hold on individual properties while also plotting more wide-scale cross-border interventions.

At the level of diplomacy, revolution in Mexico evolved during a period of intensifying American interventions around the globe generally and in Latin America more specifically. The interests of investors and economics drove much of this policy. Between 1865 and 1912, the United States moved from rejecting formal political footholds in the Caribbean and Central America to controlling the Panama Canal, occupying Nicaragua, economically and militarily dominating the Caribbean, and actively enforcing the Roosevelt Corollary to the Monroe Doctrine.[5] In fact, the United States sent warships to Latin American ports almost 6,000 times, an astounding number, between 1869 and 1897 to protect American commercial interests.[6] With increased interventions came what historian Walter LaFeber calls the imperial or "new presidency": the belief on the part of wealthy Americans that the presidency's main purpose was to maintain order internationally to stabilize and increase American economic opportunities. By the end of William Howard Taft's presidency in early 1913, the United States was on the verge of sending troops into Mexico to protect the interests of American investors and the $2 billion they had invested south of the border.[7] Acutely aware of American interventions in Latin America and around the globe, and subscribers to the idea of the "new presidency," Angeleno investors believed that their government must intervene on their behalf. As explored in chapter 4, they became a leading force in the lobbying campaign for armed intervention to protect American investments in Mexico. As they waited expectantly for military intervention, Los Angeles–based investors also sought to mitigate the impact of the revolution on the ground at their various investment properties, as explored in this chapter.

Ultimately, "Los Angeles" may not have been on the tongues of Mexican revolutionaries, but their actions on Los Angeles–based investment properties demonstrated an explicit rejection of precisely the type of economic ties that Los Angeles oligarchs had so carefully cultivated between the investor class of their city and the Díaz regime. Despite their varying fates during the Mexican Revolution's decade of active fighting, the conflict between employees, dissidents, and revolutionaries and the Quimichis Colony, the Colorado River Land Company, and the Mexican Petroleum Company illustrates the local nature of a national revolution and the ways in which this revolution explicitly challenged international capitalism and empire. The Mexican Revolution was an unambiguous critique of the type of imperial alliances forged between the city-empire of Los Angeles and Mexico's executive branch. In response, Angeleno investors held ever more tightly to their Mexican properties and to their steadfast belief that core should control periphery. Rather than selling out and settling up, Los Angeles–based investors tried to tighten their grip on south-of-the-border investments and called for American intervention.

Revolution in Los Angeles

Ironically, empires, including city-empires, not only produce profits but also breed the very insurrections that ultimately cause them to crumble. While the bloodiest episodes in the Mexican Revolution certainly unfolded south of the border, the very start of the revolution lurked on the street corners and in the alleyways of Los Angeles. Certainly, Southern Californians in Mexico, such as Windham, would come to live in far riskier conditions in a place like the Quimichis Colony. However, the spark that ignited revolutionary fervor in Mexico flared in Los Angeles several years before Windham met his fate at the hands of revolutionaries in Nayarit. Many scholars credit brothers Ricardo and Enrique Flores Magón, known as the philosophical patriarchs of the Mexican Revolution, with lighting the spark of revolt from their modest house at 111 East Pico Street, just blocks from the headquarters of the *Los Angeles Times*, a stone's throw from Doheny's mansion at Chester Place, and within a few miles of the hopeful Quimichis investors who lived on the idyllic suburban streets of Pasadena. In the heart of the city-empire, revolutionary anarchists plotted to bring down the Díaz regime, challenge the Colossus of the North, and empower the proletariat on both sides of the border. In fact, the revolution that cost Windham his life owed much of its origins to the writings and organizing efforts of the anarchist brothers who escaped prison sentences in Mexico by relocating to Texas and the American Midwest and then settling in Los Angeles by 1907.

Before the Flores Magóns relocated to Los Angeles, they frayed the edges of Díaz's thirty-five-year rule in Mexico. By 1905, it was apparent to many Mexicans that the dictator's policies had resulted in a gaping divide between the rich and the poor, the dispossession of the nation's largely indigenous and mestizo agricultural class, a drop in wages for urban workers as well as the violent repression of their organizing efforts, and the political dissatisfaction and disenfranchisement of the country's upper middle class and wealthy citizens. This unhappy tapestry, already wearing at the edges, unraveled even more as manufacturing workers protested poor wages and working conditions, the Mexican middle class felt an economic tightening, and educated elites pushed for political reform between 1905 and 1910.[8] Cognizant of the deep political and economic dissatisfaction in Mexico, the brothers began organizing a resistance movement to the Díaz regime through their anarchist newspaper, *Regeneración*.

The shorter-term triggers of dropping wages and growing strikes stemmed from long-simmering economic problems in Mexico. International capitalism like that promoted by the Los Angeles investor class shifted economic patterns in Mexico, particularly in northern territories. Massive land acquisitions by U.S.-owned oil, railroad, timber, mining, livestock, and agricultural companies consolidated land formerly used by the rural poor, disrupted peasant patterns of life, and bred discontent in Mexico's agricultural areas. The revolution, initiated in 1910, coincided with both a rise in American investment and an increase in investments originating in Los Angeles. Revolutionaries recognized the role of U.S. capital in their economic circumstances and targeted American property and businesses during the conflict.[9]

The Flores Magóns, anarchists from the state of Oaxaca, condemned the Díaz government through *Regeneración*, founded in 1900. They also founded an alternative political party, the Partido Liberal Mexicano (PLM), and through it advocated the overthrow of Díaz and supported social reforms such as the eight-hour workday and free public education. Dictators do not generally like anarchist revolutionaries, and in 1904 Díaz dispatched arrest warrants for the Flores Magóns, driving them north of the border. The brothers' revolutionary sentiments did not change with the shift in venue. After living briefly in Laredo, San Antonio, and St. Louis, Ricardo and Enrique settled in Los Angeles in a house on Pico Street. From this modest headquarters, the brothers continued to publish *Regeneración* and promoted the PLM. They also organized Mexican Americans and Mexican immigrants living in Los Angeles and built alliances with the political left in the city and across the country, including with anarchist Emma Goldman and Angeleno socialist Job Harriman. Copies of *Regeneración* circulated south across the border, helping to ignite protests and unrest in the Mexican mining industry in Cananea in 1906 and developing into armed raids by PLM members on borderland communities. This labor organizing and unrest served as a precursor to the violence that would surround the presidential election of 1910 and launch the Mexican Revolution.[10]

The Los Angeles elite, friends and supporters of Díaz with deep financial interests in Mexico, carefully monitored the activities of the revolutionary brothers. They often colluded with Díaz emissaries to track their publications and their movements. In partnership with the Díaz government and the Mexican consul in Los Angeles, the Los Angeles police department trailed the brothers to their house in the heart of downtown Los Angeles and burst in to arrest them in August 1907. Their arrest came in direct response to the radical political ideas advocated by the brothers. The Los Angeles investor class felt that the Flores Magóns represented a particular threat to their city-empire. Having carefully cultivated a mutually beneficial relationship with Porfirio Díaz and his government, invested heavily in Mexico, and tied their city's future to transnational capitalism south of the border, Angeleno oligarchs had a vested interested in preventing a revolt fomenting in the heart of Los Angeles against their most important and powerful political ally in Mexico. The morning following the arrest, the *Los Angeles Times* excitedly reported, "'Reds' Caught Red-Handed, Terrific Struggle Attends Capture of Plotters against Mexican Republic."[11] The Los Angeles police and federal authorities charged that the Flores Magóns had violated American neutrality laws that forbid plotting against the government of a friendly foreign nation.

Despite their arrest in Los Angeles in 1907, the political writings and organizing of the Flores Magón brothers shook the political foundation of Díaz's rule. The rising discontent of the Mexican population from a variety of different sectors as well as widespread political discontent set the stage for armed revolt in 1910. When Díaz first promised to step down from power by not running in the 1910 election but then ran anyway, Mexico's political elite, led by Francisco Madero, challenged Díaz's reign. In a serious miscalculation, Díaz had Madero arrested for running against him in the presidential election and claimed his own reelection by a suspiciously wide margin. Released from prison a few months after the election, Madero regrouped in El Paso and planned an armed insurrection with other upper- and middle-class Mexican leaders, including future presidents Venustiano Carranza and Adolfo de la Huerta. Peasant groups already under arms also joined the 1910 rebellion and gave rise to the iconic revolutionary leaders Emiliano Zapata in the south and Francisco Villa in the north. This coalition helped oust Díaz in the spring of 1911 and elect Madero the first new president of Mexico in thirty years. All of this stemmed, in part, from the Flores Magóns and their organizing in Los Angeles. From Los Angeles, the first social revolution of the twentieth century had erupted.

It was in the context of the 1910 rebellions, led by Madero and Villa, that revolution pierced the geographic center of the city-empire of Los Angeles. Although the Flores Magóns faced arrest in 1907, they initially escaped significant jail time, maintained their headquarters in Los Angeles, and used the city as a base for their organizing efforts across Mexico and the American Southwest. Despite being tracked by the Mexican and U.S. governments and facing several highly publicized charges of violating American criminal syndicalism laws, they began developing a plan to overthrow the Díaz regime in late 1910. Given the city's proximity to sparsely populated Baja California, Ricardo Flores Magón assessed that the PLM could easily seize the territory and establish a base there. From Baja, the PLM planned to challenge both Díaz and then the Madero movement and launch a class-based social struggle that would soon have as "its stage the surface of the whole planet, and was designed to smash tyranny, capitalism, and authority."[12]

With arms supplied by the International Workers of the World (IWW), a small force of PLM members seized the border town of Mexicali, just steps from the CRLC property, in January 1911. Over the next few days, they also seized Algodones, Tecate, and Tijuana. The PLM rebels held portions of northern Baja through the spring of 1911, but limited resources and the arrival of pro-Madero troops forced the collapse of the invasion. The arrest of both Ricardo and Enrique in Los Angeles further deteriorated the movement. The U.S. government charged the Flores Magóns with conspiracy to overthrow a foreign government and with recruiting American nationals to join their movement. Following their arrest, Eugene V. Debs described the two men as "comrades in the social revolution who were being ground between two capitalist governments."[13]

Revolution so close to home no doubt elevated blood pressures and raised adrenaline levels in the homes and offices of the Los Angeles oligarchy. Newspaper headlines made public their shrill anxiety. Otis and Chandler ran sensational stories in the *Los Angeles Times* describing the Flores Magóns as "reds of the most virulent type" and leaders of a "red junta."[14] Another headline read, "Revolutionists in Los Angeles Den. Terrific Struggle Attends Capture of Plotters against Mexican Republic."[15] Foreshadowing their later demands for American intervention in Mexico, Chandler and the CRLC, discussed in more depth later in this chapter, suggested forming a joint American-Mexican military force to regain control of Baja California from the Magonistas. The paper also nervously reported on events unfolding along the U.S.-Mexico border, including the discovery of the Plan de San Diego in Texas. The Plan, drawn up by revolutionaries in the Texas-Mexico borderlands, called for a general uprising of Mexican Americans and Mexicans to reclaim territory seized by the United States between 1836 and 1848, including Texas, New Mexico, Arizona, Colorado, and California. The discovery of the Plan incited considerable hysteria across the American Southwest. For the Los Angeles investor class, revolution did indeed lurk around every corner, and they believed it incumbent on their government to restore stability along the border and in Mexico.[16]

The actual armed revolution led by the Flores Magóns in Baja California, however, was short-lived. The brothers themselves remained in Los Angeles, directing operations from their offices downtown, which likely contributed to the breakdown of their revolutionary movement. As a result, their revolt, launched in January 1911, had been crushed by Mexican national troops by June of the same year.[17] While the Baja revolt failed to achieve what the Magonistas had hoped for, it provided the impetus for interim president Francisco León de la Barra (who took power after Diáz fled and prior to the election of Madero) to station additional federal troops in Baja California. The Flores Magón brothers remained in the United States, constantly harassed and persecuted by American authorities. While he continued writing and organizing, Ricardo Flores Magón spent much of the rest of his life in prison and died in Leavenworth in 1922. The revolution he had helped unleash from Los Angeles, however, proved more difficult to contain.

The revolutionary activities of the Flores Magón brothers, while explicitly critical of the type of imperial relationship that Los Angeles oligarchs extended across the border, also demonstrated the intimate bond between the two regions. Ricardo and Enrique did not just land randomly in Los Angeles, but found the city's Mexican community and proximity to the border a strategic location from which to publish their revolutionary newspaper and call for the uprising of the Mexican people against precisely the type of financial alliances that investors such as Otis and Doheny had cultivated between the Los Angeles investor class and Mexico's executive branch. As the emerging financial center of the U.S.-Mexico borderlands, Los Angeles served as the nucleus not only of the fiscal borderlands but also of the revolutionary borderlands. The city-empire had bred its discontents, and they found it prudent to attack the beast from its heart.

Revolution in the Hinterland

The events at Los Angeles–owned properties, from the revolt in Baja California to the fighting in Nayarit, during the decade of the Mexican Revolution exemplify the Mexican rejection of U.S. imperialism, the Los Angeles city-empire, American notions of private property, and the close relationship that had developed between Los Angeles investors and the Porfiriato. Although the Baja revolt failed to yield the political and economic transformations that idealists such as the Flores Magón brothers hungered for in Mexico and the rest of the world, Mexican revolutionaries had far more command over other Los Angeles–based and American-owned properties, particularly in regions farther from the border. Returning to the dramatic plight of Windham and the Quimichis Colony reveals precisely how profoundly Mexican revolutionaries could transform power relations between themselves and their employers or the American investors in their midst. In fact, the aggressive capitalism that emanated from Los Angeles, explored in the previous chapter, met an aggressive and violent response in the form of the Mexican Revolution beginning in 1910.

Organized and persistent resistance to Quimichis management and its Southern California owners arose shortly after the outbreak of revolutionary activity in 1910. This trend drastically shifted the relations of power between the ranch's Anglo-American owners and their Mexican employees in ways previously unimaginable in the strictly controlled labor system of the Los Angeles agricultural empire. While renters and workers had tried to challenge their American landlords and employers prior to the arrival of the revolution in Nayarit and Sinaloa, the rhetoric of the revolutionary movement, which championed the needs of the working class and opposed foreign investment, coupled with the turmoil of civil war, inverted power relations at Quimichis. Although the territory of Nayarit did not experience the heaviest revolutionary fighting, particularly in comparison to the other northern states of Durango, Chihuahua, and Sonora, some factional battles and the instability caused by the conflict provided space for Nayarit's agricultural workers to challenge the power of hacienda owners.[18] Mexican workers, farmers, and revolutionary forces disrupted the daily operations of the ranch, looted stored crops and supplies, declared themselves members of the revolution, challenged the legality of Quimichis land titles, expressed their opposition to the United States, and kidnapped and killed ranch staff. Ultimately, Mexicans challenged the economic system that Quimichis owners had tried to institute on the ranch and the ability of Los Angeles investors to link their city's fortunes to Mexico.

As a result of loss of land and harsh labor policies on haciendas, many Mexican revolutionaries fixated their animosity and resistance on large landholders when the uprising erupted in 1910.[19] Historian Adolfo Gilly argues that the hacienda "came to stand as the material form of the peasants' oppression and the principal object upon which their revolutionary fury would be vented after 1910." Examining the oral history of peasant soldiers and revolutionaries, Gilly found that many articulated the seizure of haciendas, rather than the overthrow of the central state, as their ultimate goal.[20] The ultimate goal of soldiers and peasants is the subject of intense historiographic debate. What is clear, however, is that local revolutionary fury often targeted area haciendas and ranches. Workers and peasants saw them as the most immediate and oppressive institutions in their lives. It was in this context of land privatization and worker anger that revolution came

Agricultural workers at the Quimichis Colony, 1910. Museum of Ventura County.

to Quimichis. At Quimichis, however, residents and workers directed their unhappiness against the hacienda while also identifying American policies and investments as a widespread problem in Mexico.

Although Nayarit was insulated from prolonged revolutionary violence, it did experience some disruptions as a result of the armed struggle. Initially, the Porfirian forces retreated peacefully from Tepic and Nayarit in 1911 when revolutionary general Martín Espinosa arrived with troops from Sinaloa. He was able to secure the region without firing a single shot. Tepic celebrated Espinosa's arrival, and Madero, following his own election, appointed him territorial governor of Nayarit. Following Huerta's military coup against Madero and Madero's subsequent assassination in February 1913, General Álvaro Obregón led a group of constitutionalists into Nayarit in 1914. As the constitutionalists, led by Carranza and Obregón, fought Villa for control of the country, violence overtook Nayarit. Hundreds of Villista and Carrancista troops fought for control of Tepic, each side winning and losing the city and its surrounds several times.[21] Even if they were not directly involved with the conflict, the local population suffered as a result. The fighting destroyed crops and resulted in famine, illness, and death throughout 1915 and 1916. The fighting and chaos of war, however, opened opportunities to challenge American investment strategies and ideas about the organized development of Los Angeles–based capitalism in Mexico.

Mexican revolutionaries defied the agents of empire who implemented control of American-owned properties on the ground. In the case of the Quimichis Colony, Windham served as the foreman charged with implementing extractive policies for the benefit of Southern California–based investors. Windham also embodied the exportation of Southern California race and labor systems from Los Angeles to Mexico. The period of Windham's life before it intersected with the Quimichis Colony is difficult to piece together. Sources show that Windham arrived in Pasadena, the affluent suburb of Los Angeles, in the mid-1880s after a stint working as a shipping agent for the Southern Pacific in the Southwest.[22] Once in Pasadena, he worked as the cashier for the National Bank of Commerce, served as the city's fire and police commissioner, and, just prior to accepting a post as Quimichis manager, ran the Pasadena Hardware Store.[23] A thirty-year Pasadena resident, Windham witnessed the city's rapid growth and emerging exhibitions of ostentatious wealth and affluence. While he was always referred to as "well-respected" and an "upstanding citizen," Windham's financial situation appears to have been uneven; he was never able to advance from employee to employer, was chronically in debt, and had a difficult time supporting his wife and daughter.[24] Sinking all the spare cash he could gather into 720 shares of stock in the Quimichis Colony in 1910 may have been an investment he hoped would finally elevate him to the upper economic echelons of wealthy Pasadena.[25] Windham shared his economic and class aspirations with other American investors and empire builders who hoped to improve their own class position by exploiting Mexican resources and labor. Windham would discover, however, that Mexican workers did not acquiesce easily to investment strategies and imperial plots hatched in Los Angeles.

Revolution arrived at Quimichis in the form of the plundering of private property. Looting, certainly a common by-product of war, also constituted a direct challenge to American property owners in Mexico. Appealing for help to the American consul in Mazatlán, Sinaloa, in April 1912, Windham reported that between 200 and 300 men, "mounted and armed," arrived at the ranch: "They took by force some 35 or 40 horses and mules, all our saddles, all the money we had at the hacienda, our rifles . . . In fact, it was a general looting of what movable stuff was to be found on the outside."[26] Bandits and soldiers traveling through the states of Nayarit and Sinaloa over the next three years continued to help themselves to Quimichis tools, food, horses, and cattle. Dunn observed that they "took corn for their horses just as though it belonged to them." On another occasion he noted: "We are having a lot of trouble with Carranzistas. They are pure thieves. They respect nothing, take everything, just as though it belonged to them. During the last week they have taken 11 horses, 10 mules, 2 saddles, and a lot of smaller things, besides some money. They are the most thieving lot we have had for a long time and yet they keep saying they have orders to not molest Americans. If this is true, I wonder what they would do without such orders."[27] His observations are telling, especially in the context of the economic nationalism that was a part of revolutionary ideology. Opposed to American and European control of Mexico's resources, revolutionaries at Quimichis treated it as their own and took what they needed. Dunn also commented that "they are an independent insulting lot," inferring that any expression of autonomy and self-determination by a Mexican was an affront.

Some of the looters and bandits were former Quimichis employees, making their actions even more explicitly a repudiation of their Los Angeles–based employers. In the fall of 1912, for example, Guido Hidalgo, who had worked as the butcher at Quimichis, arrived with a band of men and demanded that Windham hand over all arms and horses on the ranch. Windham refused, and Quimichis staff exchanged a volley of shots with the group of Mexican men. During a respite, Windham decided to evacuate the ranch.[28] Reports written after he left said that the ranch was in the hands of Hidalgo, other bandits, and ranch employees. In fact, at various points between 1912 and 1916, Windham and Dunn reported to Bard that bandits, rebels, and local residents had taken control of the entire ranch. In 1912, for example, Bard reported to his stockholders that bandits and rebels were in possession of the entire ranch and using it as their own.[29] In 1916, Dunn wrote to Bard that residents at three Quimichis villages—Mariachi, Quelele, and Tacote—had openly declared themselves "out and out bandits, their excuse being that I am persecuting them."[30] Local residents clearly identified Quimichis policies as the source of their discontent and aligned themselves with bandits and revolutionary forces to challenge ranch management. Their occupation of the Quimichis property also offered a direct defiance of Los Angeles–based private property. Quimichis investors, determined to enrich themselves and their city, had purchased part of the city's "periphery" and attempted to run it as they would have an agricultural ranch in Southern California. By taking over the property, Quimichis residents and workers disrupted that scheme, claiming what had been private property as their own.

Windham intensified his restrictive policies, many of which mimicked labor practices in Southern California, in an effort to maintain control of the ranch. Although he periodically evacuated the ranch, staff would return as fighting eased. During one such episode, Windham seized the opportunity presented by the presence of federal troops to request that they "make a thorough clearing of Quimichis and all that section of the country."[31] He wanted federal troops to clear the local region of anyone who might have revolutionary sympathies. A few revolutionary skirmishes provided Windham with even more reason to use antirevolutionary forces to clear out unwanted villages and workers:

> We have asked them to completely destroy every village on the property—except the one at Q. proper. These outside villages are and have been for a long time dens of thieves and places of meanness. During this war and the last one corn that was stolen was hidden in these villages. Now if [we] can get them destroyed may be the people will many of them leave which is what we want. Any who do not leave, if they chance to be not too undesirable we can make them move to Q. if they wish to remain on the property. With them all living at Q. if we can have a guard of 20 to 25 good men we can protect our selves and property. I hope that not a house or a shack outside of Q. proper is left standing.[32]

Windham's letter shows a man struggling to maintain his control of the property and its residents as well as to uphold the geographic and financial structure instituted by his employers and Los Angeles–based investors. His job was to create an orderly and lucrative investment property, which included the mandate to control his laborers. He hoped he could rely on Mexican federal troops to help by completely destroying long-standing homes and communities and moving anyone who wished to stay under the direct supervision of ranch staff. Mimicking labor regimes in Southern California agriculture, he wanted direct control over all workers on the ranch and complete supervision of anyone who lived there. His deep desire to restore order hints that disorder reigned. Mexican soldiers and residents had crossed the boundaries of private property, and Windham desperately wanted to regain control. A few weeks later, he admitted that his employees and tenants considered him harsh: "Darn it, I guess they think me a hard boss."[33]

Angelenos charged with policing properties in the periphery soon conceded their impotence and recognized the strength of Mexican resistance to the economic system of the Los Angeles city-empire and the American empire. The realization dawned more slowly on company officers, comfortably quartered in the urban core. The realization arrived with some force when defending properties required capital. Thomas Bard complained to Philander Knox, secretary of state under President Taft, that revolutionary activity had cost the company over $100,000 due to robberies, threats of violence, destruction of crops and property, and general "acts of violence and disorder."[34] Notably, the tumult of the revolution forced Bard to appeal to his own government rather than the government that oversaw Quimichis because he could not expect support or sympathy from revolutionary leaders. In short, he needed his federal government to protect the city-empire, even outside of the national boundaries of the United States, a concept explored in more depth in chapter 4.

Quimichis investors and officers viewed this destruction of their property as blatantly anti-American, perhaps even anti-Angeleno, and most certainly anticapitalist. They proclaimed that they suspected a strong anti-American sentiment in their Mexican employees, renters, and neighbors. Writing to a fellow congressman to request federal protection for his ranch and ranch manager, Bard argued that the "general character of the people gives special ground for alarm as their antipathy against Americans is marked."[35] While it is difficult to determine the exact extent of anti-Americanism felt by Quimichis workers and renters, the historical record reveals that local people, revolutionary forces stationed in the region, and groups of bandits (these groups often overlapped) intentionally turned the chaos and confusion of the revolution to their advantage and to challenge the economic structure that Los Angeles–based investors hoped to impose on Mexico. As the tables turned and power relations shifted, Quimichis residents and revolutionaries found they could wield a significant amount of power against their former employers and landlords. Their affiliation with revolutionary forces and their targeting of Americans and American-owned properties demonstrated a specifically anti-American and anti-landowner agenda, and, implicitly, an anti–Los Angeles and anti-imperial sentiment. According to the experiences of Americans living in the Quimichis Colony, the efforts of rebels, revolutionaries, and workers also dynamically transferred power from landowners into the hands of ordinary people and actively deconstructed the relationship that Los Angeles investors and boosters had so carefully fostered with Mexico.

One anecdote from 1913 reveals this shift in power relations and this defiance of Americans, including Angelenos. Urged to evacuate the ranch by the American consul in Mazatlán, Windham and Dunn set off via boat for the nearest major seaport. Federal soldiers met them at Puerta del Rio, ostensibly to guard them as they evacuated.[36] According to Windham, the soldiers "cursed, abused and insulted" the Americans, "using all the vile names known to the Mexican language."[37] Windham and Dunn did not contest the name-calling, however, because they felt they were "entirely in their power."[38] Rather than the overseers of a powerful and successful Los Angeles–based company, Quimichis staff found themselves completely powerless—powerless to control their own lives, much less their property. Windham also reported that "it appeared to us they really wished to kill us, but wanted us to give them some kind of a pretext or excuse for the deed, for they had us surrounded within a circle of about 10 feet, they loaded and cocked and leveled their guns on us . . . After a few rounds of abusive language addressed to us and 'gringoes' in general, we were let go."[39] Once in Mazatlán, Windham and Dunn were even afraid to appear in public. They predicted "much drunkenness and rowdyism" as Mexicans commemorated their independence from Spain and reported that anti-American sentiments at these celebrations were strong, especially in response to a recent reiteration of the Monroe Doctrine.[40] In fact, Windham reported to Bard that anti-Americanism in Nayarit was "strong and increasing everyday, because of the actions at Washington . . . We who are down here think the U.S. should talk less and no[t] more, should do something worthwhile or drop the matter altogether, wash her hands of Mexican affairs, and never mention the 'Monroe Doctrine' again."[41] The story, as reported by Windham, is particularly fascinating because his observations reflect strong anti-American sentiments at the local as well as the international level. Ranch workers, revolutionaries, and neighboring communities opposed the Americans running Quimichis as well as American foreign policy and the American empire, which threatened to intervene in their revolution and nation.

The story of Windham's encounter with bandits that opens this chapter further illustrates the Mexican rejection of American imperialism and Los Angeles–based capitalism. This did not signify a break in the relationship between Los Angeles and Mexico but rather that the city's embrace of its hinterland had become a deadly one. The revolutionaries' disregard for private property even extended to the body and life itself. The dispute that ultimately led to Windham's death emerged from a conflict with Vicente Arías, an *arrendatario*, or tenant farmer, on Quimichis who had eventually become the ranch's butcher. Windham and Dunn accused Arías of stealing a company cow, an accusation that resulted in Arías's arrest but no conviction. Angry over accusations that he claimed were false, and affiliated with a local group of Villa sympathizers, Arías confronted Windham on several occasions. According to Dunn, he and Windham were "being threatened daily by bandits."⁴² Eventually, one of these confrontations led to violence, and one of the Villa sympathizers shot and killed Windham.

Issues of bodily harm and private property became further entwined as Dunn tried to avenge Windham's killing. Dunn turned immediately to the local military authorities, who also happened to be Villistas (followers of Pancho Villa), to apprehend the murderers. As retribution he also asked the local *jefe de armas* (military official) to raze three villages on Quimichis property, Quelelle, Mariachi, and Naranhal. In a report to the Quimichis board, Dunn asserted that "these ranch [villages] are nothing but bandit strongholds and the proper thing to do with them would be to burn them down, as you know I have made every possible effort to accomplish this."⁴³ For Dunn, the proper response to the loss of Windham's life, in many ways the most sacred form of private property, was through the destruction of another type of property—the ancestral village and home. When the jefe de armas refused to raze the villages, Dunn argued that the houses were actually private Quimichis property and that he suspected the families of harboring cattle thieves and Villistas. Dunn threatened to appeal to his superior, General Carrasco, to which the jefe responded, "Force me to destroy these homes and I will destroy the Quimichis hacienda."⁴⁴

Windham's murder and its aftermath embodied, in the most dramatic way, the violence that resulted when expansive capitalism and aggressive empire building encountered a forceful social revolution. Dunn, Windham, and the Quimichis investors all felt entitled to control a property they had purchased in fee simple. For them, the land and its buildings, crops, livestock, trees, and supplies belonged to them explicitly, and they expressed astonishment when local residents, employees, and revolutionary soldiers challenged them, simply took what they needed or wanted, or retaliated against them with violence. Protests lodged with the U.S. and Mexican governments following Windham's death demonstrated the anguish that Quimichis staff and owners felt at these confrontations to their "rights" as property owners. Their complaints also revealed their economic worldview: their company, they believed, had provided work, wages, food, and shelter to poor Mexicans, and the violent response they received seemed unfathomable. In a letter from Quimichis board member John Cave, for example, he appealed to Carranza and General Obregón to apprehend Windham's murderers because he had "benefitted the people of that section . . . He doctored and helped the people not only of the ranch but of that whole section."⁴⁵ For Quimichis investors, their commercial project was not simply supposed to benefit them but also improve the lives of their employees. This perspective permeated discussions of Windham's death and appeals for justice and protection for the ranch.

After Windham's death, the Quimichis Colony board turned to an experienced imperialist to administer their property. Moray Applegate, a veteran of the U.S. war in the Philippines, described himself explicitly as an empire builder and had lived in the Philippines and Mexico for two decades prior to taking on the Quimichis project. Notably, he suggested a conciliatory approach to dealing with Mexican revolutionaries, from local insurrectionists to the Carranza administration (1917–1920). While fortifying the Quimichis headquarters, transforming it into a private citadel, he simultaneously brokered a deal with the head of the local Villistas, known as El Molacho. El Molacho promised not to attack the ranch directly if Applegate would provide him and his men with some provisions. Villa had broken his alliance with Carranza in 1914 and engaged in a civil war against Carranza's leadership through 1920, supported by forces and communities in the northern part of the country (Zapata led a similar resistance to Carranza in southern Mexico). El Molacho, a supporter of Villa in Nayarit, stated that he had no direct issue with the ranch, as long as they supported his campaign against Carranza and the Constitutionalists: "He claimed he was fighting only for a political cause against the government and would not harm any private persons or interests."[46] Applegate also advocated a friendly relationship with the Carranza government and adopting some of the language of the revolution to promote the company's private interests: "Much can be done eventually I think in working in harmony with the new government and in adapting ourselves to the plan and ideals of the revolution, rather than opposing or resisting them and resorting to appeals to our own government for protection. Nearly anything in this country can be arranged if one is able and willing to pay the price, and the price is usually ridiculously low."[47]

Ultimately, the Los Angeles–based owners of the Quimichis Colony found themselves still in possession of most of their property but forced to negotiate with both the revolutionary Mexican state and its even more revolutionary dissenters. They had not had to relinquish their property to the revolutionary state, at least not yet, but they did concede that Applegate, the experienced empire builder, had a legitimate point: the investment and investors in the city-empire were better off if they negotiated with revolutionary leaders, both local and national, rather than resisting them. Forming a practical alliance with revolutionary forces allowed them to continue to operate the ranch and hope for future profits. An aggressive and violent retaliation against their forceful expansion of the Los Angeles hinterland and empire building efforts obliged them to reconsider their position as investors in Mexico. They no longer had a supportive state in the form of the Porfiriato and had to deliberate on unsavory alliances with their revolutionary adversaries.

Revolution and Corporate Empires of Scale

At the end of the nineteenth century and the dawn of the twentieth, large American corporations, with the backing of U.S. political and military strength, enjoyed remarkable success around the globe, particularly in Latin America. Indeed, adventures in the nation's commercial empire succeeded largely due to the size and power of American companies that could negotiate support for their foreign operations from their own government (and its military), leverage backing from local officials, and generally compel state cooperation for corporate interests. Even as the Mexican Revolution destabilized and overthrew the Porfiriato, several large Los Angeles–based enterprises survived, even thrived, due to their continuing ability to forge alliances with American and regional officials. Negotiating with Mexican leaders in the unstable political terrain of the Mexican Revolution proved much more advantageous for Quimichis's larger and more influential Los Angeles–based associates. Chandler and Otis's Colorado River Land Company and Doheny's Mexican Petroleum Company survived where Quimichis floundered. Perhaps because of their sheer size and the political influence of their owners, as well as their early recognition that revolutionary alliances might be more advantageous than resisting the revolution, the CRLC and the MPC fared far better than their smaller counterpart in Nayarit. Due to the extent and scope of their investments, Chandler, Otis, and Doheny had far more at stake in Mexico; this alone may have convinced them to establish alliances with Mexican leaders, revolutionaries or not, as soon as it became evident in 1911 that the days of the supportive Díaz were numbered. Their immense wealth (they were valued to be some of the richest men in Los Angeles) also awarded them a significant amount of power at the local, national, and international levels. Finally, the geographic location of their investments in Mexico helped them protect their properties and even make them prosperous during the first decade of the revolution. Ultimately, the alliances that the CRLC and MPC built with regional Mexican leaders allowed them to continue to operate and even thrive during the period between 1910 and the 1920s.

The Colorado River Land Company

Along the border between Baja California and California, the CRLC forged the strategy of alliance building with revolutionary leaders. Shrill and jingoistic in their response to the Magonista revolt in 1911, the CLRC ownership also tactically marshaled their considerable economic and political interests to build alliances and protect their property south of the border. Once the Madero regime and internal disputes put an end to the Magonista revolt, CRLC investors began to explore ways to either sell their property or ensure its protection despite its location in a nation undergoing massive social unrest. While angry about the ouster of their friend and political ally President Díaz, Otis and Chandler moved quickly to establish a productive relationship with Francisco Madero, who served as Mexico's moderate president from 1911 to 1913. Madero's administration even began talks with CRLC ownership to purchase the property and colonize it with Mexican farmers. Madero's presidency, however, was cut short by the violent coup initiated by Victoriano Huerta in early 1913, abruptly stopping this plan. Although Huerta eventually stepped down after military losses to the more reformist forces of Obregón and Carranza, continued fighting between moderates and the more radical Pancho Villa and Emiliano Zapata squelched the CRLC owners' hope that the Mexican government would take the ranch off their hands.[48]

Despite these challenges to maintaining a peaceful relationship between the Los Angeles core and its Mexican periphery, geography and alliances with local Mexican leaders contributed to the revolutionary-era success of the CRLC. Rather than relinquish their hold on Mexican properties, CRLC owners buckled down and implemented a new set of strategies to maintain links between core and hinterland. Located in the Mexican periphery and more closely knit, both economically and geographically, to the center of the city-empire in Southern California, the CRLC was able to forge productive relationships with Baja California officials, particularly Esteban Cantú Jiménez, who oversaw the region's territorial government from 1914 to 1920. Like the alliance Doheny would forge with territorial leaders in Veracruz, CRLC owners formed an alliance with a regional leader that protected their property, shielded them from the harshest impacts of revolutionary fighting, and allowed them to grow their commercial operations during the tumultuous decade of the Mexican Revolution.

Chandler's attempts to control Mexican political leadership in Baja California from his offices in Los Angeles, however, initially landed him in serious trouble with U.S. and Mexican authorities. He found himself, along with the manager of the CRLC, facing charges of violating neutrality laws and conspiring to interfere in a foreign government in 1914 and 1915 (ironically, these were the same charges brought against the Flores Magóns a few years earlier). Before building a mutually beneficial relationship with Cantú, who professed to support Carranza, Chandler backed his political opponent, Balthazar Avilés, who assumed the governorship of Baja California under the authority of Pancho Villa in the fall of 1914. In the context of the rapidly shifting political milieu of the Mexican Revolution, particularly the chaos engendered by the Magonista revolt, it was likely that Chandler and the CRLC were unsure which Mexican faction or political official would best protect the rights of foreign property owners. Taking a political gamble, the CRLC initially decided to support Avilés, and, although the historical record is murky, likely showed their support by sending him several thousand dollars through a third party. They earmarked the money to help Avilés recruit and arm Mexicans and Mexican Americans in San Diego in his struggle with Cantú over control of the territory south of the border. Despite the CRLC's support, Avilés found himself outwitted by Cantú and fled Baja for San Diego, but not before emptying the territory's treasury. In Los Angeles, the prosecution in the Chandler case found their witnesses unreliable and eventually dropped the charges against him and several CRLC employees. Even before the courts dismissed the case, Chandler and the CRLC had begun building a productive alliance with the man they were charged with undermining—Esteban Cantú. While difficult to untangle and subject to some debate among historians of Baja California, this episode in the history of the CRLC does clearly illustrate one key point—that Los Angeles–based investors were willing and actively sought to strategically ingratiate themselves with the various factions that held local or regional power during the decade of the Mexican Revolution. As explored in the next chapter, for example, Chandler also busily built an alliance and a personal friendship with revolutionary leader—and later, president—Álvaro Obregón.[49]

The tactical alliance between the CRLC and its former foe, Cantú, led to a period of relative prosperity for the company, despite the violent revolution that continued in the rest of Mexico. Cantú organized and maintained a small personal army with which he ensured his position as Baja California's executive chief as well as the region's relative wartime peace and prosperity. He levied territorial taxes, many on foreign-owned companies such as the CRLC, which he used to pay his troops (in U.S. currency, which retained its value throughout the revolution), develop infrastructure, and expand public services, including schools. Although reluctant to pay additional taxes on property they worried they might eventually lose to revolutionary land redistribution policies, the CRLC assessed that new taxes trumped a complete loss of their land or the instability that would inevitably come if the revolution encroached on Baja, and dutifully paid what Cantú charged them. Although they generally paid taxes rather than outright bribes, as Doheny would claim he paid in Veracruz, the CRLC investors did offer Cantú certain perks to grease administrative levers.[50] For example, they gave Cantú the use of CRLC land on very favorable terms, so favorable that he built one of his official offices and homes on CRLC property. In addition, Chandler and one of his business partners, Moses Sherman, arranged for Sherman's Los Angeles–based bank to lend money to Cantú and even personally guaranteed the large loans.[51] This was less coercive than the local leadership Doheny would encounter in Veracruz, and Cantú achieved similar results. He avoided having to align himself or the territory of Baja California with a revolutionary faction, kept revolutionary fighting at bay, and provided a stable environment in which foreign companies could conduct business.[52]

Cotton became the agricultural gold that made the CRLC a prosperous investment, despite the political and economic chaos that existed in the rest of Mexico. High prices for the commodity held firm during World War I, and the Colorado River delta proved an excellent environment for cultivating the crop. The CRLC also sought to minimize the amount of cash they had to invest in the property, fearful that they might lose control of the ranch in the context of the revolution. Instead, CRLC leadership established a profitable program of leasing large tracts of the property, mostly to American lessees who then assumed the costs of planting and harvesting the cotton fields. Some lessees, often farmers who also owned or leased land north of the border in the Imperial Valley, leased enormous tracts of up to 12,000 acres of CRLC land. Finding a shortage of labor in and around Mexicali as Mexican laborers sought better-paying jobs further north, American lessees also began employing Asian workers, particularly from China and Japan. Unable to enter the United States due to laws banning immigration from Asia, many migrants from China and Japan capitalized on the opportunity to work south of the border.[53] The combined efforts of American lessees on CRLC land and the Asian workers they employed yielded 123,000 acres of cotton under cultivation in 1923 and recorded a higher per acre production level than cotton farms in the American South. Ranch properties also produced crops on 70,000 acres planted with alfalfa and sugarcane.[54]

The economics of the CRLC ranch proved lucrative enough through the 1910s and into the 1920s to prompt CRLC ownership to leverage their financial affiliations in Los Angeles for the benefit of their property below the border. In 1922, for example, Chandler petitioned his business acquaintance Henry M. Robinson, president of the First National Bank, for an enormous loan of $3 million. Chandler reported that the company would use the funds to build a canal from Calexico (just north of the border) to the Gulf of Mexico, as well as a highway running from the company's property south of the border into Calexico. Used together, the highway and the canal would connect the CRLC property more directly to Southern California and the Pacific trade world and allow the CRLC and its lessees to transport their agricultural goods more easily by sea. According to Chandler, "The money we are asking for will make available many thousands of acres which it is not now possible to cultivate because of [the property's] isolated position and distance from transportation . . . Our stockholders now feel that they have such a large investment of their own cash in the enterprise that we are justified in making a large loan to enable us to develop the property on a larger scale than we have theretofore been able to do." More significantly, Chandler called attention to the fact that the CRLC property was still positioned in such a way as to be more closely tied with Los Angeles than with Mexico: "Our property is in the region which makes it just as much tributary to the commercial and business interest of Los Angeles as though it was located on the American side of the line, and anything you can do to assist us in a financial way will be contributing to the development of general business and industrial growth of Los Angeles . . . Los Angeles financiers as a matter of good morals and good business policy, can afford to show a broad-guaged [sic] and progressive spirit in their dealings with our close neighbors of the South."[55] Years after initially securing the property, and a decade after the start of the Mexican Revolution, Chandler still maintained that the Mexicali Valley and Baja California more generally were more closely tied to Los Angeles than they were to greater Mexico and that these geographic and commercial links would serve the best interests of the city-empire. In many ways, history proved him right. In 1926, Baja California officials reported that 95 percent of goods brought into the territory came from California and that 98 percent of Baja California's exports ended up directly north across the border.[56]

The mutually beneficial arrangement between Cantú and the CRLC continued into the 1920s, when a Sonoran elite challenged Carranza's administration. Their revolt shifted political alliances in Mexico City and across the country, forcing Carranza to flee the presidential palace (he died in subsequent fighting) and opening space for the appointment of Adolfo de la Huerta as president and then the election of Álvaro Obregón. Annoyed that Cantú did not contribute to their rise to power, the de la Huerta and Obregón administrations doubted Cantú's loyalty to the new regime and decided to replace him. Rather than resist the power of a rapidly solidifying national government, Cantú resigned his position and retired—to Los Angeles.[57]

The Mexican Petroleum Company

Doheny's sizable investments in the Huasteca region, explored in the previous chapter, also provide an excellent example of Los Angeles's commercial empires of scale during the Mexican Revolution. Doheny's significant investment in Mexico, coupled with the fortune he had already amassed through oil ventures in the American Southwest, intersected with the growing importance of petroleum in the global market and helped protect him through the tumultuous decade of the 1910s. By the time the Mexican Revolution erupted in the 1910s, Doheny and his Mexican companies were extracting $4 million a month in liquid profits on the eastern coast of Mexico, six hundred miles east of the Quimichis ranch and sixteen hundred miles southeast of the CRLC.[58] According to one historian, oil was the only industry in Mexico that boomed during the violent revolutionary period between 1910 and 1920.[59] This position attracted the attention of revolution-era politicians but also allowed the oil magnates a sizable profit margin from which to protect their even more sizable investments. The dependence of the United States on Mexican oil during this period also prevented Mexico's revolutionary leaders from intervening in the industry in significant ways. They worried that too much disruption in oil production might incite the Colossus of the North and threaten Mexican sovereignty with an American invasion or protectorate.

From the start of the armed period of the Mexican Revolution, Doheny and the MPC guarded their oil interests, cautiously leveraging support from the U.S. government as well as the support of local and national officials in Mexico. In 1913, for example, Doheny requested permission from the administration of Huerta, the conservative who ousted Madero, for the right to arm MPC employees to protect his interests from revolutionaries operating in the Huasteca. Given that the revolutionaries wanted to overthrow the Huerta regime, Doheny and the MPC assessed that Huerta would allow American and Mexican MPC employees to carry arms to quell revolutionary activity. Doheny also offered to pay the cost of arming pro-Huerta troops near MPC properties to protect his investments and suppress rebels.[60] Doheny and the MPC also enthusiastically supported the American occupation of the port of Veracruz, discussed in more detail in the next chapter, in the spring of 1914. Doheny even lent the U.S. military his personal yacht to use as a central command center during the operation. Doheny hoped that President Woodrow Wilson's intervention in Veracruz would lead to further intervention in Mexico and increased U.S. aid for the Huerta regime, which the president supported. Instead, Wilson's intervention hastened Huerta's fall and facilitated the consolidation of the Mexican federal government under Venustiano Carranza, a moderate and, at that point, an ally of Pancho Villa and Emiliano Zapata.[61]

In the Huasteca, the presence of a powerful hacendado class in the oil region of Huasteca allowed a symbiotic relationship to develop between oil producers, particularly Doheny, and a local oligarchy. The hacendados, led by Manuel Peláez Gorrochótegui, consistently shifted allegiances at the national level, pragmatically supporting whoever seemed most beneficial for their financial interests. They initially supported Díaz and opposed Madero; they then supported Huerta, but when he appeared to be losing, they abandoned him in favor of Villa; ultimately, Peláez and his cohorts declared themselves *pelaecistas*, a more honest name for their perennially self-interested movement. Although they had originally lacked the economic resources to exploit the Huasteca's extensive oil resources for themselves, the revolution opened a power vacuum in the region and allowed a local elite to force a bargain with the oil producers. In trade for protection of oil production sites from the ravages of the revolution, the pelaecistas demanded cash to hire mercenary soldiers, arm them, and pocket a bit for themselves.[62] According to the various oil companies, they paid Peláez "tax collectors" approximately 30,000 pesos every month in the early years of the revolution. In 1919, however, Doheny's Huasteca Petroleum Company reported paying the substantial sum of 380,000 pesos (roughly $190,000) to Peláez, often delivered to him in cash by William Greene, the company's vice president.[63]

Doheny labeled Peláez and his fellow hacendados "extortionists" but dutifully paid what they demanded to protect his land and oil investments in the Huasteca. The armed protection of the pelaecistas, however, allowed

Doheny to continue oil production as well as the repressive labor practices he had established before the revolution. For example, when the indigenous Teenek tribe tried to repel crews of Doheny's men who had arrived near one of their villages to drill in 1919, Doheny's crew overwhelmed them and removed the Teenek population from the property altogether. According to a Mexican engineer, the Teenek village was "transported in its entirety, with all its inhabitants, in one night, by force, to another place to be able to explore the terrain where it stood."⁶⁴ This alliance between the region's elite population, led by Peláez, and Doheny and his companies constituted a continuation of Porfiriato-era collusions between American investors and the Mexican government. Although the national state was disintegrating between tides of the revolution, the emergence of Peláez to fill a power vacuum, at least in the Huasteca, allowed Doheny to protect his investments and to continue to capture vast rivers of oil from those investments. According to historian Myrna Santiago, Peláez guaranteed that "the Golden Lane remained a Porfirian oasis amidst revolutionary chaos: a site of 'remarkably rapid progress,' according to the [oil] companies."⁶⁵

Doheny's relationship with Peláez, combined with his regulation of petroleum workers along racial and class lines, allowed him to continue high levels of oil production and enjoy record profits despite the revolutionary violence that wracked the rest of the country and the presence of a strong workers' movement in the oil regions of Veracruz. Within the context of the revolution, defiant oil workers organized into militant anarcho-syndicalist groups. Worker organizing sparked more than twenty walkouts and strikes in the oil industry between 1915 and 1920. Despite their militarism, oil workers gained only limited changes in an industry controlled by some of the most powerful corporations in the world. Their demands included eight-hour workdays, higher wages, equal pay for equal work, and the promotion of Mexican supervisors (a clear reaction to Doheny's labor color line). The administrations of Carranza and Obregón, concerned that militant unionism in Veracruz threatened their regimes, also worked to repress oil worker militancy. As a result, the number of union actions plunged in the late 1910s. This, coupled with the presence of Peláez and his troops, allowed Doheny and his Mexican Petroleum Company to continue bonanza levels of production through the early 1920s. According to reports created by the Mexican government in the early 1920s, oil production during the violent decade of the Mexican Revolution gushed from 3.6 million barrels in 1910 to an astounding 163 million barrels in 1920, making Mexico the producer of 25 percent of the world's oil.⁶⁶

Peláez's activities, however, aroused the suspicions of the Mexican federal government and placed him in the prickly position of taking money from Doheny while simultaneously trying to appease a new national government. In a telegram to the Obregón administration, one of Obregón's generals reported that he had investigated Peláez's activities and conducted an interview with Peláez. Obregón had suspected the pelaecistas of possibly planning an armed revolt against his brand-new government and dispatched this unnamed general to scrutinize activities in the Huasteca. The general reported back that Peláez, unsurprisingly, adamantly maintained that he had never intended to arm himself against Obregón. Instead, Peláez suggested that he had "various reasons" to act as he had relative to foreign oil interests—primarily to maintain regional stability and oil production.[67] Obregón's emissaries in the Huasteca also suggested partnering with Peláez to quell friction between foreign oil interests, workers, and the federal government as the 1920s opened. One of Obregón's representatives reported that oil workers had gone on strike for "no reason" and suggested that Obregón's troops needed to partner with Peláez to reestablish order.[68] Obregón's government also paid careful attention to Doheny and the MPC's activities. One internal memo reported that Doheny was working "constantly and without justification" against Mexico.[69] Other American oil producers, likely trying to garner support for their companies from the Obregón administration, reported that Peláez not only supported Obregón but was also the individual needed to curb the power of Doheny and the MPC.[70]

Doheny did not limit his activities to fostering alliances with regional leaders such as Peláez. His beneficial relationship with Peláez kept Doheny's extraordinarily profitable wells pumping a steady stream of *oro negro* out of the ground in the Huasteca and into tankers bound for the United States. Doheny also worried, however, that rumblings about land confiscation and redistribution—the "Mexico for Mexicans" platform of the revolution—threatened to bring those oil wells to a screeching halt and that gushing flow of oil to a sad trickle. While greasing the wheels of the pelaecista political machine in the Hausteca, Doheny had larger political ambitions that he hoped would push U.S. intervention in Mexico and shape Mexican policy in his favor, even at the cost of Mexico's autonomy and sovereignty. Doheny, part of the Los Angeles city-empire, did not hesitate to plan empire building on a much larger scale, a story explored in more depth in chapter 4.

The City of Los Angeles versus the Government of Mexico

While Windham wrestled with armed revolutionaries, Chandler negotiated with Esteban Cantú, and Doheny brokered alliances with pelaecistas in Mexico, Angelenos at home in the core of the city-empire felt similarly aggrieved and under attack. Mortal attacks on Angelenos such as Windham, the city's long history of investment south of the border, and Los Angeles's proximity to the borderlands resulted in shrill demands for more incisive protection from the revolution. Newspaper coverage from the period reveals that Angelenos felt uniquely and personally under attack during the war.

For example, Angelenos had no doubt that the Mexican Revolution lurked around street corners in Los Angeles. Sightings, real and imagined, of Mexican revolutionaries fed this paranoia. In early January 1916, for example, the *Los Angeles Times* reported that a Mexican secret service agent working on behalf of President Carranza spied a man resembling General Francisco Villa slip onto a westbound train in El Paso, Texas. Although the figure lacked Villa's trademark mustache, the secret service agent wired the presidential palace in Mexico City that he was certain the westbound man was Villa, who had gone undetected for several weeks. Two days later, another secret service agent, this one "disguised as a laborer," spotted the same figure leaving the railroad station in Colton, California. The agent observed the man climbing into a "large automobile, its top up and curtains down," idling at the back of the station. According to the agent, the car sped off in the direction of Los Angeles. Worried that Villa, who had broken from Carranza, might be organizing against him from the Mexican barrio in Los Angeles, Carranza dispatched additional secret service men to monitor activities in Los Angeles's "Sonoratown" and to keep a watchful eye on the purported residence of Villa's wife on South Grand View Avenue.[71]

In the end, it turned out that Villa was not clandestinely visiting his wife at a large Craftsman home in the MacArthur Park neighborhood of Los Angeles. He resurfaced in northern Mexico to orchestrate the attack on Columbus, New Mexico, a few days after the January reports of sightings in El Paso and Los Angeles. However, repeated dispatches on his uninhibited border crossings in papers such as the *Los Angeles Times*, coupled with consistent attacks on Americans in Mexico, particularly Angelenos, frightened the Los Angeles oligarchy. Just a month after Villa allegedly materialized in Los Angeles, the *Times* reported that his supporters were congregating in the city and joining forces with the Flores Magón brothers, who had recently returned from prison, taken up residence in the city's Edendale neighborhood, and resumed publication of their revolutionary newspaper, *Regeneración*. One *Times* article breathlessly proclaimed, "Advices received from all parts of the country that many former chieftains of various Mexican rebel factions are en route to Los Angeles to confer with the numerous Villa adherents known to be here caused Assistant Chief of Police Home to order an investigation yesterday afternoon into the report that a junta is being formed in Los Angeles as a base for a new revolutionary party."[72] In the minds of Los Angeles's elite, rebels, juntas, and reds prowled not only American-owned plantations in Mexico but also the street corners and alleyways of Los Angeles. They fretted over the possibility of reds and juntas crossing into the United States and congregating in the hidden corners of Los Angeles's Mexican barrio.

Los Angeles, the oligarchy felt, was the target of Mexican revolutionaries. Despite this self-important paranoia in Southern California, Villa would cross the border into New Mexico and attack the town of Columbus just two months after his supposed sighting in Los Angeles, retribution for the U.S. recognition of the Carranza government. While Mexican revolutionaries attacked a town in New Mexico rather than a city in Southern California, the Los Angeles oligarchy felt a clear sense of persecution as a result of the revolution. This sense of trepidation not only permeated life on investment properties in Mexico but also seeped into life in Los Angeles. Los Angeles, instead of being just the center of an urban empire, was also the hinterland of a Mexican Revolution. While Quimichis investors worried about the fate of their ranch manager in Nayarit, the Los Angeles investor class also waited apprehensively for an attack on the city itself.

In 1919 a *Los Angeles Times* headline announced that the city was virtually at war with Mexico: "The Case of the City of Los Angeles vs. the Government of Mexico." The piece demanded government fortification to protect Los Angeles lives and property south of the border.[73] The Anglo-American Los Angeles investor class clearly felt under attack south of the border and called for a swift and decisive intervention in Mexico. Subtitles tantalized readers with stories of violence: "Citizens of Los Angeles Tortured and Murdered! True Stories of Revolting Crimes of Mexicans against Angelenos Here Told for the First Time." The lengthy piece, complete with photographs of Americans who had lost their lives during revolutionary violence in Mexico, including Windham, indicted President Venustiano Carranza and his government for the "wandering hordes of bandits" responsible for the torture and murder of "inoffensive" Angelenos. The *Times* also maintained that Los Angeles bore a "big and bitter share" of Mexican violence against

Americans under Carranza's administration. While noting the deep concern of the entire country over the plight of Americans in Mexico, the *Times* argued that "Los Angeles is directly interested in the American case against Mexico" because of hefty Angeleno investments in Mexican industries and because of the physical violence inflicted on citizens of the city by Mexican revolutionaries. To combat this infringement on Angeleno rights, the *Times* advocated collecting evidence of Mexican atrocities and lobbying Congress and the president to intervene on behalf of suffering Angelenos. The author of the piece noted with approval that Congressman Henry Z. Osborne was spearheading the Southern California campaign and assembling a dossier of evidence to submit to the State Department. For gruesome impact, the *Times* reported that Osborne's docket of evidence included the cut-off fingers of two Angelenos held hostage by Mexican bandits. The National Archives and Records Administration still has Osborne's dossier of proof, including a Libby's pickle jar with the disembodied fingers.[74]

Despite the generative alliances between companies such as Doheny's MPC and Otis and Chandler's CRLC during the most violent decade of the Mexican Revolution, Angelenos felt under attack between 1910 and 1920. Precisely because they envisioned Los Angeles as a city with an empire—or at least an important periphery—in Mexico, the city's investor class felt particularly targeted by the demands and violence of the Mexican Revolution. Proximity to the border and the deaths of Angelenos at the hands of Mexican revolutionaries only heightened this paranoia. The threat posed by the revolution to private and personal property, including the lives and bodies of the city-empire's imperialist vanguard, such as Windham, left wealthy Angelenos with the sense that their city, their empire, and their lives were in danger. The aggressive and expansionist capitalism of boom Los Angeles had met the aggressive and violent revolution of an angry proletariat that had the power to overthrow the investment-friendly Porfiriato. As suggested by the evidence in this chapter, however, revolution in Mexico did not eject Angeleno investors from the country. Instead, investors continued to post emissaries like Windham at the outpost of empire, requiring them to put their lives on the line to maintain the relationship between urban core and revolutionary periphery.

For example, "outrages" committed against Americans, particularly the death of Windham, revealed the deadly embrace between Los Angeles and Mexico. Enraged Southern Californians began to fixate on the vulnerabilities of their city-empire rather than abandoning investments in or connections with Mexico. Southland newspapers carried detailed descriptions of

Windham's death, and editorials called for federal intervention in Mexico to protect American lives and property. Jingoistic Southern California newspapers and the company's officers concurred that Windham's death and Dunn's capture were clearly the result of inaction on the part of the American government. Speaking to a reporter, Dr. Livingston, a Quimichis investor, declared, "No other nation would permit its citizens to be treated so. No other nation would permit 100,000 of its citizens to be driven away from their property in one country . . . No other nation would permit its citizens to be held for ransom and to be killed."[75] Critical of the Taft administration's and later the Wilson administration's anemic response to the Mexican Revolution—particularly because American private property was at stake—Quimichis officers flatly declared the United States negligent in fulfilling its duties to its citizens and its responsibilities to the world as a "strong nation." Force, Livingston maintained, was the only way to deal with Mexico and Mexicans: "Demands are all right with a civilized nation, but when you are dealing with half-civilized people like the Mexicans they must know that the force is behind the demand. That is the only way to handle the Mexicans . . . When they know the force is back of the demand they are docile."[76] The quote reflects Livingston's personal philosophy in dealing with workers and renters at Quimichis as well as his expectations of his nation in dealing with its southern neighbor. When an aggressive and "half-civilized" revolution threatened an aggressive city-empire, the appropriate response seemed clear to Livingston—an aggressive response from the U.S. government. In the context of American global interventions on behalf of capital and corporate interests, this expectation was not outlandish. Rather than giving up and walking away, Los Angeles investors insisted on bigger and more forceful intervention on their behalf.

Conclusion

The first decade of the Mexican Revolution had a dramatic impact on Los Angeles investors and the city-empire they envisioned developing south of the border. Immediately up to the outbreak of the revolution in the final months of 1910, Los Angeles investors and capitalists touted Mexico as the safest place in the world to send investment funds—a protected periphery to their rapidly growing city. Díaz, they maintained, had created a well-ordered and briskly developing nation that happily worked with American investors. American investments, they eagerly believed, would benefit capitalists in Los Angeles as well as the Mexican people and the Mexican nation. Such investment had the potential, they maintained, to develop Mexico along the lines of the United States. As a result, companies such as the Quimichis Colony, the CRLC, and the MPC continued or developed new productive relationships with wealthy Mexicans and Mexican officials.

With the arrival of the revolution, however, American investors found their economic agency severely limited by revolt. The economic system they sought to build triggered the revolution that would often prove the undoing of American investments south of the border. This phenomenon was not limited to the revolution in Mexico. As historian Walter LaFeber argues, American investments and foreign policy helped trigger revolutions around the globe, from Mexico to China to Russia.[77] On the ground in Los Angeles and Mexico, the companies discussed in this chapter struggled, albeit to varying degrees, to institute the economic system they had envisioned unfurling out of Los Angeles. Instead of a cooperative government, they found warring factions, emerging anti-Americanism, covert and explicit challenges to their status as landowners and to the web of investment they were trying to construct between Los Angeles and Mexico, and outright violence. As a result, Quimichis was never able to create a profit for its investors, and the ranch witnessed the death of its manager, who was also a stockholder and one of its most ardent promoters. Enraged at challenges to their presence in Mexico, the investors turned to the U.S. government to protect the lives and property of American citizens in Mexico. Due to their size, location, and ability to forge productive alliances with regional leaders during the revolution, the CRLC and the MPC fared better. They found a niche for wartime prosperity despite the violent and disruptive revolution unfolding around them. Despite the profits extracted from Baja cotton fields or Huasteca oil fields, however, executives like Chandler and Doheny worried incessantly that the coalitions they had formed with local leaders such as Peláez or Cantú might disintegrate and put their investments in danger. They worried particularly about the rhetoric of the Mexican Revolution, which demanded "land and freedom" and "Mexico for Mexicans." These demands, paired with the rewriting of the Mexican Constitution in 1917 along revolutionary lines, placed Angelenos at the forefront of challenging the Mexican revolutionary state. Instead of heeding the calls of revolutionaries for foreign investors to abandon their Mexican properties, Angelenos clung to their investments and their belief that Los Angeles was inseparable from Mexico.

Like many other American foreign investors and participants in the nation's commercial empire who faced challenges to the economic hegemony they were trying to establish in other countries, Los Angeles investors began to rely increasingly on their own national government to protect financial interests outside the country. Like many American corporations, they launched bellicose demands that their federal government intervene to protect private property. Unique to Los Angeles and the city-empire were understandings that a Southern California core and its Mexico periphery were inimitably bound by ties of investment, region, and history. As a result and as explored in the next chapter, Angelenos led the national call for American intervention in the Mexican Revolution.

4   Like Cuba and the Philippines

Los Angeles–based lawyer Thomas Gibbon liked wealth and proximity to the levers of political power. Perhaps that is why he cherished his friendship with Woodrow Wilson's secretary of the interior, Franklin K. Lane, a relationship forged through Gibbon's deep ties with the Progressive-Era Democratic Party. For reasons that likely bordered on self-promotion, Gibbon counted Lane a close personal friend, even keeping a framed photo of Lane in a place of honor in his office. With a not-so-subtle subtext of flattery, the regional lawyer declared to the cabinet member that Lane's photo was one of a "very few people whose pictures I care to have near me."[1] In addition to wealth and power, Gibbon also valued investments in Mexico and often worked as the "errand boy" for Los Angeles elites, particularly his partners in Mexican investment schemes, Harry Chandler and Harrison Gray Otis.[2] As policy changes resulting from the Mexican Revolution threatened Los Angeles–based investments, Gibbon served as Los Angeles's unabashed spokesman for extending formal American imperial control over Mexico. Representing the interests of the city's investor class, Gibbon arrived in Washington, D.C., to convince Lane and anyone else who would listen that the United States had to intervene, definitively and militarily, in Mexico to protect American investors. And Gibbon had the perfect blueprint for this intervention: follow the configurations of American control of Cuba, Puerto Rico, and the Philippines. Gibbon said this explicitly and repeatedly to Lane: "There is a feeling among the majority of our people [in Los Angeles] that something should be done . . . being Mexico's nearest neighbor, and in view of the experiences which we have had in giving to Cuba, Porte Rica [sic], and the Philippines the sort of government which such populations require."[3] Gibbon described American control as a "gift," albeit one that involved armed intervention, political control, racial hierarchies, and protection of property, particularly the property of foreign investors. American empire redux.

Drawing from the activities of investors and propagandists such as Gibbon, this chapter explores how Angeleno investors expected the U.S.

government to intervene on their behalf to protect both personal and urban interests. Historically and at the regional level, the state, from local police officers to the National Guard, helped dispel acts of labor organizing and racial resistance and enforce the interests of Angeleno capitalists north of the border. Generally speaking, a white Los Angeles elite maintained both its racial and its class positions with assistance from state agencies. When Angelenos first began investing in Mexico, they enjoyed similar support from the Mexican government, and ideas and practices they perpetuated regarding race, capitalism, and empire found an easy home south of the border. As the revolution remade relationships between foreign investors and Mexico, however, the system of capitalism that functioned so well for the benefit of the investor class in Los Angeles failed in Mexico. As a result, Los Angeles investors such as Gibbon argued vociferously for American constitutional protection of private property, backed by U.S. troops. He insisted that both should cross the border to guard investment dollars and ensure the orderly functioning of white landownership and nonwhite labor.[4]

Like much of what Los Angeles investors did during this period, and as reflected in Gibbon's global imperial blueprint for intervention in Mexico, their investment and lobbying activities were embedded not just in city building but also in a larger system of American empire and the complex relationship between the United States and Mexico. As historians such as Walter LaFeber and Noel Maurer argue about American policy following the close of the Spanish-American War, Americans with international investments made good use of their political and economic power to shape U.S. foreign policy in ways that benefited them. Rather than uniformly pursuing annexation or formal rule, as in the Philippines, investors pushed presidents for a creative variety of imperial protections, from creating spheres of influence to engaging in strategic interventions to protect American property, to formal imperial control. Theodore Roosevelt, for example, intervened in the Dominican Republic in 1904 on behalf of the powerful San Domingo Improvement Company, headquartered in New York. His involvement in the Dominican Republic at the behest of New York investors led to his proclamation of the Roosevelt Corollary to the Monroe Doctrine, which declared that the United States would intervene in Latin America to maintain order and "behave with a just regard for their obligations to outsiders."[5] Los Angeles investors were well aware of the precedent being set by investors and policy in locations such as the Dominican Republic and were part of a world of international corporate capitalism that had begun to not just demand but expect intervention on their behalf when political instability threatened American investments overseas.

White investors in Los Angeles also eagerly participated in a larger system that linked race, labor, and property ownership to American imperial exploits—the "gift" that Gibbon hoped to give Mexico. Those white Americans, often wealthy, who favored imperial expansion animated racial hierarchies to justify and organize domination, from labor regimes on investment properties to American foreign policy. In other words, turn-of-the-century empire building emerged hand in hand with paternalistic notions of "the white man's burden"—buttressing the right of American investors and policymakers to intervene in nonwhite nations for the benefit of investors as well as the "uplift" of nonwhite peoples.[6] As discussed later in this chapter, pro-intervention Angelenos deployed the language of "civilization" and the "uncivilized" to gain traction in their campaign to push the Taft and Wilson administrations to intervene definitively in Mexico on their behalf.

Los Angeles investors operated in this broader world of race and imperial intervention. However, what makes the case of the Los Angeles oligarchy unique is their use of the racialized rhetoric of both empire and civilization for an urban region in Southern California as well as their promotion of that idea in what they considered their financial backyard. They believed they had created a "white spot" in Los Angeles, where nonwhite workers labored quietly (and without unions) for white gentleman farmers and investors.[7] In their visualization of core and periphery, a workable racial and labor regime existed in the core and should function properly in the periphery, even one that extended across an international border. Attempts to realign labor and property regimes in Mexico during the revolution came in the form of a carefully organized public relations and lobbying campaign spearheaded by Gibbon (also an investor in the Colorado River Land Company [CRLC]) and the city's oil titan, Edward Doheny, whose activities provide the narrative for this chapter. And, as explored in the previous chapter, Angeleno investors responded to a revolution demanding their exit from Mexico with a fortified commitment to maintain ties between core and periphery.

The lobbying campaign directed by Gibbon and Doheny came in part from the fact that the revolution challenged the power of the city-empire beyond its capacity to control the hinterland. While there had been a cooperative executive in the presidency in Mexico, the Los Angeles oligarchy could bend policy in the United States and Mexico in its favor. With the onset of the revolution, however, Angeleno investors found their power and the diplomatic power of their city and its civic and private institutions severely curtailed. As explored in the previous chapter, Mexican revolutionaries had no interest in cooperating with an investor class in a city, no matter how self-important, across the border. Instead, revolutionaries specifically attacked Angelenos and Americans precisely because they represented the omnipresence of American dollars and power in Mexico.

Mexico was in the throes of a social revolution that was making radically different claims on the state. Mexican revolutionaries demanded state action on the part of ordinary Mexicans to meet their basic needs for land and freedom. They insisted that a thoroughly revised Mexican government protect the survival of the *peon*, or the ordinary Mexican, rather than the private property of the *patron* or the property rights of the Yankee. In Los Angeles, the oligarchy could push the chief of police to "strictly observe" the movements of suspicious characters in a city known for its brutal repression of the political left and harsh racial and geographic divides between white and nonwhite. Additionally, they could rely on the U.S. federal government and policies such as the Espionage Act to add extra muscle to the repressive arm of the Los Angeles police state. After all, it was the federal government that arrested the Mexican anarchists Ricardo and Enrique Flores Magón in Los Angeles and imprisoned them several times under antisyndicalism and neutrality laws.

South of the border, jittery Angelenos devoted themselves to managing tattered properties and fortifying battered egos. They watched anxiously as the revolution unfolded, and while still in the tumults of competing factions and leadership, the nation moved toward rewriting the Mexican Constitution. By 1916 it was becoming clear that whatever state emerged from the revolution, it would not protect the system of foreign investment and capitalism that had flourished under the Díaz regime. Embedded in the city-hinterland economic and racial structure, elite Angelenos struggled to come to terms with a government system that might not prioritize the protection of private property, particularly the private property of wealthy whites, against the demands of nonwhite laborers. In the Los Angeles core, landowners and investors successfully repressed strikes and imprisoned labor leaders and political dissidents. The Mexican periphery, however, was in revolt, and an international border bisected core and periphery. The Los Angeles investor class suddenly faced the challenge of trying to use the arm of their state, the United States, to control labor and property in a new Mexican state. And this new Mexican state radically questioned the function of government—to protect the private property of a few or to ensure the economic well-being of the majority?

This chapter focuses on how the Los Angeles oligarchy coupled the racialized regime of capitalism they had created in Southern California with their expectations of their rights and power in Mexico. As explored in chapter 2, the Los Angeles oligarchy fully expected to replicate the racial system of labor, investment, and state support they had carefully created in Southern California on their plantations and haciendas and oil fields south of the border. Nonwhite labor fueled the machine of Southern California agriculture, where white investors could harvest the power of the state to suppress resistance, strikes, and revolt. Before 1910, this system intersected with Mexican racial hierarchies and a sympathetic Díaz regime. During the Mexican Revolution, however, this system unraveled. Despite this unraveling of the fluid expansion of Los Angeles–based systems of race and capitalism, revolution in Mexico did not sever ties between core and periphery. Instead, Los Angeles investors reached further up the hierarchy of power in the United States to demand protection for their hinterland properties.

Article 27 and the Los Angeles Oligarchy

More grim than the possibility that Villa might invade the United States and more terrifying than that the Flores Magón brothers might partner with the IWW to overthrow Los Angeles capitalists was Article 27 of the rewritten Mexican Constitution. The article defined the right of private property as subsumed by the "national interest" and gave the state the power to expropriate private property when deemed necessary for the public good. The policy made the Mexican Constitution the first in the world to delineate social rights instead of individual or property rights. Pastor Rouaix, one of the delegates and framers of the new Constitution, argued, "The financial prosperity the country acquired with the dictatorial regime of General Díaz only served to deepen even more that abyss that separated the plutocracy from the proletariat and to augment the animosities that were impregnating the popular soul with the constant abuses suffered by the disinherited classes, which formed 90 percent of the Mexican population."[8] In an effort to address this problem, the reformist faction at the constitutional convention successfully persuaded the majority to accept a constitution that, according to historian Friedrich Katz, was considered "one of the most radical adopted anywhere."[9]

A far-reaching reformist constitution south of the border thrust Angeleno investors into the arena of international diplomacy, where they made a case for protecting the investments of the core in the periphery. Radicalism in their own city and revolutionary skirmishes along the border proved less terrifying for Doheny and Gibbon than the confiscatory and antiforeign tenets of the 1917 Constitution. The new Constitution promoted land reform; granted rights to labor, including an eight-hour day and the right to strike; drastically curtailed the rights of foreign landowners and investors; and defined all subsoil resources as the property of the nation. The Constitution also gave the Mexican government the right to expropriate foreign-owned properties for the common good and limited the rights of foreigners to own land along the country's coasts and international borders.[10] Article 27 outlined many of these new policies, and it became notorious among American investors. Article 27 demonstrated the resentment against foreign investors the Mexican middle class had fostered throughout the Porfiriato, along with its desire to bring Mexico's natural resources under national control.[11] The article also reflected the needs of the Mexican federal government to institute some reforms to mollify followers of both Emiliano Zapata and Pancho Villa. The article promised to break up large estates, return lands taken from villages, and create new communally held landholdings.

Venustiano Carranza, the first Mexican executive to lead the country following the ratification of the new Constitution, applied the new Constitution in an extremely limited and selective way. Despite his limited interpretation of the new laws, these policy shifts ignited a panic among American investors in Mexico. Doheny and Gibbon placed themselves at the forefront of efforts to challenge the new Constitution and its antiforeign policies. The two men believed they needed a robust lobbying organization to protect their interests; American policymakers, they maintained, simply did not understand the monumental changes taking place in Mexico. In the fall of 1917, a few months after the ratification of the new Mexican Constitution, Gibbon told Harry Chandler: "You would be astonished to learn how little of the truth is known in Washington about Mexico. For instance, last Saturday, while talking with Secretary Lane, I mentioned the fact that two weeks before the Mexican Congress had passed a law suspending constitutional guarantees in that country . . . He was astonished to know this which shows the extent of the ignorance of our public men about Mexico."[12] Doheny and Gibbon agreed that if they could improve Washington's understanding of the situation of American investors in Mexico, they could influence the Wilson administration to intervene more decisively on their behalf. They predicated this belief on a convincing history of American interventions on behalf of investors: if the United States willingly occupied, administrated, and annexed locations such as Hawaii, Cuba, Puerto Rico, the Philippines, and Haiti, Los Angeles investors had reason to believe that their federal government would extend this imperial protection to their properties in Mexico.

From the heart of Los Angeles, Gibbon and Doheny hatched a plan for Angeleno support of American empire in Mexico along the lines of American control of Cuba, Puerto Rico, or the Philippines. In the fall of 1917, Gibbon and Doheny, along with Harry Chandler and a handful of other wealthy Angelenos with interests in Mexico, met to form an organization specifically to counter Article 27 and protect Angeleno and American interests in Mexico. They signed a secret document pledging financial support for the effort and designated Doheny, then the world's largest independent petroleum producer, as custodian of the confidential document. Doheny signed the agreement as the president of the Mexican Petroleum Company (MPC), and Gibbon and Chandler signed as major investors in the Colorado River Land Company. The agreement stated: "We, the undersigned, hereby agree to become members of an Association organized for the purpose of endeavoring to protect the rights of foreign investors in Mexico by taking steps to secure appropriate action on the part of the governments whose nationals are interested in Mexico and by pursuing proper efforts to inform the world as to the conditions existing in that country."[13]

In short, they argued that their government had not upheld their rights as property owners in Mexico. To remedy the problem and secure support from the U.S. government, they proposed forming an organization to oversee an extensive media and lobbying campaign to "inform the world" about the problems property owners faced in Mexico. They were also willing to contribute heavily, albeit discreetly, to push American foreign policy in their favor. They hoped to create a propaganda machine to produce and disseminate information on what they considered an alarming political situation in Mexico without the appearance of bias or special interests. If it was properly managed, they believed their new organization, the National Association for the Protection of American Rights in Mexico (NAPARM), could generate "a lot of publicity which will, before very long, force the hand of the Government for the protection of our interests in Mexico."[14] Although they couched their campaign as one for the "protection of our interests," NAPARM members wanted imperial intervention and control of Mexico, pure and simple. From their city-empire, they advocated the expansion of formal American empire south of the border.

In the context of American foreign policy, empire, and U.S.-Mexico relations, American investors fully expected a well-coordinated set of demands to yield desired outcomes. NAPARM members, in Los Angeles and across the country, certainly watched closely when the United States intervened in other Latin American countries in the first decades of the twentieth century. As noted earlier, Theodore Roosevelt acted at the behest of a group of private investors when he intervened in the Dominican Republic, which in turn led to the declaration of the Roosevelt Corollary of the Monroe Doctrine. The corollary not only protected the interests of a private American firm but also reassured American investors in the Caribbean and across Latin America that the U.S. government would defend the private property rights of its citizens. The U.S. market bore the evidence of investor approval: after American intervention, bonds in many Latin American countries rose precipitously. This happened again after Roosevelt dispatched marines and nine warships to Cuba in 1906 in response to political unrest. Investors were often the driving force behind these types of interventions precisely because they created or ensured favorable circumstances for investments. Following this pattern, in 1907 the United States also sent marines and the navy to protect American banana investors during a dispute between Nicaragua and Honduras. The same held true in Mexico, even under the welcoming administration of Porfirio Díaz. During Taft's first year in office, Díaz proposed to reform property rights in Mexican mines to benefit political allies and at the expense of foreign investors. Under pressure from American mining investors, Taft met personally with Díaz and persuaded him to drop the stipulations against foreign investors. In the end, Díaz acquiesced. Even Woodrow Wilson, who espoused democratic ideals more vocally than his presidential predecessors, continued Latin American interventions, including in the Dominican Republic, Haiti, Nicaragua, and Mexico. As discussed in this chapter, however, Los Angeles investors did not always get what they demanded, despite Wilson becoming "the most interventionist American president of his era."[15]

Ambassadors for the Los Angeles Empire

When the Mexican Revolution began at the end of 1910 and Díaz fled to France in May 1911, Doheny hoped to be able to work with Francisco Madero and subsequent Mexican executives.[16] His Mexican wells were producing rich rivers of oil, he had growing financial support in Los Angeles and New York, and he believed that political unrest in Mexico would be short-lived. New taxes levied by the Madero and Huerta governments in 1912 and 1913 were also small and, according to oil producers, easily absorbed by their companies. As the conflict and political instability in Mexico continued, however, Doheny decided that he needed a political plan to ensure that Washington, D.C., recognized the strategic value of his oil holdings in Mexico and would provide protection from a nationalist attack on the oil industry.[17] New policies that challenged foreigners' rights to own property alarmed him, and he felt the structure of empire shifting rapidly under his feet. A nation composed predominantly of indigenous or mestizo people had revolted against a racial and economic system controlled by a handful of wealthy Mexicans and Anglo-American investors. The racial and economic system, bolstered by a supportive state, that functioned in Los Angeles and had expanded as an imperial regime into Mexico now faced fierce opposition.

An intensely secretive and guarded man, Doheny instructed his wife to burn all of his personal and business correspondence and papers upon his death. As a result, the historical record demonstrating Doheny's worldview in his own words is thin. However, a book about Mexico that he commissioned and financed reveals much about how Doheny understood the relationship between himself, the United States, Mexico, and the rapidly shifting political relationship between property owners and the state south of the border. In 1916, Doheny had asked his friend Clarence Barron to visit his holdings in Mexico and publish a book on the significance of the Mexican oil industry for the security of the United States. Significantly, Barron was also the owner of Dow Jones & Company and the publisher of the *Wall Street Journal*. Barron's book, *The Mexican Problem*, outlined a perspective that matched Doheny's while simultaneously promoting Doheny's more prosaic economic and political interests in Mexico. Based on his observations traveling through Mexico in 1916, Barron argued that "national disorder must not be allowed anywhere in the world, for it leads to international disorder."[18] Throughout his well-publicized and widely read book, Barron maintained that American capitalism and empire provided the best solution to economic and political chaos in Mexico. As many scholars have demonstrated, issues of race defined the rhetoric of imperial order in early twentieth-century America. While Barron couched his argument in a discussion of order versus disorder, his book essentially spoke to the assumption that nonwhite revolutionaries lacked the racial capacities necessary to create an orderly (and Anglo-run) capitalist system: "That is the need of Mexico today—opportunity to labor, opportunity for the family, opportunity for food, clothing, better shelter, and better social conditions." And, according to Barron's estimation of prerevolutionary Mexico, "this is exactly what American and European capital and organization have brought . . . This is what will ultimately redeem Mexico and forward her people."[19] Demands for the redistribution of communal and indigenous lands ran against the grain of one of the main tenets of American capitalism—white ownership of property and control of labor and capital. Barron put it bluntly: "Mexico will never be for the Mexicans or for humanity until American and European enterprise has had fair play in that country."[20]

At the point Doheny dispatched Barron to Mexico, the Mexican Constitution had not yet been rewritten, but the position of American investors was precarious, and American foreign policy was in flux. Mexican revolutionaries opposed the violent ascendancy of President Victoriano Huerta in a 1913 coup, and their antiforeign rhetoric, particularly that regarding foreign investment, was still viscerally apparent to American investors. By 1914, violence and political instability had also forced many investors to abandon mines, ranches, and even oil fields. When Woodrow Wilson took office, he opposed Huerta, who had come to power in part with the backing of Taft's ambassador to Mexico, Henry Lane Wilson. At the same time, President Wilson found himself under immense pressure from American oil interests, whose fields were threatened by revolutionary fighting, and began preparing for an armed invasion of Mexico to protect strategically important materials such as oil, rubber, copper, and zinc. The administration used a minor skirmish between American sailors and Mexicans in Tampico as an excuse to occupy Veracruz in April 1914. Doheny offered the use of his private yacht as part of the operation. Huerta resigned, not because of the American occupation but because his opponents, Venustiano Carranza and Pancho Villa, had combined forces and defeated his military forces. Wilson withdrew from Veracruz in November 1914. Events in Europe and the invasion of Haiti and the Dominican Republic occupied much of the administration's foreign policy agenda through the end of 1914 and into 1915. In March 1916, however, Pancho Villa crossed the border in a raid on the New Mexican town of Columbus, likely in retribution for Wilson's tacit recognition of the Carranza government (which Villa now opposed). Wilson's cabinet worried that rebels in Latin American countries occupied by U.S. forces, including the Dominican Republic, Haiti, Cuba, Panama, and Nicaragua, might follow Villa's example and decided that they had to capture and punish Villa. Wilson dispatched General John J. Pershing and

6,000 U.S. troops across the border into Mexico in the spectacularly unsuccessful Punitive Expedition to find Villa. The expedition pursued Villa without any luck across Mexico from March 1916 through February 1917.[21]

It was in this context that Barron's book, published in 1917, disavowed American exploitation in Mexico but maintained that economic and commercial development would provide Mexico with the political, social, and racial stability that he believed it desperately needed. Oil, he contended, provided the ideal solution to the "Mexican Problem." Oil was a valuable commodity, Mexico possessed rivers of it, and the Americans involved in its extraction could provide high wages and stable employment for Mexicans. The solution, he unequivocally argued, was "Business with a big B . . . Business is expanding wages all around, wages to labor, wages to capital; incentive to labor to accumulation, to luxury—luxury of freedom in body and mind."[22] The United States, according to Barron, had the economic and political experience that could help Mexico achieve stability. The solution could look like Cuba under the Platt Amendment, which gave the United States de facto control over the island and which Barron argued had made the island more productive and stable than at any other time in its history. In essence, the amendment was an instrument created by the U.S. government to "formally" grant Cuban independence while preserving control over people "unfit" for self-governance. Of course, the Platt Amendment also rested on the same racial assumptions about economics and property that Barron believed would be so beneficial to Mexico.[23] Allow a white capitalist class to create the conditions of prosperity, and Mexican workers could fill the demand for wage laborers.

Barron saw the intervention of the United States in Mexico not as an unwelcome imperialistic project but as a strategy for creating international and racial peace and order. Racial uplift, so common in imperialistic rhetoric about Cuba or the Philippines, permeated all of Barron's observations. The United States could help Mexico establish "protection for order, courts, contracts, industries for a brief space,—one, two, or three decades . . . keep order, create courts, educate a generation . . . [and the] Mexican can be trusted to maintain what it secures under tutelage, and to add to it."[24] Good jobs, provided by American businesses, would create "technical training, higher wages, bank accounts, financial independence, and the rights of citizenship and accumulation."[25] According to Barron, Mexicans would not mind an "invasion" of businesses able to create political and social tranquility through the establishment of an American-style economic system. As argued by American interventionists around the globe, white racial and economic tutelage would help Mexico while simultaneously protecting the rights of white property owners.

To lobby the Wilson administration to win American imperial intervention in Mexico on behalf of Angeleno investors, Doheny partnered with a fellow Democrat and investor in Mexico, Thomas Gibbon. James Miller Guinn, Gibbon's contemporary and a regional historian, described Gibbon as "one of the busiest men in Los Angeles." Like his close friend Harry Chandler, Gibbon arrived in Los Angeles an ailing consumptive. Gibbon fell in love with his adopted city after his arrival in 1888 and seemed to relish opportunities to promote his region. Over the course of a long life in Los Angeles, he zealously pursued both private and public success; he coupled a booming law practice with civic leadership. He also aligned himself with the city's politically and racially conservative elite and backed the efforts of men like Harrison Gray Otis to keep Los Angeles anti-union, antiradical, and strictly divided along racial lines.

Gibbon was born in Arkansas in 1860 to a farming family. He studied law in Little Rock, where he opened a law practice in the Jim Crow South in 1883. While living in Little Rock, Gibbon also ran for a position in the Arkansas legislature and served from 1884 to 1885 (because of his age, twenty-five, his colleagues referred to him as the "boy member").[26] In 1888, he moved to Los Angeles, likely because he suffered from tuberculosis, and started a prosperous law practice. According to historian William Deverell, Gibbon was extraordinarily ambitious and strategically allied himself with the city's wealthy elite, including Harry Chandler, with whom he had a close friendship.[27] In 1891, he joined the Los Angeles Terminal Railway Company and served as the vice president and attorney for the organization until the San Pedro, Los Angeles, and Salt Lake Railway absorbed the line in 1901. Gibbon was one of the organizers of the San Pedro/Salt Lake line and also served as its vice president and general counsel.[28] Gibbon also led the fight for a "free harbor" in Los Angeles, which brought him into contact with major Democratic politicians. By the 1910s, these would include Secretary of the Interior Franklin K. Lane and President Woodrow Wilson. Just prior to his death, Gibbon also lobbied hard for the construction of what would eventually become Union Station in Los Angeles. In a *Times* tribute published after his death in 1921, likely penned by his close friend, business partner, and pallbearer Chandler, the paper eulogized Gibbon's life as a reflection of the growth of Los Angeles: "To mark the stages by which he rose to eminence in the city and the community which he loved so well would be to narrate the progress of Southern California during the last quarter of a century; and to count his friends would be to enumerate the greater part of its population."[29] Gibbon, Chandler intoned, was Los Angeles.

Gibbon's interest in Mexico, coupled with his work on behalf of the San Pedro harbor, brought him into close contact with Otis and Chandler at the moment they decided to expand their investments into Mexico. As a result of these personal and professional affiliations, Gibbon became a founding member of Otis and Chandler's Colorado River Land Company. With other syndicate members, Gibbon invested heavily in the purchase and development of CRLC lands in northern Baja California.[30] As in Doheny's case, Gibbon and his fellow CRLC investors initially believed the Mexican Revolution would be short-lived. As violence increased, however, and spilled across the border, Gibbon became increasingly concerned about his investment and the status of Mexico's economy. Ultimately, rumors that a new Mexican constitution would redistribute foreign-owned properties pushed him to join with Doheny and other investors in Mexico to lobby for the protection of their properties and their city-empire.

In addition to his investments in the CRLC, Gibbon also vocally supported increased international trade in Los Angeles. He likely saw promoting trade, particularly with Mexico, as a strategy beneficial to his transportation interests and as a tactic to increase the city's national and international profile. Comparing the city's current trade with Mexico with that of its northern rival, San Francisco, Gibbon maintained that with a new port and Los Angeles's expanding railroad network, the city could easily eclipse San Francisco's trade with Mexico.[31] Gibbon suggested maximizing Los Angeles's transportation system by chartering a steamship company capable of transporting 2,000 tons of goods between Southern California and Mexican ports each month. His suggestions moved the Los Angeles Chamber of Commerce and the Merchants and Manufacturers Association to place increased trade with Mexico high on their list of priorities for the city. Gibbon also described himself as a friend, ally, and "student of Mexico" because of his "proximity in Southern California to that country."[32] Of course, racial and class undertones tinged Gibbon's friendship with Mexico. He counted Mexican elites as his friends and colleagues, whom he often referred to as "Spanish gentlemen," allowing their social class to elevate their status in relationship to the Mexican workers who likely helped build Gibbon's railroad or farmed on the CRLC property.

Strict ideas about the roles of capital and labor and white and brown skin commanded Gibbon's actions as he launched an intense lobbying campaign at the federal level. A self-described "student of Mexican conditions," Gibbon wrote frequently about his perspective on events unfolding south of the border.[33] These writings explicitly related race to the revolution in Mexico and, in Gibbon's assessment, the country's failed experiment with democracy. Gibbon argued, "I believe that a survey must be made of the racial history of the Mexican people, the character and result of their efforts during ninety-eight years to maintain a democratic government."[34] Reflecting on Mexican history from its independence from the Spanish Empire to the outbreak of the Mexican Revolution, Gibbon linked the country's struggles to build a stable democracy directly to its racial composition. Observing the preponderance of nonwhite peoples in Mexico, Gibbon argued that racial mixing and the country's large indigenous and mestizo population had resulted in an untenable experiment in democracy. The results, he maintained, were "the misfortunes which have overtaken foreigners having interests in the country and which have resulted in untold misery to both its native and foreign populations."[35] In Gibbon's estimation, had Mexico followed the tenets of imperialism, allowing wealthy whites to run an economic system that enriched them and relegated darker-skinned peoples to the position of "docile" laborers, Mexico's history would look remarkably different.

As explored in the introduction to this chapter, Gibbon did not hesitate to promote a formal American empire in Mexico. Reflecting on the imperial relationship between the United States and other regions that had once been ruled by the Spanish Empire, Gibbon lobbied his contacts in Washington, D.C., to simply extend American political and military control over Mexico. Gibbon maintained that American proximity to Mexico and the countries' shared border provided even stronger justification for imperial intervention and control. In Gibbon's estimation, however, the strongest justification was racial. In a letter to the Wilson administration, Gibbon wrote that American involvement in Mexico would "eventually elevate them [the Mexicans] to a respectable place among the people of the world," with the added benefit of protecting American financial interests.[36] Gibbon laid out what he believed to be a compelling case. The United States shared a border with a troubled Mexico. The conditions in Mexico were "intolerable," at least for American investors. The United States had more than two decades of imperial experience in Cuba, Puerto Rico, and the Philippines. Those populations required a certain "sort of government," in Gibbon's mind, a government run by white investors. Therefore, it was the imperial responsibility of the United States to intervene. This was much more than simply protecting property; it was an imperial mission with moral overtones. In Gibbon's words, "We probably gained more honor and moral distinction as a nation by our intervention on behalf of the Cuban people than by any other thing we have done in our national life. It seems to me that the same conditions which called for intervention in Cuba, call for intervention even more loudly in the case of Mexico because the welfare of so many more people are [sic] involved."[37] With this worldview, Gibbon charged from Los Angeles into Washington politics and U.S. foreign policy, determined to protect American investments in Mexico and, hopefully, to return Mexico to the system of imperialism that had proven so profitable in the past. If informal imperialism was not an option, Gibbon was happy to support a more formal system of rule for the benefit of foreign investors.

And the Los Angeles oligarchy relied on Gibbon to push precisely this agenda in the nation's capital. As they witnessed the control over their Mexican properties slip through their fingers, from the local level at ranches such as Quimichis to the national level embodied in the rewriting of the Constitution and Article 27, Los Angeles investors turned to their federal government to advance their regional agenda. Gibbon's extended national network of political connections stretched from Southern California to Sacramento to Washington, D.C., and made him an ideal liaison between Los Angeles and the federal government. Fellow investors like Chandler had already frequently leaned on Gibbon to serve as a link between Los Angeles business and political interests and the federal government. In 1916, for example, the CRLC employed Gibbon as its attorney to "represent us in Washington for the purpose of assuring us such protection as we believe American citizens are entitled to for their investments in foreign countries."[38]

Through his friendship with Franklin Lane, Gibbon had access to the highest-level diplomatic negotiations between the United States and Mexico and could advocate for Los Angeles investors and for increased intervention and control south of the border. For example, he regularly sent lengthy epistles directly to the president outlining precisely how he thought the United States should proceed in Mexico.[39] In addition, Gibbon used his close relationship with Lane to attend negotiations between the United States and Mexico for the withdrawal of the Pershing Expedition (Gibbon vehemently opposed the withdrawal). Gibbon stopped by the Griswold Hotel in Connecticut, where the commission met, to observe proceedings and meet with U.S. and Mexican diplomats. While there, Gibbon attended commission meetings as well as a meeting between the joint commission and President Wilson.[40] During a subsequent trip to Washington, D.C., Gibbon reported back to Harry Chandler in Los Angeles that he had just lunched with Secretary Lane and advocated an embargo on ammunition shipments to Mexico. Gibbon seemed excited to report that "the Secretary left me after lunch to attend a meeting of the Cabinet, at which he said he was going to protest against the lifting of the embargo."[41] Continuing an arms embargo did not quite constitute the imperial rule that Gibbon sought, but at least it might slow the process of revolution and perhaps set the stage for more forceful intervention.

Gibbon also considered himself a spokesperson for the American Southwest and thought it his responsibility to utilize his relationships in Washington for the benefit of the region. In correspondence to Lane and Wilson he referred often to the feelings and sensibilities of "Southern Californians" and "southwesterners." According to Gibbon, his interest in Mexico came about "partly by the fact that I have financial interests in Mexico, and also by our proximity in Southern California to that country."[42] He believed that Los Angeles's proximity to Mexico and commercial ties to the country uniquely positioned him to understand and fear political unrest in the neighboring state. In correspondence with Wilson, Gibbon wrote, "For myself, and in behalf of your fellow countrymen in this part of the West, I want most heartily to thank you for your recent letter dealing with conditions in Mexico. I assure you it has been received with enthusiasm by the people of this section of the country, whose proximity to Mexico has enabled them to know more probably than the average American does of the frightful conditions now prevailing in that country."[43] Gibbon maintained that people of the American Southwest had witnessed the destruction of their property, the killing and imprisonment of their relatives, and the threat of losing the right to own land in Mexico. They needed, he argued, the federal government to understand their financial and *geographic* position and to respond to the revolution on their border.[44]

As tensions between American investors and the Mexican revolutionary state intensified prior to the passage of the new Mexican Constitution, an alarmed Gibbon appealed immediately to his allies in Washington on behalf of investors and southwesterners. He sent a hasty telegram to Lane in December 1916, alerting him that all Los Angeles–based "holders of large development interests" in Mexico were "greatly concerned" over the possible passage of a constitution that would eliminate protections for private property owners in Mexico and "establish machinery of spoliation evidently designed to facilitate the confiscation of property of foreigners."[45] The telegram included strongly worded advice to Wilson regarding his policy toward Mexico: "Cannot our president as protector of American rights and also the true friend of Mexico intervene to prevent such a constitution as will certainly lead to robbing Americans and other foreigners of hundreds of millions of property, to condemnation of Mexico by every civilized nation and inevitably to forcible aggression upon that country by European nations the property rights of whose nationals may be invaded, and may thus involve our nation in serious complications."[46] Significantly, Gibbon linked the concept of "civilization" with the protection of private property. Racially loaded, the terms "civilization" and "civilized nations" made reference to a world racial hierarchy in which those nations with populations less white and economies less capitalist ranked below nations where Anglo-Saxons ruled and capitalism triumphed. Question the sanctity of private property, Gibbon intoned, and you questioned the very foundation of the civilized—and white—world.

Foreign Policy for the Los Angeles Empire

In mid-1917, against a rapidly shifting global backdrop of war and a rewritten Mexican constitution, Doheny and Gibbon decided to join forces in their effort to protect Los Angeles (and American) financial interests in Mexico. In January, Wilson ordered Pershing's troops home following an utter failure in their campaign to find Villa back to the United States. In February, the Zimmermann telegram came to light, offering an alliance between Germany and Mexico in the war, with the conquered borderlands of Texas, New Mexico, and Arizona dangled as a reward. Later the same month, constitutional delegates approved a rewritten Mexican constitution, including Article 27. Declaration of war against Germany in April preoccupied the Wilson administration and left normalization of relations with Mexico, and the fate of American investors, in limbo. Events in Mexico seemed to be rapidly moving in the opposite direction of the desires of the Los Angeles oligarchy. This was the moment that required organizing in the interest of investors in Mexico, from Los Angeles, and across the country. City elites had so far failed to successfully marshal foreign policy on their behalf, and perhaps the situation demanded a more coordinated and nationwide effort.

Doheny and Gibbon agreed on this point and organized the meeting in the fall of 1917 that launched NAPARM.[47] Together, their goal was to ensure the financial rights of American investors in Mexico by establishing a nationwide media network to influence public opinion and by building a strategic lobbying campaign in Washington, D.C., to bend foreign policy in their direction. Their unstated goal was also significant: they infused demands for the protection of American property in Mexico with the racialized language of the civilized versus the uncivilized, the propertied versus the landless, and the investor versus the revolutionary. This was a fully developed lobbying campaign to promote a formal American empire in Mexico. According to their plan, companies headquartered in Los Angeles and New York would contribute monthly sums of cash to start a new special interest organization that would raise public awareness of the treatment of Americans in Mexico and influence federal policy. These corporations, including the CRLC and Doheny's Mexican Petroleum Company, would each contribute between $500 and $1,000 a month depending on the size of their Mexican investment. Through a variety of strategies NAPARM would collaborate to raise "a lot of publicity which will, before very long, force the hand of the Government for the protection of our interests in Mexico."[48]

The plan reflected the Angeleno elite's acknowledgment that the diplomatic power they had wielded in Mexico prior to the revolution had rapidly dwindled. To their disbelief, Mexican revolutionaries, bedraggled peons in the eyes of Los Angeles investors, might now control the destiny of their investment dollars. This threat demanded an oligarchy that had imagined itself as a powerful centrifugal political and economic force in Los Angeles to call on the support of other centers of power, namely, the political power represented by Washington, D.C., and the economic power represented by the nation's leading financial center, New York City.

To draw on the support of these financial and political cores, NAPARM leadership envisioned a Washington-based organization headed by a man "who has had considerable experience as the Washington correspondent of some leading newspaper and a wide acquaintance with other Washington newspaper correspondents."[49] Gibbon believed it prudent to hire someone whose professional networks and personal friendships would enable him to secure publication of news stories that promoted the organization's agenda. In other words, Gibbon strategized that they needed an organizational director who could successfully direct a pro-investor and pro-imperial propaganda campaign in the nation's capital. The organization planned to have their director release daily news bulletins relative to events in Mexico "immediately after they occur and get them reproduced by the newspapers."[50] A bilingual assistant would provide translation services, particularly for Mexican news items. The office would subscribe to all of the major Mexican newspapers and use them as the main source of information for its own bulletins and news pieces.

While Angeleno investors and their ideas of city, empire, and race initially drove the organization, NAPARM also planned for a nationwide network of pro-interventionists. To expand the organization's membership beyond Los Angeles, Doheny organized a meeting of forty leading American investors in New York City in January 1919 to discuss the mission of NAPARM. According to the association's report, the attendees represented every American industry in Mexico, including agricultural interests, cattle ranchers, irrigation companies, railroad corporations, mining companies, oil producers, and bankers. After discussion of the situation in Mexico and the goals of the association, the group agreed to join and finance the effort. They also outlined some additional policies and goals. First, NAPARM would organize as large a membership as possible. They would circulate news briefs to members regularly to keep them apprised of political events in Mexico. They would meticulously document any illegal or unfair treatment of Americans and their property. They would coordinate a press campaign to correct "false" impressions of events in Mexico. They would provide assistance to the U.S. government in understanding the position of American investments in Mexico. They would champion the well-being of the Mexican people, as they perceived it, particularly around issues of good government. Finally, they would push the U.S. government to "sternly insist" to the Mexican government that it respect the rights of Americans and American property in Mexico.[51] These ideas, espoused during the organization's New York meeting, reiterated and amplified Doheny and Gibbon's perspective on the role of Anglo-Americans and American capital in Mexico.

In an effort to extend its geographic and political influence even farther than New York and Washington, NAPARM also planned an expansive nationwide circulation for the organization's publication, *Mexican Outlook*. The organization would write, publish, and circulate the bulletin at its own expense. The total circulation amounted to 25,000 copies. Gibbon and Doheny designated 2,650 copies for all of the daily English-language newspapers in the country. They also reserved 2,350 for all weekly publications across the country, such as the *Argonaut* of San Francisco and the *Graphic* of Los Angeles. The remaining 20,000 copies they allocated to a circulation list composed of "the men in each community who are known as reading, thinking men and leaders of thought."[52] Gibbon clearly stated his objectives in this distribution plan: he wanted a publication that influential citizens and decision makers considered a leading source of information on Mexico. Gibbon hoped that NAPARM, directed by a handful of venture capitalists in Los Angeles, would become the leading source of information on Mexico in the United States. The organization, also directed by individuals and companies with significant financial interests in Mexico, anticipated becoming the driving force behind American public sentiment and policy toward Mexico.

Considering himself a leading expert on the "Mexican question," Gibbon penned the first issue of *Mexican Outlook* himself and used the opportunity to promote American imperial intervention in Mexico. According to him, farsighted Mexicans under Díaz had made the wise decision to invite Anglo-American investors into the country. Unfortunately, the lower "masses" of Mexico failed to understand their role in this system of empire and revolted against an economic framework that, according to Gibbon, offered them nothing but benevolent benefits. He outlined the history of foreign investment in Mexico, noting that by the beginning of the revolution, Americans had invested at least $1 billion in Mexican commercial enterprises: "The foreign element in Mexico was the backbone of the business of the country."[53] As a stakeholder in the CRLC, Gibbon could not help but highlight American reclamation work in Mexican desert landscapes as a significant success: "Of great importance to Mexico was the fact that foreigners were investing many millions of dollars in great reclamation projects, planned for placing water for irrigation upon lands, that, without water, were unproductive by which, with it, would become among the most productive in the world."[54] This ability to transform wild land into productive farmland firmly attached "civilization" to American efforts in Mexico. What Mexicans had been unable to achieve, Anglo-Americans and American capitalism and empire had succeeded in. This American investment, Gibbon argued, provided jobs for hundreds of thousands of Mexicans with wages substantially higher than those offered by Mexican employers. The revolution, he maintained, "seriously injured" these enterprises and, as a result, harmed the Mexican working class. The revolutionary government had rewritten the Mexican Constitution, confiscated privately owned American property, and stalled the Mexican economy. *Mexican Outlook*, Gibbon maintained, would provide a vehicle to inform the American people about what was happening in Mexico and why Mexico was in its current state, and to "fix the responsibility for them."[55]

Doheny and his public relations team repeated the jingoistic calls for American intervention in Mexico. T. F. Lee, who worked for Doheny's publicity office, wrote in a widely circulated pamphlet: "The Philippines and Cuba point the real solution of the Mexican problem . . . Mexico will only be a breeding ground for chaos and anarchy and bolshevism until some strong moral force—some outside force—reaches into that unhappy land, pulls together the raveled threads of government, places them in the hands of such capable men as may truly guide and represent the real Mexican people and then stands back of such constituted government with every force necessary to protect its own citizens as well as the aliens within its bounds."[56]

Undoubtedly reflecting his employer's convictions, Lee argued that the only resolution for the turmoil in Mexico was armed imperial intervention. That intervention might not result in formal rule or annexation, but would select some sympathetic Mexican figurehead through which the United States (and its investor class) could rule the country to their benefit. The phrase "reaches into that unhappy land" left little ambiguity—the hand that reached into Mexico would be the American state and its armed forces, which would remain to ensure that its chosen head of state protected the "aliens within its bounds."

By 1918, the conclusion of the war in Europe fully occupied Wilson's attention, and Doheny, Gibbon, and other NAPARM members decided to intensify their campaign for armed intervention in Mexico to protect their financial interests. With allies in the State Department as well as the support of pro-intervention Senator Albert Bacon Fall, NAPARM leaders worked with the Senate Committee on Foreign Affairs to conduct a series of hearings on "damages and outrages" committed against American citizens in Mexico. Fall was the self-appointed expert on Mexican issues in Washington, D.C., and had already conducted hearings on attacks on Americans in Mexico in 1913. He wanted the United States to intervene in Mexico, and it seems he needed little prodding from NAPARM to resurrect the issue in 1919. The subcommittee that he composed to conduct the hearings was particularly concerned with personal damages such as injuries, accidental deaths, and murders as well as destruction and confiscation of private property.[57]

Three decades of friendship between Fall and Doheny helped facilitate the hearings. Their friendship demonstrates the type of links between the Los Angeles oligarchy and state policymakers at the federal level that Angelenos hoped would help them deploy the power of the American state south of the border. The two men established a friendship when they both resided in New Mexico in the mid-1880s, and it was their collaboration on the Senate investigation that solidified their friendship and political alliance. Fall served as a senator from New Mexico from 1912 until 1921, when

President Warren G. Harding appointed him secretary of the interior. During Fall's tenure at the Interior Department, he leased oil land in Wyoming to Doheny without a competitive bidding process and received cash gifts in return for the favor. When the transaction became public in 1920 it was dubbed the Teapot Dome Scandal and ruined Fall's career. Doheny was put on trial and was in danger of serving prison time. The emotional pressure of the scandal may have also contributed to the mysterious murder-suicide of Doheny's son, Edward Jr., and his secretary, Hugh Plunkett.

In 1918, however, Los Angeles investors, led by Doheny and supported by Fall, were more concerned with orchestrating intervention in Mexico. In Los Angeles, Doheny hoped he could manipulate the federal government to intervene on behalf of his personal financial interests, often disguised as in the interest of the greater nation. Working with Doheny, Gibbon, and NAPARM, Fall organized a subcommittee to hear testimony from American business interests and political leaders familiar with the political situation in Mexico and to push the Wilson administration to intervene on their behalf. The Fall Committee held hearings from September 1919 through May 1920, traveled over 12,000 miles during their investigation, and held hearings in ten cities, including Los Angeles. They called 257 witnesses and produced a 5,000-page report documenting testimony and findings.[58] In its concluding report, the committee recommended armed intervention in Mexico if the Carranza administration failed to guarantee protection for American property. Referencing Cuba as a successful example of intervention, the Fall Committee argued that the United States had the obligation to intervene for the benefit of both the United States and Mexico. This recommendation, to intervene in Mexico as the United States had intervened in Cuba, carried obvious racial and imperial overtones. Mexico, the report argued, had allowed its nonwhite population to revolt. That nonwhite population was uncivilized and incapable of self-rule and thus in need of the tutelage of its northern neighbor.

Los Angeles played a major role in the work of the congressional committee. This was not just the work of concerned federal officials. Instead, it stemmed from the careful machinations of a public relations campaign coordinated and funded in Southern California. Oilmen, including Doheny, comprised most of the witnesses in support of armed intervention in Mexico. Many of the interventionist witnesses were also members of NAPARM. In his testimony, Doheny emphasized the "legal" and racial dimensions of empire building south of the border. He highlighted his legal acquisition of land in Mexico and the benefits his company had provided the Mexican people. He discussed his major acquisitions and underscored the legality of their titles and his purchases. He did not, he stressed, receive any properties as concessions from the Díaz administration, nor did he illegally dispossess any Mexicans of their land.[59] In fact, Doheny maintained, the MPC had paid well above market value to obtain its Mexican properties. Like Barron, Doheny also emphasized the benevolent and civilizing work of his oil enterprise. He noted that when his petroleum company arrived, Mexican workers in the Tampico region earned thirty-six cents a day. In comparison, the Mexican Petroleum Company offered employees a wage of seventy-five cents to a dollar a day.[60] He also noted that the company provided decent housing, schools, and good working conditions for almost 15,000 employees. While on the stand, Doheny produced photographs of his Huasteca property, showing schools built at the expense of the company: "Here are some more photographs showing how the people live down there. I would like to place these on file to show we take care of our employees . . . These show the homes of the peons."[61] According to Doheny, his millions in oil money also had the benevolent benefit of uplifting the Mexican "peon." In fact, Doheny argued that the Mexican government under Carranza had intervened in his efforts to assist the people of Mexico: "They have tried to prevent me from doing the things I would like to do to help out those people down there, and for whom I lay down to no man in desire to give assistance, both as a friend of humanity and a friend of the people who have always been friends of mine."[62] According to Doheny's line of thought, oil fields did not just produce wealth for him but also provided the benefits of racialized imperialism—the uplift and civilization of a nation of peons. A series of strikes organized by the workers he purported to help on his oil properties, however, belied his humanitarian claims.[63] Finally, Doheny argued that the United States needed to protect American oil holdings around the world, not just for their owners, but also for the well-being of "the people who use the flivver, as well as the people who ride in the limousine."[64] Oil holdings, he argued, benefited not only investors but also the stability and security of the entire population, regardless of social status. This perspective, of course, reflected Doheny's belief in the organizing power of both the core-hinterland relationship and race and capitalism. From Los Angeles, he had helped coordinate the capitalist development of a nonwhite hinterland. In so doing, his oil empire provided the "appropriate" type of labor for a nonwhite population while also "uplifting" an entire nation.

While Doheny took the witness stand and Fall caravanned the committee hearings across the American Southwest to promote intervention by

Washington, D.C., Gibbon coordinated the release of his book on the "Mexican situation," *Mexico under Carranza: A Lawyer's Indictment of the Crowning Infamy of Four Hundred Years of Misrule*. The book reiterated the hearings' findings that the United States had the imperial obligation to intervene in Mexico not just to protect the investments of its own (white) citizens but also to protect the interests of nonwhite Mexican workers in Los Angeles's hinterland. A national best seller, *Mexico under Carranza* was a collection of his self-proclaimed expertise on events unfolding in Mexico. In a letter to his good friend Chandler just before the book's publication, Gibbon revealed, "The manuscript has been read by several people and I am very much gratified at the universal expression of approval that it has won. Everybody says that they believe its publication will mark an epoch in Mexican affairs and will force the Government to give that protection to Americans and American interests in Mexico, which it has so far not accorded."[65] In anticipation of the book's publication, Gibbon traveled to Washington, D.C., to circulate the manuscript and build publicity for the book's release. He met with political friends in the capital and reported to friends in Los Angeles that their network of federal allies believed the book would promote protection of their interests in Mexico. In another letter to Chandler, Gibbon reported that "my book is going to be most timely, as it will furnish a great deal of ammunition to the people in and out of Congress who propose to insist on justice for American interests in Mexico."[66]

Gibbon opened his book with an inscription, dedicating the work to "The submerged eighty per cent of the Mexican people—the peons—who, for four hundred years, have been the victims of an industrial slavery almost without parallel in history, and to those who have been their greatest friends and benefactors in that dark period, the heroic American pioneers who, at the risk, and oft-times at the cost, of their lives, have invaded the mountains, deserts, and jungles of Mexico to discover and develop the hitherto unknown natural resources of that country for the benefits of its workers and of civilized mankind."[67] Gibbon's dedication encapsulated his economic worldview and his perspective on U.S.-Mexican diplomatic relations during the Mexican Revolution. Dismissing the populist origins and demands of the revolution, Gibbon's inscription linked the well-being of the Mexican people to the Americans who had invested in developing the country's natural resources. Gibbon uncoupled foreign investment from the hardships faced by Mexico's industrial workers and agricultural laborers, arguing instead that American capital development of Mexican natural resources provided an essential service for the Mexican people and, indeed, the world. International capitalism, Gibbon intimated, offered the solution to rural poverty and urban discontent in Mexico. According to Gibbon, an American-style economic system could provide stability and order for a poor country overwhelmed by revolutionary violence. Gibbon's inscription included an implicit critique of Mexico's ruling class—they had failed to create a classed but stable society, like the one Gibbon believed existed in the United States and functioned exceptionally well in Los Angeles.

Gibbon also provided a scathing critique of his own government's failure to act on behalf of its citizens in Mexico and an explicit plan to save American investors and the Mexico "peon"—direct imperial intervention. He stated bluntly that Mexico required intervention for its own salvation: "What Mexico needs, and what I believe she must have, is the intervention in her affairs of saving power such as . . . our own nation has afforded to the Philippines, and to Cuba."[68] Gibbon felt free to articulate a very specific strategy for Mexico in his book: bring it under the imperial control of the United States, at least until the nation could be deemed sufficiently stable to oversee its own affairs. This type of imperial oversight, Gibbon argued, would rescue Mexico's twelve million people from a chaotic situation that represented an affront to civilized nations. In proposing radical interventionism, Gibbon recognized that he diverged from many Americans, but he maintained that he was a conscientious student of Mexico and that his careful research and reflection on the revolution had brought him to this conclusion.

The people of Mexico suffered, Gibbon believed, because their leaders had failed to establish a stable country open to enterprising settlers and investors from the United States. Economic development, led by American investors, had offered the promise of employment, steady wages, and growth in Mexico. The revolution, in challenging the presence of American investors and threatening their private property, had not only violated the rights of American citizens but had also submerged the Mexican people in disorder, anarchy, and misery. Intervention led by the United States, he maintained, would resolve both of these issues by reestablishing a welcoming environment for American dollars, teaching Mexicans about democracy, and providing stability and economic opportunities for Mexicans. He ended his treatise with a question designed to lead his readers to the same conclusion: "Would it not be better now for us to go back to the idea of doing our simple duty to our own people . . . [and] rescuing the suffering masses of [Mexicans] from the criminals who are imposing upon them so many of the miseries of 'self-government' as it exists in Mexico?"[69] Presumably the "suffering masses of Mexicans" were the nonwhite citizens of Mexico whose racial makeup made them incapable of effective self-rule.

Despite what NAPARM leaders hoped would be the one-two punch of the Senate hearings and Gibbon's treatise on Mexico, they failed to reignite the desire for war in the Wilson administration. Working with the State Department, NAPARM did succeed in stalling the full normalization of the relationship between the United States and Mexico until the mid-1920s.[70] Ultimately, two factors likely prevented NAPARM from winning the type of successful (at least for American investors) intervention they had seen in places such as the Dominican Republic and Haiti. First, World War I occupied much of Wilson's time and attention and that of U.S. military forces after the Pershing Expedition. Second, as historian Noel Maurer argues, Mexico was "too big to invade." While varying factions controlled the Mexican government and presidency between 1914 and 1917, the United States could not impose the types of sanctions, or "dollar diplomacy," and strategic interventions that had worked effectively in other nations, particularly in the Caribbean. Instead, protecting American investments in Mexico would have required a full-scale invasion and the occupation of a vast nation. Various contingency plans drawn up by the U.S. Army between 1911 and 1914 estimated that occupation of Mexico would require between 114,000 and 352,985 troops and would cost $238 million. In 1914, the U.S. Army had 98,000 active personnel, and the entire U.S. defense budget totaled $347 million.[71] This type of massive military operation would have also required the political support of the American population, not just the zealous jingoism of a small number of wealthy investors. As a result, Wilson simply left Mexico alone during the final years of his presidency. And, despite his repeatedly interventionist actions in other Latin American nations, he continued to state that he feared the "extremist consequences" that might result from American occupation of Mexico and announced that "INTERVENTION (that is the rearrangement and control of Mexico's domestic affairs by the U.S.) there shall not be either now or at any other time if I can prevent it."[72]

Despite this failure to achieve their goal of intervention in Mexico, Doheny and Gibbon's efforts reveal two important themes in the history of Los Angeles and its relationship with Mexico as well as its connections to Washington, D.C. Between the ascension of Porfirio Díaz and the Mexican Revolution, Angeleno elites could utilize their location in Los Angeles to promote their regional interests in Mexico and with Mexican elites and the Mexican state. They coordinated from a regional capital just north of the border and successfully manipulated international relationships for their benefit. Relying on class-based alliances with Mexican elites and policymakers, Angeleno investors wielded enough power and influence to negotiate international water rights or relocate a federal office, efforts that could be accomplished at the regional level. As the revolution toppled the Díaz regime and began to rewrite the social contract between citizens and their government, Angeleno investors enjoyed far less power in Mexico. Their regional core seemed in danger of losing its clout and muscle on an international level. Angelenos suddenly shifted tactics; since they could no longer rely on the Mexican state to do their bidding, they turned to their own capital and center of power, Washington, D.C. What they found there appalled and incensed them. Their president refused to intervene in Mexico on their behalf. The regional empire, bisected by an international border, flailed.

Mexico and the Regional Empire

While the Los Angeles investor class plotted in the regional core north of the border, the Mexican state also followed the activities of NAPARM and its members from south of the border. In particular, Doheny's activities sparked marked interest and understandable concern about what his interventionist agenda would mean for Mexico. In June 1918, for example, the Mexican embassy in Washington, D.C., reported to the Carranza administration that they believed Doheny had a cache of weapons stored in central California and that he was offering them to the state government.[73] The embassy was not sure what Doheny's intentions were but found the situation alarming. They speculated that Doheny had purchased the arms in anticipation of the world war but also reported that the Mexican consul in San Francisco harbored suspicions of that explanation.[74] Reportedly, the cache included 750,000 rounds of ammunition and 500 new rifles that the Mexican government feared might be used against Mexico. Clearly, Mexican officials in both the United States and Mexico City worried that Californians might make use of the weapons stash against Mexico or that Doheny might be planning an armed insurrection. Carranza also paid close attention to Doheny's trip to the League of Nations meeting in Versailles in 1919. Although Doheny's efforts to lobby representatives at the treaty negotiations failed to win support for intervention in Mexico, his presence there clearly signaled a challenge to Carranza's presidency on an international level. Carranza also cleverly maneuvered against intervention by leveraging intervention against the interventionists; while Doheny pushed armed intervention in Mexico, Carranza threatened to set fire to oil fields if American troops landed on the country's Gulf Coast.[75]

Relationships between oil producers and the Mexican presidency did not immediately improve after Álvaro Obregón's coup against Carranza in 1920.[76] However, Obregón did express a desire to reach an agreement with foreign oil producers, particularly if it could help him secure recognition of his presidency from the Harding administration. A decision by the Mexican Supreme Court finding Article 27 not retroactive for the oil companies also improved Obregón's position vis-à-vis Doheny and other oilmen. Although generally satisfied with the decision, Doheny was not fully appeased. He argued that despite the Court's decision, private property was still not safe in Mexico, and he continued to push for American military intervention. While struggling to win support from Wilson, Doheny also took intervention into his own hands. According to one biographer, Doheny backed a 1921 scheme by the governor of Baja California, Esteban Cantú, and his Los Angeles–based brother Frederico Dato to use arms and money supplied by Doheny to overthrow the Obregón presidency.[77] Nothing came of the plan, but it reveals Doheny's increasing desperation to control Mexican politics and protect the source of his substantial oil fortune.

Reports on schemes like the one involving Cantú reached the Obregón administration, and Obregón continued to carefully monitor Doheny's activities in Southern California, along the U.S.-Mexico border, and in Washington, D.C. In 1924, for example, the Obregón administration connected Doheny to an American named John Camp who, according to an informant for the Mexican government, was conducting suspicious activities in Los Angeles, along the Texas-Chihuahua border, and in the Mexican capital. The head of the Mexican federal police reported that Doheny had retained Camp to try again to foment a coup against Obregón with Dato, who continued to reside in Los Angeles.[78] The federal police dispatched agent C. Modesto Nemer to Ciudad Juárez to investigate the issue. Nemer reported that Camp had been apprehended with documents that showed plans on the part of Doheny to back Obregón's political opponents.[79] Although Camp's relationship to Doheny is not clear, the Mexican federal police did intercept a cryptic telegram from Dato to Camp asking, "Did you receive my wire of the twenty sixth last from news received we still have good opportunities let me know if we are going to go ahead with our plans answer me to 28 Clubhouse Ave. Venice Calif."[80] Doheny did have a relationship with Dato and could very well have been involved with the plans referred to in the telegrams exchanged between Dato and Camp. The Mexican government also obtained receipts clearly documenting Camp's purchase of large supplies of guns and ammunition in El Paso, including 200 Colt .45 pistols and 3,000 rounds of ammunition.[81] On another occasion, Camp purchased 20 carbines, 500 Colt .45s, and 200 machine guns at the Toepperwein Hardware and Sporting Goods Company in San Antonio.[82] Camp's activities may have been linked to the machinations of Adolfo de la Huerta, who had been part of the Obregón administration but who orchestrated a failed revolt at the end of 1923. Just prior to the failed coup, de la Huerta had been negotiating a loan deal with Doheny for the Mexican government, and Doheny may have provided him with financial support for a coup.[83] According to an investigation conducted by Obregón, de la Huerta did meet with Doheny in Los Angeles shortly after the failed coup, and he fled Mexico for Southern California.[84] A story of intrigue and espionage at the border is fascinating in and of itself but also points to the lengths to which Los Angeles capitalists would go to protect assets south of the border. Doheny and his cohorts appeared willing to intervene in Mexico militarily even without the approval or support of the federal government.

Conclusion

After decades of investing south of the border and carefully constructing ties between Los Angeles and Mexico, Los Angeles investors now called for formal imperial control of their southern neighbor. They drew from the developments they had witnessed in other imperial locales, such as Cuba and the Philippines, to argue loudly and unwaveringly that the United States owed both its investor class and the people of Mexico a definitively military and political intervention. American empire should now move officially into Mexico. However, the intricate political maneuverings of Doheny, Gibbon, and NAPARM failed to yield the result they desired in Mexico. Wilson eventually refused to bend to their demands and even grumbled to his personal physician during a game of golf, "I sometimes have to pause and remind myself that I am president of the whole United States and not merely of a few property holders in the Republic of Mexico."[85] Although Doheny and Gibbon complained, cajoled, harassed, badgered, planned, and schemed to push the Wilson administration to intervene more forcefully in Mexico's internal affairs, their efforts never achieved the outcome they desired—a full-scale invasion and occupation of Mexico. Instead, Wilson left the relationship with Mexico unsettled when he left office in 1921. By then, Álvaro Obregón had succeeded Carranza as Mexico's head of state. Obregón and the Harding administration used recognition of the Mexican administration and protections for American investors as leverage in negotiations between the two nations in 1922 and 1923. The resulting Bucareli Treaty, also discussed in the next chapter, provided some protections for American investors, particularly those involved in the oil industry, from retroactive application of Article 27, and resulted in recognition for Obregón's government. These negotiations generally protected large international oil interests in Mexico until President Lázaro Cárdenas announced plans for nationalization in 1938.[86]

Despite the failure of their efforts to orchestrate invasion in 1917 and 1918, the lobbying campaign American investors coordinated from their palatial homes and plush offices in Los Angeles reveals both the reach and the limitations of a city that hoped to control an international empire. They had successfully coordinated with President Díaz to the mutual benefit of elite Angelenos, the Mexican state, and Mexican elites. Revolution, however, realigned the goals of the Mexican state and undermined the significant power of Americans, particularly Angelenos, to get their financial way in Mexico. The Mexican state that emerged out of the Constitution of 1917 refused, at least initially, to do the bidding of a capitalist class in an urban core in Southern California. In cases such as this in Los Angeles, the oligarchy could rely on the armed power of the state—the police, and even the National Guard—to help it align labor to its interests. Faced with armed revolutionaries and an uncooperative state south of the border, Doheny and Gibbon realized that the reach of their city-empire did not quite extend to the presidential palace at Chapultepec. And while they owned arms, particularly Doheny, they could not deploy them with enough force in Mexico to counter the revolution. Instead, they turned to one of the strongest executive powers and armed forces in the world, the U.S. president and military, to do their bidding south of the border.

In essence, this was an imperial plan designed and promoted by a municipal elite who had invested heavily south of the border. While revolution challenged Angeleno aspirations in Mexico, these investors remained in a tight encirclement with their city's hinterland. Empire, for men like Doheny and Gibbon, was intimately linked to their hometown of Los Angeles. Ultimately, however, the city-empire could not coordinate an armed defense of property in Mexico. An international border bisected core and periphery and forced Angeleno investors to lean on their federal government to support their financial interests in another nation. Their expectation that the executive and other federal agencies would support their cause certainly had precedent. Doheny and Gibbon were keen observers of American foreign policy and empire building, both formal and informal, throughout Latin America and beyond. Given the promiscuous empire building on the part of the U.S. government and the country's investor class in the three decades leading up to 1920, Angelenos certainly had reason to believe that if they pushed hard enough, raised shrill, bellicose voices for intervention and war, and explained that Mexicans were simply unable to govern themselves, they could convince an American president to cross the border on their behalf. What they had not anticipated was Wilson's reluctance to take on a country as large and densely populated as Mexico, his preoccupation with world war, and his waffling position on self-determination for Latin American countries. Had one of these variables been slightly different, Angeleno investors and the lobbying campaign they spearheaded might have been more successful. Ultimately, however, the moment for armed intervention passed, and Angeleno investors had to contemplate alternative strategies for protecting their property or, at the very least, selling out and settling up. As explored in the next chapter, Angeleno investors began, frantically, to find buyers for their Mexican properties or to negotiate for the highest possible payment from the Mexican government for confiscated properties.

A number of trends shaped the perspective of Los Angeles investors such as Doheny and Gibbon, from global expansion of American economic and political power to their positions as the builders of a city with a great international hinterland. Gibbon and Doheny viewed the revolution unfolding south of the border less as a national issue confined to Mexico than as a threat to both their city and a world economic system that benefited them personally. Just as the federal government had tried to control labor unrest across the United States since the 1870s, just as the Merchants and Manufacturers Association had strictly regulated labor and labor organizing in Los Angeles, and just as the federal government had intervened regularly on behalf of American investors around the globe, Gibbon and other Angeleno investors believed the United States could and should regulate the economic and labor regimes of Mexico for the simultaneous benefit of Americans, particularly Angelenos, and Mexicans. Respecting international borders appeared less important than reinforcing an economic and class system that elites such as Doheny and Gibbon believed maintained balance and order, whether in Los Angeles, the United States, or Mexico.

5   Against Capital and Foreigners

In early 1921, Moray Applegate, the manager of the Quimichis hacienda following the death of William Windham, sent an urgent telegram to his employers in Southern California. Applegate reported that a group of "extreme radicals highly prejudiced against both capital and foreigners" now controlled the local agrarian commission and that there were rumblings of land takeovers and the expropriation of foreign-owned properties along the west coast of Mexico. Local families and indigenous communities, he feared, would soon start to take the situation into their own hands and simply seize American-owned properties, with or without the backing of the Mexican federal government. Sensing that the local agrarian commission in Nayarit would back their land claims, even if they began as squatters' movements, *agraristas* on and around the Quimichis ranch decided to implement the tenets of the 1917 Constitution independent of the Mexican federal state.[1] As Applegate noted, "These people, knowing that the [local] government is back of them are getting much excited and will be hard to satisfy. I think we are up against a hard desperate fight."[2]

Applegate's agitated telegram and his observations regarding the demands of Mexican agraristas exposed the transfigured power dynamics in Los Angeles's Mexican hinterland. Applegate, a veteran of the U.S. war in the Philippines and thus uniquely qualified as an agent of empire, was on the ground in the periphery to observe the seismic shift. As he noted, Mexican peasants, farmers, and revolutionaries, staunchly anticapital and antiforeign, had seized local political power. Unwilling to wait on federally mandated land reforms under the 1917 Constitution, they were simply seizing the lands they wanted. The telegram sent from Nayarit to Los Angeles embodied the transformation in power and property that had so frightened Angelenos such as Edward Doheny and Thomas Gibbon. Los Angeles investors could no longer maintain physical control over their employees or their properties in Mexico. Revolution in the hinterland had overthrown the power of the urban core and challenged American empire. In fact, American empire had never faced a challenge as pervasive and successful as it did in the form of the Mexican Revolution.

As explored in the previous chapter, the failures of Doheny and Gibbon to secure American intervention in Mexico and the protection of private investment properties had lasting consequences for Angeleno investments and the structuring of Los Angeles as the center of a transnational city-empire. As Mexico entered its postrevolutionary period and began overhauling national land policies, power tilted precipitously from the metropolitan center of Los Angeles toward the city's Mexican hinterland. Instead of residing in the gilded homes and plush offices of Los Angeles oil titans or the craftsman parlors of middle-class Pasadena investors, power came to reside in the periphery itself. Los Angeles investors who for so long had carefully tried to lace together core and periphery became themselves drawn into the Mexican Revolution. In the liminal space of the borderlands where the U.S. federal government had refused to intervene decisively, where individual investors, no matter how wealthy, never had arsenals ferocious enough to quell a revolution, and where revolutionaries and peasants were determined to redistribute land and realign power, Los Angeles investors lost the imperial authority they had so carefully cultivated. Revolution had slashed investment ties, and the Los Angeles investor class found itself at the mercy of Mexican farmers, local government agencies, and the Mexican state. Despite this reconfiguration of power between core and periphery, Los Angeles and Mexico remained tightly bound together. The nature of the relationship shifted, but Mexico and Mexican properties remained at the forefront of Angeleno investment schemes.

Despite the determined and aggressively imperial campaigns of Doheny and Gibbon for American intervention in Mexico, Mexicans and the Mexican state began commandeering American-owned properties in the 1910s and 1920s. Between 1920 and 1940, individual Mexicans, agricultural associations, and the Mexican government laid claim to over 100 million acres of Mexico's surface area for redistribution to agrarian families.[3] Agrarian and labor unrest pushed Mexican presidents, from the fiscally conservative Álvaro Obregón (1920–1924) to the more populist Lázaro Cárdenas (1934–1940), to fulfill the populist and nationalist demands of the Mexican Revolution through the confiscation and reallocation of the country's natural resources, particularly its agricultural lands.[4]

Local land seizures also had a lasting impact on foreign policy and placed ordinary Mexicans at the center of the relationship between the United States and Mexico. At the level of international diplomacy, efforts to mediate disputes over properties, particularly agrarian and oil properties, defined the relationship between the United States and Mexico in the 1920s. In 1921, the Mexican Congress laid out the process through which agrarian communities could seek redistribution of land under Article 27 of the Constitution. At the same time, the United States and Mexico agreed to establish the Special Claims Commission, a binational committee charged with settling disputes resulting from damages suffered during the revolution or property lost due to the Constitution of 1917. Oil companies also received assurances from the Obregón regime and confirmation from the Mexican Supreme Court that Article 27's provisions regarding subsoil resources would not be retroactive and that oil producers would not lose oil properties purchased before 1917. While this interpretation of the Constitution generally protected oil producers until 1938, when Cárdenas announced plans to nationalize American oil companies, agrarian investors did not fare as well. In fact, as explored in this chapter, international agreements had little impact on agrarian land seizures, which accelerated due to local organizing efforts and demands in the 1920s and 1930s.[5] This point, that ordinary people played a pivotal role in the relationship between the United States and Mexico, is an important one. Throughout this chapter I emphasize the power that Mexicans, many of them poor farmers, exercised to access land. These local land seizures had a lasting impact on the relationship between Los Angeles and Mexico as well as on that between the United States and Mexico. As historian John Dwyer argues, the power of peasant agency forced administrations on both sides of the border to respect tenets of the Mexican Constitution and limited investor options for recourse.[6]

During the several-decade period discussed in this chapter, Angeleno property owners, the Mexican federal state, agraristas, local Mexican officials, and the U.S. government clashed over definitions and uses of private property. Angeleno property owners asserted that the right to private property was sacrosanct and pressed the American and Mexican federal states to recognize and protect their position as property owners. The Mexican federal state, headed by a series of fiscally conservative executives, implemented Article 27 of the Mexican Constitution extraordinarily slowly and usually only in cases of political pragmatism. In response, agraristas, many of whom participated in the Mexican Revolution because they wanted a redistribution of privately held agricultural lands, took interpretation of the Mexican Constitution into their own hands. Local Mexican officials, at both the state and municipal levels, often backed the demands of agraristas because they wanted to build political support or because they prioritized the rights of Mexicans to use Mexican land over the rights of foreign capitalists. This matrix of local, national, and international interests led to the dispossession of Angeleno properties and rendered Los Angeles as the urban core of a transnational empire largely impotent. This chapter explores the unraveling of a city-empire through the transfer of American property to Mexicans and the Mexican state, looking most closely at the cases of the San Isidro Ranch Company (SIRC), the Quimichis Colony, and the Colorado River Land Company (CRLC). On these investment properties, which up until the Mexican Revolution had been peripheral to both Los Angeles and Mexico City, peasants overturned the imperial geography of urban core and rural hinterland.

Los Angeles investors also operated in a world where the United States had had extraordinary success in defending the rights of property owners around the world, and they reacted with utter shock that they, en masse, faced the loss of private property with no guaranteed compensation. Considering the successful history of American interventions on behalf of investors in the Pacific, the Caribbean, Latin America, and around the globe following the Civil War and into the twentieth century, their disbelief is not startling. From the confrontation between American sugar planters in Hawaii and Queen Liliuokalani in 1893 forward, American government interventions on behalf of investors were "astoundingly successful."[7] The United States was able either to protect investors and their properties outright or extract compensation for expropriated properties without significant financial damage to investors. Successful strategies ranged from overturning elected leaders, to outright annexation and eventual statehood, to imperial rule, both formal and informal.[8] Thus, when Angeleno investors specifically and American investors generally faced the expropriation of properties without diplomatic decisions about compensation, they had trouble comprehending their drastically transformed position in Mexico.

Dude Ranchers versus Squatters

One of the most striking inversions of the urban-periphery geography of power unfolded on a dude ranch just south of the U.S.-Mexico border. The San Isidro Ranch Company offered its well-heeled Los Angeles membership a vast pleasure park approximately twenty miles southeast of San Diego and within sight of the opulent Hotel Coronado. Purchased by a group of twenty-nine wealthy Angelenos in 1911, the ranch provided a rugged and undeveloped landscape for riding, shooting, and rustic living. As one member wrote to another, "I am sure that you agree with me that the chief charm of [San Isidro] is the primitive life that still exists in Mexico and it is a relief after the bustle of a new American city. My idea is to retain the simple wild appearance and maintain a real hunting preserve for real hunters."[9] Despite the pride that Angeleno city builders felt in their booming city, they also had a nostalgic longing for an escape from urban living through "primitive" experiences in a less "civilized" landscape south of the border. The purchase of the San Isidro ranch allowed members to safely indulge in their more "savage" sides in their city's hinterland.[10] For example, as the club got off the ground, founder Henry Workman Keller wrote to his friend William Edwards, "If we can get this thing started we will certainly have a fine club and some good times." Edwards replied, "Do not let us let this thing fall through, there is fun for all of us for many years yet. Don't work so hard, get fat and lazy the way I am!!! Shoot quail eat them and have a good time. Is that not a good prescription for all our ills?"[11] In particular, Edwards's response is revealing, suggesting that too much time in the urban core might result in one getting "fat and lazy," while some rigorous activity in the undeveloped periphery would provide a "prescription" for the indulgences of the city.

Precisely because rugged activities south of the border offered a prescription to the softening effects of the city, a number of prominent Los Angeles businessmen joined the club, including banker and oilman William L. Valentine, developer William G. Kerckhoff, and Automobile Club of Southern California official Henry Workman Keller. Harry Chandler also joined the club a few years after they purchased the property. Like many wealthy white men early in the twentieth century, the group described themselves in the terms of both rugged masculinity and refined white manliness; they were "wealthy sportsmen . . . [and] reputable citizens of Los Angeles, in fact among the best people in that locality."[12] Individuals purchased the right to enjoy the ranch and its activities by becoming a shareholder in the SIRC holding company for the substantial sum of $2,000 per share.[13] For that amount, they could gather at the Jonathan or California clubs early on Saturday mornings and motor south of the border with their friends. Once on the SIRC property, they bunked in the company's cabins, rode horses, hunted quail and deer, and enjoyed rugged adventures in masculinity on the property's 35,000 acres of undeveloped "wilderness." According to the club's articles of incorporation, the property was a "famous game preserve" and boasted over one million quail as well as doves, rabbits, deer, antelope, and mountain sheep.[14]

Despite enactments of rugged masculinity on the club's 35,000 acres of prime game preserve, the Mexican Revolution posed a threat to these performances as well as to the corporate and municipal power that the club's members cultivated in their urban core. Between its purchase in 1911 and its complete expropriation in the 1940s, the ranch's history demonstrates the severe restrictions on American power, particularly the power of the Los Angeles investor class, in revolutionary and postrevolutionary Mexico. Although SIRC members self-identified as members of a Los Angeles elite and as "friends of Mexico," the circumstances that confronted them in the northern territory of Baja California undermined their ability to protect their hunting grounds and investment.[15] The chaos engendered by the revolution resulted in a territorial government in Baja California that disregarded traditional property rights on the SIRC ranch in favor of its own needs. More broadly, it also resulted in a collision of two interests and ideologies—economically conservative Angelenos who passionately believed in the power of white manhood and the sanctity of private property, on the one hand, and Mexican revolutionaries and agraristas who demanded "land and liberty" and "Mexico for Mexicans," on the other.[16]

As explored in chapter 3, Colonel Esteban Cantú established himself as governor of Baja California in 1914 and set out to build a loyal personal army and improve the territory's financial situation. In addition to building military loyalty by paying high wages, Cantú initiated a period of infrastructure building and economic development.[17] His projects included a highway between Mexicali, Tecate, and Enseñada as well as the construction of schools such as the Escuela Primeria Cuauhtémoc. To fund his projects, Cantú raised property taxes to levels more than 1,000 percent of the amounts levied during the Díaz administration and charged a head tax on every immigrant laborer he allowed into the territory from China.[18] Cantú and his policies had supporters and detractors. For Mexican residents in Baja California, his investments in state infrastructure and educational programs were appealing. According to his adversaries, however, including the SIRC, Cantú functioned as a miniature dictator who overtaxed their properties; they derisively described him as Baja California's "de facto" governor and as a "soldier of fortune."[19]

The SIRC's leadership may have cast Cantú in these terms because they found his policies an affront to their position as urban empire builders. Key to this was Cantú's refusal to respect American property rights in Mexico. While Cantú did not necessarily set out to undermine SIRC members or the position of Los Angeles investors writ large, the property's owners certainly found his actions a challenge to their power in Mexico and, by extension, their historically privileged position as city builders and property owners. For example, in 1916, Cantú issued a proclamation allowing him to create military bases on American-owned properties across Baja California. At the San Isidro ranch, he began by taking over pastureland and using it to cultivate crops to feed his army. He expanded his farming enterprise on SIRC property a few months later by taking over a parcel known as El Morro, where he raised wheat.[20] He also began stationing troops on the property to oversee his agricultural projects and created a military colony known as Hacienda de Remonta. Finally, and most alarming for the SIRC, Cantú began constructing permanent structures on the property, including several barracks, a barn, and fences. SIRC owners and members found Cantú's construction of permanent barracks particularly troubling. Through a military building, the Mexican governor was inserting a postrevolutionary militia directly into a property owned by Los Angeles investors who understood themselves to be paragons of urban power.

In addition to farming the SIRC property himself, Cantú usurped the rights and privileges normally reserved for property owners and inconceivable under American traditions of landownership. He rented out portions of the ranch to local residents as pasture and farmland. He also offered pieces of the property for free to poor residents who wished to live and farm on the ranch. SIRC's Mexican attorney, a Mr. Gonzalez, traveled to Baja California to investigate the issue and reported that Cantú had posted signs informing local residents that Mexican citizens were "free to enter upon [the lands] and occupy them."[21] The SIRC superintendent reported that by the end of 1919, dozens of squatters were residing on the property. Efforts to build political support among Baja California's residents likely initiated Cantú's policies. By offering an American property for use by Mexican citizens, Cantú could build political allegiances. In taking over the property, however, he also commandeered the power normally reserved for property holders and empire builders who resided in Los Angeles.

When SIRC vehemently protested Cantú's occupation of their property, he skillfully maintained his position of power. His soldiers occupied the ranch, and he assessed that the company's only recourse was a lengthy legal and administrative process. His actions demonstrated a new imbalance of power that deeply frustrated SIRC ownership: Cantú had armed agents of the Mexican state on his side, while SIRC members could do nothing but file petitions. The company lodged dozens of complaints with Cantú's office as well as the Baja California courts. Cantú even suggested that the company file a legal case, knowing that he had appointed all of the district's judges and that they would likely decide any case in his favor. Cantú also evaded the SIRC's protests by simply refusing to acknowledge in writing that he was the one occupying their property, referring instead to "those persons unlawfully in possession of your lands."[22] Cantú also claimed that the state had the right to establish military colonies on *terrenos baldíos*, or vacant lands, under the proclamation he had issued in 1916. When the SIRC sent their lawyer to negotiate with Cantú in 1919, he promised to vacate the property at once, but as soon as the SIRC lawyer left, he moved his headquarters to the very center of the ranch and built another barn.[23] While the building may have served a practical purpose on an agricultural property, it also served a powerful symbolic purpose: Cantú could build a permanent structure at the heart of a piece of property that technically belonged to a group of Anglo-American men from Los Angeles, and they could do nothing but protest with a burst of pointless paperwork in a rigged judicial system.

In early 1920, four years after initially occupying the ranch, Cantú finally relinquished his claim on the property. Instead of returning it to the SIRC, however, he handed it over to the Mexican government, claiming that its titles were incorrect and did not prove SIRC's ownership. The Departamento de Fomento, charged with handling agricultural properties following the revolution, did not immediately address the issue of ownership of the ranch, and in this administrative vacuum additional squatters entered the property in "goodly numbers."[24] According to Keller, the Departamento de Fomento stalled around the issue of the ranch to allow local residents to continue to occupy the property. He was right; instead of returning the property to its Los Angeles owners, the Departamento de Fomento settled several dozen additional colonists on 1,700 acres of the ranch's best land.[25] Borrowing from the racialized rhetoric of civilization and incivility, SIRC owners referred to the new residents as the "horde of settlers that squat upon our lands."[26] Keller despaired because the presence of individual families meant that the company had to bring legal suits against each one to have them expelled from the property, rather than simply suing the state to regain control of the land.[27] Like Cantú, the Departamento de Fomento likely shied away from evicting Mexican squatters from an American-owned property because they wanted political support and did not want to appear to side with a foreign company.

Ordinary peasants and farmers further challenged the power of the dude ranchers from Los Angeles. Organizing among workers and agraristas was strong in Baja California, particularly in communities along the border, in the 1920s and 1930s, and likely contributed to squatters' willingness to invade and take over foreign-owned properties such as the SIRC. Agraristas in the Mexicali Valley, for example, organized into workers' associations to demand better wages and working conditions and, later, to petition for land grants. When petitions for *ejidos* failed to win support from the Department of Agriculture, groups often simply took over properties to farm or in some cases staged armed invasions of American-owned lands.[28] Although the SIRC's accounts did not record the political perspectives of the squatters who invaded its property, it seems likely that these squatters were inspired by the strong culture of organizing and agrarian demands in northern Baja.

The dude ranch, a place white Angelenos had purchased to engage in rugged leisure in their city's hinterland, remained in a state of limbo throughout the 1920s and 1930s. Colonists and squatters thwarted every SIRC effort to regain control of the hunting grounds and continued to live on and cultivate SIRC property. Feeling extraordinarily powerless in the face of a group of squatters and an unsympathetic state, SIRC stockholders continued to pay taxes on the property to the Mexican government. They feared that if they stopped paying taxes, the Mexican government would be able to officially lay claim to the property. The SIRC board also continued to offer leases to the colonists, but only if the Mexican government would assure them that they would respect their land titles. Instead, agraristas encroached on more SIRC land. The ranch manager reported in September 1931 that members of the agrarian movement, along with Mexican officials, had driven ranch employees off the property at gunpoint: "[They] have taken possession of all the houses and all they contained . . . This all came about through the encouragement given these people by the Bolshevik Governor."[29] Squatters and colonists were aware that the local government would support their cause over that of a group of wealthy Americans and seemed unconcerned with possible repercussions.[30] In fact, when SIRC members or their representatives traveled to the property, colonists, *ejeditarios*, and squatters all refused to discuss the ranch with any Americans or to "give any information to Americans as they feared they would be doing something that would prove detrimental to the above mentioned classes."[31] On the SIRC property, the revolution had overturned prerevolutionary power relationships between core and periphery. Formerly formidable foreign property owners from the urban center of Los Angeles now found themselves at the mercy of Mexican "Bolsheviks" in the periphery.

To counter the "Bolsheviks," SIRC members consciously described themselves as "friends of Mexico," hoping that long histories of investment in Mexico and friendships with elite Mexicans might help their cause. Used in the context of the early twentieth century by Anglo-American men, the phrase "friends of Mexico" also carried with it undertones of paternalism. The rhetoric of "friendship" had long denoted the extension of a fatherly white hand held out to assist a less civilized Mexico. Drawing from this idea, Keller and Chandler in particular identified their connections to Mexico and argued that "by their past acts [they had] proven themselves friends of the Mexican nation." They maintained that they knew of "no one among our stockholders who is not well disposed and friendly to Mexico."[32] The SIRC board also adamantly denied being what they described as "exploiters" in Mexico. Rather, they understood themselves as wealthy investors anxious to help develop the northern region of Baja California as long as Mexico protected their rights as property owners. If given the opportunity, Keller wrote, we would "develop our holdings to the benefit of the territory where our lands are found."[33] SIRC members even maintained that they had remained friendly to Mexico despite "very harsh treatment" at the hands of the Mexican government. In the early 1930s, both Henry Workman Keller and Harry Chandler also reminded their friends in the Mexican government that they were key players in the effort to build a highway to connect Los Angeles to Mexico City, a highway, they pointed out, that would be extraordinarily beneficial to Mexico.[34]

The property's geographic position as part of the periphery of both Los Angeles and Mexico and its location within the borderlands also proved crucial to its fate. In the 1930s, the Mexican government admitted that it had been reluctant to return the SIRC property to its North American owners because of its location directly on the boundary line between the United States and Mexico. In fact, the ranch lay within the *zona prohibida* (prohibited zone) where Mexican law restricted landownership to Mexican citizens, precisely to limit the type of foreign investment and control represented by companies such as the SIRC.[35] *Licenciado* Eduardo Cortina reported to the company in 1932 that "the fundamental objection that the government of Mexico has to recognizing the rights of the San Isidro Rancho Company is that it consists of lands situated on the border and the partners that constitute the company are North Americans. Taking into account historical antecedents, the government of Mexico does not desire to have American citizens as property owners on the border."[36] Cortina's letter referred to an understandable reluctance on the part of the Mexican government to having strategic regions of the country's borderlands heavily populated or owned by noncitizens. The company protested, without success, that it had obtained an exception to the zona prohibida in order to purchase the property. Precisely because the ranch was located in Mexico's far northern periphery where the United States had proven itself an unreliable respecter of sovereignty, SIRC investors found themselves subject to closer levels of scrutiny from the Mexican state.

Reluctant to displace the Mexican citizens now residing on the ranch and return property in the zona prohibida to Americans, the Mexican government did nothing to restore the ranch to the SIRC. Instead, in 1928, the company filed a claim with the U.S.-Mexico claims commission, requesting $108,000 in damages and lost property.[37] Under the commission, designed to adjudicate claims by American citizens against Mexico for damages sustained as a result of the revolution, American property owners had the right to petition for reparations from the Mexican government. While the SIRC waited for a decision from the claims commission, the Mexican government continued to settle Mexicans on the property. The administration of Lázaro Cárdenas increased land redistribution in the 1930s, and as a result more and more Mexican citizens petitioned for properties, including on the San Isidro property. In 1938, after the passage of Cárdenas's agrarian land reform laws, a group of colonists "without notice met on a hill of the San Ysidro Rancho and denounced about 10,000 acres of that property for *ejidos*."[38] Aware of the federal government's new approach to land expropriation and redistribution, residents of Baja California did not hesitate to apply the law and petition for an ejido. They were successful, and the SIRC board reluctantly relinquished the property and received a judgment of $73,000 in 1943.[39]

In the clash between the SIRC owners, Mexican colonists and squatters, and the Mexican government, the geography of power that had existed between Los Angeles investors and the city's Mexican periphery flipped. The postrevolutionary Mexican state at both the local and federal levels had an interest in appeasing the demands of Mexican farmers as well as protecting national interests in the borderlands. Lacking the support of the American federal government and finding their interests now running in the opposite direction of the postrevolutionary Mexican state, SIRC owners found their power eclipsed in a hinterland they had recently dominated. They recognized that they had purchased the San Isidro ranch almost entirely for recreation and leisure—they wanted a vast and undeveloped tract of land where they could escape from the pressures of urban and corporate life—but they also asserted that they owned the property in fee simple and had the right to enjoy it in any way they wanted. Finding their power incredibly reduced in the periphery, they even adopted the language of the revolution to defend possession of their property. Keller implored a friend in Mexico to explain to the Departamento de Fomento that he and his "friends are not exploiters, we are not interested in the profits that might be derived from the land . . . Our principal desire is to restore the game and indulge in hunting in season."[40] Hoping to salvage the property, Keller divorced SIRC's interests from economic gain and simply emphasized the recreational function of the ranch—to provide a place to indulge in the rugged aspects of what it meant to be rich, white, and male in the first decades of the twentieth century. When this approached failed, and as squatters and colonists continued to steadily eat away at SIRC landholdings, the company's board invoked the discourse of civilization to remind the Mexican government that the laws of "civilized nations do not permit the appropriation of private property without due action of law and compensation to the owner for the property taken."[41] Neither approach worked in the shifting terrain of power in the periphery.

Instead, SIRC members discovered a fundamental reordering of power relationships in their city's hinterland. A social revolution profoundly opposed to their presence in Mexico, their status as recreational ranchers, and their position as private property holders had restructured relationships of power in the borderlands. As one of the company's Mexican lawyers noted, "The general tendency is to favor the poor workman against the capitalist."[42] Rather than recognizing the rights of white capitalists, the postrevolutionary Mexican government favored a different social class—"the poor workman." This altered philosophy on property, outlined in the 1917 Constitution and put into practice by local agrarianists, made men like Keller and Edwards nostalgic for the Díaz administration, its support of American capitalists, and the geography of power they had enjoyed before the revolution. Edwards wistfully noted, "We sometimes sigh for the good old days under Diaz but they are gone forever."[43]

Rather than a compliant Díaz regime, SIRC investors came face to face with Mexican agraristas who believed they had an inherent right to the land to support their families. Abelino Romero, working as a SIRC representative in Baja California, reported to Keller that "la Compañía had a very serious and difficult problem . . . [I don't see how SIRC] would ever be able to get all these lands back by ejecting all the squatters and others who have applied to the government for titles to the lands they now hold and were granted provisional titles . . . These people felt that they rightfully own these properties and would die defending them."[44] As Romero observed, agraristas believed they had an inherent right to SIRC property because it belonged to them as Mexican citizens. They seemed to assert that American ownership in fee simple meant little when Mexican citizens were in need of land and entitled to parts of the nation owned by foreigners.

The Hacienda versus the *Ejido*

Within the social and political upheaval of the revolution, communities in Nayarit also laid claim to Angeleno properties, further transforming the relationship between Angeleno investors and Mexicans in the city's hinterland. In Nayarit, local Indian and agrarian communities utilized the chaos of war, the support of the military, and the backing of sympathetic local governments to reclaim lost lands. Landless campesinos made use of the distance between the ranch's owners in Los Angeles and the ranch's location in Nayarit to utilize the property for themselves. The policies and positions of local policymakers also played an enormous role in the administration of revolutionary reforms. As in the case of the SIRC, Quimichis owners attempted to maintain control of their ranch but struggled as local government officials backed agrarista petitions for and occupation of American-owned lands. And, as in the case of the SIRC, Quimichis owners and ranch managers found themselves fundamentally at odds with emerging Mexican ideas about private property and the distribution of land.

Moray Applegate assumed the management of day-to-day operations at Quimichis after the death of William Windham in 1915 and fashioned himself an empire builder. Richard Bard, who directed the company following his father's death in 1915, recalled that Applegate loved to ride his horse across the hacienda, the head of his own little "domain." He was stationed in the Philippines following the Spanish-American War and reported on native industries for the U.S. government. After the Philippines, Applegate shifted colonial locales and moved to Mexico, where he married a Mexican woman named María Pastora Perez. She owned 2,400 hectares of land near Acaponeta, Nayarit, which Applegate managed in addition to the Quimichis ranch. Although he lived in Nayarit for several decades, he worked as manager of the ranch only from 1916 to 1922. The Bard family disliked his management style, especially his tendency to ignore their directives, and fired him in 1922. Part of the problem lay in managing corporate affairs from afar.

Quimichis owners resided in Los Angeles. They distrusted their manager on the ground in Nayarit. As power shifted between core and periphery as a result of the revolution, investors found it increasingly difficult to keep control of affairs in the hinterland and often blamed Applegate, the company's imperial agent. As discussed later in this section, given the distance between Los Angeles and Nayarit, local workers and indigenous communities dealt most often with Applegate as they made demands for land.

The presence of revolutionary troops and the absence of American military intervention created the space for indigenous communities on and around the hacienda to challenge the company's land titles. For example, in 1916 and 1919, the Tecuala Indians, whose land bordered Quimichis, relied on support from Mexican revolutionary forces to challenge a land dispute that dated back to 1909. The Tecuala held a communal piece of property adjacent to Quimichis and argued that the Quimichis Company had moved the boundaries to encroach on their land. They utilized the presence of revolutionary troops in Nayarit in 1916 to regain the portion of land they had lost seven years earlier. Deeply concerned, Applegate telegraphed the company's Southern California headquarters to report, "Tecuala Indians trying to get possession part Hacienda thru Military. Have State Department request Carranza to suspend action until conditions permit fair legal defense our interest."[45] Still courting support from the U.S. government, Carranza intervened on behalf of the company and protected its property from the Tecualas' claim.

As the political terrain shifted north and south of the border, however, the Tecuala community would have more success. By 1919, when the community resubmitted their petition to the Comisíon Agraria in Tepic, Mexico had rewritten its constitution to favor national ownership of natural resources. Additionally, the war in Europe and its aftermath had fully claimed Woodrow Wilson's attention and shifted it away from intervention in Mexico. Local actors capitalized on these national and international events to challenge traditional structures of power between Angeleno investors and Mexican workers and farmers. With the assistance of Captain Espinosa, a member of the Tecuala community and the military commander of Acaponeta, the community resubmitted its claim for part of the Quimichis hacienda. Espinosa argued that the Indians had not been fairly represented in the original property negotiations and deserved the rights to a piece of Quimichis several square kilometers in size.[46] He pointed out that while the company held an agreement ceding the Tecuala lands to Quimichis, the tribe had been represented by the municipal president of Acaponeta and not by a member of the community. Applegate noted that Espinosa "admitted [the title's] probable legality but claimed that the purpose of the revolution is to rectify the injustice done by the municipal residents to the unrepresented Indians."[47] Espinosa explicitly applied the ideas of the revolution to the dispute over land at Quimichis. The revolution, he maintained, had occurred precisely to provide redress in situations like this one.

The San Felipe community also relied on ideas of the revolution and the shifting relationships of power between core and hinterland to regain access to land, and petitioned the government for restitution of its land in 1917. As historian Veronica Castillo-Muñoz documents, the indigenous San Felipe community identified the policies of the Díaz administration as directly responsible for the dispossession of their lands and the growth of foreign investment companies such as the Quimichis Company. Adopting the language of the revolution, they argued that since the Díaz administration, they had lost their land to ambitious investors in the Quimichis hacienda. They respectfully requested the return of their ancestral property.[48] The National Agrarian Commission ruled in their favor despite appeals from Quimichis management.

The power of local decision makers over Los Angeles–based enterprises resurfaced in Applegate's reports on the Mexican Congress's decision to appoint General José Santos Godínez as the governor of Nayarit in 1919. According to Applegate, Godínez was "extremely radical and a pronounced enemy to 'capital' . . . He is an extreme partisan and his following is what would be called the 'Bolsheviki' element in any other country."[49] The company complained that it was virtually impossible to get local officials to protect its property under the administrations of revolutionary leaders such as Godínez. Even if the federal government or a district court issued an edict or ruling in favor of the company, local officials simply refused to enforce it.[50] In 1925, for example, Quimichis residents received a telegram from the office of President Obregón stating that portions of their property along the Acaponeta River were designated a "federal zone" and therefore were ineligible for redistribution under Article 27. Local officials in Nayarit, however, refused to remove local residents who had already begun to cultivate tobacco and corn along the river.[51]

As the country entered a period of relative stability in the 1920s, the company feared that the Mexican state could turn its attention to implementing the property reform laws outlined in the Constitution of 1917. In addition to facing local challenges to their property rights, as in the case of the Tecuala tribe, Quimichis directors realized that they would face additional pressure from a Mexican federal government looking for strategies to implement some revolutionary reforms. Applegate, for example, recommended selling off some of the property before the "obnoxious Article 27" went into full effect. He predicted that the Mexican government would eventually divide up large agricultural holdings and redistribute them, and he advised selling off surplus land before "radical legislation" forced subdivision.[52] He assessed that the Mexican people would not abandon redistributive policies, regardless of the position of the United States, and pushed the company to unload some of its underutilized lands before forced to do so by the Mexican state.

Applegate's assessment about policy change in the hinterland may have spurred action in the core. In Los Angeles, Richard Bard and the Quimichis board decided to pursue an option to sell large chunks of the property beginning in the late 1920s. Such was the changed landscape of Angeleno imperialism in Mexico, however, that even selling off investment properties proved an arduous task in the postrevolutionary context. The Quimichis board and even some members of the Mexican federal government supported selling the property in large chunks to Mexicans with enough cash to purchase land outright rather than establishing community-held ejido lands. Although the Quimichis board desperately wanted to dispose of the property and had found well-off Mexicans anxious to buy, local agraristas vigorously objected to the sale, demanding land distributed as ejido properties. The interested buyer, José Zuloaga Vizcaíno, declared that negotiating the deal had jeopardized his physical well-being because campesinos so forcefully opposed the sale. In a report to the company's Mexican representative, Ramón Sánchez-Albarrán, he wrote, "I have put forth my best efforts, made use of all my friendly connections, and, above all, I have been calm through it all, with the idea of being able to meet a situation which could have cost me my life; for you haven't any idea of how excited the people were by their leaders."[53] Vizcaíno assessed the local political situation and concluded that communities resented the sale of Quimichis to those who could afford to pay cash. He claimed that a deadly atmosphere met him when he arrived in Acaponeta and that agrarista leaders had been actively organizing against the sale.

This understandably frustrated Quimichis investors no end. Not only could they not operate their investment property as a profitable ranch; they could not even dispose of the hacienda in the way that they wanted. Instead, Quimichis residents organized forcefully for the expropriation and redistribution of the hacienda as ejidos. Their petition took place in a shifting political climate in Mexico. Demands for the redistribution of agrarian properties fueled the popularity of Lázaro Cárdenas, and following his election as president in 1934, the Mexican state took decisive steps to break up large landholdings and parcel them out as ejidos. As part of this push, campesinos and Nayarit demanded ejido properties and vigorously opposed the sale of American investment properties to wealthy Mexicans. One Quimichis company representative reported that representatives of the communities greeted him with open hostility during a meeting. He pushed for each community to consider becoming "small farmers" rather than pursue their petitions for ejidos. They staunchly refused.

In fact, in their official petition for ejido lands, the people of Quimichis argued that "since time immemorial" their families had lived and worked as peons or temporary laborers at the Quimichis hacienda and therefore deserved access to the property. According to their observations, Quimichis owners had practically abandoned the ranch, and now its proposed sale threatened their ability to continue farming the property as they had for years and endangered their ability to provide for their families. They also referenced the rhetoric of the revolution, arguing that the policies of the Díaz administration had dispossessed them and that the policies of the Quimichis owners had negatively impacted their lives. Consequently, under the Código Agrario (Agrarian Code) they were applying for parcels of land sufficient to support their families. The representatives of almost 300 Quimichis families signed the petition.[54] In effect, 300 families in Nayarit had become more powerful than the family of an American senator and their fellow investors in Southern California.

In 1935, Albarrán regretfully wrote to Richard Bard to inform him that President Cárdenas had approved yet another application for an ejido carved out of the Quimichis property. The Mexican government's official paper announced the grant of 4,177 hectares to the people of Milpas Viejas under the provisions of the country's Agrarian Code. The ejido included 21 hectares already occupied by Milpas Viejas residents, 704 hectares of "choice moist land," 192 hectares of dry farming land, land for an educational center, and 3,200 hectares of grazing land.[55] As a result of the ejidal petitions, the Mexican government expropriated 23,000 hectares of the 30,000-hectare Quimichis property in 1935. The company estimated that the expropriated lands were worth 1,840,000 pesos or $750,000.[56] Herman Lyttle, secretary of the Quimichis board, reported, "This year the Mexican Government practically confiscated the entire ranch so that at the present writing it is evident there is no value whatever to either the common or preferred shares."[57]

Mexican expropriation of privately owned land had rendered American investments worthless.

After the confiscation, and in spite of the constitutional rule that property owners would be reimbursed for expropriated properties, the Quimichis owners held little hope that they would see compensation. Bard wrote despairingly, "We of course have made a legal protest to the Government of Mexico and have demanded that the land either be returned or compensated for but as everybody knows such a protest will avail nothing and we consider the property as having been confiscated. Therefore, it is our opinion that the stock of Quimichis Colony is worthless."[58] A few years later, after the company had filed a claim against the Mexican government, they hoped cautiously to receive $100,000 of the $285,000 they had requested.[59]

Local communities continued to take over pieces of the company through the 1940s. In 1942, for example, José Sainz claimed 1,500 hectares of prime agricultural land as *terrenos baldíos*, or unclaimed public land. The section, known as Las Flores, was located just down the river from the Quimichis Company headquarters. Applegate, sent to oversee the surveying of the ranch for expropriation, urged Bard to dispute Sainz's claim, arguing that they could sway the local agrarian engineer in their favor.[60] Local residents, however, had made good use of the property while its owners were absent. Pablo Hernández, the former Quimichis foreman, lived in the company headquarters building with his family. Other families from the area occupied additional rooms in the building and utilized land around the headquarters complex to farm.[61] Local residents also occupied all of the buildings surrounding the headquarters, including warehouses and the former mill.

Ultimately, the Quimichis ownership expressed disappointment in the failure of their own government to protect their right to private property as it had done so successfully in other nations where American investors faced economic challenges. Correspondence between Moray Applegate and Richard Bard articulated profound dissatisfaction with what they perceived as the acquiescence of the United States to the demands of Mexican peasants. Rather than intervening to ensure that American citizens preserved their property, the U.S. government refused to intervene militarily, negotiated nominal reparations from Mexico, and eventually announced a new era in U.S.-Mexico relations in the form of the Good Neighbor Policy, discussed in more depth in the next chapter. The impact of the revolution, also discussed in more detail in the next chapter, had reshaped the relationship between the two nations. As Applegate commented bitterly in 1943, he considered it useless to appeal to either the U.S. or Mexican government because neither side would be willing to risk any action that might "dispel the happy illusion of our diplomats that there exists perfect harmony under the 'good neighbor policy.' Of course we all know that all will be sweet and lovely as long as Mexico gets what she wants and has to concede nothing. The first time we refuse to give them what they want we will again suddenly become 'El Coloso del Norte' threatening them with our policy of 'imperialism.'"[62] In Applegate's assessment, Mexico held the power in the relationship between the two nations. It wielded the epithet "imperialism" as a weapon to win demands from the United States. Both Appleby and Bard noted with embarrassment and chagrin that the United States had bowed to the Mexican people and the Mexican state. While the revolution and new land policies had certainly not achieved complete economic equality or overthrown capitalism in Mexico, Mexican peasants had successfully forced a well-connected American company to cede its lands to organized campesinos. And the powerful "Coloso del Norte" had decided not to intervene in any meaningful way on behalf of its citizens and the former owners of private property in Mexico. Mexican agriculturalists had proven more powerful than the Los Angeles investor.

Harry Chandler versus Presidents Obregón and Cárdenas

Other Los Angeles capitalists utilized relationships with elites in a Mexican center of power—Mexico City—to try to salvage and defend their properties south of the border. In the context of postrevolutionary Mexico, Harry Chandler, a paragon of self-made Angeleno capitalism, turned to a revived sense of class-based and core-to-core brotherhood in an attempt to protect his substantial interests in the Colorado River Land Company. While also a member of the SIRC, Chandler was likely more concerned with his other sizable financial investments south of the border than with the fate of the hunting club. Taking a different approach than SIRC members and the Quimichis Colony, Chandler tried to leverage power in Mexico through alliances with postrevolutionary Mexican executives. Observing the changing core-periphery relationship, Chandler assessed that building relationships with the seat of power in a Mexican core might serve to protect the investments he had made in his city's borderland periphery.

As a result, Chandler set to work in a different geographic and political plane than his Quimichis or SIRC associates. Rather than just negotiating with local power brokers and elected officials in the Los Angeles periphery and borderlands, he cultivated relationships directly with the seat of Mexican power, the presidency and Mexico City. Remarkably, Chandler counted every Mexican president from Porfirio Díaz (1876–1911) to Abelardo Rodríguez (1932–1934) as personal friends. When Álvaro Obregón (1920–1924) traveled to Los Angeles, for example, he stayed at Harry Chandler's home as his personal guest. The two men became friends in 1919, just before Obregón assumed the presidency. Although they had conflicts over the course of their fifteen-year friendship, the two men were very close. Chandler described Obregón as "my consistent and fine friend" and as having the utmost "confidence in his ability and patriotism."[63] Chandler lobbied for the United States to recognize Obregón's government from 1920 to 1923, and he and his wife and daughter traveled to Mexico City in 1924 to attend the inauguration of Obregón's hand-picked successor, Plutarco Elías Calles (1924–1928).[64] Chandler and the CRLC had also championed Mexican sovereignty and water rights along the Colorado River because their Mexican property needed irrigation waters provided by the Colorado. As the Mexican Revolution waned and the country settled into its postrevolutionary phase, Chandler and the CRLC hoped that these types of personal relationships—alliances between elite power brokers on both sides of the border and in geographic capitals in the United States and Mexico—would shield them from agrarian movements and confiscatory policies such as Article 27.

As is evident in the postrevolution history of the CRLC, however, economic power in the United States and political alliances between Chandler and a series of Mexican presidents did little to protect American-owned lands in Baja California. Chandler built close friendships with postrevolution Mexican presidents, agreed to finance development projects in Baja California, and even agreed to a colonization plan that would sell off CRLC holdings in small parcels to Mexican campesinos. Despite these efforts, his company failed to protect its holdings from expropriation. The experiences of the CRLC also demonstrate how the Mexican federal government could utilize Article 27 and the threat of expropriation to extract economic investment and political support from American investors. Despite the position of men like Chandler—white, wealthy, American, and politically well connected—the Mexican state was able to leverage significant concessions from investors hoping to hold onto their properties in the context of postrevolutionary Mexico. For example, in the 1920s, Obregón, who did not support expansive land expropriation programs, nevertheless used them as a tactic to leverage Chandler's support for other projects. In other words, as Chandler appealed to several postrevolution Mexican presidents and tried to build friendships based on development plans that he argued would benefit Mexican citizens, he and his fellow Los Angeles–based investors often found their friendships leveraged against them. Alliances built on a shared position of power did not necessarily result in the protection of American-owned properties. Instead, Los Angeles–based investors such as Chandler found themselves answering to the demands of their Mexican friends and colleagues.

As discussed previously, the interwar period was relatively profitable for the Colorado River Land Company. Sheltered from the worst violence of the revolution, Baja California enjoyed an economic boom created by a tremendous global demand for cotton. As this demand spurred steadily rising cotton prices, the CRLC leased out large tracts of its property for cultivation by individual growers. Most of these growers were Americans who had the resources to lease and cultivate up to 10,000 or 12,000 acres. They also assumed the costs of improving the properties they leased. Chinese immigrants filled an intense need for laborers in these vast cotton fields.[65] High cotton prices in 1923 and 1924 brought the syndicate some of its first significant returns since they had invested in the property twenty years prior.[66]

A population boom in the Mexicali Valley in the early 1920s, however, also brought new settlers to the Colorado River delta, some of whom settled on CRLC land. Emboldened by the Constitution of 1917, families looking for agricultural land simply moved onto undeveloped pieces of the CRLC property and began farming. By March 1921, more than seventy families were squatting on CRLC land.[67] According to historian Dorothy Kerig, these families fully expected Mexico's new land policies to challenge the CRLC's titles and uphold their right to portions of the ranch. As in the case of the Quimichis Colony, groups of peasants on and around the CRLC also called for the Mexican federal government to begin carving the enormous investment property into ejidos. And, as in the case of the SIRC and the Quimichis Colony, the Los Angeles owners of the CRLC found the presence of squatters and their inability to remove them, despite their position as wealthy Angelenos, extremely unsettling. As Chandler watched squatters eat away at his property, profits, and power, he hoped that a friendly alliance with Mexico City and Mexico's president would help him retain power in the hinterlands and regain control over his borderland property.

In the seat of power in Mexico City, however, the country's executive had alternative development plans. President Obregón likely cultivated a friendship with Chandler based on a shared position as power brokers and to leverage Chandler's support for an Obregón-driven national agenda. A

The Lopez family rented land from the Colorado River Land Company and raised cattle, early twentieth century. Colorado River Land Company Collection, Sherman Library.

political and economic conservative, Obregón believed that economic development in Mexico required private investment. For example, he appointed a succession of pro-business governors in Baja California—Salazar, Balarezo, Ibarra, and Rodríguez—to succeed Cantú. Obregón also believed that Mexico needed foreign investment and did not hesitate to utilize his friendship with Chandler to solicit Angeleno capital. In 1921 he extended an invitation to Chandler to visit Mexico City and discuss how his administration and the CRLC could cooperate to promote economic development in Baja California.[68] Chandler replied that he and Henry Workman Keller planned to travel to the Mexican capital together to discuss American capital and Baja California with Obregón in person.[69] A few years later, Chandler tried to leverage banking interests in Los Angeles and San Francisco to financially support development projects directed by Obregón.[70] Powerful elites on both sides of the border saw a postrevolution opportunity to leverage an alliance based in overlapping economic interests for personal and

Against Capital and Foreigners   163

political gain. What Chandler did not realize, however, was that he would lose.

Chandler eagerly cultivated this friendship with Obregón, assessing that an alliance based loosely on shared political and economic power would be the best way to maintain the CRLC property. He and Obregón shared an interest in protecting Mexico's water rights along the Colorado River, and both supported infrastructure development in Baja, including a railroad, a port, and roads.[71] In particular, Obregón hoped to attract foreign investors to construct a rail line from Mexicali to the bay of San Felipe on the Gulf of California. In 1921, he asked Chandler and the CRLC to spearhead the effort. Chandler responded that the CRLC did not have the resources to tackle the project but promised Obregón to find investors in Los Angeles and Washington, D.C., to finance the line. Chandler worked on piecing together financing for the railroad throughout the early 1920s. He reported regularly to Obregón on his progress and always presented a positive spin on his efforts.[72] Chandler also lobbied the U.S. government to recognize Obregón's government. The United States refused to acknowledge his presidency until he made concessions regarding Article 27, particularly for the oil industry.

The relationship between Obregón and Chandler unfolded against and contributed to a broader terrain of improving U.S.-Mexico relations in the 1920s. In 1920, Wilson refused to recognize Obregón's administration as leverage to win protections for U.S. investors from Article 27. When Harding assumed power the following year, he followed this precedent. While corporate interests like NAPARM had cooled their jingoistic calls for an invasion of Mexico, they still sought a solution to conflicts over American investment properties. Both administrations saw benefit to an agreement to resolve these conflicts and met in Mexico City in 1922 and 1923 to hammer out the details, eventually known as the Bucareli Treaty. The agreement established the claims commission to oversee awards for damages sustained during the revolution and gave assurances that Article 27 would not be applied retroactively in the petroleum industry. In return, the United States agreed to recognize the Obregón government.

Chandler's desire to see the United States recognize Obregón's government, which he hoped would in turn protect his own investments in the postrevolutionary period, was so intense that he regularly ferried information from Washington, D.C., to Mexico City via Los Angeles throughout international negotiations in the early 1920s. For example, drawing from information given to him by a source in Washington, Chandler wrote a letter marked "personal and confidential" to Obregón in May 1923 just as

General Álvaro Obregón, far right, and Harry Chandler, second from right, discuss the extension of a railroad line in Baja California, undated. Colorado River Land Company Collection, Sherman Library.

the two nations were deep in talks. Although he would later claim that it was "very much out of place for any foreigner having interests in Mexico to mix up in the politics of [Mexico]," he assessed that his friendship with Obregón might protect his interests, that he needed the United States to recognize Obregón, and that he would do whatever was necessary to make that happen.[73] To accomplish this, Chandler alerted Obregón to exactly what the U.S. government would agree to so that he would "have it in hand at the earliest possible moment that it may enable you to give the subject consideration so that in the event such a question arises you will have advance confidential knowledge of it." Realizing the unauthorized role he was playing in international treaty negotiations, Chandler closed the letter to his friend, "You will understand, my dear President Obregon, that this is entirely confidential and I ask that in whatever use you may make of it that my name shall on no account be connected with it."[74]

At the local level, however, agrarian activists pushed back against influential elites north and south of the border and demanded immediate land reform in the territory. In 1922, for example, former revolutionary colonel Marcelino Magaña y Mejía organized campesinos to petition for parcels of irrigated land. Mejía also organized invasions of private property to

Against Capital and Foreigners 165

underscore the farmers' demands. His strategies included revolutionary rhetoric regarding land; he argued that property owned by foreign companies actually belonged to the Mexican nation.[75] In response to peasant organizing, and perhaps to motivate Chandler, Obregón expropriated three pieces of CRLC land and appointed a governor who appeared more sympathetic to the campesino demands.[76] Obregón's move seemed more a political strategy to prove he meant business to Chandler than a decision in sympathy with the rights of Mexican peasants.

Obregón's strategic actions spurred Chandler's desire to have an even closer working relationship with Mexico City and the Mexican executive. Although the friendship might be an uneasy one based loosely on the considerations of realpolitik, it moved both men toward results in Baja California. Hoping to appease the agraristas with at least temporary access to CRLC lands, Obregón used the expropriations to leverage further work on the rail line. Although the project seems reminiscent of Porfirian-era railroad concessions, Obregón maintained far more political leverage over the project in the postrevolutionary context. He communicated regularly with Chandler about financing for the proposed route and insinuated that a successful railroad could help protect the CRLC from encroachments on its land. Worried that the expropriations set a dangerous precedent, Chandler acquiesced and began aggressively recruiting investors for the railroad. For example, in 1922 he organized a large banquet to bring together Los Angeles–based investors, particularly the Los Angeles Chamber of Commerce, and representatives of the Obregón administration.[77] An Obregón aide reported to the president that he understood the event as an honest effort on Chandler's part to raise the investment capital necessary to build the railroad.[78] Obregón's aide also noted that the banquet brought together exactly the type of businessmen with which the Mexican executive hoped to cultivate relationships. The aide also pointed out, however, that the Los Angeles business executives gathered at the meal demonstrated "a vehement desire to resume official relations between the two republics without any conditions affecting [Mexico's] national honor."[79] In other words, Los Angeles investors, much like Chandler, were willing to temper their imperial tone of the previous decades and the aggressive expansion of their city's periphery to respect their southern neighbor's honor. Such was their enthusiasm for a relationship in the postrevolutionary era that banquet attendees declared they would visit their Mexican compatriots in Mexico City within the year, and made commitments to send letters in support of

Obregón to the White House. Also, Chandler promised to publish only positive reports on Obregón in the *Los Angeles Times*.[80]

Occasional demonstrations of executive power also spurred action north of the border. While Chandler hurried to work his political connections in the United States, Obregón continued to threaten the CRLC's land titles to leverage further concessions from his tenuous ally in Los Angeles. At one point in 1922, he went so far as to sign a decree canceling all of the CRLC's titles.[81] These fairly drastic actions frightened Chandler and pressed him into a number of large concessions. Chandler agreed to invest in new industries in Baja, pay for additional irrigation systems, develop a colonization scheme for placing Mexican farmers on portions of CRLC land, and gift a large portion of the property to the Mexican government if Obregón agreed to reinstate the CRLC's titles. Chandler also continued to provide evidence to Obregón that he was pushing hard in Washington, D.C., for American recognition of the Mexican administration. In April 1923 he wrote Obregón referencing his involvement in the upcoming Bucareli negotiations, "Confidentially, I have a plan working out to make the hardest drive that has yet been made upon the Administration for recognition. I would not pretend to predict that we will win but I will say that we are getting a lot of interests mobilized to make the most effective drive we know how to make in order to put it over."[82] Chandler's efforts appeared to appease Obregón and resolve the company's troubles with agrarian reform. In exchange for recognition of its titles, the CRLC essentially agreed to reinvest any profits it earned from the property in the infrastructure of the ranch and Baja California.[83] Chandler's machinations also sought to leverage his power in Los Angeles between Washington, D.C., and Mexico City. Although Chandler was working under duress, his position as a wealthy transnational investor with relationships in the capitals both north and south of the border, paired with his long history of promoting Southern Californian interests, put Los Angeles into conversation between Washington and Mexico City.

As the Mexican federal government and the CRLC negotiated the company's future in Baja California, Chandler made sure to highlight the alliance between himself and the Mexican executive as well as between Los Angeles and Mexico. He thanked Obregón for his personal attention, his interest in the company, and his "chivalrous" dealings with Chandler himself. In a letter to the Mexican executive in 1923, for example, Chandler expressed appreciation for Obregón's selection of an upstanding representative in dealings related to Los Angeles and Baja California. Although he was undoubtedly frustrated with his friend's maneuverings, Chandler made sure to thank him for assigning a man of "honor and character" to deal with the company's complaints and for Obregón's "invariable consideration and goodness in dealing out even-handed justice as you have done in all of our relations."[84] Chandler accompanied the letter with a flattering depiction of Obregón's representative, General Manuel Perez Trevino, in the *Los Angeles Times*. The *Times* piece described Trevino as a "gallant gentleman," a "notable guest," and a "soldier of high attainment." The piece publicly put Chandler into diplomatic conversations with Obregón via the mouthpiece of Los Angeles's leading newspaper. The title of the article strategically placed Los Angeles at the center of negotiations: "High Mexican Official to Visit L.A."[85]

The alliance brokered between Chandler and Obregón, based on shared and divergent interests in the Colorado River delta, continued to protect the CRLC's holdings through the 1920s. Obregón's successor, Calles, generally followed Obregón's policies, and Obregón continued to wield a significant amount of power, even outside of the executive seat in Mexico. Obregón and Chandler also continued their close association, working together on projects to promote economic development in Baja California and the Imperial Valley. In 1925, for example, Chandler arranged for Obregón and executives from the Southern Pacific to meet in Baja California to talk about agricultural development in the region and to view the CRLC's holdings.[86]

As the 1930s opened, however, Mexican agraristas in Baja California became more vocal and forceful in their calls for land redistribution. As Dwyer argues, peasants in the Mexicali Valley organized into militant "peasant leagues, aligned themselves with national labor unions, filed ejidal petitions, held marches and demonstrations, performed political plays, voted for representatives, gathered arms, and invaded an enormous private property owned by a powerful U.S. company."[87] These organizing efforts, designed as a counter to the alliances being cultivated between the regional and national capitals of Los Angeles and Mexico City, also coincided with a more sympathetic Mexican chief executive in the form of Lázaro Cárdenas, who oversaw more sweeping agricultural land reforms.

Militant peasant organizing in the Mexicali Valley heralded the end of the CRLC's land monopoly in the region. Organizing efforts coupled with Cárdenas's presidency resulted in the compulsory sale of CRLC property to Mexican farmers. In addition to the carving up of CRLC land for sale to individual farmers, local Mexicans also organized to demand ejidal land grants as they had in Nayarit and on the SIRC property. For example, in

January 1937 a group of nearly 400 armed agraristas invaded the CRLC property demanding ejidal land grants. They described the CRLC as "a horrible company that hoarded land" and expressed profound frustration that the government had ignored their petitions for ejidos.[88] Cárdenas considered these land invasions "treasonous," primarily because he wanted agraristas to rely on his government, rather than their own organizing efforts, for land grants. Several powerful workers' organizations, however, supported the CRLC invasion, and Cardenás ultimately felt forced to concede to them. He met with their leadership and agreed to requests for land grants carved out of the CRLC property. He also ordered the Agrarian Department to conduct an agrarian census in the Mexicali Valley to assess peasant needs and authorized the establishment of a Mixed Agrarian Commission in the territory to review ejidal petitions. All of this unfolded quickly. By March 1937, the Mixed Agrarian Commission had begun creating ejidos out of the CRLC property. In 1938, the U.S. consulate in Mexicali reported that nearly all land belonging to Americans had been redistributed to Mexicans. At the end of Cardenás's presidency in 1940, the CRLC had lost 412,000 acres of its land to expropriation.[89]

Even this late in the long arc of negotiations between the CRLC and the Mexican government, Chandler continued to draw on the rhetoric of civilization, implicitly arguing that this civilizing influence had emanated from the urban core of Los Angeles to defend his company's right to private property. In a 1939 letter to one of the Agrarian Claims Commission members, for example, Chandler pointed to the work he and the CRLC had invested in transforming an uncivilized desert into a "very fertile garden spot," much as land developers had done in Southern California. In Chandler's estimation, Los Angeles–based businessmen had led the way in applying the tools of advanced agriculture and civilization to convert the inhospitable Colorado River delta into the "flower of civilization in the Western Hemisphere, if not in the world." Chandler also employed the language of paternalism to describe the CRLC's colonization agreement with the Mexican government, arguing that the company had "gathered together a loyal, efficient and highly trained personnel" to help "guide" a new populace of Mexican farmers as they took over CRLC lands. The CRLC's program, according to Chandler, had hired Anglo-American experts to train Mexican colonists and help to "form a body politic . . . and so be a source of pride to all concerned, and particularly to our sister Republic."[90] When the Mexican government reneged on colonization agreements, Chandler accused them of lacking civility and abandoning law and order.

More significantly, while shrewd, Chandler's maneuvers to establish a clear alliance between Los Angeles and Mexico City still did not protect his borderland investment. Unlike his company's cozy relationship with Díaz, a close relationship with postrevolutionary leaders such as Obregón did not protect the CRLC. Díaz had had no interest in or impetus to protect peasant interests in the valley, instead building tight connections with American investors while ignoring the needs of Mexico's agricultural workers. These types of policies were impossible following the revolution, when Mexican executives assessed that they had to meet at least some of the demands of a population that had recently revolted against oligarchies and monopolies. Straddling the boundary between the United States and Mexico and teetering between the metropolitan cores of Los Angeles and Mexico City, the CRLC became ever more forcefully pulled into the political orbit of Mexico City as a result of the demands of local agricultural workers.

U.S.-Mexican Claims Commissions

Under the Cardenás administration, every American-owned property in Mexico faced expropriation by the Mexican state. Los Angeles–based investors in Mexico certainly took this loss as an affront to their civic and imperial powers. Not only did they face the loss of private property, something they considered a sacrosanct part of their rights as American citizens, but their government had acquiesced to the government of a revolutionary nation, and, more troubling still, to the demands of Mexican peasants. Giving in to poor Mexican farmers, many of whom had participated in an anticapitalist revolution, signified a blow to capitalism, a setback to American diplomatic power, and an undercutting of American status on an international stage. Importantly for this study, the revolution and postrevolutionary policies represented the largest rejection of American commercial and informal empire building in the first half of the twentieth century.

This blow to Los Angeles investment strategies and the city's financial periphery cultivated by Los Angeles investors was negotiated at the national level. The United States and Mexico initially met in September 1923 to discuss hundreds of complaints by American citizens against the government of Mexico for damages sustained during the Mexican Revolution. The convention resulted in the establishment of several claims commissions, including the Special Claims Commission and the General Claims Commission.[91] The commissions reviewed cases intermittently between 1924 and 1934 but put all decisions on hold in the spring of 1934 pending further negotiations between Mexico and the United States. In April 1934 the two countries agreed to create a new General Claims Commission to settle all claims on the part of American citizens against Mexico *en bloc*, with the exception of claims for lands expropriated under agrarian reform programs.[92]

After the creation of the new General Claims Commission, the U.S. State Department collected information regarding the claims of U.S. citizens against the nation of Mexico for losses suffered as a result of the revolution.[93] Companies submitted dossiers of information to the State Department, which in turn passed the cases to a commission composed of two national appointees and a neutral umpire. The commission reviewed each claim, including the alleged damages, and requested monetary awards. It also requested independent audits of damage amounts in some cases and estimated that valid claims would be paid at a rate of 50 to 75 percent of the appraised value. The treaty required the commission to submit a joint report to each government that summarized the claims and the total amount of liabilities by 1937. It also required that this "global amount" be paid off by the Mexican government at the rate of $500,000 per year beginning in 1935 and continuing until the entire sum was paid. Over 3,000 Americans filed claims under the Claims Commission, of which 148 were from Southern California. In total, Southern Californians claimed $16,715,030 in damages, second only to the $33,694,430 claimed by 135 residents of New York City.[94]

These Los Angeles–based investors were particularly incensed by what they perceived to be a Mexican rejection of their generous incorporation of Mexico into the city's periphery. Both the CRLC and SIRC cases included long commentaries on their mistreatment in Mexico and anger about what they considered a betrayal of their efforts to assist Mexico. They reiterated that their projects had been investment ventures, but they also sincerely believed that their development of commercial enterprises in Mexico would ultimately benefit the Mexican people. Writing to the Agrarian Claims Commission in 1939, for example, Chandler reminisced that the CRLC's work had transformed the property from a harsh desert into bountiful and productive farmland. According to his estimate, "over 250,000 acres have been leveled, plowed, planted to crops and an irrigation system consisting of several thousands of miles of canals and levees, as well as roads, have been built to bring about this result."[95] In addition, Chandler pointed to the larger diplomatic role he believed his company had played: "Over the years we have endeavored to co-operate with successive Administrations of the United States of North America and the United States of Mexico and in every way to build up friendly and cooperative relationships between Mexico and the United States—especially those states of California and the Southwest adjacent to the United States of Mexico."[96] Chandler's letter outlined what he believed to be the role of the CRLC in the Colorado River delta—transforming a desert region into fertile farmland while simultaneously promoting friendly diplomatic relations between the United States, particularly Southern California, and Mexico. Chandler's reflections also mirrored the geography of power that his cohort of investors believed existed between Los Angeles and Mexico. In his estimation, an economic system radiated from an urban core in Los Angeles and transformed a periphery both above and below the border into productive farmland.

The Mexican state, however, insisted that Los Angeles's productive periphery be returned to Mexico and Mexicans. The Mexican Revolution demanded that property in Mexico be transferred from the hands of foreign investors, including many Angelenos, to the control of ordinary Mexicans and the Mexican state. When the U.S. government failed to protect the interests of American investors, not even friendships with Mexican executives could protect foreign investors. Companies such as the CRLC had to tally up their losses, estimate the value of the properties they were about to lose, and pack their bags for a return to Los Angeles. As they submitted claims to the joint commission, the CRLC estimated the value of their property at $6,297,208 (they paid $533,359 for the property in 1902).[97] Chandler and the remaining members of the syndicate received payments from Mexico annually from 1943 through 1956.[98] It is not clear what percentage of the total claim they ultimately received.

Both the SIRC and Quimichis Colony also requested monetary settlements, although no amount of cash was likely to assuage bruised egos, as Los Angeles capitalists had to admit they had lost to a motley army of Mexican revolutionaries. The SIRC filed a claim with the Special Claims Commission for $108,348 in 1928, but the commission appraised the value of the property at a much lower amount—$37,500.[99] Including interest and damages owed to the company, it would receive a settlement of $73,500, which Keller encouraged his fellow stockholders to accept (they had paid approximately $141,000 for the property in 1910).[100] The remaining stockholders agreed to the settlement and began receiving payments in 1943. In their claim, Quimichis investors estimated the value of their property at $284,313. The commission awarded them $201,955 in 1943 (they had paid $242,500 for the property in 1909).[101]

Conclusion

Revolutionary policies ultimately truncated the flow of profits from the periphery to the city while also continuing to lock Angelenos and Mexicans in a troubled relationship and reshaping the relationship between the United States and Mexico. This was the moment when the expanding commercial empire of the United States met its first significant challenge, and many of the American investors in Mexico, particularly in the agricultural sector, lost significant properties.

All the investors and urban empire builders discussed in this chapter eventually lost their Mexican investments, although some were able to extract great wealth before this occurred. Even if they eventually lost properties, all of the major investors involved in the three companies were wealthy men before they ventured into Mexico, and they remained wealthy men despite the confiscation of their properties. Keller and his friends had enough disposable income in 1910 to invest $2,000 each in a dude ranch south of the border, and all emerged with their wealth intact. Thomas Bard was already a millionaire as a result of his oil and real estate investments in Southern California before he bought the Quimichis hacienda in 1909. He died before the Quimichis expropriations began, but his sons and heirs inherited a sizable fortune from him despite his losses in Nayarit. Although his investments in the CRLC were hefty, Harry Chandler also maintained his status as an extraordinarily wealthy man despite the confiscation of his immense property in Baja California. At the end of his life he was estimated to be one of the wealthiest men in the United States. Doheny does not make an appearance in this chapter for a variety of reasons. Although he had been intimately involved in trying to direct American foreign policy in Mexico and actively protected his Mexican investments through the mid-1920s, in 1925 he decided to focus on his domestic assets. He sold most of his Mexican holdings to Standard Oil in 1925. As a result, he withdrew from dealings with the Mexican government and American foreign relations south of the border well before the nationalization of the oil industry in 1938. The Teapot Dome scandal and Doheny's subsequent trial also occupied much of his time and attention until his acquittal in 1930.[102]

Perhaps because peasant activism successfully undercut their investment strategies and imperial aspirations, Keller, Chandler, and the Bard family all expressed disbelief that they had lost their economic and political battle in Mexico. Those strategies had proved successful for them closer to home in Los Angeles, and it startled them that they failed below the border after the revolution. As Chandler reminisced in the 1940s, his generation of Los Angeles–based capitalists had foreseen lucrative possibilities south of the border. They sincerely believed that Los Angeles capital applied to Mexican natural resources would yield good profits for investors while simultaneously developing Mexico into a modern nation. In many ways, they encountered the Mexican Revolution with puzzlement and disbelief. They had difficulty wrapping their minds around a social revolution that had such radically different ideas about the ownership and use of property.

More specifically, the investors discussed in this chapter had trouble comprehending how a generation of generally poor Mexican revolutionaries had successfully undercut the political and economic power of Los Angeles–based investors and even reshaped the relationship between the United States and Mexico. For men like Keller, Chandler, and the Bards, personal identities were bound up in their successful promotion of their city and its hinterland. For them, investment schemes and ideas about race and civilization marked the various rings of their city-empire's geography. In this geography, power emanated from the core, from Los Angeles, and from the white elite who resided there. As revolutionary violence subsided in Mexico, and Mexican agriculturalists and policymakers alike grappled with how to remake the Mexican economy, Los Angeles investors assumed that their power, which resided in their privileged class, as well as the power of their city and nation, would continue to protect their rights to property ownership. Instead, they found peasant movements that not only could successfully challenge their investment properties but also undermine their social position. Even paternalism, so often invoked in dealings between the United States and Latin America, failed to yield the outcome they desired.

In 1910, investors such as Bard, Keller, and Chandler had little doubt they had secured stable and profitable properties and the ability to link Los Angeles to international investment. American power and economic innovation, they firmly believed, would turn the Mexican countryside into profitable properties, much as they had done in Los Angeles. Mexico had invaluable natural resources. They believed the labor force was stable, adaptable, and willing to work. The revolution, however, undermined these easy assumptions. After witnessing the impact of the revolution and the expropriation of American properties, Bard lamented, Mexico was "beautiful . . . rich in soil and rich in forests, where as the old hymn goes, 'every prospect pleases and only man is vile.'"[103] While Bard's quote likely invoked "man" in its universal sense, his use of the term may also have referred to his assessment of Mexicans who had undermined the power he and his fellow investors had hoped to wield in "uncivilized" Mexico. Instead of acquiescing to the civilizing influences of the city-empire, Mexicans had revolted—and won. Despite the state and peasant takeover of properties, however, Angelenos remained deeply embedded in their Mexican periphery. Even as they lost investment dollars and properties, they continued to maintain close connections with Mexican workers and policymakers. Any hope of maintaining a property or receiving compensation for it required carefully cultivating relationships with Mexicans at the local, state, and national levels. Angeleno investors found themselves locked in a losing war but unable to leave or sever ties with their Mexican hinterland. Some, as explored in the next chapter, also began to envision other ways to bind Los Angeles to Mexico in the postrevolutionary era.

6   Highway for the Hemisphere

∙∙

Early on the soggy morning of March 15, 1930, a crowd of 500 Automobile Club of Southern California (ACSC) staff, well-wishers, reporters, and photographers milled around a caravan of five touring cars in the courtyard of the club's headquarters in Los Angeles. Equipment for a rugged journey packed the big Fords—a portable radio transmitter, camping gear, emergency rations, distilled water, cameras and film, spare car parts, first aid kits, medical supplies, ropes, picks, shovels, gas cans, oil, tools, and a "liberal supply" of high-powered rifles, shotguns, revolvers, and ammunition. Nine men squeezed into the laden vehicles. Each wore a uniform they thought appropriate to their journey—heavy boots, khaki knickerbockers, and pith helmets. With a shout to clear the way and a rattling of motors, the crowd parted, and the caravan passed under the Spanish Colonial Revival archways of the club building and jostled onto Figueroa Street. The convoy, with the flags of the United States and Mexico fluttering from radiator caps, quickly turned southeast toward Arizona and the U.S.-Mexico border.[1]

The motorcade was also part of a project proposed in 1929 by a group of Angeleno businessmen and a team of Mexican policymakers who hoped to capitalize on a far-reaching and postrevolutionary borderlands relationship. It would be launched in Los Angeles but developed along a shared coast and proximity to the Pacific Ocean. As explored in the previous chapter, revolution south of the border and subsequent changes to the Mexican state and the Mexican Constitution that led to the redistribution of Los Angeles–based investment properties to Mexican nationals undercut ideas that Los Angeles could be an empire. The investment periphery that Angeleno investors had envisioned and bought up in Mexico no longer belonged to capitalists in the core. However, some of the same investors who lost properties to Mexican expropriation, including Harry Chandler and Henry Workman Keller, remained confident that Los Angeles must remain closely knit to the borderlands and beyond. This postrevolutionary web of relationships between Los Angeles and Mexico would take the physical form of transborder infrastructure, an eye toward commercial partnerships in trade and tourism, and the rhetoric of American hemispheric fraternity.

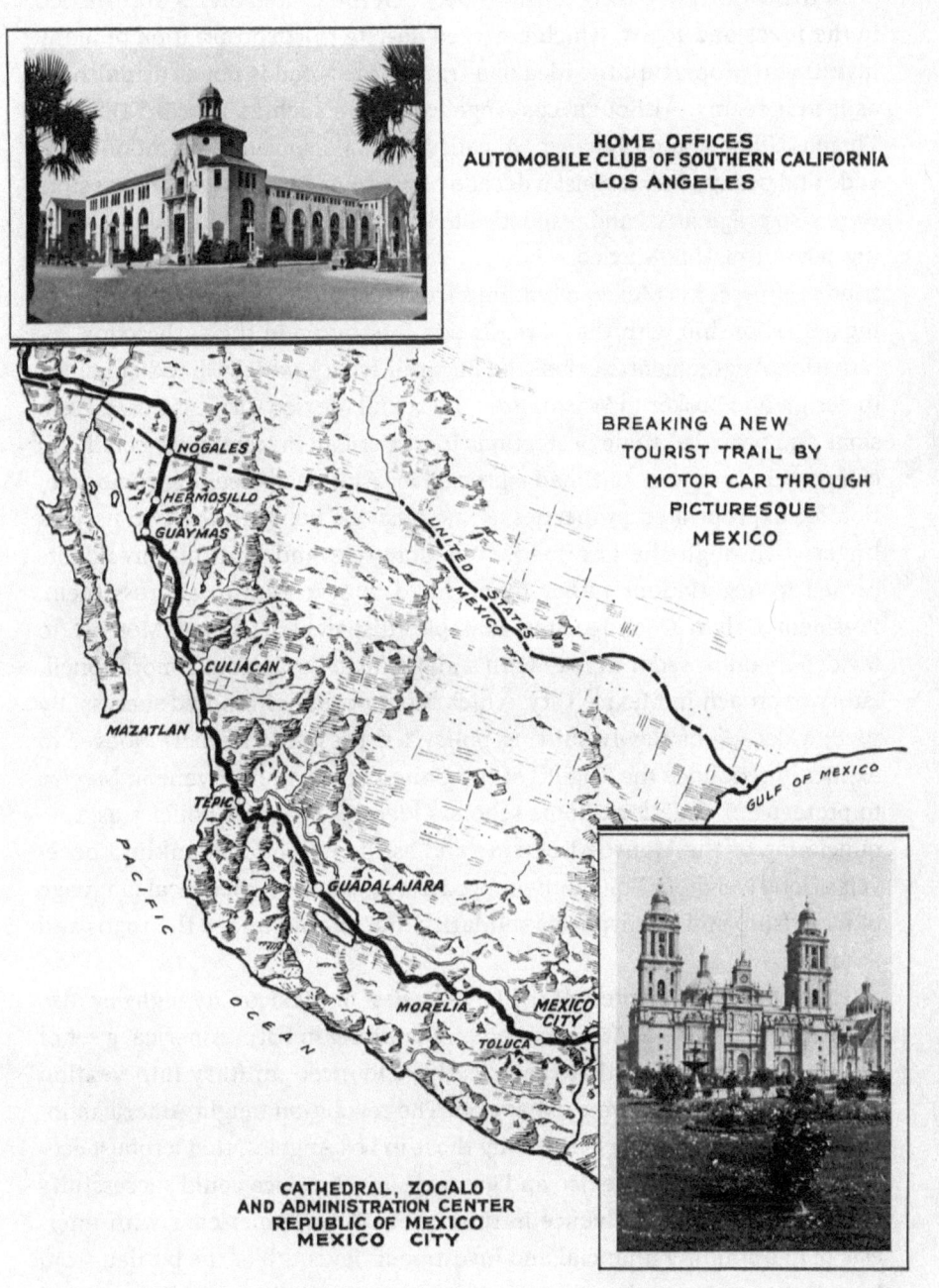

Map of the route of the International Pacific Highway from the Automobile Club of Southern California headquarters in Los Angeles to the Zócalo in Mexico City (*The International Pacific Highway: Los Angeles to Mexico* [Auto Club, 1931], frontispiece). © Automobile Club of Southern California Archives.

In the context of easing tensions between the United States and Mexico in the 1920s and 1930s, which emerged despite the expropriation of many investment properties, the idea of a transborder road is not as astonishing as it first seems. Although Los Angeles figures such as Edward Doheny, Thomas Gibbon, and Chandler led calls for the Wilson administration to invade and occupy Mexico just a decade earlier, Los Angeles–based investors were also pragmatists and responded to both their bottom line and the shifting terrain of U.S.-Mexico relations. As explored in chapter 5, Chandler tried to protect his Mexican holdings from revolutionary policies by building a relationship with the Obregón administration in the early 1920s. International agreements such as the Bucareli Treaty, which Chandler helped to design and broker in Washington, D.C., and Mexico City, also eased tensions and provided some protections for American investors, especially oil companies, or at least outlined a process for Americans seeking compensation for expropriated properties. Some tensions between the two nations lingered through the late 1920s, but Congress and multiple presidents turned to negotiations rather than armed intervention to address them. President Calvin Coolidge, for example, dispatched Dwight Morrow to Mexico as ambassador in 1927 with a mandate to implement a more conciliatory approach in Mexico City, which Morrow did with noted success. By 1928, a decade of slowly shifting policy led President Herbert Hoover to explicitly renounce the "right" of the United States to intervene in Mexico to protect U.S. investors. Some scholars identify Hoover's policies as a renunciation of the Monroe Doctrine and as the parent of Franklin Roosevelt's Good Neighbor Policy, announced in 1933, and the rhetorical language of friendship and hemispheric solidarity that characterized the 1930s and 1940s.[2]

However, the promoters of the Los Angeles–to–Mexico City highway also typified a new type of American empire building in Latin America, a set of policies and strategies that rhetorically renounced military intervention while embracing economic expansion. The revolution taught American investors and policymakers, including those in Los Angeles, that a robust economic nationalism in Mexico and greater Latin America could successfully challenge American influence in the region. Those Americans with interests in maintaining financial and investment ties south of the border, from local investors in Los Angeles to policymakers in Washington, D.C., turned instead to negotiating trade treaties, finding markets for American goods, establishing manufacturing facilities and production chains, and developing infrastructure.³ In short, the Mexican Revolution forced the U.S. government and American investors to renounce the strategies of "hard power" while they simultaneously honed other "soft power" tools of empire, including economic growth and integration, political coercion, consumption and travel, and, after World War II, an obsession with containing communism.⁴ In Mexico, many American investors returned in the 1930s and after World War II with the same aspirations they had carried across the border thirty or forty years earlier but with some new strategies, including tourism, travel, and increased trade. Their rhetoric also shifted and championed hemispheric fraternity even while they sought economic gain.

As the international tensions caused by the Mexican Revolution eased and hemispheric cooperation increased, particularly around issues of trade and economic development, Los Angeles investors and promoters and their Mexican partners reconceptualized Los Angeles and western Mexico as part of a shared Pacific alliance, one that would run from north to south along the Pacific Ocean and would promote tourism and trade. Their plan was to construct a transnational highway to connect Los Angeles to Mexico City via a road down the Pacific coastline. The road was part of the much-heralded International Pacific Highway (IPH), a 12,000-mile road linking the west coasts of North, Central, and South America along the Pacific. Initiated by members of the Automobile Club of Southern California, the nation's leading motoring association, the road began in Anchorage, Alaska, and headed south through every country in the Americas that bordered the Pacific Ocean. When it was completed in 1957, it traversed thirteen nations and became one of the longest highways in the world. In 1929, when Mexicans and Angelenos began working on the project, most of the route from Alaska to Baja California had already been paved, due in part to enthusiasm for the automobile and the Good Roads movement in the United States. As a result, road promoters in Los Angeles and along Mexico's west coast turned their attention to mapping, paving, and posting signage for the 1,600-mile section from Los Angeles to Mexico City.⁵ The highway project, promoted by several investors who had just lost properties in Mexico, demonstrates that revolution forced Angeleno promoters to relinquish many of their explicitly imperial aspirations, but they still hoped to capitalize on their proximity to Mexico. As explored in the epilogue to this book, the highway project also epitomized a new type of American empire in Latin America, one that promoted free market capitalism and globalization.⁶

In addition to reflecting the abatement of hostility and incipient strategies in a "new" imperialism of free trade, the highway project also demonstrated the ways in which Los Angeles elites reconfigured their relationship to Mexico to prioritize the movement of people, goods, and services. Promoters conceived of the IPH as a physical artery between Los Angeles and Mexico, one that would likely have thrilled more bellicose urban empire builders such as Harrison Gray Otis. It was also, however, reflective of the impact of the revolution, the shifting economic priorities of Los Angeles investors and promoters, and the broader context of U.S.-Mexico relations. By the 1920s, the city's population had boomed (again), and new industries now dominated the geography and imaginations of Angelenos. Although the city had a long history of population booms, the boom in the 1920s was particularly spectacular. Los Angeles more than doubled its population between 1920 and 1930, from 577,000 to 1.2 million. Economic growth was equally impressive, particularly in the area of trade and in industries such as motion pictures, oil equipment and production, tires, glass, aircraft, steel, and tourism. Tourism had long been a key industry in Los Angeles and saw a significant boost in the 1910s and 1920s with the growing popularity of the automobile. Boosters encouraged both residents of and visitors to Los Angeles to take advantage of the city's location and temperate weather to explore Southern California, the greater Southwest, and the borderlands via highway. The borderlands also enjoyed an increase in auto tourism from Los Angeles because of prohibition, and cities like Tijuana capitalized on this opportunity by building spectacular hotels and resorts to attract American clientele.[7] By 1929, the year that launched the IPH, Angelenos boasted one of the highest rates of automobile ownership in the nation—two cars for every three residents.[8] Finally, trade also enjoyed spectacular growth in 1920s Los Angeles, due in large part to the completion of the Panama Canal. In 1923, the Los Angeles Chamber of Commerce boasted that the city's port had quadrupled its trade in a single year.[9] By 1926, Los Angeles had surpassed every city except New York in tonnage of foreign exports.[10]

This period of remarkable growth in population, tourism, and trade in Los Angeles, coupled with more amicable relations between the two bordering nations, reshaped the relationship between city and hinterland and, to some extent, undid the rhetoric and dreams of a city-empire that had preoccupied earlier city elites and promoters. Although the borderline running horizontally between the two countries was an increasingly important and rigid political marker during this period, the construction of a transnational highway demonstrates the ways in which some elite regional promoters hoped to strengthen ties between Los Angeles and Mexico and increase the movement of tourists and trade goods along the Pacific coast. A shift away from resource extraction, an emphasis on trade and tourism, and the rhetoric of cross-border cooperation and hemispheric friendship brought these Los Angeles businessmen and Mexican policymakers together. The shift, however, did not completely undo the process of empire building but instead traded bellicose calls for military intervention for softer proposals of partnerships in tourism and lifted trade barriers across the border and along the Pacific coast.[11]

Road Builders for the Hemisphere

The IPH promoters hailed from Southern California and the western states of Mexico, embodying not just a set of relationships between city and hinterland but also a lateral relationship between Los Angeles and the Pacific coast of Mexico. The group also represented a set of regional and urban elites who used proximity to the border and distance from their respective capitals to promote the Pacific borderlands. They credited Chandler with the initial idea for the highway. By 1929, Chandler had been investing in Mexico for almost forty years and represented an Angeleno elite that had deep economic roots in Los Angeles as well as an expanding commercial interest in Mexico and the Pacific. As discussed earlier in this book, he held extensive property investments from Southern California to southern Mexico. The IPH effort was not his first attempt to link Los Angeles to both Mexico and the Pacific Rim. In 1916, he helped to found *Pan Pacific Progress*, a magazine dedicated to the "friendly development of COMMERCE among ALL countries bordering the Pacific Ocean."[12] While based in California, the magazine boasted associated editors and staff correspondents in Mexico, Japan, India, Hawaii, Australia, Chile, Peru, and China. Chandler utilized this magazine and his newspaper to promote trade around the Pacific basin, from Mexico to Japan. He believed that infrastructural development in Mexico, particularly development that promoted tourism, would have a reciprocal benefit for Southern California and the Pacific regions of both countries.

Chandler enlisted the support of his friend, business partner, and auto club board member, Henry Workman Keller, in the highway project. Keller joined the club's board of directors in 1909 and became its first vice president in 1921. He was born in the heart of Los Angeles and grew up bilingual, learning to speak fluent Spanish from the Mexican American children in his neighborhood and school. Perhaps as a result, Keller invested heavily in Mexico as an adult and used his language skills and business relationships in Mexico to promote economic ventures in the borderlands. He owned mines in Sonora and spearheaded the founding of the San Isidro Ranch Company, the dude ranch along the California–Baja California border discussed in chapter 5.[13]

Keller maintained close friendships with the two most enthusiastic IPH promoters in Mexico—Filiberto Gómez and Cayetano Blanco Vigil. Gómez served as the governor of the state of Mexico from 1929 to 1933 and also presided over the Partido Nacional Revolucionario (National Revolutionary Party, or PNR). He led fellow governors in state road-building projects, enthusiastically securing state funds and establishing road councils to oversee local and regional projects. Friends called him "the road builder."[14] According to a *Los Angeles Times* correspondent, Gómez had already built roads as flat and wide as "billiard tables" across his state prior to joining the IPH project and had extensive experience in road building.[15] Gómez founded and headed the Comisión Permanente for the Carretera Internacional del Pacífico (Permanent Commission for the International Pacific Highway) in 1930 and organized local committees to promote the IPH across northern and western Mexico. Vigil spearheaded the IPH following the death of Gómez in 1934. He was one of the founders of the Mexican Automobile Association and the head of one of Mexico's largest auto insurers, and worked closely with Keller on the IPH through the 1940s and 1950s.[16] Intensely interested in completing the highway, Vigil networked with public and private interests on both sides of the border and provided a link between the ACSC and local Mexican governments to push work forward on the road.

These networks and the shifting relationship between city and hinterland also reveal shifting demands for an imperial relationship between Los Angeles and Mexico. To promote new routes of trade and tourism, boosters relied on shared cultural interests and what they saw as historical affinities between Los Angeles and Mexico during the era of the "Good Neighbor" and a growing American obsession with Mexican history and culture. This confluence took the form of the "Spanish fantasy past" in Los Angeles, California, and the American West and *mexicanidad* (Mexico's pre-Spanish roots and identity) in postrevolutionary Mexico. IPH promoters on both sides of the border rooted their relationships in celebrating a nostalgic interpretation of Southern California's and Mexico's pre-Columbian and Spanish periods. As a number of scholars have demonstrated, the perceived exoticism of Los Angeles's Spanish colonial history captivated Anglo-Americans at the end of the nineteenth century. This fascination drew American tourists to the region and launched Spanish festivals, Spanish revival architecture, and the preservation of Spanish-era missions across Southern California and beyond. IPH promoters in Los Angeles hoped to capitalize on their proximity to the "real thing" in Mexico through the highway. For example, at the same time that he suggested the idea for the IPH, Chandler was also providing political and financial support for the development of a tourist attraction deeply rooted in the city's "Spanish past" in the heart of downtown Los Angeles.[17] As noted earlier, leisure, commerce, and tourism in cross-border communities such as San Diego and Tijuana, and El Paso and Ciudad Juárez, also grew in the first three decades of the twentieth century. As the IPH project shows, however, the landscape of tourism and the Spanish fantasy past in the borderlands region stretched far beyond the border itself—in this case, extending south from Los Angeles along thousands of miles of the Pacific coast.[18]

South of the border, Mexican governors recognized that Los Angeles's love of a Spanish fantasy past intersected with a growing national attention to mexicanidad. Built around the celebration of Mexican history and culture following the Mexican Revolution, mexicanidad paralleled the nostalgia of the Spanish fantasy past while simultaneously promoting Mexican nationalism. While not drawing on the same set of cultural, national, or racial archetypes, Southern California's obsession with a Spanish fantasy past and the growth of mexicanidad in Mexico did overlap in a common West Coast interest in promoting tourism. Although the two movements were often thought of as mutually exclusive, with the Spanish fantasy past developing north of the border and mexicanidad to the south, the construction of the IPH illustrates the ways in which both Mexicans and Anglo Angelenos sought to profit from the promotion of a nostalgic romanticization of their region's yesteryears. They believed this overlapping identity spanned the Pacific coast.[19]

This network running from Los Angeles, north to south along the Pacific coast, provided the relationships necessary to both build a road and remap the relationship between Los Angeles and Mexico in the postrevolutionary period. Chandler, Keller, Gómez, and Vigil, along with additional city boosters in Los Angeles and regional policymakers in Mexico, believed that the Pacific coastline provided an opportunity for cooperation between Southern California and western Mexico based in the rhetoric of hemispheric solidarity, cultural overlap, and the business of trade and tourism rather than in extractive industries and the language of empire. Given this belief, their focus on the Pacific coast may have also been an attempt to draw attention at the federal level in both nations away from their respective national cores and toward a western periphery. For example, the idea for the IPH emerged just a few years after the proposal for the well-known Pan-American Highway launched in 1923 at the International Conference of American States. Promoters of this highway planned to connect road systems already running through the American Midwest and have the highway cross into Mexico by way of Laredo, Texas, and Nuevo Laredo, Tamaulipas. The Pan-American Highway would span the length of the United States' central states and Mexico's central and eastern states and eventually end in Buenos Aires, Argentina.

Boosters in both Los Angeles and western Mexico supported the project to promote regional interests. The focus of both the U.S. and Mexican governments on the Pan-American Highway likely alarmed them and may have prompted IPH promoters such as Chandler and Goméz to propose their Pacific route. Although Chandler secured a letter of support for the IPH from President Herbert Hoover in 1930, it was primarily a borderlands elite in Southern California and western Mexico that designed and lobbied for the completion of the IPH.[20] The West, particularly the Pacific coast, provided the geography around which regional elites on both sides of the border could organize relationships and shift national attention to Los Angeles, the state of California, and Mexico's western states. Imbuing the highway with a providential future, *Los Angeles Times* writer Harry Carr described the IPH as the "destiny" of the West Coast.[21] Like Carr, highway promoters on both sides of the border saw historic and future connections between Los Angeles and Mexico's Pacific coast. Earnest East, engineering director of the ACSC, wrote, "The west coast is one of the most entrancing and richest sections of Mexico and is closely connected, by business and sentimental ties, with the southwestern United States."[22] In Baja California, elected official Miguel Angel Menéndez stated more succinctly, "Mexico has left the luminous wake of its potent spirit in California."[23] IPH promoters also understood the significance of the highway in the postrevolutionary period. Undoubtedly Gómez had the tensions of the revolution in mind when he observed, "I believe that we shall manage to understand each other and that this understanding will bring with it the complete disappearance of all suspicion substituting in its place an era of harmony and mutual understanding."[24]

Remapping the Borderlands

Highway promoters on both sides of the border viewed a highway mapping expedition, composed of ACSC staff and several Los Angeles–based journalists, as an opportunity not just to map the most drivable route from Los Angeles to Mexico City but also to cement a postrevolutionary network of relationships between Los Angeles highway enthusiasts and supportive political and business allies along the Pacific coast. While regional elites, boosters, and policymakers reflected on the historic relationship between borderlands regions and predicted a new era in the relationship between Los Angeles and Mexico, the practical work of remapping the borderlands region fell to this "pathfinding" expedition from Los Angeles to Mexico City organized and financed by the ACSC in 1930. IPH boosters in Los Angeles, including Chandler and Keller, initiated and organized the expedition in careful coordination with allies south of the border. They also hoped to use reporting from the trip in outlets like the *Los Angeles Times* to promote interest in the highway project. Members of the expedition included East, Carlos Ariza, the club's Spanish-English interpreter, and Carr. With an additional six members drawn from ACSC staff, the group drove some 2,000 miles, stopped in more than thirty west coast Mexican cities and towns, and met dozens of Mexican officials.[25]

Although they made brief stops at familiar borderland landmarks, including Tijuana and Nogales, the expedition quickly drove past the political boundary between the United States and Mexico and focused their attention on building relationships with elected officials further south, along Mexico's west coast. Their carefully planned trip, in many ways as much a publicity stunt as an engineering expedition, included meetings with numerous elected officials from Nogales, Sonora, to Castillo de Chapultepec, the presidential palace in Mexico City. At each stop, the "pathfinders" and Mexican businessmen and elected officials negotiated the terms under which they would attempt to knit together Los Angeles and Mexico and their countries' respective western regions.

Elected officials along Mexico's coastline were particularly welcoming of the highway because they were keen to promote tourism and believed that the success of tourist attractions in Los Angeles and border towns such as Tijuana could be replicated along the coast. In 1920 alone, over 60,000 Americans, many from Southern California, drove south to Tijuana.[26] Tourism in Mexico proved almost as alluring as tourism in Los Angeles. As noted by a number of scholars, postrevolutionary Mexican officials turned to industries such as tourism and infrastructural development, including roads, as a key component of nation building in the postrevolutionary period. In 1928, the Mexican federal state no longer required Americans to present passports to enter the country and instructed customs officials to expedite the oversight of their luggage. The government also supported Mexico's first national congress of tourism and the creation of the National Commission of Tourism in 1930. Fully aware that cross-border tourism and travel had brought thousands of Americans and their dollars into border towns, regional Mexican policymakers hoped to extend border profits along the nation's Pacific coast. Mexican officials were also not hesitant to capitalize on their culture and history to attract tourists. Federal agencies advertised their country as a tourist wonderland, "rich in romance and history."[27] Finally, Mexican officials were also cognizant of the tremendous growth of automobile ownership and travel by their own citizens.[28] As a result, Mexican highway promoters generally welcomed a partnership with the auto club, Los Angeles highway boosters, and the expedition when it arrived in Mexico in the spring of 1930.

For example, in Hermosillo, the capital of the northwestern state of Sonora, Governor Francisco Elías greeted the ACSC travelers with a well-appointed reception. He had helped the ACSC plan the trip and was pleased to see it realized.[29] The Mexican regional press also gave the pathfinders favorable coverage, following their progress through West Coast states with interest and providing readers with detailed reports on their activities. In April 1930, for example, *El Informador*, the newspaper of Guadalajara, the capital of the western state of Jalisco, published a series of extensive articles about the highway. Front-page headlines informed readers that the governor, members of the state government, the Club Rotario, the Comité Pro-Turismo, and members of local automobile associations would greet the expedition as they arrived on the road from Tequila. The paper also cautioned citizens that "the visit of these businessmen is of great importance to us and it is expected that all groups interested in the construction of roads will greet the grand idea with enthusiasm." The IPH, the paper noted, would benefit all aspects of the Mexican economy. And, in an appreciative tone, the paper noted that the ACSC travelers were "enchanted" with the beauty of western Mexico.[30]

And indeed, members of the auto club delegation were enchanted with Mexico. They packed nostalgia for a Spanish fantasy past in their tour cars next to their camping equipment and surveying tools. For example, as they traversed Mexico's west coast they brought the language of Southern Cali-

Outdoor luncheon during the IPH expedition in Mexico, undated. Automobile Club of Southern California Collection of Photographs and Negatives, courtesy Huntington Library, San Marino. © Automobile Club of Southern California Archives.

fornia's Spanish fantasy past and applied it to what they encountered. In a daily log of the trip, published in the auto club's magazine, *Touring Topics*, members of the delegation recounted their observations of the town of San Blas: "Numerous antiquities remain to testify to the quondam glory of San Blas and tourists of the future will find in this beautiful but drowsy little pueblo by the sea one of the many entrancing phases of Mexico."[31] As this observation demonstrates, members of the convoy thought that they had discovered the past in Mexico. For them and for the American tourists they envisioned traveling the IPH, Mexico provided a place to encounter the romance of the Spanish colonial past. What boosters had conjured out of the relics of Spanish missions in Southern California also existed in Mexico, and members of the IPH expedition encouraged American tourists to use the highway to hunt down a fantasy created in the United States but seemingly around every corner in Mexico. Phil Townsend Hanna, a member of the expedition and managing editor of *Touring Topics*, noted that California's mission system was better known than Mexico's, thanks to the advertising and tourism machine that transformed decaying mission structures into one of the state's most popular tourist attractions. While in Sonora, he noted for his readers that northern Mexico had a historically more significant string of missions, but that they were lesser known because they had yet gone undiscovered by the American tourist.[32]

As a number of historians of culture and American empire have argued, tourism and tourist encounters often became important sites of conflict, containment, and management of America imperial power.[33] This was certainly true in encounters around the IPH. For example, although a common history of Spanish colonization linked Los Angeles with Mexico's Pacific coast, Mexican officials were certainly less charmed by this nostalgic view, and in the context of the postrevolutionary period had the power to express it. While they appreciated the expedition's romantic view of their nation's history and natural beauty, they countered the Americans' sentimental discussions of Mexico's colonial past with assertions of Mexico's modernity.[34] Mexicanidad was not simply about a romantic past but also about nationalism and nation building. Reform and modernization, they asserted, were also part of the agenda of a generation of postrevolution political officials. Discussions regarding the highway's route illustrate this point of contention. Governors in western states agreed that the region needed more roads and that the IPH would be beneficial for western Mexico, but diverged from the auto club's commitment to sticking to the coastline. For example, during the expedition's stop in Hermosillo, Sonora, Governor Elías welcomed the party and took its members on a tour of roads he was building in the state. A borderland resident, Elías spoke English fluently and had extensive relationships with American businesses along the U.S.-Mexico border. Like his IPH allies north of the border, Elías was interested in expanding borderlands commerce throughout his state. During his tenure as governor, he aggressively promoted highway construction in Sonora and purchased the most up-to-date equipment to build an extensive network of roads for his state. While showing the IPH expedition over some of the state's newly constructed thoroughfares, however, Elías informed them that the region's most pressing need was for adequate roads to connect agricultural areas with market centers. He recognized the significance of the IPH and promised to apply some resources to its proposed route, but his priority, he reminded them, was to build a network of roads and highways that would promote the local and regional interests of the state of Sonora. Elías did, however, take advantage of the visit of an experienced road engineer such as Earnest East to discuss and compare best practices for road building.[35]

As these exchanges between Elías and members of the expedition demonstrate, the eagerness for a Pacific road and a network of relationships between Los Angeles and Mexico's Pacific coast spanned the border. Visions for the use and route of the highway, however, often rested on two different sets of desires and needs. The ACSC and the highway's Southern California backers wanted an artery to Mexico City, a road that would take tourists from the constructed romance of Los Angeles to the "real thing" in Mexico. Mexican IPH promoters welcomed the promise of tourists and their dollars but also prioritized the pragmatic needs of Mexico's west coast regions. They balanced the tourist appeal of mexicanidad with the practical need for roads.

Other governors and the Mexican press echoed Elías's enthusiasm as well as his concerns; they welcomed the road but managed plans for its route with Mexican priorities. In *El Informador*'s extensive coverage of the expedition through the west coast state of Jalisco, the paper coupled an article welcoming the American travelers with a piece announcing the route preferred by Mexico on the first page of its April 17, 1930, edition. In another article discussing a meeting with Jalisco governor José María Cuéllar, the paper highlighted that Mexican policymakers preferred the IPH to cross the Los Altos region in the eastern and more inland side of the state via San Juan de Los Lagos rather than adhering an older route that followed the Southern Pacific Railroad. As *El Informador* noted, Mexican policymakers believed the road would be more beneficial if it linked agricultural regions not already located along a railroad route to urban centers. According to the paper, members of the expedition argued that the road needed to stay as close as possible to the Pacific Ocean and could not deviate too far inland unless absolutely necessary. In response, Jalisco officials pointed out that the IPH had the potential to link one of the most populated and highly productive agricultural regions of the state to larger urban markets. Ultimately, Mexican policymakers simply ignored the ACSC's recommendation, and the IPH followed the route preferred by Mexicans. Their decision still located a segment of the road in western Mexico but tugged it eastward and away from the coast. The decision was certainly pragmatic. While celebrations of Mexican heritage or mexicanidad might attract tourists, other mandates sometimes governed road building.[36]

Regional governors also utilized meetings organized during the trip to promote Mexico's language and cultural heritage. Their efforts fit in with the desire of Los Angeles's white population to find "Old Mexico" but also served to assert mexicanidad as part of a nationalist agenda in Mexico. For example, Colonel Leopoldo Gallardo, chief of staff for Governor Lázaro Cárdenas, welcomed the convoy party for a lavish luncheon in the countryside of the state of Michoacán.[37] Gallardo refused, however, to allow members of the expedition to speak English with his guests. He politely but firmly informed them that they were in Michoacán and had to speak the local language. He had previously instructed his staff to ignore any conversation in English, and they obediently disregarded any requests for food or other accommodations that were not made in Spanish. Gallardo's language policies demonstrated that he wanted to convey a sense of nationalist pride in both his country and its language and that he had the power to remind the expedition that they were guests in a country with its own language, heritage, culture, and future. They were not colonizers, he reminded them, who could impose their own language on another country. The English-speaking members of the ACSC delegation struggled through some conversation in Spanish and finally interpreted Gallardo's language restriction as a joke.[38]

Ultimately, the expedition, which reached Mexico City late in April 1930, demonstrated the successes and challenges of efforts by both Southern Californians and Mexicans to link Los Angeles to Mexico City following the revolution and to create a strong regional network along the Pacific coast. It also served as a site for negotiation between Americans and Mexicans interested in bringing Americans to Mexico via a highway. Both groups approached the highway as beneficial to Mexicans and Americans on the Pacific coastline. Members of the ACSC expressed their enchantment with Mexico's "charming" coastline and proclaimed a historic link between California's and Mexico's west coasts based on a shared Spanish colonial past and proximity to the Pacific Ocean. Mexican elected officials along the route welcomed the expedition warmly and touted the advantages of the highway project while also countering notions of a romantic Mexico of the past. They emphasized the nationalism of mexicanidad as well as the modernization efforts of postrevolutionary Mexico. Through a road, regional boosters on both sides of the border negotiated the relationship between the United States and Mexico.

Building Mexican Roads in Los Angeles

Building on momentum from the expedition, IPH promoters from both sides of the border met in Los Angeles, envisioned as the epicenter of the highway, in October 1930 to discuss concrete steps to see the highway through to completion. While celebrating opportunities for cross-border travel and trade, the conference also reflected some of the tensions inherent in building regional alliances between Los Angeles and Mexico and along a binational coastline and constructing a north-south highway across an international border. Mexican delegates continued to voice their support of an IPH project that met the national and regional needs of Mexico. American delegates tempered some of their romantic characterizations of Mexico with the increasingly popular language of fraternity in the Americas. The location of the conference, Los Angeles, also exposed the innate problem of trying to construct a road to connect the western edges of two nations across a border that was becoming increasingly regulated and policed in the context of a crippling economic depression.

In the fall of 1930, Los Angeles was the center of xenophobic calls for the repatriation of Mexican nationals, which many Anglo-Americans believed would alleviate their own economic hardships. As the IPH delegates gathered at the ACSC headquarters downtown, however, they largely ignored local and increasingly virulent demands for repatriation. Instead, to promote their own highway agenda, both Mexican and American conference delegates launched their event with the language of trans-American fraternity.[39] For example, the conference opened with a deliberately bilingual event. When the thirty-eight Mexican and thirty-one American delegates gathered for the opening speech on the morning of October 15, ACSC vice president Henry Keller delivered his address in both Spanish and English. Drawing on the language he had learned from Mexican American childhood friends, Keller argued that Los Angeles was a border city that intimately understood Mexico's past, present, and future. Translating his original statement from Spanish, Keller explained to his English-speaking audience, "It is fitting that this Convention should meet in Los Angeles, bordering the International Line, for because of our historical background and constant intercourse with our neighbors to the South there exists a friendly status builded [sic] on mutual respect and confidence."[40] Keller spoke with enthusiasm about the ability of the IPH to unite the people of the Western Hemisphere into a cohesive Pacific entity—a lateral network of sovereign nations that would collaborate to create better lives for its citizens.[41]

At the same time, however, Keller's speech and subsequent speeches by both Angeleno and Mexican delegates ignored ideas about who could travel the road and in which direction. Presumably, Keller meant that Anglo-American tourists as well as trade products could move freely north and south along the IPH. If asked about Mexican migrants, his response might have been more tempered. By late 1930, when Keller gave his address, more than 18,000 Mexicans had returned to Mexico, many of them deported forcibly by the U.S. government. This number represented more than double the number returned in 1929 and reflected the increasingly troubled state of the American economy and the growing nativism and xenophobia of Anglo-Americans in Los Angeles and the American West.[42] Mobility, in the case of the IPH, referred to Anglo-Americans and commercial goods, and not to Mexicans.[43]

Keller's audience, however, still held men and women from both sides of the border who hoped that connecting Los Angeles to Mexico along the lateral coastline, rather than through empire and extractive industries, would benefit both Los Angeles and western Mexico. The group representing Los Angeles business interests included Keller and Chandler (as noted in chapter 2, Chandler opposed repatriation and restrictions on Mexican migration because he saw their labor as invaluable to California's agricultural sector), members of the ACSC, the governors of twelve Mexican states, and road engineers from both sides of the border.[44] Delegates from Mexico included many of the regional policymakers and road builders who had greeted the expedition in Mexico a few months before, including Filiberto Gómez, Francisco Elías, Alejandro Villaseñor, mayor of Nogales, Sonora, and Luis Pastor, head of the National Tourist Commission in Mexico City.[45] The Mexican consul in Los Angeles and the Mexican secretary of foreign relations also played key roles in organizing the conference and in coordinating with the Mexican delegates. Even Mexican president Pascual Ortiz Rubio sent a telegram to the governors of the states of Sonora, Sinaloa, Nayarit, Michoacán, Mexico, Puebla, Oaxaca, and Chiapas requesting that they attend the conference. He considered it an excellent opportunity to expand Mexico's tourism industry and highway system.[46]

The proceedings of the conference tried to highlight Los Angeles as at the forefront of American foreign relations in Latin America. The conference also reflected efforts on the part of highway promoters to create a bilateral atmosphere that recognized the importance of a Pacific relationship as well as Mexico as a nation equal to the United States. For example, as the delegates launched the conference, formalities such as appointing a conference chairperson offered the opportunity for Mexican delegates, rather than American ones, to drive the agenda. While welcoming Mexican delegates, ACSC representatives noted that the city of Los Angeles considered it a high honor to host more Mexican officials in one meeting than any time before in the history of the neighboring nations. Los Angeles, they suggested, was the capital of a hemispheric partnership. They also repeatedly

Harry Chandler, far left, and Filiberto Gómez, second from left, next to a map of the IPH during the highway conference in Los Angeles, 1930. Automobile Club of Southern California Collection of Photographs and Negatives, courtesy Huntington Library, San Marino. © Automobile Club of Southern California Archives.

deferred decisions on the structure, agenda, and leadership of the conference to Mexican delegates, insisting that this was their conference and that the ACSC representatives attended solely as technical advisers. As the conference began, Keller announced that it would be left entirely to the Mexican delegates to chair and run the proceedings. He politely declined a nomination made by the governor of the state of Mexico, Filiberto Gómez, to chair the conference and deferred to Mexican leadership. He stated that he hoped the delegates would "consider this a Mexican conference," although, importantly, in Los Angeles, and pushed for a Mexican delegate to preside over the proceedings. Mexican delegates assumed the conference's leadership positions and conducted most of the meetings in Spanish.[47]

As before the revolution, much of this alliance between Angeleno and Mexican road builders emerged from their position as regional elites; while the border was certainly hardening for Mexican workers in 1930, IPH promoters in positions of political and economic power still saw the potential

Highway for the Hemisphere   193

for mutually beneficial transnational trade and tourism. Los Angeles could act as a friendly portal to Mexico and Latin America. The explicitly imperial tone of the prerevolutionary era was gone, however. Visions of empire had morphed into desires for trade networks and commercial corridors. The three days of speeches from both American and Mexican delegates resounded with both Mexican modernity and Pacific fraternity. Elías, for example, echoed many of Keller's sentiments and proclaimed that the IPH would "bring about an additional link in the complete understanding and union of all the nations of this continent." While certainly optimistic, Elías's statement did reflect the perception that a highway could not only link the American and Mexican Pacific but could also bring about a better diplomatic relationship between American nations. Elías also alluded to the tensions that had historically strained the U.S.-Mexico relationship but argued that the IPH would help the two countries transcend those conflicts. Mexicans, he noted, had their own traditions and culture, as did Americans, but the highway would "serve to bring about a mutual understanding."[48] Like Elías, most of the Mexican delegates diplomatically reminded their American audience to get to know postrevolutionary Mexico and Mexicans, ideally via the IPH. Cultural sensitivity and understanding, facilitated by transnational infrastructure such as highways, would help Americans fully appreciate their southern neighbors.

Angeleno conference organizers also reassured Mexican delegates that a lateral relationship would not replicate prerevolution patterns of American investment in their country. During conference proceedings, they reiterated that the ACSC and affiliated Los Angeles investors had no direct financial interest in promoting the IPH and would not attempt to dictate the route, construction, or use of the highway. In an effort to allay the suspicion expressed in the Mexican press, for example, club representatives emphasized that their interest in the highway stemmed from a desire to promote good trade, international neighborliness, and transnational tourism. The club's status as a nonprofit organization, Keller stated explicitly, prohibited it from making loans or investing in for-profit enterprises in Mexico. Their interest was solely to promote international tourism between Southern California and Mexico and to enjoy the auxiliary profits that a booming tourist industry would bring to Los Angeles. In many ways this reflected the prerevolutionary alliances between Mexican and American borderland elites, often based on common class interests.[49]

Governor Gómez repeated the sentiment from a Mexican perspective, reiterating that the IPH could benefit the Pacific coast regions of both countries but without reestablishing American imperialism in Mexico. In his address to the convention he stated unequivocally, "Mexico, a young and pushing country, is open rather to spiritual conquest by men of good faith than to capitalistic colonizing. We are eminently understanding and understandable to whoever comes with his mind made up to understand us and respect us in the sacred spot of our nationality."[50] For Gómez and Mexico, Los Angeles–Mexico and north/south infrastructural partnerships that brought tourists to his nation were acceptable; imperialism was not. Nevertheless, Gómez seemed to believe Angeleno assurances of goodwill and neighborliness. During the conference he sent a telegram to President Ortiz Rubio stating that the gathering represented a group of Americans sincerely interested in assisting Mexico in expanding its tourism industry.[51]

Following the conference meetings, organizers hoped to promote their Pacific interests and cement friendships between Mexican and Los Angeles delegates through a road trip across Southern California and a brief excursion to Baja California. In a luxury bus, conference delegates toured the local Pacific coast from Los Angeles to San Diego and Tijuana, returning along an inland route through Calexico, the Salton Sea, and San Bernardino. These locations also gave the ASCS representatives a chance to indulge in the Spanish romanticism that they associated with Southern California. They again drew on the region's fantasy past to demonstrate to Mexican delegates what they considered the historic and spiritual connections between the two regions. As they had pointed out during the expedition's trek through Mexico, IPH promoters used this imagined past to envision a future that would bind Southern California and Mexico along the Pacific.

In his coverage of the road trip, for example, Harry Carr noted that Mexican delegates were "tickled pink" when the expedition stopped for lunch in San Clemente and found that the "illustrious caballero, Don Ole Hanson, has built a beautiful Spanish city where all other architecture is forbidden. It also impressed them to notice the names of the towns as they dashed by—Balboa, Laguna, San Juan Capistrano, San Clemente, San Luis Rey, La Jolla, San Diego—the flavor of Old Mexico."[52] Although told from the perspective of an American journalist fully invested in the fantasy of California's Spanish past, Carr's reporting on the trip suggested that Mexican delegates found the landscape and architecture both familiar and intriguing. They discussed the many ways in which Mexico's history and landscapes would appeal to American tourists already familiar with Southern California and would strengthen the Mexican tourism industry. Reflecting on a day of travel with the expedition, Carr reflected, "It has been a day of riding along new pavements laid on top of old, old trails."⁵³ In other words, the IPH may have been new, but its Spanish past had led directly to a prosperous Mexican and American future.

When conference members reached Tijuana, they paused to meet with Baja California officials, relax in a deluxe tourist resort, and toast the success of the highway and amicable relations between the two nations. In language that dramatically reversed the saber rattling of interventionists such as NAPARM members, Carr enthusiastically observed, "When the Americans are not standing up toasting health, wealth and joy to President Ortiz Rubio, the Mexicans are standing up toasting President Hoover. At the end of the dining room are the Mexican colors flanked on both sides by the Stars and Stripes. Mexicans who can't speak English are exchanging heart beats of eternal friendship with Americans who have no Spanish."⁵⁴ In spite of language barriers and their varying interests in road building, delegates eagerly celebrated the new relationship they were forging between the United States and Mexico. Indulging in the links between Southern California and western Mexico rooted in a common Spanish past and the promotion of tourism allowed the conference delegates to ignore the racialized hardening of the border by focusing on the movement of Anglo-Americans and American and Mexican goods along the proposed highway.

Notwithstanding promises of eternal friendship, the conference delegates still had to grapple with the impact of the Depression and U.S. immigration policy when they arrived back in Los Angeles a few days later. Fully cognizant of repatriation efforts at the federal level, many of them supported by Los Angeles elected officials, Mexican delegates to the conference utilized their time in the city to promote Mexico to Mexican Americans and Mexican nationals residing in the United States. Mexican delegates, including Gómez, used their visit to Los Angeles to speak directly to an audience of workers that they hoped would return to postrevolutionary Mexico. For example, in an interview with Los Angeles's Spanish-language newspaper, *La Opinión*, Gómez argued that the IPH would help to reconnect Mexican expatriates to a homeland that needed and valued their labor. Gómez invoked the movement of Mexicans and Mexican Americans along the highway, but only in a southward direction. In his state of Mexico, for example, Governor Gómez noted, probably optimistically, that there was no problem of unemployment. Echoing the sentiment of the Mexican federal government as well as the Mexican consul in Los Angeles, Gómez urged *La Opinión*'s readership to consider returning to Mexico, utilizing one of the new highways that connected border towns to the country's interior.⁵⁵ "In the

State of Mexico," Gómez maintained, "everyone has an occupation and misery does not exist."[56] Interestingly, some of the Mexican delegates may also have discouraged Mexican nationals from utilizing the IPH to enter the United States. As Kelly Lytle Hernández found in her study of the U.S. Border Patrol, many Mexican officials along the international boundary actively discouraged Mexicans from crossing illegally into the United States in the late 1920s and 1930s.[57]

Gómez's statements at the IPH conference illuminate how discussions of the Los Angeles–Mexico City highway and hope for continued connections between Los Angeles and a Mexican hinterland intersected with a severe economic depression, American racism, and repatriation, as well as the increased monitoring of the U.S.-Mexico border in the 1920s and 1930s.[58] Gómez hoped that Mexican nationals and Mexican Americans would utilize cross-border infrastructure to travel south, escape American racism, and help rebuild Mexico. Albeit implicitly, Anglo-American IPH promoters emphasized the flow of presumably white tourists and American dollars southward, rather than the movement of Mexican workers into California. With anti-Mexican sentiment running high in Los Angeles and other southwestern cities, Anglo-American and Mexican IPH promoters were hesitant to underscore the obvious—that the road might well be used by Mexican migrants in the labor and economic circuits between the American Southwest and the Mexican North. While both Mexican and American IPH promoters could tout the lofty notions of hemispheric fraternity, very different notions of who could and would move between the two countries ran beneath the surface of the conference proceedings.

Participants may have wanted the highway to bisect the international border and unite the western coasts of the United States and Mexico, but in reality the border was becoming increasingly rigid and policed, limiting the movement of Mexican nationals and even Mexican Americans between the two nations. Gómez's statement during a conference speech may have contained both a critique of U.S. border policy in 1930 and a hope regarding what the IPH could offer as an alternative: "Humanity's laboratory is in America but in order that America fulfill its historical destiny it is necessary that America be a . . . unity of wills, and a confederation of free peoples . . . International highways blot out frontiers . . . AMERICA FOR HUMANITY."[59]

As Gómez's hopeful proclamations in the fall of 1930 reveal, IPH promoters did not comprehend the deep and lasting impact that the economic crash of the previous year would have on their two nations and their road.

While economic conditions were less severe south of the border, both the United States and Mexico faced the problems of an economy in free fall, including rising unemployment and a decline in the activities that IPH promoters cherished most—international tourism and trade. Nevertheless, the promoters pushed forward following the conference in Los Angeles. Angeleno highway supporters likely believed that the IPH could attract tourists from around the nation who still had the resources to travel and that Los Angeles should fight to remain the "gateway" to Latin America. Indeed, historian Helen Delpar argues that the "enormous vogue of things Mexican" reached its apex between 1927 and 1935. Improved diplomatic relations between the two nations as well as an Anglo-American fascination with the "primitive" element of Mexico attracted a significant amount of attention from tourists, and Los Angeles still wanted to capitalize on this. Despite the deepening Depression, Americans spent $33 million in Mexico in 1933, representing 17 percent of all American dollars spent on foreign travel that year.[60] Angeleno boosters eyed that amount jealously. If Mexico still attracted tourists, they were determined that Los Angeles would provide the point of departure. While simultaneously supporting "bum blockades" and advocating repatriation, organizations such as Los Angeles's All Year Club (established to promote tourism in Southern California) also declared that the city continued to welcome wealthier tourists.[61]

So, notwithstanding the Depression and the unstated implications about who could and would travel the IPH, or in what direction, both Mexican and American delegates deployed the rhetoric of hemispheric friendship rather than empire to push for the road's completion and used the setting of the conference to identify concrete next steps. While still in Los Angeles, Mexican delegates organized a formal International Pacific Highway Association to advance the project. They also voted unanimously to lobby their federal government for funds for each state to complete their respective portions of the highway. They also agreed to reconvene in Mexico the following month to continue planning logistics for the project. Finally, they telegraphed President Ortiz Rubio to inform him of their progress and to call for his support of the IPH. Presumably, both American and Mexican delegates returned home pleased with their progress. Their road, which built on old connections between city and hinterland, also reflected a new lateral relationship between Los Angeles and Mexico and felt well under way to completion.[62]

Building a Los Angeles Road in Mexico

Mexican participants in the IPH conference pursued road building with zeal upon their return to Mexico. Their enthusiasm, however, often bumped up against the more local interests and concerns of towns and communities in postrevolutionary western Mexico. The efforts of Gómez, elected president of the Comisión Permanente for the Carretera Internacional del Pacífico (Permanent Commission for the International Pacific Highway), characterized these tensions among local, regional, and transnational interests. While in Los Angeles, he organized a follow-up meeting of the delegates in December 1930 in Mexico City and from there launched an aggressive campaign to see the road to completion.[63] He organized local IPH committees, regularly traveled the west coast of Mexico to inspect progress on portions of the highway, and initiated a press campaign to build support for the road.[64]

As Gómez traversed Mexico's west coast, he discovered the tensions inherent in mobilizing communities hundreds or even thousands of miles away from Los Angeles to construct a Pacific-based highway. Local officials and policymakers supported the idea in theory, but also prioritized municipal or state needs over those of IPH promoters. In Magdalena, Jalisco, for example, Gómez called together a meeting of the mayor, various municipal officials, and the chamber of commerce to organize a *comité local* for the IPH. The new comité noted that their city lacked any reliable system of transportation or communication and enthusiastically supported the IPH project as a solution to this problem.[65] Their immediate need, however, was for a more reliable network of regional highways that would link Magdalena with market centers in the state. When questions of how to allocate funding arose, local and state officials often prioritized these needs over constructing what was seen as a tourist route from Los Angeles.

Gómez's meetings with communities in Nayarit also reflected the tensions between regional interests and the IPH. According to the local press, "The announcement of the construction of the IPH has awakened an interest in all of the local population because it will benefit them directly and the authorities and local population have offered their help and all kinds of items for the work."[66] As this quote reflects, the idea of the IPH generated enthusiasm but local interests also reiterated local priorities. They asked the question about which parts of the road project would "benefit them directly." Although aware that the road would eventually connect the region with California, most of the local IPH commissions identified the local needs that road building would fulfill. El Comité Local de Guadalajara reported to Mexico City, "[This work] is of great importance to this region . . . Everyone here recognizes its importance."[67] The IPH represented something important to officials in Guadalajara, but regional interests trumped those of the IPH promoters. This emphasis on state and national interests likely reflected the nationalism and state-building aspirations of the postrevolutionary Mexican state. As a number of scholars have noted, postrevolutionary federal administrators promoted roads at the regional and national levels as a strategy for strengthening the national government and connecting a nation torn by factionalism and a long revolution. In other words, roads often served a national purpose, not a transnational one.[68]

Gómez tried to address this tension between local and regional interests and the completion of a coastal highway in his own state. In his annual gubernatorial report, published in the state of Mexico's official newspapers, he devoted a significant amount of space to reporting on his activities and what he believed a Pacific coast highway might offer his constituents. He noted that during the Los Angeles meeting and the subsequent IPH meeting in Mexico City, Mexican IPH delegates had agreed, with "great enthusiasm," to finish construction of the highway as quickly as possible, alluding to the fact that Mexican IPH promoters saw value in a trans-state coastal highway that provided the connective tissue between Los Angeles and Mexico's western coast. In Gómez's account to his state constituents, he emphasized that Mexican IPH delegates had committed to completing the IPH not just for local reasons but also to promote Pacific coast tourism, which would ultimately yield regional benefits. He noted that his own state, as well as others, should use all methods possible to encourage tourism, including printed materials describing historic and picturesque locations to draw American tourists to attractions far south of the border.[69]

Even in the face of continued IPH-regional tension, Gómez continued work on the long lateral Los Angeles–Mexico City route, and promotional campaigns in Los Angeles sent increasing numbers of tourists south along the IPH. Newspapers announced that the first section of the IPH, from Nogales to Magdalena, was open for travelers in the fall of 1932. American travelers, still entranced by Mexican culture, responded enthusiastically. The *Los Angeles Times* reported a "magical" increase in the number of tourists motoring south.[70] While exact numbers for IPH travelers are hard to determine, the Mexican secretary of foreign relations reported a steep rise in requests for tourist maps and pamphlets in 1931, particularly in Mexico's Los Angeles consulate.[71] In a letter to the Mexican foreign secretary's office,

Los Angeles consul Rafael de la Colina wrote, "In view that we have exhausted all of the pamphlets regarding tourism in this office and in view of the fact that many people continually ask for them, I would like to ask for more to be sent this consulate as soon as possible, particularly materials relative to automobile roads."[72] As a result of this request, the office of the Mexican foreign secretary appealed to a number of government and private agencies to begin publishing more material for American, and particularly Southern Californian, tourists. The office argued that tourism would not grow as fast as Mexican officials wanted if tourists did not have adequate maps and guides.[73] The Mexican government also increasingly highlighted the nation's characteristics most alluring to Southern Californian tourists— its pre-Columbian past and Spanish heritage. With or without maps, crossings into Mexico at Nogales (the entry point for the IPH) steadily increased in the 1940s and 1950s. By the 1950s, more Americans entered Mexico through the Nogales crossing than at any other place along the border.[74]

As more and more Americans entered Mexico via automobile, work on the IPH continued steadily, if slowly. Despite the fact that Mexico weathered the Depression better than its northern neighbor, thanks in part to postrevolution economic policies, work did slow due to the economic crisis. Although he supported the construction of highways, Ortiz Rubio and his administration cut government spending by 23 percent during the first few years of the 1930s. Lázaro Cárdenas, president from 1934 to 1940, was committed to government spending and the development of the country's infrastructure, including roads. His concurrent commitment to nationalizing the nation's agricultural and petroleum properties, however, ate up much of the federal government's budget and impinged on its ability to invest in public works projects such as roads. While committed to Keynesian-style economics, Cárdenas simply could not afford to increase spending on highway construction.[75]

World war, security concerns, and an increased need to move goods from the United States sped up road building as the 1930s came to a close. A diplomatic alliance engendered by World War II transformed the IPH from a scenic tourist byway into a strategic piece of war infrastructure for the Western Hemisphere. The United States worried that Mexico might serve as a staging ground for Axis powers. Consequently, the two governments worked to increase the interconnectedness of Mexican and American road systems in case the need arose to move troops and military equipment. For example, as a result of the war, the Mexican Congress appropriated 3 million pesos to work on the IPH section between Magdalena and Tepic in 1941. In the same period, the ACSC reported to the *Los Angeles Times* that the governments of both the United States and Mexico recognized the significance of the IPH in their joint fight against Axis enemies.[76] According to the *Times*, "Attack upon Mexico, if it comes, will almost certainly be from the Pacific side and the [IPH] would be of great help in getting troops and supplies to the scene thereof."[77] The war also increased the significance of trade with the United States for the Mexican economy, further promoting the integration of transnational road networks. By the end of the war, over 90 percent of Mexico's foreign trade was with the United States, with most goods shipped by truck rather than railroad.[78] These connective networks of roads and trade were also harbingers of a new type of economic empire characterized by free trade and globalization, as discussed in the epilogue.

As a result of these war concerns and wartime collaboration, by the early 1940s the Mexican federal and state governments had completed much of the construction of a drivable route from Nogales to Mexico City, with some segments being leveled and graded dirt roads and others paved. By the 1950s, a period historian Benjamin Fulwider describes as the apex of Mexican road building, only a short section through a mountainous area of Nayarit had yet to be completed. The Mexican government finally finished the section in 1957 and laid a large bronze plaque commemorating the efforts of Cayetano Blanco Vigil and Henry Workman Keller, both aged but still alive and active in the IPH project, in seeing it through to its final completion. Blanco Vigil prophesized a future of robust free trade between the United States and Mexico when he mused in 1957 as he stood next to the final stretch of the completed highway, "This *camino* has linked our two countries with new bonds. Too it has opened a great region of commerce for many small cities and villages that hitherto were isolated . . . Now chickens and melons and pigs and beef are carried freely over the pavement by big trucks and little trucks and station wagons and cars; it has opened a new world."[79] Reflected in Blanco Vigil's words were the shifting ideas about the usefulness of the IPH and the relationship between Mexico, Los Angeles, and the United States. By the 1950s, air travel was rapidly replacing the automobile for tourists. While American tourists certainly still turned south for vacation, they often flew to locations such as Acapulco and newly designed resort destinations such as Cancún. Los Angeles as a trade center, however, continued to make transnational roads vital. The rise of trucking as the primary means for moving a staggering amount of goods between the United States and Mexico shifted the significance of international roads, making the IPH most importantly a route for truck drivers and trade goods rather than for tourists. Although near the end of their lives, Blanco Vigil and Keller both felt strongly enough about the continued significance of the road as a trade route that epitomized the economic relationship between the United States and Mexico that they worked on the project well into their eighties.

Conclusion

Despite the changing role of the IPH, from Los Angeles–Mexico City artery, to scenic tourist drive, to strategic wartime infrastructure, to trade route, the efforts of regional Mexican and Southern Californian highway promoters, from its inception in 1929 to its completion in 1957, reflect the ways in which elites in Los Angeles and along the Mexican west coast envisioned and negotiated a regional, more specifically a Pacific, relationship between two borderlands regions. Just as the international boundary helped organize opportunities for cross-border enterprises, including trade and tourism, regional elites in Los Angeles and along Mexico's west coast also saw possibilities for organizing postrevolutionary relationships along a lateral geographic marker—the Pacific coastline between Los Angeles and Mexico City. For boosters in Los Angeles, the highway also served as a concrete piece of infrastructure suturing the city to regions south of the border in the service of two of the city's most important industries—tourism and trade.

As noted in the introduction to this book, a number of borderlands scholars argue that although it is a rich field of study, much of the scholarship on the twentieth-century U.S.-Mexico borderlands sticks close to the border, telling "small-scale tales." As this book and this chapter explore, however, other geographies also organize the borderlands. In particular, cities, hinterlands, coastlines, and regions highlight broader sets of geographic ties that crossed borders and stretched borderlands. These alternative geographies, however, are still defined by the tensions at the crux of borderlands histories, including questions of sovereignty, paradoxes of division and union, regulations around inclusion and exclusion, and links between cores and peripheries. Pulling back from the "small-scale" narratives of communities immediately adjacent to the political border brings additional borderlands actors and relationships into relief and illustrates that borderland dynamics stretch north to south, in this case from Los Angeles to Mexico City. IPH promoters grappled with issues of national sovereignty as they tried to knit together two nations through a highway. In particular, they had to contend with an increasingly policed international border. Despite these paradoxes, they utilized the common language of a nostalgic past to draw tourists to Mexico. They also built on their positions as West Coast elites to promote the interests of their shared Pacific coast, often working without the support or interest of their national governments. They exploited the ambiguities of national power, so characteristic of borderland regions, to promote an aligned set of regional interests that spanned almost 2,000 miles of coastline. IPH promoters also grappled with the politics of inclusion and exclusion, simultaneously pushing Anglo-Americans to travel north and south along the highway and limiting the mobility of Mexican nationals and Mexican Americans. Ultimately, the International Pacific Highway demonstrates that what characterizes the borderland region did not just stretch east to west along the international boundary, but also along the alternative geography of Los Angeles and the Pacific coast.

As the IPH stretched the borderlands, it also signified a new era in the imperial relationship between the United States and Mexico, one that would unfold over the second half of the twentieth century and that had eerie echoes of the prerevolutionary period. While Washington, D.C., coupled the Good Neighbor Policy with strategies of economic development and stability, American policymakers and investors coupled this approach with demands for lifted trade barriers, increased globalization, and free market capitalism. When Blanco Vigil stood on the side of the IPH in 1957 and observed that the road would serve as an artery to carry chickens, melons, pigs, and trucks "freely" between regions and nations, he made an accurate prediction about opening a "new world" of trade and international relations. During the negotiations over the North American Free Trade Agreement (NAFTA) in the 1990s, Henry Kissinger would use similar language to declare in the *Los Angeles Times* that unrestricted trade constituted "the new world order." Beginning in the 1960s and accelerating through the 1970s and 1980s, the United States in its policy toward Latin America would increasingly call for lifting regulations, freeing up trade, opening markets, and promoting private investment. One historian dubbed this the "third conquest of Latin America" and America's "new imperialism."[80] Transportation corridors, such as the International Pacific Highway, that link global cities such as Los Angeles to cross-border manufacturing and production centers made much of this possible.

Epilogue
Global City

A drive through contemporary Los Angeles reveals Mexican resources still embedded in the city's iconic sprawl. Angeleno investors who sought opportunity in Mexico bequeathed the city tangible remembrances of their wealth. Griffith Park remains one of the city's most popular outdoor attractions, and tourists still tiptoe into the Bradbury Building for a peek at its unusual interior. Harry Chandler's imprint lives on in many locales, including at Olvera Street, the city's Spanish and Mexican core. In the 1920s he helped raise money for the campaign that would conjure a bucolic and fabricated Mexican village from the deteriorating historic neighborhood. Part of the renovation of Olvera Street included inviting the famed Mexican artist David Alfaro Siqueiros to paint an eighty-foot mural on the side of the neighborhood's Italian Hall. A veteran of the Mexican Revolution, Siqueiros chose European and American imperialism in Mexico as the dramatic subject for his mural. A bald eagle, symbolizing the United States, hovered over the crucifixion of an indigenous man. Chandler's partner in the Olvera Street renovation, a horrified Christine Sterling, immediately had the mural whitewashed. Critiques of empire had no place in her bucolic reimagining of Mexico in Los Angeles's historic core.[1]

Edward Doheny's presence also still haunts the Los Angeles landscape. He showered the returns of his Mexican oil across the city, building a gilded library on the University of Southern California campus in honor of his deceased son. A street linking Beverly Hills to Los Angeles still bears his name. Doheny's Mexican fortune also constructed a library and chapel at St. John's Seminary in Camarillo, just north of Los Angeles. Notably, the library's facade is based on the Catedral Metropolitana de la Asunción de María, the church located in Mexico City's Plaza de la Constitución and the largest cathedral in the Americas. This mirroring of Mexico in Los Angeles, paid for by Mexican resources, is more than just symbolic. As reflected in the city's topography, Los Angeles is a twenty-first-century global metropolis because its early promoters and investors oriented the city toward Mexico, the borderlands, and empire at the end of the nineteenth century.

That a replica of a Mexican cathedral stands in Southern California, built with wealth wrought from Mexican oil, is the result of imperial design, not chance.

By the end of the twentieth century, the city-empire that Angeleno city builders envisioned in the final decades of the nineteenth century had come to spectacular fruition in the form of a "global city." At the dawn of the twenty-first century, Los Angeles's size, influence, and global reach, so crucial to these early city builders, placed it firmly within the small set of what geographers describe as "global city-regions" such as New York, Tokyo, Bombay, and Mexico City.[2] In a twenty-first-century metamorphosis of the city-empire, global city-regions such as Los Angeles are home to multinational corporations, major centers for manufacturing and trade, and media and finance complexes, and often function as "the basic motors of the global economy."[3] In Los Angeles, transnational highways and relaxed trade policies created one of the world's busiest trucking and trade corridors between Southern California and Mexico. The Los Angeles harbor was, and continues to be, the largest in the nation and the third largest in the world, daily loading and unloading a dizzying array of goods. Likewise with the city's airport, the second-largest cargo airport in the United States and the fourth-largest in the world. Trade continues to fuel the region, transforming the Los Angeles metropolitan area into one of the world's largest economic regions. By 2000, greater Los Angeles had an economy larger than the entire nation of Mexico.[4] If men such as Henry Workman Keller and Harry Chandler were still alive, they would undoubtedly embrace this growth as the fulfillment of their turn-of-the-century urban and imperial aspirations.

In the early decades of the twenty-first century, Los Angeles is still deeply embedded in the networks of American empire. In what John Mason Hart deems the "neo-Porfirian economy" and Greg Grandin dubs "the third conquest of Latin America," American investors, including Angelenos, returned to Mexico with gusto in the last three decades of the twentieth century. Building on foundations laid in the nineteenth century, more American investment capital flowed into Mexico at the end of the twentieth century than into any other national economy in the world.[5] This process of economic empire building, in the form of transnational investment and trade, is rooted in globalized cities. In 1990s Los Angeles, for example, one of the city's largest investment firms bought up more than a third of the Mexican insurance market, giving one Los Angeles company major control over an entire national industry.[6] In a recognizable transmutation of older forms of imperialism, such as cross-border trade and investment, American investors and the American state have promoted neoliberal policies throughout Mexico and beyond that emphasize increased foreign investment, privatization, free market economies, open trade, and limited social spending.[7] Global cities such as Los Angeles serve as the geographic nexus for these policies and their aftermath.

Nineteenth-Century Imperial Roots

As *Imperial Metropolis* argues, Los Angeles's global connections and influence were firmly rooted in urban expansion, capitalism, and empire in the borderlands at the end of the nineteenth century. Since the moment Los Angeles became an American city in 1848, its Anglo elite has imagined and manufactured a transnational network of investment and trade emanating from Southern California, extending across the border into Mexico, and eventually circumnavigating the globe. Anglo Angelenos sketched their personal fortunes and the future of their city on the blueprint of an imperial metropolis. When they did this, there was no guarantee that Los Angeles would become the capital of the American West and the Pacific Rim. Ambition and anxiety, however, powered single-minded Anglo-Americans to leverage their class and racial positions to grow their city beyond its Southern California locale. At the end of the nineteenth century, they looked longingly at San Francisco's success, glanced uneasily over their southern shoulders at San Diego's advances, and tenaciously harnessed Los Angeles to Mexico.

Imperial aspirations originated with figures such as William Rosecrans, who planted the seeds of an imperial and global Los Angeles on his rancho in Southern California. More than any other figures in early Anglo Los Angeles, Rosecrans and fellow Civil War veteran Harrison Gray Otis articulated a future for their city in Mexico and vociferously championed the growth of an American commercial empire. Eyeing the transfer of land from Californios to Anglo settlers and the proletarianization of Mexicans in California, figures such as Rosecrans and Otis saw no reason that south-of-the-border Mexican land, resources, and labor could not be drawn into Los Angeles's commercial orbit. Urban development and American capitalism in the form of "informal" empire could proceed hand in hand across the border.

When revolution threatened Angeleno investment properties in Mexico, it also tightened a now dangerous embrace between an imperial core and periphery. While city builders and investors struggled to control what they had hoped would be a lucrative hinterland, Mexico became their singular preoccupation. They hoped revolt in the periphery would not mangle dreams of a city-empire rooted in Mexico. The revolution ruined some investors, such as the ill-fated Quimichis Colony. Yet, larger operations, such as Otis and Chandler's Colorado River Land Company and Doheny's Mexican Petroleum Company, profited. While their efforts to coordinate American intervention (a violent and formal type of empire building) in Mexico ultimately failed, they had the resources and political savvy necessary to negotiate with local and national Mexican policymakers and to continue depositing Mexican profits in Los Angeles bank accounts.

Maneuvers for intervention also placed Angelenos at the forefront of American foreign policy toward Mexico in the 1910s and 1920s. Careful observers of American "informal" empire in other Latin American and global locales, investors in Los Angeles had every reason to believe that the U.S. government would intervene on their behalf. Had they been successful, a handful of capitalists and city boosters in Los Angeles and the network of financial allies they built across the country would have extended the power of the federal government into a sovereign nation in order to protect their investments, city-empire, and urban hinterland. As the Mexican Revolution shifted Mexico toward economic nationalism, Los Angeles investors faced the painful process of expropriation and profit loss. Efforts to prevent expropriation or win compensation, however, continued to link the urban core tightly to its Mexican periphery. Nevertheless, the grassroots power of ordinary Mexicans reshaped not only investment patterns that had siphoned Mexican wealth to the United States, but also the larger imperial relationships between Los Angeles and hinterland and the United States and Mexico.

Interest in Mexico continued to orient Los Angeles toward the borderlands and the Pacific world. Revolution, however, had tempered imperial bombast, and Los Angeles boosters proceeded into the 1930s and the postwar period with a rhetoric of hemispheric friendship as they promoted new projects south of the border. Some of the same figures who had faced expropriation of investment properties worked tirelessly for the better part of three decades to link Los Angeles to Mexico through a concrete ribbon of highway. While individual investment properties might be taken over by Mexican peasants, a cross-border Pacific highway could be used by Angelenos, other Americans, and Mexicans in search of alternative ways to make money in the borderlands. Highways, tourism, cross-border trade, and the migration of millions of Mexicans across the border would knit Los Angeles to the borderlands ever more tightly as the twentieth century proceeded. These ties would also continue to have imperial imbalances into the twenty-first century.

American Empire, Mexico, and Los Angeles in the Postwar Era

As argued in the last chapter of *Imperial Metropolis*, fanfare around the completion of the International Pacific Highway, trumpeted during a period of international "goodwill" between the United States and Mexico, also pointed to the many contradictions in the postwar relationship between the two nations. Moreover, it generated echoes of empire that would continue to reverberate across the second half of the twentieth century. With the context laid out in this book, we are better able to appreciate the early and urban foundations that enabled the rise of American empire in the twentieth century, a topic with a rich historiography. Looking to the relationship between the United States, including Los Angeles, and Mexico from World War II to the present reveals ever-tightening diplomatic, economic, and social ties between the neighboring regions and nations. These ties continued an imperial trajectory launched a century earlier.

Initially, following the iteration of the Good Neighbor Policy and during World War II, the United States and Mexico cooperated on defense efforts, particularly in the borderlands. In the name of wartime defense, the two countries worked together on transborder transportation, infrastructure, and trade through institutions such as the U.S.-Mexican Commission for Wartime Cooperation. A period of transnational cooperation, however, did not necessarily negate American empire in Mexico. Instead, as Grandin argues, in the second half of the twentieth century Latin America also served as the test site for a "new" American imperialism. This new empire coupled free market capitalism and coercive economic and lending policies with military interventions purportedly intended to contain communism or spread American democratic values.

As the United States honed its imperial economic policies in the second half of the twentieth century, it put increasing pressure on countries like Mexico to follow economic regulations dictated by international loan conditions and organizations such as the International Monetary Fund. These included lowering spending on social programs, deregulating the financial sector, returning state industries to the private sector, rolling back labor and environmental protections, and opening up trade policies. Foreign investment and international loans poured into Mexico in the 1980s and 1990s and fueled economic growth. American investment flowed into the country at rates not seen since the Porfiriato. Americans again invested in older extractive industries, including oil and mineral production. American corporate interests also expanded into Mexico, including Goodyear, Ford, General Motors, Sears, Coca-Cola, and Walmart, to name just a few. Increased trade and investment in the postwar era reached its zenith in the implementation of the North American Free Trade Agreement in 1994. On the pages of the still boosterish *Los Angeles Times*, Henry Kissinger declared NAFTA the harbinger of a "new world order," characterized by export-oriented economies, foreign investment, and open trade.[8] Positive results of this "new world order" in Mexico, however, were short-lived and favored a few Mexican elites and foreign corporations at the expense of the many. Wages declined, poverty reached shocking rates, and deals such as NAFTA undercut Mexican production and led to the displacement of workers and communities, particularly in rural areas.[9] These dire economic conditions prompted new waves of migration into the borderlands and borderland cities, including Los Angeles.

Steady, even dazzling, economic growth in Los Angeles attracted these Mexican workers and migrants from around the world following World War II. These workers played a key role in helping Los Angeles cement its position as a major economic player in the United States and around the globe. Their labor expanded the region's economic base in agriculture, oil, and film and helped extend it into steel, iron, aircraft assembly, shipbuilding, chemical production, and tire manufacturing. The city's industrial and manufacturing sectors continued to grow at a stunning rate, even as late as the 1980s, and continuous waves of immigrant workers, from agricultural workers to engineers, fueled this growth. Census data on immigration from Mexico, for example, reflects a Mexican population in Los Angeles of approximately 7 percent of the city total in 1950 and 14 percent by 1960. A decade later, Los Angeles was home to 1.7 million Latinos, most from Mexico. By 1990, 3.7 million people of Mexican descent lived in greater Los Angeles. These postwar migrations not only fueled the region's economy but also remade Los Angeles into the city with the largest Mexican population outside of Mexico City.[10]

Los Angeles's economic development in the latter part of the twentieth century also depended on global connections and the nation's "new empire" in ways reminiscent of the nineteenth-century city-empire. NAFTA lifted many of the trade barriers that traditionally demarcate sovereign nations and economies, blurring the economic border between north and south, and allowing cities with transnational reach such as Los Angeles to benefit from lowered tariffs and increased trade. The city's growth machine supported the policy and believed a new era of free trade heralded good things for Los Angeles. In the early 1990s, the *Los Angeles Times* published a series of editorials that had eerie echoes of the nineteenth century. Still pro-growth, pro-trade, and run by the descendants of Harry Chandler, the city's paper of record promoted a resounding yes in the heated debates on the passage of NAFTA. One editorial argued that the doctrine of free trade was "profoundly important for long-term relations between two geographically close . . . neighbors."[11] In this way, NAFTA met many of the desires and demands of early twentieth-century Los Angeles capitalists such as Chandler, Otis, Doheny, Bard, Gibbon, and Keller. It coordinated investment and trade between the two nations, protected the interests of investors while sacrificing the welfare of workers, and opened Mexico to the United States' economic needs.

In the materialization of these booster and imperial dreams, NAFTA further integrated the Los Angeles and Mexican economies, with Los Angeles continuing to serve as a node of power and wealth in the U.S.-Mexico borderlands. Billions of dollars cross the border every year in transactions between transnational companies in Los Angeles and their Mexican partners.[12] Los Angeles has benefited from a growth in high-end, high-tech jobs, many of which specialize in trade with the maquiladoras that sprouted along the border.[13] Between 1990 and 2001, this type of international trade revitalized the Southern California economy; during this period 60 percent of California's NAFTA trade originated in or was destined for Los Angeles and represented 60 percent of the region's export growth.[14] At the same time, however, inexpensive manufactured and agricultural goods from the United States, often shipped via transnational highways like the IPH, flooded Mexico and washed away native industries and jobs.[15]

Although free trade policies opened trade routes north for a staggering number of consumer goods, from clothing to toys to electronics, they have failed to offer the same freedom of movement to people, many of them seeking refuge from the consequences of America's new empire of free trade. As it was a century ago, Los Angeles is still a major destination for immigrants headed north from Mexico.[16] However, changes in immigration policy since 1965 created the new category of "illegal" or undocumented immigrants from the Western Hemisphere and gave rise to the growth of the U.S. Border Patrol and the violent scrutiny of those who cross the border. As NAFTA became law in the 1990s, Anglo Californians renewed campaigns to barricade their border against Mexicans looking for jobs and economic opportunity. Draconian proposals such as Proposition 187, passed by the California electorate the same year NAFTA became law, sought to deny undocumented immigrants access to public schools, hospitals, health services, and nearly all publicly funded social programs. Despite these nativist movements, many Mexicans still sought (and continue to seek) employment north of the border. Many head to Los Angeles. With centripetal force, the economy of a globalized city draws people from the devastated Mexican countryside across a militarized border and into the urban core.[17] As explored in *Imperial Metropolis*, this phenomenon and the economic configurations behind it are nothing new under the Southern California sun.

As we journey into the twenty-first century, American economic empire and cities such as Los Angeles will continue to intersect and play ever-increasing roles in the global economy. As geographers observe, it is through a handful of growing cities that economies connect beyond national borders to global capital and trade. The relationship between globalization and global cities is also reflexive. Enormous city-regions are at once the product of and the mediators of global phenomena such as trade and migration. For example, global city-regions, growing in size and influence, are also characterized by the inequality of globalization and divides between the rich and the poor. Some scholars go so far as to argue that globalization has shaped the internal spatial patterns of cities, physically separating wealthy, often white, professionals from an ever-increasing population of the nonwhite urban poor. A drive across the rapidly gentrifying landscape of Los Angeles reveals this to be true.[18]

Yet, even as I type this conclusion, global cities such as Los Angeles are also confronting the intense challenges of American empire, globalized economies, inequalities, and migrations in the twenty-first-century city. As Donald Trump's presidency unfolds, rooted in a virulently anti-immigrant and even anti-urban platform, Los Angeles municipal leaders have declared the city a "sanctuary city." Preemptively resisting an anticipated federal crackdown on undocumented immigrants and the building of a border wall, Angelenos, from the mayor and city councilmembers to university students and union members, are declaring their support for all Los Angeles residents regardless of race, ethnicity, religion, or immigration status. The city is also resisting the federal dismantling of social welfare programs and environmental policies. This outlook, so different from the transnational relationships imagined by nineteenth-century Angeleno boosters or promoted by trade policies like NAFTA, is the product of the city's now robust labor movement, its base of progressive nonprofit and immigrants' rights groups, and the growing power of an immigrant and nonwhite electorate. Together, these communities have spent the better part of three decades organizing to demand that city officials support and protect Los Angeles's stunningly diverse population and promote more progressive social and economic policies. Los Angeles, they demand, will provide refuge for those most vulnerable to the vagaries of American empire and globalization. As observed by journalist Juan Gonzalez, the revolt in Los Angeles is part of a "new grassroots urban political revolt in America . . . [with] huge swarms of voters rallying behind a crusade against income inequality and roundly rejecting a conservative free-market worldview that has dominated American urban [and foreign] policy for the past fifty years."[19] It is too early to know if this urban-based resistance to the violent tightening of borders, appalling xenophobia, and the ever-deepening local and global chasm between the rich and poor will work. One thing is evident, however, to any close observer of Los Angeles. In the twenty-first century the city will continue to be the major crossroads for the United States and Mexico, urban growth and the borderlands, and capitalism, empire, and resistance.

Appendix

List of Companies Incorporated in Los Angeles County to Conduct Business in Mexico, 1886–1931

Note: This list is not a complete overview of Los Angeles investments in Mexico. Some companies, although headquartered in Los Angeles, incorporated in other counties or states.

Source: Data from the Seaver Center for Western History Research, Natural History Museum of Los Angeles County.

Company Name	Year Incorporated	Primary Purpose	Location
Mexican Oil and Gas Company	1886	Oil and natural gas	Mexico City
Guadalupe Mill and Mining Company	1886	Gold and silver mining	Chihuahua City, Chihuahua
California and Mexican Land Company	1887	Real estate, water rights, telephone service, electricity	Mexicali, Baja California Norte
Los Angeles Rubber Plantation	1889	Rubber and hardwood cultivation	Tuxtla Gutiérrez, Chiapas
Mexico Mining and Development Company	1891	Real estate, water rights, mining	Mexico City
Cayaltepee Land and Improvement Company of Mexico	1895	Real estate	Cuicatlán, Oaxaca
Mexican Water Pipe Company	1895	Irrigation supplies	Mexico City
Los Angeles Coal Company	1895	Coal mining	
Piramide Mining Company	1895	Gold, silver, copper, and lead mining	La Paz, Baja California Sur
Mexican Petroleum Company	1900	Real estate, petroleum production, coal mining	Ebano, San Luis Potosí
Mexico Oil and Development Company	1900	Real estate, petroleum production, coal mining	Cuidad Victoria, Tamaulipas; Xalapa, Veracruz; Monterrey, Nuevo León; San Luis Potosí, San Luis Potosí; Santiago de Querétaro, Querétaro; Guanajuato, Guanajuato; Pachuca, Hidalgo; Toluca de Lerdo, Mexico; Tlazcala, Tlazcala; Puebla, Puebla

Suaqui Grande Mining Company	1900	Mining	Suaqui Grande, Sonora
Los Angeles–Oaxaca Mining and Milling Company	1900	Mining	Oaxaca de Juarez, Oaxaca
Mexican Colonization Land and Development Bureau	1901	Real estate, land management, railroads	
California and Mexico Mining and Development Company	1901	Gold and silver mining	
Coahuila Development Company	1901	Agriculture	Saltillo, Coahuila
California-Mexico Land and Cattle Company	1902	Agriculture	Mexicali, Baja California Norte
Mexican Asphalt Paving and Construction Company	1902	Road and highway construction	Mexico City
San Antonio de Zaragoza Mining Company	1902	Gold, silver, copper, lead, and borax mining	San Antonio, Coahuila
Santo Nino Mining and Smelting Company	1902	Smelting and mineral refining	
Guadalupe Cattle and Development Company	1902	Agriculture	
Artesian Company a.k.a. Sinaloa Land and Water Company a.k.a. Sinaloa Land and Water Company, Ltd.	1902	Real estate and water rights	Culiacán, Sinaloa
Mexican Medicine Company, Limited	1903	Pharmaceuticals	
American White Lead and Paint Manufacturing Company	1903	Paint manufacturing	Mexico City

(continued)

Company Name	Year Incorporated	Primary Purpose	Location
American-Mexican Mining and Smelting Company	1904	Mining	
Esmeralda Mining and Development Company of Mexico	1904	Gold, coal, and salt mining	
American-Mexican Vitro Tile Company	1904	Marble and granite mining, tile production	
San Pedro De Tobacachi Mining Company California	1904	Oil production and coal mining	Cumpas, Sonora
Nieves Mining Company	1904	Mining	
Tampico Sugar Company	1904	Agriculture	Tampico, Veracruz
Awawatz Mining Company	1904	Mining	
La Cienega Gold Mining Company	1904	Gold, silver, and copper mining	Victoria de Durango, Durango
Mexican-American Cattle Company	1905	Agriculture	
Mexican Colonization and Transportation Company	1905	Irrigation and transportation	
Mexican Information Bureau	1905	Financial services	
Rio Antiguo Mining Company	1905	Gold and silver mining	
Sinaloa Mining Company	1905	Mining and timber	Culiacán, Sinaloa
Chiapas Land and Stock Company	1905	Real estate, water rights, burglar and fire alarm production, agriculture	Tuxtla Gutiérrez, Chiapas
Red Hill Mining and Smelting Company	1905	Mining	Chihuahua City, Chihuahua

Guadalajara Steam Laundry Company	1905	Steam laundry service	Guadalajara, Jalisco
Mexican Pearl Company	1905	Pearl and oyster fisheries	
Reed Mexican Mining and Development Company	1906	Mining and electricity production	
Valladares Gold Mining Company	1906	Mining	Ensenada, Baja California Norte
Gulf Coast Development Company	1906	Railroad, road, and telegraph line construction	Zacapoaxtla, Puebla
Papantla Vanilla Plantation Company	1906	Agriculture	Chihuahua City, Chihuahua; Zacapoaxtla, Puebla
Lewis & Udell Company	1906	Import and export of manufactured goods	
Pittsburg Placer Mining and Milling Company	1906	Mining and mining supplies	
Southwestern Mining and Improvement Company	1906	Mining	
El Refugio Mining Company	1906	Mining and mining supplies	El Refugio, Jalisco
Mexican Mining Company of Long Beach	1907	Mining	
Mexico Sinaloa Colonial Incorporation	1907	Agriculture	Culiacán, Sinaloa
Mexican Hardwood Lumber Company	1907	Lumber	Salina Cruz, Oaxaca
Mexican Commission Company	1907	Financial services	Salina Cruz, Oaxaca
Mexican Hardwood Lumber Company	1908	Lumber	Salina Cruz, Oaxaca

(continued)

Company Name	Year Incorporated	Primary Purpose	Location
Mexican Colorado River Land Company	1908	Agriculture and irrigation	Mexicali, Baja California Norte; Hermosillo, Sonora
Sierra Madre Club	1908	Trade organization	
California Jalisco Land Company	1908	Agriculture	Guadalajara, Jalisco
Union Annex Oil Company	1909	Oil production	
Mexican Guano Company	1909	Fertilizer	La Paz, Baja California Sur
Julieta Mining Company of Mexico	1909	Mining	Jiménez, Chihuahua
Mexico West Coast Mining and Development Company	1909	Mining	
Culiacan Land Company	1909	Real estate	Culiacán, Sinaloa
Sanborn Brothers Successors	1909	Drug manufacturing	Mexico City
Mexican Mines Company	1910	Mining	Mazatlán, Sinaloa
Calimex Plantation Company	1910	Water power and irrigation	
South Mexico Development Company	1910	Rubber cultivation and agriculture	
Mexican Oil & Asphalt Company	1910	Oil production and asphalt	
Culiacan Land Company	1910	Real estate and agriculture	Culiacán, Sinaloa
Colegio Mining and Development Company	1910	Mining	
California Mexican Development Company	1911	Real estate	
California-Mexican Petroleum Company	1911	Mining and oil production	

Company	Year	Business	Location
West Mexico Trading	1911	Import and export of manufactured goods	
Mexican Fruit and Transportation Company	1911	Agriculture, oil production, mining	Manzanillo, Colima
Liberty Land Company	1911	Real estate	
Mutual Agricultural Company	1911	Real estate and agriculture	
America Mexico Land and Colonization Company	1912	Real estate	Parral, Chihuahua
P. F. & D. Mining Company	1912	Mining	
Rio Michol Development Company	1912	Rubber cultivation	Tuxtla Gutiérrez, Chiapas
Pelton System Concrete Tank Company	1912	Manufacturing	
Mexico Trading Company	1913	Trade and agriculture	
Mexican-American Iron Company	1913	Mining	
Mexico Western Investment Company	1913	Real estate and mining	
Mexico West Coast Land Company	1914	Real estate and agriculture	
Black Hawk Mining Company	1914	Mining equipment and machinery	
Mexicano Products Company	1914	Real estate, irrigation, and agriculture	
American-Mexican Canneries Corporation	1914	Real estate, irrigation, and agriculture	
Mexican Fertilizer and Exploitation Company	1915	Fertilizer and mining	Los Figueroa, Baja California Norte
Mexico-American Exploitation Company	1915	Real estate and timber	

(continued)

Company Name	Year Incorporated	Primary Purpose	Location
California and Mexican Steamship Company (later changed to California and Mexico Steamship Company)	1915	Transportation, shipping, and trade	Ensenada, Baja California Norte; La Paz, Baja California Sur
Latin American Publishing Company	1915	Advertising and trade publications to promote commerce between California and Latin America	
Los Angeles, Mexico and Pacific Steamship Company	1916	Transportation, shipping, and trade	
Latin American Trading Company	1916	Transportation, shipping, and trade	
Tetamecha Cattle Company	1916	Trade and agriculture	
Mex-American Trading Corporation	1916	Trade and financial services	
Mexico Arizona Reduction Company	1917	Fertilizer	
Maizarina Manufacturing Company Inc.	1917	Agriculture and food processing	Bamoa, Sinaloa
California Farming Company	1917	Real estate and agriculture	
Caipatria Land & Cattle Company	1917	Agriculture	
Lower California Mexican Land and Development Company	1918	Real estate and agriculture	La Paz, Baja California Sur
American-Mexican Packing Company	1918	Agriculture and food processing	

Mexican Mercantile Association	1918	Trade	
Mexican Commercial and Agricultural	1918	Trade organization	
Hispano American Company	1918	Manufacturing	
New Mexico Petroleum and Refining Company	1919	Real estate and oil production	
Mexican Guano Company	1919	Fertilizer	
Compania Mercantil Mexicanos Unidos	1919	Trade	
Latina Productions	1919	Film	
Pan American Trading Company	1919	Trade	
Cal-Mex Oil and Refining Company	1920	Real estate and oil production	
Mexican National Film Company	1920	Film	
Mexican American Finance Development Corporation	1920	Real estate and oil production	
West Coast Annalist & Mexican Year Book Company	1921	Magazine and newspaper publishing	
Mexican Pacific Exportation Company	1921	Real estate, agriculture, and brewing	Tepic, Nayarit
Partido Liberal Mexicano, Inc.	1931	Political party established by the Flores Magóns	
New Mexico Development Company Ltd.	1931	Real estate	
Carmex Investment Corporation Ltd.	1931	Real estate	

Notes

Abbreviations

ACSC	Automobile Club of Southern California Archive, Los Angeles
AHSRE	Archivo Histórico de la Secretaría de Relaciones Exteriores, Mexico City, Mexico
AMM	Archivo de Municipio de Mexicali, Baja California, Mexico
BC HL	Bergman Collection, Huntington Library, San Marino
BC UCD	Bradbury Collection, University of California, Davis
CFL	Coleccíon José Y. Limantour, Centro de Estudios de Historia de Mexico, Mexico City, Mexico
CPD UI	Coleccíon Porfirio Díaz, Universidad Iberoamericana, Mexico City
CP HL	Cleland Papers, Huntington Library
CRLC SL	Colorado River Land Company Records, Sherman Library, Corona del Mar
CSCC SL	Chandler-Sherman Corporation Collection, Sherman Library, Corona del Mar
GFP UCLA	Griffith Family Papers, University of California, Los Angeles
HWKC HL	Henry Workman Keller Collection, Huntington Library, San Marino
LAT	*Los Angeles Times*
LC AGN	Fondo Lázaro Cárdenas, Ramo Presidentes, Archivo General de la Nación, Mexico
NARA	National Archives and Records Administration, College Park, Maryland
OC AGN	Fondo Obregón-Calles, Ramo Presidentes, Archivo General de la Nación, Mexico
POR AGN	Fondo Pascual Ortiz Rubio, Ramo Presidentes, Archivo General de la Nación, Mexico
SCWHR	Seaver Center for Western History Research, Museum of Natural History, Los Angeles
TBC HL	Thomas Bard Collection, Huntington Library, San Marino
TBC QCA HL	Thomas Bard Collection, Quimichis Colony Addendum, Huntington Library, San Marino
WSRP UCLA	William Stark Rosecrans Papers, University of California, Los Angeles

Introduction

1. Starr, *Material Dreams*, 181–84.

2. On empire, European capitals, and imperial landscapes, see Driver and Gilbert, *Imperial Cities*. Contributors to the volume argue that imperial ventures are mapped on the topography of imperial centers and cities.

3. Calculated using www.measuringworth.com.

4. "His Race Is Run: Death of L. L. Bradbury, the Millionaire Mine-Owner," *LAT*, July 16, 1892, and BC UCD.

5. For details on Griffith's life, see his unpublished autobiography. Unpublished autobiography of Griffith J. Griffith, box 15, GFP UCLA.

6. Griffith autobiography, box 15, GFP UCLA.

7. Letter from Griffith to Mayor Alexander and City Council, December 21, 1912, box 15, GFP UCLA.

8. A number of urban historians, particularly those interested in the U.S. West, have explored the relationship between urban cores and peripheries. See, for example, William Cronon's iconic study of nineteenth-century Chicago, *Nature's Metropolis*. Gray Brechin also explores this phenomenon, particularly its cultural components, in *Imperial San Francisco*. Eugene P. Moehring argues that the core-hinterland relationship existed across the American West in *Urbanism and Empire in the Far West*. For an older treatment of the same process, see Donald W. Meinig, "American Wests." For a discussion of the growth of city and hinterlands in the East, see Roberta Balstad Miller, *City and Hinterland*. These historians owe a scholastic debt to Immanuel Wallerstein and his studies on empire and "world-systems" theory. See, for example, *The Capitalist-World Economy*. Geographer Neil Smith makes a similar argument while paying particular attention to cities and empires in *Uneven Development*. More specifically, Smith argues that urban spaces play important roles in global capitalism and in the core-periphery model.

9. "An Opening for an Extension of Trade," *LAT*, December 4, 1894, 4.

10. "The Land We Live In," *LAT*, December 31, 1892, 5.

11. Angelenos invested $17,715,030 in Mexico compared to New Yorkers' $33,694,430. Amounts calculated from a list of damages filed by U.S. citizens against Mexico and organized geographically by state and city. "Geographical List of United States Claimants," Research and Information Section, International Claims Commissions, box 1, Record Group 76, NARA. Hundreds of millions of international investment dollars poured into Mexico during this period. Per capita, Angelenos invested the most. New Yorkers and New York–based corporations invested the most in terms of dollars. Other large investors included British and German companies. See Hart, *Empire and Revolution*.

12. For an overview of the emerging field of the history of capitalism, see the following sources. Many of these scholars pay implicit, if not explicit, attention to cities and the development of American capitalism. Beckert, "History of American Capitalism"; Beckert, *The Monied Metropolis*; Beckert, *Empire of Cotton*; Levy, *Freaks of Fortune*; Cohen, *A Consumers' Republic*; Hoganson, *Consumers' Imperium*; Maggor, *Brahmin Capitalism*. On the rise of corporate capitalism and white-collar

work in Los Angeles, see C. Davis, *Company Men*. For a recent work arguing for a local approach to understanding American empire, see Lipman, *Guantánamo*.

13. Paul Kramer argues that the intersection between urban history and the history of American empire is an area ripe for development. He maintains that an imperial lens would allow U.S. historians to "see American cities as the hubs of imperial systems." Kramer, "Power and Connection," 1355.

14. The literature on resistance to Gilded Age capitalism and incorporation is vast, although not all works in this area bring together histories of both investors and labor, particularly across international borders. Maggor's *Brahmin Capitalism* is a notable exception, although his work is focused on the United States. For a recent synthesis, see Edwards, *New Spirits*. Edwards argues that economic incorporation produced violence from the Reconstruction South to the western frontier to urban centers across the country. She relies on older arguments regarding "incorporation" and resistance put forward by Alan Trachtenberg in his classic *Incorporation of America*. Walter LaFeber provides an international analysis of this process, arguing that American industrialization drove centralization, both at home and abroad. The growth of American economic power thus not only fueled domestic revolts but also triggered revolutions from Mexico to China to Russia. LaFeber, *The American Search for Opportunity*. For a more recent treatment of the American Gilded Age in international context, see Fink, *The Long Gilded Age*. Historians of the Mexican Revolution also point to the tremendous role of foreign capital in creating the conditions for revolt. See Hart, *Empire and Revolution*, and Katz, *The Life and Times of Pancho Villa*.

15. This analysis has roots in the work Saskia Sassen, Allen J. Scott, and Michael Storper. According to these scholars, the decreasing power of national states and concurrent trends of globalization and deregulation have led to the growing significance of alternative spatial units or scales, most notably subnational entities such as cities, territories, and cross-border regions. Some scholars also argue that the phenomenon is not just the product of late twentieth-century capitalism but instead has deep historical roots in places such as New York, London, and Amsterdam. Sassen, *The Global City*; Scott, Agnew, Soja, and Storper, "Global City-Regions," 11–30. Scott et al. define cities with transnational hinterlands as "essential spatial nodes of the global economy and as distinctive political actors on the world stage." See also Abu-Lughod, *New York, Chicago, Los Angeles*.

16. There is some debate over the artificial dichotomy created between "formal" and "informal" empire in U.S. history and historiography. "Formal" empire is commonly defined as state-territorial control. "Informal" was a concept utilized by New Left historians of American foreign relations, notably William Appleman Williams and Walter LaFeber, to argue that the expansion of the United States' commercial power around the world constituted a form of empire, albeit "informal." More recent historians, including Paul Kramer, argue that the distinction between "formal" and "informal" empires is not so neat or clearly delineated. For example, commercial enterprises cannot be separated from "formal" state power because national governments often supported the interests of capitalists and their global investments. I try to use the term "informal" carefully in this book and often

in quotation marks or paired with the term "formal" to remind us that "informal" American expansion did not mean a lack of state support or enthusiasm and that the two often traveled together across the globe. Kramer, "Power and Connection," 1374–78.

17. Kramer's definition of empire is useful here. He argues that empire is a process or category of analysis rather than a specific thing or entity. He also argues that empire is about the organization and control of space as well as nonterritorial networks; that empire is based in hierarchical distinctions among populations; and that in imperial systems, power is exercised over "long-distance connections" and results in the uneven development of societies. Kramer, "Power and Connection," 1348–50.

18. Self, "City Lights," 414.

19. See Self, "City Lights." On Boston investors in the West, see Maggor, *Brahmin Capitalism*.

20. Chang, *Pacific Connections*, 11–12. On American conquest of the West as part of empire building, see Limerick, *Legacy of Conquest*. Kramer makes a similar argument about linking continental expansion with overseas empire. See Kramer, "Power and Connection," 1354–55. Paul Sabin makes a more extended argument related to this topic. He contends that there are "profound connections between western development and the role of the United States in international capitalist expansion. Many of the processes, people, and institutions that actively shaped [Latin America] are well-known from the drama scripted by U.S. expansion through North America." See Sabin, "Home and Abroad," 305–35.

21. As discussed in an earlier note, "New Left" historians of U.S. foreign relations history revolutionized the field by arguing that the United States had long had an imperial role in the world, driven primarily by the search for markets. See LaFeber, *The New Empire*, and Williams, *The Tragedy of American Diplomacy*. This historiographic trend was followed by a focus on the role of culture in shaping and spreading global American imperialism. On this, see Kaplan and Pease, *Cultures of United States Imperialism*.

22. For an excellent definition of "boosters" and their role in western cities, see Naylor, *Frontier Boosters*. Naylor defines boosters as "community residents who actively or directly promoted county development and those who espoused development thinking and/or supported boosterist goals." On elites in borderlands regions, see Baud and van Schendel, "Toward a Comparative History of Borderlands," 217.

23. As Tony Ballantyne and Antoinette Burton write, "Historically, the building of empires was about the wresting of land—whether through military might, economic encroachment, or purposeful settlement—from its traditional owners or imperial rivals and accumulating these pieces of territory in an extended economic and political system . . . At a fundamental level, empire building was about the extraction of rent, revenue, and resources from land overtaken." Ballantyne and Burton, "Empires and the Reach of the Global," 306.

24. On elites and their particular role in borderlands regions, see Baud and van Schendel, "Toward a Comparative History of Borderlands." Recent histories of elites and capitalism blend social, intellectual, and political history to illuminate

business activities, social lives, politics, and views of the world in relationship to critical histories of race, gender, labor, and culture. See Beckert, *The Monied Metropolis*. The Los Angeles investor class also lived and worked during a period in which the status of the speculator and investor, particularly in the American West, had been rehabilitated, made over from selfish and cavalier into a useful and productive member of society. As Ann Fabian notes, investors at the end of the nineteenth century described themselves as key pillars in the development of capitalism: "They brought land into 'use.' They 'worked' as capitalists and provided a 'social service' as taxpayers and moneylenders. The speculator was transformed from a selfish gambler to a self-sacrificing pioneer and from an exceptional figure of evil to a benign aspect of every settler." Fabian, *Card Sharps and Bucket Shops*, 169–70.

25. The literature on empire, both "formal" and "informal," is extensive. One foundational text is Cooper and Stoler, *Tensions of Empire*. See also Cooper, *Colonialism in Question*, and Burton, *After the Imperial Turn*. For an analysis of global empires in world history, see Burbank and Cooper, *Empires in World History*. For an excellent overview of American expansion and formal and informal empire, see Immerwahr, "The Greater United States," 373–91. Additional overviews include Immerman, *Empire for Liberty*, and Ninkovich, *The United States and Imperialism*. For a history that links American territorial expansion in the West with its imperial expansion, particularly in the Pacific, in the twentieth century, see Cummings, *Dominion from Sea to Sea*. For classic histories of American "informal" empire, see LaFeber, *The New Empire*, and Williams, *The Tragedy of American Diplomacy*. On American foreign interventions to protect property and business interests, see Maurer, *The Empire Trap*. For an overview of American corporate imperialism and culture, see Domosh, *American Commodities in an Age of Empire*. On culture and American empire, see Kaplan and Pease, *Cultures of United States Imperialism*.

26. Smith, *American Empire*, xvii–xviii.

27. See for example the history of the San Domingo Improvement Company in the Dominican Republic or the role of United Fruit in Central America. Veeser, *A World Safe for Capitalism*; Colby, *The Business of Empire*.

28. I am indebted to Philip J. Ethington's work in my thinking about Los Angeles as a global city with deep ties to the borderlands and empire. He treats these subjects in two essays. In one, he argues that Los Angeles was deeply "integrated with the Borderland political culture . . . The *porfiriato* enriched the Los Angeles Anglo ruling class, and the Revolution deeply threatened it." Ethington, "Ab Urbis Condita," 192. He also discusses Los Angeles as a global and imperial city, noting that "a globalizing metropolis is also an imperial one, whether or not that city is a capital, such as London, Paris, or Rome . . . The histories of twentieth-century San Francisco and Los Angeles show that cities can become imperial without or within nation-states." Ethington, "Global Spaces of Los Angeles," 58.

29. In my thinking on this subject, Beckert's work was very influential, particularly his argument in *The Monied Metropolis*. For excellent analysis of Los Angeles's growth and the role of elites between 1885 and 1915, see Jaher, *The Urban Establishment*, 612–54.

30. On boosterism in Los Angeles, see Jaher, *The Urban Establishment*.

31. "Interview on the Philippines," *LAT*, October 9, 1902.

32. See Hart, *Empire and Revolution*, 260–62.

33. See McWilliams, *Southern California*, 274–83; Fogelson, *The Fragmented Metropolis*, 129–31. Following events such as the 1894 Pullman Strike and the bombing of the *Los Angeles Times* building in 1910, elite Angelenos believed that the city should be free of unions and that the federal government should protect industry against the exigencies of organized labor. It was a labor dispute that ended in the bombing of the *Times* building on October 1, 1910. The event strengthened the power of Los Angeles's conservative population as a result. Deverell, *Railroad Crossing*, 79–82; Perry and Perry, *A History of the Los Angeles Labor Movement*.

34. Nell Irvin Painter highlights the role of the "producer-centered" worldview in *Standing at Armageddon*. Emily Rosenberg outlines a similar ideology but on an international scale. Rosenberg, *Spreading the American Dream*.

35. For more on this worldview, see Painter, *Standing at Armageddon*, as well as Wiebe, *The Search for Order*, and Trachtenberg, *The Incorporation of America*.

36. Rosenberg, *Spreading the American Dream*, 7.

37. Los Angeles historians have argued that Los Angeles boosters emphasized a "regional tradition of white supremacy" to overcome the area's Mexican past and assert its Anglo, even Aryan, future. See Avila, *Popular Culture in the Age of White Flight*, 20–24; Mike Davis, *City of Quartz*, 28; Deverell, *Whitewashed Adobe*; Lewthwaite, *Race, Place, and Reform*; and Wild, *Street Meeting*, 38–39.

38. On reconsidering the relationship between imperial cores and periphery and the nuanced interchanges between the two, see Cooper and Stoler, *Tensions of Empire*, and Norton, "Tasting Empire," 660–91.

39. Mexicans and Mexican Americans profoundly shaped Los Angeles not just through revolution and resistance to transnational investment but also through migration, community building, labor, political protest, language, and culture, to name but a few. The literature on Mexican Americans and Mexicans and the shaping of Los Angeles is rich and growing. For two excellent examples, see Monroy, *Rebirth*, and Sánchez, *Becoming Mexican American*.

40. Hart, *Empire and Revolution*, 260. There is a wealth of work on the causes, trajectory, and results of the Mexican Revolution as well as American intervention in the revolution. See Gilly, *The Mexican Revolution*; Hart, *Revolutionary Mexico*; Katz, *The Secret War in Mexico*; Katz, *The Life and Times of Pancho Villa*; Knight, *The Mexican Revolution*, vols. 1 and 2; Knight, *U.S.-Mexico Relations*; Nugent, *Rural Revolt in Mexico*; Ruíz, *The Great Rebellion*; Womack, *Zapata and the Mexican Revolution*.

41. Katz, *The Secret War in Mexico*, 3.

42. Hämäläinen and Truett, "On Borderlands," 338–61. Some scholars are calling for broader and comparative understandings of borderlands. See Johnson and Graybill, *Bridging National Borders*. There are a few later studies that are beginning to explore urban histories in the context of borderlands, including Cadava, *Standing on Common Ground*; Chang, *Pacific Connections*; and Karibo, *Sin City*

North. For one of the definitive works on North American borderlands, see Adelman and Aron, "From Borderlands to Borders," 814–41.

43. In studying capitalism in the borderlands, I also owe an intellectual debt to the work of scholars such as Samuel Truett, Rachel St. John, and Katherine Benton-Cohen. See Truett, *Fugitive Landscapes*; St. John, *Line in the Sand*; Benton-Cohen, *Borderline Americans*.

44. As Self observes, "Urbanization and urban influence cross scales and geographies, making cities the architects of the countryside . . . Western urbanists must learn to act more like geographers in exploring the spatial extension of urbanization across multiple scales—regional, national, and international." Self, "City Lights," 416. An excellent example of reconsidering cities, scale, and region in the West is Needham, *Power Lines*. On planning and the rise and history of Los Angeles, see Hise, *Magnetic Los Angeles*.

45. On "identity of interest," see Painter, *Standing at Armageddon*, and Rosenberg, *Spreading the American Dream*.

46. Scholars of race and empire caution American historians not to simply transplant domestic systems of race into American imperial projects. Kramer, for example, argues that new systems of race and governance developed during American control of the Philippines. See Kramer, *The Blood of Government*. Other scholars tackling empire and race include Briggs, *Reproducing Empire*; Love, *Race over Empire*; Renda, *Taking Haiti*.

47. Coatsworth, "Measuring Influence," 64–71. While scholars disagree on the amount of anti-Americanism demonstrated by Mexican revolutionaries, most concur that American investments in Mexico precipitated Mexico's social revolution. See Hart, "Social Unrest," 7; and Knight, "The United States and the Mexican Peasantry," 27.

48. Campbell and Heyman suggest widening the geographical boundaries of the borderlands through the study of tourism in "The Study of Borderlands Consumption," the concluding essay in McCrossen, *Land of Necessity*. As noted earlier, Hämäläinen and Truett make a similar call in their essay "On Borderlands." For more on borderlands and leisure, see Culver, *The Frontier of Leisure*; and Vanderwood, *Satan's Playground*. The study of the Pacific world, where highway promoters placed their project, is a fairly recent historiographical turn. See Cummings, *Dominion from Sea to Sea*; and Igler, *The Great Ocean*. On new forms of American empire in Latin America that emerged in the post–World War II era, see Grandin, *Empire's Workshop*; Hart, *Empire and Revolution*, particularly chapters 5 and 6; and Bacevich, *American Empire*.

49. See Margaret Davis, *Dark Side of Fortune*.

50. On Harrison Gray Otis, Harry Chandler, and the *Los Angeles Times*, see Gottlieb and Wolt, *Thinking Big*.

51. On Thomas Bard, see Hutchinson, *Oil, Land, and Politics*.

52. Part of this was the allure of trade. For an overview of the history and significance of trade in the modern world, see Pomeranz and Topik, *The World That Trade Created*.

53. For more on these statistics and an overview of Los Angeles's rise to a global city in the twentieth century, see Abu-Lughod, *New York, Chicago, Los Angeles*, 133–41; and Erie, *Globalizing L.A.* For a classic work on Los Angeles's growth, see Fogelson, *The Fragmented Metropolis*.

Chapter One

1. All data compiled from Los Angeles County incorporation records at SCWHR.
2. "Mexico," *LAT*, May 21, 1882, and "Sonora," *LAT*, January 8, 1882.
3. For recent work on the local textures of American empire, see Lipman, *Guantánamo*. For a discussion of American-driven capitalist development in the borderlands, see Truett, *Fugitive Landscapes*, and St. John, *Line in the Sand*.
4. For a succinct discussion of this phenomenon, see Rosenberg, *Spreading the American Dream*.
5. Pubols, "Born Global."
6. On the Mexican-American War in Los Angeles, see Deverell, *Whitewashed Adobe*; and Torres-Rouff, *Before L.A.* On the racial dimensions of Manifest Destiny, see Horsman, *Race and Manifest Destiny*. On the Mexican American community following the war, see Griswold del Castillo, *The Los Angeles Barrio*.
7. Quoted in Fogelson, *Fragmented Metropolis*, 12.
8. Deverell, *Whitewashed Adobe*, 11–48.
9. Pubols, "Born Global," 35; and Torres-Rouff, *Before L.A.*
10. On the Spanish fantasy past, see Deverell, *Whitewashed Adobe*; and Kropp, *California Vieja*.
11. Moehring, *Urbanism and Empire in the Far West*, xvii–xxii.
12. "Slipping Away: The Mexican Trade—Los Angeles Should Be Up and Doing," *LAT*, May 13, 1882.
13. On borderlands capitalism, see Truett, *Fugitive Landscapes*; St. John, *Line in the Sand*; and Benton-Cohen, *Borderline Americans*.
14. Quoted in Truett, *Fugitive Landscapes*, 4. Truett also discusses Díaz's belief that the American West offered a blueprint for economic development in Mexico.
15. *Congressional Record*, February 28, 1884, 1454. Also quoted in Schoultz, *Beneath the United States*, 85.
16. On capitalism and the incorporation of the West into the United States, see White, *"It's Your Misfortune and None of My Own."* On Americans, empire, and Mexico, see Hart, *Empire and Revolution*. On American investors in Mexico following the Civil War, see Pletcher, *Rails, Mines, and Progress*. On informal empire and American foreign policy, see Williams, *The Tragedy of American Diplomacy*. For a comprehensive history of American policy in Latin America, a policy predicated on American self-interest, see Schoultz, *Beneath the United States*. Truett also points out that Americans tested a new kind of "informal" empire in Mexico, often led by San Francisco capitalists. Truett, *Fugitive Landscapes*, 55–57.
17. Truett, *Fugitive Landscapes*, 56.

18. William H. Knight, "William Rosecrans," *LAT*, August 8, 1897; Tatum, "General William S. Rosecrans and the Rancho Sausal Redondo," 275–312.

19. Appointment letter from Andrew Johnson to His Excellency the President of the United States of Mexico, undated, legajo 42-30-141, AHSRE.

20. Hart, *Empire and Revolution*, 32.

21. Quoted in Hart, *Empire and Revolution*, 46.

22. Hart, 260.

23. "Shall Our Government Render Aid to Mexico? A Letter from General Rosecrans," March 17, 1870, clipping, folder 14, box 89, WSRP UCLA.

24. "The Rosecrans Memorial on Mexico," undated clipping, folder 14, box 89, WSRP UCLA.

25. William Rosecrans, "Manifest Destiny, the Monroe Doctrine, and Our Relations with Mexico: A Letter from Gen. Rosecrans to the People of the United States," folder 15, box 89, WSRP UCLA.

26. William Rosecrans to Benito Juarez, May 28, 1869, folder 15, box 89, WSRP UCLA.

27. "The Development of Mexico," March 17, 1870, clipping, folder 14, box 89, WSRP UCLA.

28. William H. Knight, "William Rosecrans," *LAT*, August 8, 1897.

29. Schell, *Integral Outsiders*, 2–5. On the Southern Pacific in Mexico, see Lewis, *Iron Horse Imperialism*. Hart, *Empire and Revolution*, 31–55.

30. Corporate charter, Mexican Colonization and Industrial Company, August 10, 1885, folder 20, box 15, WSRP UCLA.

31. Hart, *Empire and Revolution*, 31–55.

32. St. John notes the significance of brokers in borderlands capitalism. See *Line in the Sand*.

33. Jaher, *The Urban Establishment*, 627–30.

34. "Our Commercial Opportunities," *LAT*, November 11, 1882.

35. There is a large body of literature on local elites and empire. For one example, see Slootjes, "Local 'Potentes' in the Roman Empire," 416–32.

36. For an excellent biography of Sepúlveda, see Gray, "Judge Ignacio Sepúlveda," 141–87.

37. Gray, 155–56, and Ignacio Sepúlveda to Ignacio del Valle, June 8, 1868, Del Valle Family Papers, item no. 455, SCWHR.

38. Gray, "Judge Ignacio Sepúlveda," 169.

39. *Los Angeles Herald*, February 26, 1884.

40. Schell, *Integral Outsiders*, 13.

41. Letter from F. G. Hart to Ignacio Sepúlveda, October 7, 1915, HWKC HL.

42. Gray, "Judge Ignacio Sepúlveda," 171–87; Schell, *Integral Outsiders*, 11–14.

43. On other consular offices and the calls from Los Angeles's Mexican community for a consulate, see Balderrama, *In Defense of La Raza*, 3–5.

44. Letter from Los Angeles Chamber of Commerce to the Secretary of Foreign Relations, Republic of Mexico, September 18, 1896, legajo 1965 (II), AHSRE.

45. Letter from Los Angeles Chamber of Commerce.

46. Letter from Los Angeles Chamber of Commerce.

47. Letter from Los Angeles Chamber of Commerce.
48. Letter from Los Angeles Chamber of Commerce.
49. *LAT*, May 20, 1897.
50. "Andrade Welcome," *LAT*, June 20, 1897.
51. *LAT*, May 20, 1897.
52. American support actually helped propel Porfirio Díaz to power in 1876. He had plans to overthrow the presidency of Sebastián Lerdo de Tejada (1872–1876) and relied on American financial support in this process. Hart, *Revolutionary Mexico*, 105–9.
53. Hart, 157–62.
54. "Andrade Honored," *LAT*, June 18, 1897.
55. "Andrade Honored."
56. "Andrade Honored."
57. Calculation based on data from Los Angeles County incorporation records at SCWHR and calculated using www.measuringworth.com. Of course, $70 million does not necessarily reflect the actual amount of investment capital sent from Los Angeles to Mexico. Not all stock was purchased, and the incorporation records from which this number was calculated do not record all Los Angeles investments in Mexico. The amount is useful in suggesting the levels at which Angeleno investors hoped and expected investment capital in Mexico to yield returns.
58. Data compiled from Los Angeles County incorporation records at SCWHR. Most stock options were offered between 1890 and 1920, the majority of stock available for purchase between 1900 and 1910. Investment slowed, but did not stop, after the start of the Mexican Revolution in 1910. In the decade following the outbreak of the revolution, the number of incorporations fell to fifty-six.
59. "Trade with Mexico," *LAT*, June 22, 1897.
60. Letter from S. A. Conner to José Yves Limantour, June 25, 1903, CDLIV.2a. 1903, 20, 39, CFL.

Chapter Two

1. Testimony of Harry Chandler, United States Congress, House of Representatives, quoted in *Western Hemisphere Immigration*, 59.
2. Chandler testimony, 60.
3. Chandler testimony, 60.
4. Molina, *Fit to Be Citizens?*, 6. On constructing race in the borderlands during this period, see Stern, *Eugenic Nation*.
5. Historians of Los Angeles and California argue that racial boundaries hardened following the city's connection to the rest of the nation via railroad in the 1870s. More efficient transportation brought an onslaught of Anglo-American settlers, definitively shifted the region's demographics to majority white, and diminished the power of Californios, mestizos, and native peoples. Pitt, *The Decline of the Californios*; Deverell, *Whitewashed Adobe*; and Torres-Rouff, *Before L.A.*
6. Chandler testimony, 60.
7. For a classic work on race, labor, and immigration, see Alexander Saxton, *The Indispensable Enemy*.

8. On relational racialization and labor in the West, see Foley, *The White Scourge*. On racialization in California, see Almaguer, *Racial Fault Lines*. On relational racialization in Los Angeles, see Molina, *Fit to Be Citizens?* On labor, race, and Mexicans in Los Angeles, see Sánchez, *Becoming Mexican American*. On race in Mexico, see M. Martínez, *Genealogical Fictions*.

9. Scholars of race and empire caution American historians not to simply transplant domestic systems of race into American imperial projects. Paul Kramer, for example, argues that new systems of race and governance developed during American control of the Philippines. See Kramer, *The Blood of Government*. Other scholars tackling empire and race include Briggs, *Reproducing Empire*; Love, *Race over Empire*; Renda, *Taking Haiti*.

10. Knight is quoted in Hart, *Empire and Revolution*, 432.

11. On racialization and imperial collaboration, see Kramer, *The Blood of Government*, 159–227.

12. For more on the Imperial Valley during this period, see Andres, *Power and Control in the Imperial Valley*. For more on Andrade, see Hendricks, "Guillermo Andrade and Land Development." Much of the CRLC's work in its first decade focused on the tricky business of transnational water rights in an arid region. On this important subject, see Worster, *Rivers of Empire*.

13. In some ways, this racialization matched not only earlier alliances with Californios but also the process of purchasing a higher *casta* so common in Spanish colonies in the eighteenth and nineteenth centuries. See M. Martínez, *Genealogical Fictions*.

14. Quoted in Gottlieb and Wolt, *Thinking Big*, 17.

15. Stevens, "Two Radicals and Their Los Angeles," 44–64, 69–70.

16. Quoted in Arax and Wartzman, *The King of California*, 214.

17. Gottlieb and Wolt, *Thinking Big*, 125.

18. Lummis, *Awakening of a Nation*, 104–5. Also quoted in Ruiz, *Americans in the Treasure House*, 84.

19. Ruiz argues that Americans were fascinated by the figure of Díaz and refashioned his race and leadership to fit their own expectations; *Americans in the Treasure House*, 65–101.

20. "Welcome to Díaz," *LAT*, February 22, 1897.

21. "Welcome to Diaz."

22. "An Enlightened Ruler," *LAT*, September 7, 1900.

23. Charles Lummis, "The Man of Mexico: Remarkable Career of President Porfirio Díaz," *LAT*, October 8, 1899.

24. "General Otis Pleased with His Trip to Mexico," *LAT*, October 16, 1902.

25. "Díaz Smashes Union Octopus," *LAT*, August 23, 1906.

26. "President Díaz Ends the Mexican Strike," *LAT*, August 26, 1906.

27. Letter from Harrison Gray Otis to Porfirio Díaz, December 19, 1903, document 000430, legajo XXIX, CPD UI.

28. Letter from *Los Angeles Times* circulation manager to "Dear Sir," 1902, document 185, CDLIV 2a, CFL.

29. Letter from E. C. Butler to José Yves Limantour, November 9, 1905, document 184, CDLIV 2a, CFL.

30. Letter from Thomas E. Gibbon to Secretary of Interior Franklin K. Lane, undated, folder 1, box 35, BC HL.

31. Gibbon to Lane.

32. Letter from Harry Chandler to Henry M. Robinson, undated, folder 1B, CRLC SL. Robinson replied, "We recognize fully that the development of the [CRLC] would work most advantageously to Los Angeles and to our institutions, and we have been hopeful that a situation would arise that would warrant your undertaking the further development of the area." Letter from Henry M. Robinson to Harry Chandler, May 24, 1922, folder 1B, CRLC SL.

33. Monroy, *Rebirth*, 117.

34. For more on Mexican labor in Los Angeles, see Monroy; Deverell, *Whitewashed Adobe*; Garcia, *A World of Its Own*; and Molina, *Fit to Be Citizens?*

35. Starr, *Endangered Dreams*, 157–94.

36. F. Taylor and Welty, *Black Bonanza*, 94.

37. Almaguer, *Racial Fault Lines*, 81.

38. Almaguer, 85.

39. Camarillo, *Chicanos in a Changing Society*.

40. Quoted in Almaguer, *Racial Fault Lines*, 79.

41. Hutchinson, *Oil, Land, and Politics*, 248.

42. Letter from Joseph Rawles to W. O. Gerberding, May 25, 1914, box 18, TBC HL.

43. Letter from John Cave to Thomas Bard, January 3, 1910, box 5, TBC HL.

44. Letter from Charles Barnard to E. O. Gerberding, February 12, 1913, box 3, TBC HL.

45. Letter from W. R. Livingston to Thomas D. Boyd, September 12, 1916, box 4, TBC HL.

46. Report to stockholders, October 24, 1914, box 4, TBC HL.

47. Letter from John Cave to E. O. Gerberding, undated, box 5, TBC HL.

48. Gilly, *The Mexican Revolution*, 5.

49. Knight, *The Mexican Revolution*, 78–81.

50. Castillo-Muñoz, "Historical Roots of Rural Migration," 36–60.

51. Hart, *Revolutionary Mexico*, 158.

52. Almaguer, *Racial Fault Lines*, 72.

53. Menéndez, *Doheny el Cruel*.

54. Margaret Davis, *Dark Side of Fortune*, 285.

55. On issues of manliness, civilization, and empire, see *Manliness and Civilization*; Greenberg, *Manifest Manhood*; Hoganson, *Fighting for American Manhood*; and Renda, *Taking Haiti*. On empire, race, and gender in the domestic context, see Wexler, *Tender Violence*.

56. Abu-Lughod, *New York, Chicago, Los Angeles*, 12.

57. Letter from the Compañía Mexicana de Petróleo to José Yves Limantour, Minister of Finance, August 12, 1901, document 27719, rollo 19, 2a serie, año 1901, CFL.

58. Compañía Mexicana to Limantour, August 12, 1901.

59. Investors included Russell J. Waters, congressman from Los Angeles; E. P. Ripley, Santa Fe president; Aldace F. Walker, Santa Fe chairman of the board; and R. H. Herron, Los Angeles oilman. Ansell, *Oil Baron of the Southwest*, 56.

60. Ansell, 81–83.

61. Letter from Edward L. Doheny to Porfirio Díaz, September 10, 1902, document 011715, Legajo 27, CPD UI.

62. Ansell, *Oil Baron of the Southwest*, 140.

63. La Botz, *Edward L. Doheny*, xiv.

64. Translation of article published in *La Prensa*, Los Angeles, April 12, 1919, box 34, BC HL.

65. Letter from Edward Doheny to Joaquin D. Casasus, November 8, 1902, CFL.

66. Letter from Edward L. Doheny to Porfirio Díaz, September 10, 1902, document 011715, Legajo 27, CPD UI.

67. Santiago, *The Ecology of Oil*, 70–82.

68. Santiago, 163.

69. Letter from Edward L. Doheny to Porfirio Díaz, September 10, 1902.

70. Santiago, *The Ecology of Oil*, 168.

71. Santiago, 174.

72. Special Representative of the Department of State to Jesus Urueta, Secretary of Foreign Relations, March 17, 1915, expediente 16-14-97, AHSRE.

73. Santiago, *The Ecology of Oil*, 173.

74. Santiago, 175.

Chapter Three

1. W. C. Dunn to Quimichis Colony, November 8, 1915, box 25, TBC HL. I reconstructed this narrative of Windham's death from an extraordinarily detailed letter written by Dunn to the officers of the Quimichis Colony just a few days after Windham's death in 1915. Dunn describes all of the events of that night, including the conversation he had with Windham just prior to the latter's death, in rich detail.

2. Dunn to Quimichis Colony, November 8, 1915.

3. While scholars disagree on the amount of anti-Americanism demonstrated by Mexican revolutionaries, most concur that American investments in Mexico precipitated Mexico's social revolution. See Hart, "Social Unrest," 75; and Knight, "The United States and the Mexican Peasantry," 27.

4. On resistance to American commercial and imperial expansion during this period, see Maurer, *The Empire Trap*, 58–148. On banditry as resistance, see Frazer, *Bandit Nation*; and Hobsbawm, *Bandits*.

5. Maurer calls this the creation of the "first American empire"—a period when American investors came to expect and rely on the protection of the United States government for foreign investments. Maurer, *The Empire Trap*, 58–89.

6. Grandin, *Empire's Workshop*, 20.

7. LaFeber, *The American Search for Opportunity*, xiii–xvi, 68–72, 220–27.

8. For a concise history of the causes of the Mexican Revolution, see Joseph and Buchenau, *Mexico's Once and Future Revolution*. Two classics in the history of the Mexican Revolution include Katz, *The Life and Times of Pancho Villa*, and Knight, *The Mexican Revolution*.

9. For debates around anti-Americanism as part of the Mexican Revolution, see Hart, "Social Unrest," 75; and Knight, "The United States and the Mexican Peasantry," 27.

10. There is an extensive literature on the Flores Magón brothers and their lives in the United States. For an analysis of their significance to Los Angeles, see Hernández, *City of Inmates*. See also MacLachlan, *Anarchism and the Mexican Revolution*; Raat, "The Diplomacy of Suppression"; Samaniego, *Nacionalismo y revolución*; Sandos, *Rebelión en la frontera*.

11. "Nip Revolutionists in Los Angeles Den," *LAT*, August 24, 1907.

12. Cánovas, *Ricardo Flores Magón*, 106. Quoted in MacLachlan, *Anarchism and the Mexican Revolution*, 35.

13. Quoted in MacLachlan, *Anarchism and the Mexican Revolution*, 22.

14. "Federal Fist Crushes Nest of Reds," *LAT*, June 15, 1911.

15. "NIP Revolutionists in Los Angeles Den."

16. For a discussion of the Plan de San Diego and the violent backlash it unleashed, see Johnson, *Revolution in Texas*. For more on border violence during the Mexican Revolution, see Hall and Coerver, *Revolution on the Border*; Stout, *Border Conflict*; St. John, *Line in the Sand*; and Vanderwood and Samponaro, *Border Fury*.

17. Kerig, "Yankee Enclave," 136–39.

18. As Castillo-Muñoz notes, the revolution temporarily destabilized the political situation in Nayarit but did not lead to major mobilizations on the part of its population. The Villa and Carranza armies both passed through Nayarit, which contributed to temporary ruptures in local governance. Castillo-Muñoz, "Divided Communities," 22–66.

19. Taylor and Katz both note the long history of rebellion in rural Mexico that predated the beginning of the Mexican Revolution by centuries. See Katz, *Riot, Rebellion, and Revolution*; and W. Taylor, *Drinking, Homicide, and Rebellion*.

20. Gilly, *The Mexican Revolution*, 16–17.

21. Conservative Victoriano Huerta planned and executed a military coup in 1913 against the administration of Francisco Madero with the aid of the United States ambassador. Opposed to Huerta's rule, Venustiano Carranza (an ardent follower of Madero) joined forces with Pancho Villa to oust him. They succeeded in 1914 with support from the Wilson administration, which opposed Huerta's coup. When Carranza assumed the presidency in 1914, however, both Villa and Zapata denounced his administration. In early 1915, the factions fell into civil war, with Carranza's constitutionalist forces fighting Villa in the north and Zapata in the south.

22. Irvin, *Let the Tail Go with the Hide*, 124.

23. "Carranza Orders Americans Freed," *Los Angeles Examiner*, December 3, 1913, box 25, TBC HL.

24. Windham died deeply in debt to the Quimichis Colony. Despite his salary as ranch manager and his status as a stockholder, he constantly had to borrow money to pay for his wife's and daughter's living expenses.

25. Letter from Quimichis Secretary to W. S. Windham, September 17, 1910, box 25, TBC HL.

26. Letter from W. S. Windham to William F. Alger, April 20, 1912, box 1, TBC HL.

27. Letter from W. C. Dunn to Thomas Bard, quoted in letter from Thomas Bard to Robert Lansing, Secretary of State, July 24, 1915, box 6, TBC HL.

28. Russell, *Mexico in Peace and War*, 277.

29. Quimichis Colony Stockholders Annual Meeting Report, 1912, box 1, TBC HL.

30. Letter from W. C. Dunn to "My Dear Sir," January 11, 1916, box 18, TBC HL.

31. Letter from W. S. Windham to Thomas Bard, June 22, 1912, box 24, TBC HL.

32. Windham to Bard, June 22, 1912.

33. Letter from W. S. Windham to E. O. Gerberding, July 29, 1912, box 24, TBC HL.

34. Letter from Thomas R. Bard to Philander Knox, [1911], box 6, TBC HL.

35. Letter from Thomas R. Bard to Hon. John D. Works, U.S. Senate, May 7, 1911, box 4, TBC HL.

36. Windham does not specify who the soldiers were. From his use of "federal" and the year, 1913, they were likely Huerta's forces.

37. Letter from W. S. Windham to Thomas Bard, quoted in letter from Bard to Henry Cabot Lodge, October 1, 1913, box 6, TBC HL.

38. Bard to Lodge, October 1, 1913.

39. Bard to Lodge, October 1, 1913.

40. Bard to Lodge, October 1, 1913. It is not clear what declaration the United Stated had made regarding Mexico, but evidently the reiteration of the Monroe Doctrine was not popular.

41. Bard to Lodge, October 1, 1913.

42. Letter from W. C. Dunn to "My Dear Sir," January 11, 1916.

43. Dunn to "My Dear Sir," January 11, 1916.

44. Letter from Thomas Bard to William Jennings Bryan, February 11, 1914, box 6, TBC HL.

45. Letter from John Cave to E. O. Gerberding, undated, box 5, TBC HL. At this point, Álvaro Obregón was Carranza's highest-ranking military officer. He would go on to become president in 1920.

46. Letter from M. L. Applegate to Companía Agricola de Quimichis, May 17, 1917, box 2, TBC HL.

47. Letter from M. L. Applegate to Companía Agricola de Quimichis, May 31, 1917, box 2, TBC HL.

48. For more on the history of the CRLC during this period, see Kerig, "Yankee Enclave," 128–48.

49. To understand the historical debate on this episode in Baja, see Gottlieb and Wolt, *Thinking Big*, 172–76; Blaisdell, "Harry Chandler and Mexican Border Intrigue," 385–93; P. Martínez, *Historia de Baja California*.

50. The CRLC kept perfect records of their tax payments during this period, likely to help protect their claim on the property. See caja 19, Colleción "Chata Angulo," AMM.

51. Kerig, "Yankee Enclave," 173–74.

52. Kerig, 155–57.

53. Kerig, 152–55.

54. Clipping from the *Dearborn Independent*, August 25, 1923, folder 43, CRLC SL.

55. Letter from Harry Chandler to Henry M. Robinson, First National Bank, May 1922, folder 1B, CRLC SL.

56. Abelardo L. Rodriguez, "Enchanting Ensenada, Baja California, Mexico Will Be the Mecca of Thousands of Tourists and the Home of Many Clubs," *Pan Pacific Progress*, July 1926.

57. "Cantu Will Surrender," *LAT*, August 16, 1920, and August 21, 1920. Also cited in Kerig, "Yankee Enclave," 178.

58. Margaret Davis, *Dark Side of Fortune*, 109.

59. Brown, *Oil and Revolution in Mexico*, 172.

60. Letter from Henry Lane Wilson to Francisco de la Barra, April 26, 1913, expediente 16-9-150, AHSRE.

61. Margaret Davis, *Dark Side of Fortune*, 100.

62. Santiago, *The Ecology of Oil*; and Brown, *Oil and Revolution*, 253–78.

63. Brown, *Oil and Revolution*, 271; and Margaret Davis, *Dark Side of Fortune*, 112. According to Hart, a peso was worth approximately fifty cents in the early 1920s. Hart, *Empire and Revolution*, 348.

64. Lavín, *Petróleo*, 125. Quoted in Santiago, *Ecology of Oil*, 99.

65. Santiago, *Ecology of Oil*, 99.

66. Santiago, 243; "Produccion de petroleo crudo in Mexico, durante el periodo comprendido entre los años de 1901 a 1920," expediente 104-P1-P-22, OC AGN.

67. Telegram to Álvaro Obregón, July 17, 1921, box 34, expediente 104-H-10, OC AGN.

68. Telegram to Álvaro Obregón, July 21, 1921, box 34, expediente 104-H-10, OC AGN.

69. Undated memo, box 34, expediente 104-H-10, OC AGN.

70. Letter from Albau B. Butler to Álvaro Obregón, July 22, 1921, box 34, expediente 104-H-10, OC AGN.

71. "Gen. Villa Is Hunted Here," *LAT*, January 10, 1916.

72. "Police Investigation of 'Junta' Ordered," *LAT*, February 6, 1916.

73. F. C. Spayde, "Case of the City of Los Angeles vs. the Government of Mexico," *LAT*, December 7, 1919.

74. File 412.11, Central Decimal File Enclosures, NARA.

75. "Former Pasadena Banker and Assistant Are Prisoners in Mexico," newspaper clipping, *Los Angeles Examiner*, December 2, 1913, box 25, TBC HL.

76. "Former Pasadena Banker."

77. LaFeber, *The American Search for Opportunity*.

Chapter Four

1. Letter from Thomas Gibbon to Franklin K. Lane, January 12, 1920, folder 1, box 33, BC HL. Letter from Secretary of the Interior Franklin K. Lane to Thomas E. Gibbon, December 27, 1919, folder 1, box 33, BC HL.

2. Deverell, "The Neglected Twin," 72–99.

3. Letter from Thomas Gibbon to Franklin K. Lane, April 26, 1915, folder 1, box 33, BC HL.

4. Peter Trubowitz makes the compelling argument that regional interests in the United States have had a significant impact in shaping American foreign policy. Regional policymakers have consistently advocated for foreign policy beneficial to their specific regions. See Trubowitz, *Defining the National Interest*.

5. See LaFeber, *The American Search for Opportunity*, 199–201; and Maurer, *The Empire Trap*, 58–89.

6. See Kramer, *The Blood of Government*; Love, *Race over Empire*; and Renda, *Taking Haiti*. See also Kramer, "Race, Empire, and Transnational Identity," 199–219.

7. For a discussion of Los Angeles as the "white spot," see Avila, *Popular Culture in the Age of White Flight*, 20–25.

8. Quoted in Brown, *Oil and Revolution*, 225.

9. Katz, *The Life and Times of Pancho Villa*, 620.

10. There is a large literature on the Mexican Revolution and the Constitution of 1917. On the issue of property rights, see Elizondo, *The Concept of Property*, and Haber, Razo, and Maurer, *The Politics of Property Rights*. For excellent overviews, see Cumberland, *Mexican Revolution*; Ely, *Guardian of Every Other Right*; Hart, *Revolutionary Mexico*; Katz, *The Life and Times of Pancho Villa*; Katz, *The Secret War in Mexico*; Niemeyer, *Revolution at Querétaro*.

11. Hart, *Revolutionary Mexico*, 330.

12. Letter from Thomas Gibbon to Harry Chandler, November 17, 1917, "Mexico & C. M." folder, box 35, BC HL.

13. "Agreement," undated, "Mexico—Mr. Doheny" folder, box 35, BC HL.

14. Letter from Thomas E. Gibbon to Harry Chandler, November 17, 1917, "Mexico & C. M." folder, box 35, BC HL.

15. On these interventions and the role of American investors, see Schoultz, *Beneath the United States*, 176–219; Maurer, *The Empire Trap*, 60–118, quote from 118. On Wilson and the Mexican Revolution, see Benbow, *Leading Them to the Promised Land*.

16. Brown, *Oil and Revolution*, 114–15.

17. Brown, 151. Doheny initially tried to create strategic alliances with Mexican leaders, including Madero and Huerta. He was somewhat successful, but their short tenures in office limited political stability in the country and undermined Doheny's political alliances. When Carranza took office, the oil industry was one of the few still producing revenue in the war-torn country, and Carranza instituted a number of policies to tax foreign oil companies. Oil producers such as Doheny re-

sented Carranza's taxation policies and feared they represented a precursor to nationalization of the industry. See Brown, *Oil and Revolution*, 171-253.

18. Barron, *The Mexican Problem*, vii.
19. Barron, 34-35.
20. Barron, 71.
21. For a summary of American policy toward Mexico during this period, see Schoultz, *Beneath the United States*, 238-50. On Villa's attack on Columbus, see Katz, "Pancho Villa and the Attack on Columbus, New Mexico," 101-30.
22. Barron, *The Mexican Problem*, viii.
23. See Schoultz, *Beneath the United States*, 148-51.
24. Barron, *The Mexican Problem*, xxiv.
25. Barron, 14.
26. Deverell, "The Neglected Twin," 72-99.
27. Deverell, 72-99.
28. "Thomas E. Gibbon Dies," *LAT*, June 23, 1921.
29. "Thomas Gibbon," *LAT*, June 25, 1921.
30. Kerig, "Yankee Enclave," 58.
31. "Trade with Mexico: How It May Be Promoted by Los Angeles," *LAT*, June 22, 1897.
32. Letter from Thomas E. Gibbon to President Woodrow Wilson, March 22, 1915, folder 1, box 33, BC HL.
33. Letter from Thomas Gibbon to Woodrow Wilson, March 22, 1915, folder 1, box 33, BC HL.
34. Draft, "History of Nations," by Thomas Gibbon, undated, box 31, BC HL.
35. Draft, "History of Nations."
36. Letter from Thomas Gibbon to Franklin K. Lane, April 26, 1915, folder 1, box 33, BC HL.
37. Telegram from Thomas Gibbon to Franklin K. Lane, March 10, 1916, folder 1, box 33, BC HL.
38. Letter from the California-Mexico Land and Cattle Company to Thomas E. Gibbon, September 1, 1916, folder 1, box 35, BC HL.
39. Gibbon makes reference to his regular correspondence with the president in a letter to Franklin K. Lane. Letter from Thomas E. Gibbon to Secretary of Interior Franklin K. Lane, May 11, 1915, folder 1, box 33, BC HL.
40. Gibbon, *Mexico under Carranza*, 78.
41. Letter from Thomas E. Gibbon to Harry Chandler, January 17, 1919, folder 1, box 34, BC HL.
42. Letter from Thomas Gibbon to Woodrow Wilson, March 22, 1915, folder 1, box 33, BC HL.
43. Letter from Thomas E. Gibbon to President Woodrow Wilson, June 10, 1915, folder 1, box 33, BC HL.
44. Letter from Thomas E. Gibbon to Secretary of Interior Franklin K. Lane, October 24, 1916, folder 1, box 33, BC HL.
45. Telegram from Thomas E. Gibbon to Secretary of Interior Franklin K. Lane, December 28, 1916, folder 1, box 35, BC HL.

46. Gibbon to Lane, December 28, 1916.

47. Unfortunately, many of the records and much of the correspondence documenting the beginnings of the organization are undated. Correspondence in the Bergman Collection suggests that Doheny, Gibbon, and Chandler decided in the summer of 1917 that they needed an organization to represent their Mexican interests in Washington, D.C. Letter from Thomas Gibbon to Harry Chandler, November 17, 1917, and letter from D. J. Haff to Edward Doheny, box 35, BC HL.

48. Letter from Thomas Gibbon to Harry Chandler, November 17, 1917. Eventually, members included Doheny in his capacity as president of the Pan-American Petroleum and Transportation Company; J. S. Alexander, president of the National Bank of Commerce of New York; G. F. Kelly, vice president of the Greene Cananea Copper Company; Thomas W. Lamont, member of J. P. Morgan and Company; and Charles H. Sabin, president of the Guaranty Trust Company of New York. Lou, "Fall Committee," 5.

49. Thomas Gibbon, "Data upon the Proposed 'Mexican Outlook,'" undated, folder 2, box 33, BC HL.

50. Gibbon.

51. U.S. Senate, *Preliminary Report and Hearings of the Committee on Foreign Relations*, 66th Cong., 1st Sess., Document No. 185 (Washington, DC, 1920), I:408-9.

52. U.S. Senate, 408-9.

53. Thomas Gibbon, "The Mexican Outlook," manuscript, undated, folder 2, box 33, BC HL.

54. Gibbon.

55. Gibbon.

56. Quoted in LaBotz, *Edward L. Doheny*, 78.

57. U.S. Senate, *Preliminary Report*, I:3.

58. Lou, "Fall Committee," iii.

59. Doheny's testimony before the Fall Committee is reproduced in its entirety in Hanrahan, *The Bad Yankee*, 273-381.

60. Hanrahan, 289.

61. Quoted in Hanrahan, 355.

62. Quoted in Hanrahan, 351.

63. La Botz, *Edward L. Doheny*, 149. Unions struggled to organize workers at Doheny-held properties throughout the early 1920s. Although their wages were higher than the national average, workers opposed Doheny's paternalistic management policies. As argued by historian Myrna Santiago, native peoples in Mexico's oil region, the Huastecs, made strategic use of the presence of the industry. They wrought temporary gains through wages and royalties between 1900 and the 1920s. As the oil industry waned in the late 1920s, the Huastecs organized for ejido, or communal, land grants to reestablish their agricultural tradition. Santiago, "Rejecting Progress in Paradise," 169-88.

64. Statement of Edward L. Doheny, *Investigation of Mexican Affairs,* Hearing before a Subcommittee of the Committee on Foreign Relations, United States Senate, 1919, 254.

65. Letter from Thomas E. Gibbon to Harry Chandler, January 17, 1919, folder 1, box 34, BC HL.

66. Gibbon to Chandler, January 17, 1919.

67. Gibbon, *Mexico under Carranza*, v.

68. Gibbon, 233.

69. Gibbon, 238.

70. See Schoultz, *Beneath the United States*, 251.

71. Maurer, *The Empire Trap*, 141–42.

72. Wilson to the House, June 22, 1916, in the Papers of Ray Stannard Baker, Library of Congress. Quoted in Gardner, "Woodrow Wilson and the Mexican Revolution," 29.

73. Message from the Mexican Embassy to Carranza, expediente 976, caja 16, AHSRE.

74. Letter from the Mexican Embassy, Washington, DC, to Cádido Aguilar, Secretario de Relaciones Exteriors, June 10, 1918, expediente 976, caja 16, AHSRE.

75. Brown, *Oil and Revolution*, 217.

76. Although they had fought together against Huerta as well as Villa, Carranza and Obregón had a contentious relationship, and Obregón harbored plans to assume the Mexican presidency. In 1920, he announced his candidacy for president and rallied support from those disenchanted with Carranza's administration. He criticized Carranza for failing to fulfill the promises of the revolution and issued his Agua Prieta Plan in 1920, which called for the removal of Carranza. The army backed Obregón and forced Carranza to flee Mexico City. Members of Carranza's bodyguard killed him during his escape, and Obregón assumed the presidency later in 1920.

77. La Botz, *Edward L. Doheny*, 104.

78. Letter from El Jefe de la Policia Judicia Federal to El Procurador General (attorney general), February 20, 1924, expediente 101-RR-D-1, OC AGN.

79. El Jefe de la Policia to El Procurador General, February 20.

80. Telegram from Frederico Dato to John Camp, [1923], expediente 101-RR-D-1, OC AGN.

81. Telegram from J. F. Peterson to John Camp, [1923], expediente 101-RR-D-1, OC AGN.

82. Receipt from Toepperwein Hardware Company to John Camp, November 12, 1923, expediente 101-RR-D-1, OC AGN.

83. La Botz, *Edward L. Doheny*, 108–9.

84. Telegram from the Mexican Consul in Los Angeles to Fernando Torreblanca (Obregón's personal secretary), June 22, 1924, expediente 101-RR-D-1, OC AGN.

85. Quoted in Brown, *Oil and Revolution*, 192.

86. On this period of U.S.-Mexico relations and the oil industry, see Margaret Davis, *Dark Side of Fortune*, 118–22; and Schoultz, *Beneath the United States*, 275–77.

Chapter Five

1. *Agraristas* is a term used to describe members of the agrarian movement in Mexico in the early part of the twentieth century, particularly those who fought for a more just distribution of land. While the Mexican federal state hesitated to begin

redistributing foreign-owned land following the revolution, local agricultural communities started to move onto private properties and farm them. See Dwyer, *The Agrarian Dispute*.

2. Letter from M. L. Applegate to Compania Agricola de Quimichis, February 13, 1921, box 2, TBC QCA HL.

3. See Hart, *Empire and Revolution*, 371; and Dwyer, *The Agrarian Dispute*, 20 and 160.

4. See Nugent, *Rural Revolt in Mexico*; Castillo-Muñoz, "Divided Communities"; and Dwyer, *The Agrarian Dispute*. On the power of ordinary Mexicans in creating the revolutionary state, see Joseph and Nugent, *Everyday Forms of State Formation*; and Vaughn, "Cultural Approaches to Peasant Politics."

5. On agrarian land seizures and this period of American-Mexican relations, see Hart, *Empire and Revolution*, 343–53. On oil during this period, see Margaret Davis, *Dark Side of Fortune*, 118–22; Brown, *Oil and Revolution*, 224–29; and Schoultz, *Beneath the United States*, 272–83.

6. In this argument I draw from the intervention laid out in Dwyer's *Agrarian Dispute*. In particular, see his introduction.

7. Maurer, *The Empire Trap*, 2.

8. Maurer, *The Empire Trap*, 1–25.

9. Letter from William Edwards to Henry Workman Keller, undated, folder 13, box 23, HWKC HL.

10. For a discussion of gender and the discourse of civilization, see Bederman, *Manliness and Civilization*.

11. Letter from Henry Workman Keller to William Edwards, April 10, 1910, folder 13, box 23, HWKC HL; letter from William Edwards to Henry Workman Keller, July 25, 1910, folder 13, box 23, HWKC HL.

12. Letter from William Edwards to Chief Justice William H. Taft, November 21, 1929, folder 13, box 23, HWKC HL.

13. Letter from Edwards to Taft, November 21.

14. San Isidro Ranch Company Articles of Incorporation, 1910, folder 2, box 21, HWKC HL.

15. The peninsula of Baja California is divided into two districts—Norte (North) and Sur (South). The territory of Baja California Norte became a Mexican state in 1953.

16. For a textured history of agrarian reform in Baja California, see Castillo-Muñoz, *The Other California*, and Dwyer, *The Agrarian Dispute*.

17. León-Portilla and Piñera Ramírez, *Baja California*, 148–49.

18. Kerig, "Yankee Enclave," 157. Baja California experienced a labor shortage during this period and actively recruited workers from China to labor primarily on agricultural properties.

19. Undated memo, folder 1, box 21, HWKC HL.

20. Letter from Henry Workman Keller to American Consul Walter Boyle, January 14, 1919, folder 6, box 19, HWKC HL.

21. Letter from Henry Workman Keller to Walter F. Boyle, June 3, 1919, folder 6, box 19, HWKC HL.

22. Letter from Henry Workman Keller to American Consul Walter Boyle, January 14, 1919, folder 6, box 19, HWKC HL.

23. Letter from Henry Workman Keller to Harry Chandler, July 21, 1921, folder 26, box 21, HWKC HL.

24. Letter from Henry Workman Keller to Walter F. Boyle, January 12, 1920, folder 6, box 19, HWKC HL.

25. Letter from Henry Workman Keller to Harry Chandler, Burton E. Green, Homer E. Sargent, W. L. Valentine Estate, June 11, 1943, folder 7, box 19, HWKC HL.

26. Letter from Henry Workman Keller to Walter F. Boyle, March 15, 1920, folder 6, box 19, HWKC HL.

27. Letter from Henry Workman Keller to Walter F. Boyle, November 10, 1919, folder 6, box 19, HWKC HL.

28. See Dwyer, *The Agrarian Dispute*, 44–76.

29. Letter from Henry Workman Keller to William Edwards, September 18, 1931, folder 13, box 23, HWKC HL. Keller is referring to Governor Carlos Trejo y Lerdo de Tejada, the appointed governor of Baja California in 1931. Tejada was a nationalist who believed that the territory's problems stemmed from inequitable land redistribution and economic inequalities. See Kerig, "Yankee Enclave," 313.

30. "The intending squatters know before locating on the property that the local Fomento is probably in sympathy with their actions." Letter from Henry Workman Keller to William Edwards, November 13, 1929, folder 13, box 23, HWKC HL.

31. Memorandum from Abelino Romero to Henry Workman Keller, undated, folder 17, box 21, HWKC HL.

32. Undated memo, folder 1, box 21, HWKC HL.

33. Undated memo, HWKC HL.

34. Letter from Henry Workman Keller to Governor Filiberto Gómez, March 4, 1931, folder 1, box 21, HWKC HL. The highway referenced by Keller was the International Pacific Highway and is the subject of the next chapter. He wrote, rather testily, to his friend Filiberto Gómez, the governor of the state of Mexico, "Notwithstanding this injustice, the writer as you well know is wholeheartedly, and without compensation or hope of reward, making every effort to bring about the construction of the International Pacific Highway which when realized will do more to bring permanent prosperity and happiness to your people than anything undertaken in Mexico since your Republic was formed."

35. The *zona prohibida* prohibited non-Mexican citizens from owning property along Mexico's coasts and international borders. The policy was a reaction to the loss of Texas and lands ceded to the United States following the Mexican-American War.

36. Letter from Eduardo Cortina to Carlos Ariza, February 19, 1932, folder 1, box 21, HWKC HL.

37. Letter form Henry Workman Keller to Stockholders of the San Isidro Ranch Company, May 5, 1928, folder 7, box 19, HWKC HL.

38. Letter from Henry Workman Keller to Harry Chandler, Burton E. Green, Homer E. Sargent, W. L. Valentine Estate, June 11, 1943, folder 7, box 19, HWKC HL.

39. Letter from Keller to Chandler et al., June 11.

40. Letter from Henry Workman Keller to Jorge Correa, January 19, 1939, folder 1, box 22, HWKC HL.

41. Letter from Henry Workman Keller to Governor Filiberto Goméz, March 4, 1931, folder 1, box 21, HWKC HL.

42. Letter from Emilio Gonzalez to Henry Workman Keller, July 1, 1932, folder 1, box 26, HWKC HL.

43. Letter from William Edwards to Henry Workman Keller, October 14, 1925, folder 13, box 23, HWKC HL.

44. Memorandum from Abelino Romero to Henry Workman Keller, undated, folder 17, box 21, HWKC HL.

45. Telegram from M. L. Applegate to John A. Treher, box 2, TBC HL. For information on Applegate's life, see visa application letter from M. L. Applegate to the Mexican government, 1942, box 2, TBC HL, and letter from Richard Bard to C. H. Windham, February 9, 1931, box 5, TBC HL.

46. Letter from M. L. Applegate to Compania Agricola de Quimichis, April 25, 1919, box 2, TBC HL.

47. Letter from Applegate to Quimichis, April 25.

48. Discussed in Castillo-Muñoz, "Divided Communities," 32 and 87.

49. Letter from M. L. Applegate to Compania Agricola de Quimichis, October 31, 1919, box 2, TBC HL.

50. Telegram from Richard Bard to the Department of State, July 21, 1926, box 6, TBC HL.

51. Letter from Richard Bard to the Department of State, January 19, 1925, box 6, TBC HL.

52. Letter from Richard Bard to M. L. Applegate, May 24, 1921, box 2, TBC HL, and letter from M. L. Applegate to Compania Agricola de Quimichis, May 30, 1921, box 2, TBC HL.

53. Letter from José Zuloaga Vizcaíno to Ramón Sánchez-Albarrán, August 28, 1934, box 6, TBC HL.

54. *Periódico Oficial de Nayarit*, March 13, 1935, 1.

55. Letter from R. Sanchez Albarran to Richard Bard, June 20, 1935, box 6, TBC HL.

56. Letter from Richard Bard to Adams Chadwick Company, June 27, 1931, box 3, TBC HL.

57. Letter from H. Lyttle to Bank of America, September 10, 1935, box 4, TBC HL.

58. Letter from Richard Bard to Bank of America, February 24, 1938, box 4, TBC HL.

59. Letter from Richard Bard to Bank of America, March 17, 1941, box 4, TBC HL.

60. Letter from M. L. Applegate to Richard Bard, April 10, 1942, box 2, TBC HL.

61. Letter from M. L. Applegate to Richard Bard, June 11, 1942, box 2, TBC HL.

62. Letter from M. L. Applegate to Richard Bard, May 7, 1943, box 2, TBC HL.

63. Letter from Harry Chandler to V. H. Rosetti, July 23, 1929, folder 1, box 1, Harry Chandler Subject Files Relating to the Colorado River Land Company, CSCC SL.

64. Kerig, "Yankee Enclave," 242.

65. Kerig, 100.

66. Kerig, 257, and Stone, "Cotton Production Data of Lower California," undated, claim 54, docket 72, box 31, Records of the U.S. and Mexican Claims Commissions, Record Group 76, NARA.

67. Letter from Otto Brant to Harry Chandler, March 17, 1921, cited in Kerig, "Yankee Enclave," 203.

68. H. H. Clark to President Obregón, February 15, 1922, expediente 803-C-14, OC AGN.

69. Villareal referenced Chandler's plans in a telegram to Obregón. Telegram from Antonio Villarreal to President Obregón, May 25, 1921, expediente 421-Ch-7, vol. 154, OC AGN.

70. Letter from Harry Chandler to John Key, April 13, 1925, folder 1, box 1, Harry Chandler Subject Files Relating to the Colorado River Land Company, CSCC SL.

71. Kerig, "Yankee Enclave," 210.

72. Telegram from Harry Chandler to President Obregón, May 14, 1923, expediente 422-S-9, vol. 160, OC AGN.

73. Letter from Harry Chandler to I. P. Gaxiola, August 29, 1927, folder 5, box 1, Harry Chandler Subject Files Relating to the Colorado River Land Company, CSCC SL.

74. Letter from Harry Chandler to Álvaro Obregón, May 31, 1923, folder 5, box 1, Harry Chandler Subject Files Relating to the Colorado River Land Company, CSCC SL.

75. Castillo-Muñoz, "Divided Communities," 92–93. Mejía argued more specifically that repatriated Mexicans and Mexican Americans deserved property in Baja California more than American-owned firms such as the CRLC.

76. Kerig, "Yankee Enclave," 215.

77. Letter from Harry Chandler to President Obregón, April 4, 1922, expediente 243-B1-B, vol. 116, OC AGN.

78. Letter from Chandler to Obregón, April 4.

79. Letter from Chandler to Obregón, April 4.

80. Letter from Governor José Lugo to President Obregón, April 15, 1922, expediente 243-B1-B, vol. 116, OC AGN.

81. Letter from Harry Chandler to President Obregón, December 2, 1922, expediente 803-C-14, OC AGN.

82. Letter from Harry Chandler to President Obregón, April 10, 1923, expediente 104-B-15, vol. 25, OC AGN.

83. Kerig, "Yankee Enclave," 237–38.

84. Letter from Harry Chandler to President Alvaro Obregón, June 26, 1923, expediente 245-D1-B, vol. 123, OC AGN.

85. "High Mexican Official on Visit to L.A.," *LAT*, June 9, 1923, expediente 245-D1-13, vol. 123, OC AGN.

86. Letter from Harry Chandler to T. H. Williams, October 7, 1925, Harry Chandler Subject Files Relating to the Colorado River Land Company, CSCC SL.

87. Dwyer, *The Agrarian Dispute*, 45.

88. Dwyer, 59. The invasion of the CRLC property in 1937 had deep historical roots. As argued by Dwyer, campesinos had been organizing in Baja California since the 1920s and had long-standing radical politics.

89. For more details on the expropriation of CRLC land in the 1930s, see works by Castillo-Muñoz, Kerig, and Dwyer, as well as the claim the CRLC filed with the U.S. and Mexican Claims Commissions, boxes 30 and 31, Records of U.S. and Mexican Claims Commissions, Record Group 76, NARA. In Mexico, see expediente 437.1/413, 503.11/106, 404.1/4227, 404.2/81, 705.2/26, LC AGN.

90. Letter from Harry Chandler to Lawrence M. Lawson, American Commissioner, Agrarian Claims Commission, May 4, 1939, box 31, Records of U.S. and Mexican Claims Commissions, Record Group 76, NARA.

91. They created the Special Claims Commission to adjudicate claims emerging from the Mexican Revolution between 1910 and 1920 as the result of armed forces. The General Claims Commission arbitrated claims related to damages resulting from "other acts."

92. Woolsey, "The Settlement of Claims between the United States and Mexico," 99–102.

93. The State Department had actually been collecting this information since 1923 but began collecting more complete claims information in 1934.

94. "Geographical List of United States Claimants," Research and Information Section, International Claims Commissions, box 1, Record Group 76, NARA.

95. Letter from Harry Chandler to Lawrence M. Lawson, American Commissioner, May 4, 1939, box 31, docket 72, Approved American Claims Case Files, Records of U.S. and Mexico Claims Commission, Record Group 76, NARA.

96. Letter from Chandler to Lawson, May 4.

97. "Affidavit," February 25, 1939, box 30, docket 72, Approved Agrarian Claims, Records of the U.S. and Mexico Claims Commission, Record Group 76, NARA.

98. Kerig, "Yankee Enclave," 386.

99. Letter from Henry Workman Keller to Harry Chandler, Burton E. Green, Homer E. Sargent, Estate of W. L. Valentine, June 16, 1943, box 19, HWKC HL.

100. Letter from William A. Edwards to Henry Workman Keller, April 10, 1910, folder 13, box 23, HWKC HL.

101. Letter from James Langston, Commissioner, to Quimichis Colony, September 8, 1943, box 48, docket 107, Approved Agrarian Case Files, American Mexican Claims Commission, Record Group 76, NARA.

102. Ansell, *Oil Baron of the Southwest*, 240–41.

103. Letter from Richard Bard to H. C. Thompson, June 16, 1959, box 2, TBC HL.

Chapter Six

1. Earnest E. East, "The International Pacific Highway: Los Angeles to Mexico City Section Report," 1930, folder 611, box 19, Report Collection, ACSC; Phil Townsend Hanna, "Pilgrims to Anahuac: The Adventures and Achievements of the First International Pacific Highway Expedition of the Automobile Club of Southern California in Mexico," *Touring Topics*, July 1930, 12.

2. Schoultz, *Beneath the United States*, 281–315.

3. For an excellent overview of the "new" American empire in Latin America, see Greg Grandin's *Empire's Workshop*, 11–39. Andrew Bacevich makes a similar argument about the postwar period and American empire in *American Empire*.

4. See Grandin, *Empire's Workshop*. On the United States and Latin America, including continued economic ties, from the period of the "Good Neighbor" through World War II and into the second half of the twentieth century, see Lipman, *Guantánamo*, 7–8; Schoultz, *Beneath the United States*, 315; Maurer, *The Empire Trap*, 311–12. On American tourism and empire in Latin America, especially Mexico, see Merrill, *Negotiating Paradise*, 1–103.

5. "Road Plan to Link Coast with South America," *LAT*, August 4, 1929; "Estudian los Ingenieros Mejicanos, el plan de la Carretera Internacional," *Heraldo de Cuba*, October 26, 1930. Founded in the first decade of the twentieth century, the ACSC served as the preeminent advocate for auto enthusiasts in the nation. J. Davis, *The Friend to All Motorists*.

6. See Grandin, *Empire's Workshop*, 159–195; and Bacevich, *American Empire*.

7. On Los Angeles and cross-border tourism, particularly tourism and race, see Kun, "Tijuana and the Borders of Race," 313–26. On American tourism in Mexico, see Bloom, *Adventures into Mexico*; Vanderwood, *Satan's Playground*; Berger and Wood, *Holiday in Mexico*. On more recent California forays into Mexico related to empire and homeownership, see Fingal, "Your House Es Mi Casa."

8. Hartig, "'A Most Advantageous Spot on the Map,'" 289–312. On tourism in Southern California, see Culver, *The Frontier of Leisure*.

9. "Los Angeles Trade Booms! 12,322,213 Tons of Freight Passes through Harbor in Six Months," *New York Times*, August 19, 1923.

10. Abu-Lughod, *New York, Chicago, Los Angeles*, 151. On economic growth in Los Angeles in the 1920s, see also Sitton and Deverell, *Metropolis in the Making*.

11. On increasing restrictions on border movements during this period, see Hernández, *Migra!* On repatriation during this period, see Balderrama, *Decade of Betrayal*. Race became an increasingly important marker in restricting people's movements in Southern California and the borderlands during this period. On the subject of race and mobility in California, see Carpio, *Collisions at the Crossroads*.

12. *Pan Pacific Progress*, May 1919.

13. "Henry Keller, Pioneer, Civic Leader, Dies," *LAT*, November 11, 1958.

14. Instituto Mexicano del Transporte, *Historia de las Juntas Locales de Caminos*, 24.

15. Harry Carr, "Mexican Notables Due for Road Conference," *LAT*, October 12, 1930.

16. Berger, *Pyramids by Day*, 51.

17. On the remaking of this space, see Estrada, *The Los Angeles Plaza*.

18. On the Spanish fantasy past, see McWilliams, *Southern California*; Deverell, *Whitewashed Adobe*; and Kropp, *California Vieja*. For more on borderlands tourism, see essays in McCrossen, *Land of Necessity*.

19. On mexicanidad and tourism, see Merrill, *Negotiating Paradise*; and Berger and Wood, *Holiday in Mexico*.

20. Herbert Hoover to Phil Hanna, March 10, 1930, ACSC. Regarding the highway, Hoover wrote, "This movement holds large promise of providing a practical bond of enlarged friendly-relationship with our Southern neighbors through facilitating communications with them."

21. Harry Carr, "Road Plan to Link Coast with South America," *LAT*, August 4, 1929.

22. East is quoted in Phil Townsend Hanna, "Linking the Americas with an International Highway," *LAT*, January 2, 1930.

23. "Transactions of the First International Pacific Highway Conference," 1930, folder 1, box 46, HWKC HL. Hereafter cited as "Transactions, ACSC."

24. "Transactions, ACSC."

25. Hanna, "Pilgrims to Anahuac."

26. Kun, "Tijuana and the Borders of Race," 317.

27. Merrill, *Negotiating Paradise*, 70.

28. Delpar, *The Enormous Vogue of Things Mexican*; Romo, "Work and Restlessness," 176.

29. "With the First International Pacific Highway Expedition: A Daily Log of Progress and Experiences," *Touring Topics*, May 1930, 21.

30. "Hoy Deberá arribar a Esta Ciudad la del Auto-Club de California," *El Informador*, April 15, 1930; "Arribaron a Esta Ciudad los miembros del Auto-Club del Sur de California," *El Informador*, April 16, 1930; "Se sesea que la Carretera Internacional cruce la región de Los Altos," *El Informador*, April 17, 1930.

31. "With the First International Pacific Highway Expedition."

32. Hanna, "Pilgrims to Anahuac," 19.

33. Merrill provides an excellent analysis of this process in *Negotiating Paradise*.

34. On links between tourism and state building in Mexico, see Berger, *Pyramids by Day*.

35. Harry Carr, "Mexican Notables Due for Road Conference," *LAT*, October 12, 1930; Hanna, "Pilgrims to Anahuac," 20–21.

36. "Se desea que la Carretera Internacional cruce la región de Los Altos"; "La ruta internacional debe ser por Los Altos," *El Informador*, April 24, 1930; "Filiberto Gómez," *Gaceta del Gobierno*, October 21, 1931.

37. When the expedition traveled through Michoacán, Cárdenas was the state's governor. He became president of Mexico in 1934.

38. Hanna, "Pilgrims to Anahuac."

39. On the history of United States–Latin American relations and the roots of the Good Neighbor Policy, see Schoultz, *Beneath the United States*, 290–315.

40. "Transactions, ACSC."

41. Phil Townsend Hanna, "Conference Gives Impetus to International Highway," *Touring Topics*, December 1930, 20.

42. Hernández, *Migra!*, 122.

43. On race and mobility, see Carpio, *Collisions at the Crossroads*.

44. "A Road to Bind the Americas," *Westways*, December 1930, 11. In addition to extensive coverage in the Los Angeles press, the conference also received attention

in the Mexican press. See "Porvenir en carreteras de la nación: La Conferencia Internacional de Caminos en Los Angeles," *El Nacional*, October 19, 1930; "La Carretera Occidental en México," *La Prensa*, October 18, 1930. On the response of the Los Angeles elite to repatriation, see Sánchez, *Becoming Mexican American*, 209–26; and Gutiérrez, *Walls and Mirrors*, 44–48.

45. Hanna, "Conference Gives Impetus."

46. Rafael de la Colina to the Secretario de Relaciones Exteriores, October 2, 1930, III-23-13, AHSRE; Pascual Ortiz Rubio to the Governors of Sonora, Sinaloa, Nayarit, Michoacán, Mexico, Puebla, Oaxaca, Chiapas, October 3, 1930, expediente 13, registro 7319, año 1930, POR AGN.

47. "Transactions, ACSC."

48. Quoted in Hanna, "Conference Gives Impetus."

49. "Carretera de Sonora a Guatemala," *El Economista*, August 1, 1930; "La Carretera Occidental en México," *La Prensa*, October 17, 1930. On alliances between borderland elites, see Truett, *Fugitive Landscapes*.

50. "Transactions, ACSC."

51. Filiberto Gómez to Pascual Ortiz Rubio, October 1930, expediente 13, registro 7319, año 1930, POR AGN.

52. Harry Carr, "Road Envoys at Tia Juana," *LAT*, October 20, 1930.

53. Carr.

54. Carr.

55. L. F. Bustamante, "Se abre la Convencion de Caminos," *La Opinión*, October 15, 1930. On Mexican state support for the return of Mexican migrants, see Andres, "Invisible Borders," 5; and Balderrama, *Decade of Betrayal*.

56. Bustamante, "Se abre."

57. Hernández, *Migra!*

58. On the increased policing of the U.S.-Mexico border, see St. John, *Line in the Sand*, and Hernández, *Migra!*

59. Transcription of Gómez's speech, "Transactions, ACSC."

60. Delpar, *The Enormous Vogue of Things Mexican*, 55–58.

61. Wild, "If You Ain't Got That Do-Re-Mi," 317–34.

62. "Porvenir en carreteras de la nación," *El Nacional Revolucionario*, October 18, 1930; and "Junta para la construcción de la carretera de EE. UU. a Guatemala," *El Informador*, December 4, 1930.

63. "Se ratifican los acuerdos para la construcción de la Carretera Internacional," *La Prensa*, December 3, 1930.

64. "La gran carretera en la parte de Nayarit," *El Universal*, August 22, 1931; Filiberto Gómez to Pascual Ortiz Rubio, August 22, 1931, expediente 13, registro 7319, año 1931, POR AGN; El Comité Local de Tepic to Pascual Ortiz Rubio, August 16, 1931, expediente 13, registro 7319, año 1931, POR AGN.

65. El Comité Local de Magdalena to Pascual Ortiz Rubio, August 19, 1931, expediente 13, registro 7319, año 1931, POR AGN.

66. "La realización de un magno proyecto," *El Universal*, August 16, 1931.

67. El Comité Local de Nayarit to Pascual Ortiz Rubio, August 16, 1931, expediente 13, registro 7319, año 1931, POR AGN. Gómez also set up local committees in

Guadalajara and Tepic. El Comité Local de Guadalajara to Pascual Ortiz Rubio, August 20, 1931, expediente 13, registro 7319, año 1931, POR AGN.

68. Fulwider, "Driving the Nation," and Waters, "Re-mapping the Nation."

69. "Informe annual de Filiberto Gómez," *Gaceta del Gobierno: Peródico Oficial del Estado de México*, January 20, 1931.

70. "Dedication Set for Tomorrow," *LAT*, September 23, 1932.

71. "Ya esta lista la carretera de Los Angeles a Sonora," *La Prensa*, November 4, 1932; "Ha quedado concluido ya el primer tramo de la Carretera Internacional," *El Nacional Revolucionario*, November 4, 1932; Alfonso Sierra Madrigal to the Secretario de Relaciones Exteriores, February 4, 1931, IV-496-11, AHSRE.

72. Rafael de la Colina to the Secretario de Relaciones Exteriores, January 28, 1932, IV-492-23, AHSRE.

73. Alfonso Sierra Madrigal to the directors of El Aguila, February 13, 1932, IV-492-23, AHSRE.

74. Cadava, *Standing on Common Ground*, 78.

75. Knight, "The Character and Consequences of the Great Depression in Mexico," 213–45; Fulwider, "Driving the Nation."

76. "Mexico Pushes Work on Road," *LAT*, March 4, 1941; "Mexico Awards Contracts for Vital Link in Highway," *LAT*, April 13, 1941.

77. "U.S. and Latin Highway Seen as Friendship Link," *LAT*, November 2, 1941.

78. Fulwider, "Driving the Nation," 95.

79. Ed Ainsworth, "Mexico Marks New Highway Completion," *LAT*, May 5, 1957.

80. Grandin, *Empire's Workshop*, 159–95.

Epilogue

1. On the mural and the refashioning of the plaza, see Estrada, *The Los Angeles Plaza*, 203–29.

2. There is an extensive and growing literature on global cities. See Amen, Archer, and Bosman, *Relocating Global Cities*; Driver and Gilbert, *Imperial Cities*; Marcuse and van Kempen, *Globalizing Cities*; Prakash and Kruse, *The Spaces of the Modern City*; Sassen, *The Global City*; Scott, *Global City-Regions*; and Storper, *The Regional World*.

3. Scott, *Global City-Regions*, 4.

4. Erie, *Globalizing L.A.*

5. Hart, *Empire and Revolution*, 458–66.

6. Hart, 462.

7. Merrill, *Negotiating Paradise*, 6; and Grandin, *Empire's Workshop*, 49.

8. Henry Kissinger, "U.S. Finally Creates a New World Order," *LAT*, July 19, 1993.

9. Grandin, *Empire's Workshop*, 198–201; and Hart, *Empire and Revolution*, 432–58.

10. Abu-Lughod, *New York, Chicago, Los Angeles*, 237–68. Mike Davis argues that Latino populations are remaking and revitalizing American cities. See Davis, *Magical Urbanism*.

11. "North American Trade Talks Gather Steam," *LAT*, July 19, 1992.

12. See Herzog, "Global Tijuana," 119–42.

13. Erie, *Globalizing L.A.*, 212.

14. Erie, 166.

15. For a thoughtful analysis of NAFTA in historical context and by a borderlands historian, see Monroy, *The Borders Within*.

16. Monroy, 13–50.

17. Bobo, Oliver, Johnson, and Valenzuela, *Prismatic Metropolis*.

18. Marcuse and van Kempen, *Globalizing Cities*. It is also important to note that although Los Angeles has very high rates of poverty in Latino communities (due primarily to low wages, documentation status, and underground economies), the region is also home to the largest Latino middle class and the highest rates of Latino home ownership in the nation. See the introductions to Jerry González, *In Search of the Mexican Beverly Hills*, and Vallejo, *Barrios to Burbs*.

19. Mike Davis, *Magical Urbanism*, and Juan González, *Reclaiming Gotham*, 6.

Bibliography

Newspapers and Magazines

El Economista
El Informador
El Nacional
El Nacional Revolucionario
El Universal
Gaceta del Gobierno (Mexico City)
Heraldo de Cuba
La Opinión (Los Angeles)

La Prensa (Los Angeles)
Los Angeles Times
New York Times
New York Tribune
Pan Pacific Progress
Periódico Oficial de Nayarit
Touring Topics
Westways

Archival Collections

Archivo de Centro de Estudios de Historia de México Carso, Mexico City, Mexico
    Colección José Yves Limantour
Archivo General de la Nación, Mexico City, Mexico
    Fondo Lázaro Cárdenas
    Fondo Obregón-Calles
Archivo de Municipio de Mexicali, Baja California
Archivo Histórico de la Secretaría de Relaciones Exteriores, Mexico City, Mexico
Automobile Club of Southern California Archive, Los Angeles, CA
    Report Collection
Colecc*í*on José Y. Limantour, Centro de Estudios de Historia de Mexico,
    Mexico City, Mexico
Colecc*í*on Porfirio Díaz, Universidad Iberoamericana, Mexico City, Mexico
Comisión Agraria Mixta, Mexico City, Mexico
    Población: Quimichis, Municipio: Tecuala, Estado: Nayarit
Huntington Library, San Marino, CA
    Bergman Collection
    Henry Workman Keller Collection
    Robert G. Cleland Papers
    Thomas Bard Collection
    Thomas Bard Collection, Quimichis Colony Addendum
Museum of Ventura County, Ventura, CA
    Livingston Collection
National Archives and Records Administration, College Park, MD
    Records of U.S. and Mexican Claims Commissions, Record Group 76

Registro Agrario Nacional, Tepic, Nayarit
   Expediente: Ejidos, Ejido San Felipe
Seaver Center, Museum of Natural History, Los Angeles
   Los Angeles County Incorporation Records
Secretario de Relaciones Exteriores, Mexico City, Mexico
   Acervo Histórico Diplomático
   Archivo Genaro Estrada
Sherman Library, Corona del Mar, CA
   Anderson Portfolios
   Chandler-Sherman Corporation Collection
   Colorado River Land Company Collection
Universidad Iberoamericana, Mexico City, Mexico
   Archivo Porfirio Díaz
University of California, Davis, Special Collections, Davis, CA
   Bradbury Collection
University of California, Los Angeles, Special Collections, Los Angeles, CA
   Griffith Family Papers
   Phil Townsend Hanna Papers
   William Stark Rosecrans Papers

Books, Reports, and Government Documents

Abu-Lughod, Janet L. *New York, Chicago, Los Angeles: America's Global Cities*: Minneapolis: University of Minnesota Press, 1999.
Adelman, Jeremy, and Stephen Aron. "From Borderlands to Borders: Empires, Nation-States, and the Peoples in between in North American History." *American Historical Review* 104 (June 1999): 814–41.
Almaguer, Tomás. *Racial Fault Lines: The Historical Origins of White Supremacy in California*. Berkeley: University of California Press, 1994.
Amen, M. Mark, Kevin Archer, and M. Martin Bosman. *Relocating Global Cities: From the Center to the Margins*. Lanham, MD: Rowman and Littlefield, 2006.
Andres, Benny J. "Invisible Borders: Repatriation and Colonization of Mexican Migrant Workers along the California Borderlands during the 1930s." *California History* 88, no. 4 (2011): 5–65.
——. *Power and Control in the Imperial Valley: Nature, Agribusiness, and Workers on the California Borderland, 1900–1940*. College Station: Texas A&M University Press, 2016.
Ansell, Martin R. *Oil Baron of the Southwest: Edward L. Doheny and the Development of the Petroleum Industry in California and Mexico*. Columbus: Ohio State University Press, 1998.
Arax, Mark, and Rick Wartzman. *The King of California: J. G. Boswell and the Making of a Secret American Empire*. New York: Public Affairs, 2003.
Avila, Eric. *Popular Culture in the Age of White Flight: Fear and Fantasy in Suburban Los Angeles*. Berkeley: University of California Press, 2006.

Bacevich, Andrew. *American Empire: The Realities and Consequences of U.S. Diplomacy*. Cambridge, MA: Harvard University Press, 2009.
Balderrama, Francisco E. *Decade of Betrayal: Mexican Repatriation in the 1930s*. Albuquerque: University of New Mexico Press, 2006.
———. *In Defense of La Raza: The Los Angeles Mexican Consulate and the Mexican Community, 1929–1936*. Tucson: University of Arizona Press, 1982.
Ballantyne, Tony, and Antoinette Burton. "Empires and the Reach of the Global." In *A World Connecting: 1870–1945*, edited by Emily S. Rosenberg, 285–434. Cambridge, MA: Belknap Press of Harvard University Press, 2012.
Barron, Clarence W. *The Mexican Problem*. Boston: Houghton Mifflin, 1917.
Baud, Michiel, and Willem van Schendel. "Toward a Comparative History of Borderlands." *Journal of World History* 8, no. 2 (1997): 211–42.
Beckert, Sven. *Empire of Cotton: A Global History*. New York: Vintage Books, 2015.
———. "History of American Capitalism." In *American History Now*, edited by Eric Foner and Lisa McGirr, 314–35. Philadelphia: Temple University Press, 2011.
———. *The Monied Metropolis: New York City and the Consolidation of the American Bourgeoisie, 1850–1896*. Cambridge: Cambridge University Press, 1993.
Bederman, Gail. *Manliness and Civilization: A Cultural History of Gender and Race in the United States, 1880–1917*. Chicago: University of Chicago Press, 1995.
Benbow, Mark. *Leading Them to the Promised Land: Woodrow Wilson, Covenant Theology, and the Mexican Revolution*. Kent, OH: Kent State University Press, 2010.
Benjamin, Thomas, and Marcial Ocasio-Meléndez. "Organizing the Memory of Modern Mexico: Porfirian Historiography in Perspective, 1880s–1980s." *Hispanic American Historical Review* 64, no. 2 (1984): 323–64.
Benton-Cohen, Katherine. *Borderline Americans: Racial Division and Labor War in the Arizona Borderlands*. Cambridge, MA: Harvard University Press, 2011.
Berger, Dina. *Pyramids by Day, Martinis by Night*. New York: Palgrave Macmillan, 2005.
Berger, Dina, and Andrew Grant Wood. *Holiday in Mexico: Critical Reflections on Tourism and Tourist Encounters*. Durham, NC: Duke University Press, 2010.
Blaisdell, Lowell L. "Harry Chandler and Mexican Border Intrigue." *Pacific Historical Review* 35, no. 4 (1966): 385–93.
Bloom, Nicholas Dagen, ed. *Adventures into Mexico: American Tourism beyond the Border*. New York: Rowman and Littlefield, 2006.
Bobo, Lawrence, Melvin Oliver, James Johnson, and Abel Valenzuela Jr., eds. *Prismatic Metropolis: Inequality in Los Angeles*. New York: Russell Sage Foundation, 2000.
Brechin, Gray. *Imperial San Francisco: Urban Power, Earthly Ruin*. Berkeley: University of California Press, 2006.
Briggs, Laura. *Reproducing Empire: Race, Sex, Science, and U.S. Imperialism in Puerto Rico*. Berkeley: University of California Press, 2002.
Brown, Jonathan C. *Oil and Revolution in Mexico*. Berkeley: University of California Press, 1993.

Burbank, Jane, and Frederick Cooper. *Empires in World History: Power and the Politics of Difference*. Princeton, NJ: Princeton University Press, 2010.

Burton, Antoinette. *After the Imperial Turn: Thinking with and through the Nation*. Durham, NC: Duke University Press, 2009.

Cadava, Geraldo. *Standing on Common Ground: The Making of a Sunbelt Borderland*. Cambridge, MA: Harvard University Press, 2013.

Camarillo, Albert. *Chicanos in a Changing Society: From Mexican Pueblos to American Barrios in Santa Barbara and Southern California, 1848–1930*. Dallas: Southern Methodist University Press, 1979.

Campbell, Howard, and Josiah McC. Heyman. "The Study of Borderlands Consumption: Potentials and Precautions." In *Land of Necessity: Consumer Culture in the United States-Mexico Borderlands*, edited by Alexis McCrossen, 325–32. Durham, NC: Duke University Press, 2009.

Cánovas, Agustín Cúe. *Ricardo Flores Magón, la Baja California y los Estados Unidos*. Mexico: n.p., 1957.

Carpio, Genevieve. *Collisions at the Crossroads: How Place and Mobility Make Race*. Berkeley: University of California Press, 2019.

Castillo-Muñoz, Veronica. "Divided Communities: Agrarian Struggles, Transnational Migration and Families in Northern Mexico, 1910–1952." PhD diss., University of California, Irvine, 2009.

——. "Historical Roots of Rural Migration: Land Reform, Corn Credit, and the Displacement of Rural Farmers in Nayarit, Mexico, 1900–1952." *Mexican Studies Estudios Mexicanos* 29, no. 1 (2013): 36–60.

——. *The Other California: Land, Identity, and Politics on the Mexican Borderlands*. Oakland: University of California Press, 2017.

Chang, Kornel. *Pacific Connections: The Making of the U.S.-Canadian Borderlands*. Berkeley: University of California Press, 2012.

Coatsworth, John. "Measuring Influence: The United States and the Mexican Peasantry." In *Rural Revolt in Mexico: U.S. Intervention and the Domain of Subaltern Politics*, edited by Daniel Nugent, 64–71. Durham, NC: Duke University Press, 1998.

Cohen, Lizabeth. *A Consumers' Republic: The Politics of Mass Consumption in Postwar America*. New York: Alfred A. Knopf, 2003.

Colby, Jason. *The Business of Empire: United Fruit, Race, and U.S. Expansion in Central America*. Ithaca, NY: Cornell University Press, 2011.

Cooper, Frederick. *Colonialism in Question: Theory, Knowledge, History*. Berkeley: University of California Press, 2005.

Cooper, Frederick, and Ann Laura Stoler, eds. *Tensions of Empire: Colonial Cultures in a Bourgeois World*. Berkeley: University of California Press, 1997.

Cronon, William. *Nature's Metropolis: Chicago and the Great West*. New York: W. W. Norton, 1991.

Culver, Lawrence. *The Frontier of Leisure: Southern California and the Shaping of Modern America*. New York: Oxford University Press, 2010.

Cumberland, Charles C. *Mexican Revolution: The Constitutionalist Years*. Austin: University of Texas Press, 1972.

Cummings, Bruce. *Dominion from Sea to Sea: Pacific Ascendancy and American Power.* New Haven, CT: Yale University Press, 2009.
Davis, Clark. *Company Men: White-Collar Life and Corporate Culture in Los Angeles, 1892–1941.* Baltimore: Johns Hopkins University Press, 2001.
Davis, J. Allen. *The Friend to All Motorists: The Story of the Automobile Club of Southern California through 65 Years, 1900–1965.* Los Angeles: Automobile Club of Southern California, 1967.
Davis, Margaret Leslie. *Dark Side of Fortune: Triumph and Scandal in the Life of Oil Tycoon Edward L. Doheny.* Berkeley: University of California Press, 1998.
Davis, Mike. *City of Quartz: Excavating the Future in Los Angeles.* New York: Vintage Books, 1992.
———. *Magical Urbanism: Latinos Reinvent the U.S. Big City.* New York: Verso, 2001.
Dear, Michael, and Gustavo Leclerc, eds. *Postborder City: Cultural Spaces of Bajalta California.* New York: Routledge, 2003.
Delpar, Helen. *The Enormous Vogue of Things Mexican: Cultural Relations between the United States and Mexico, 1920–1935.* Tuscaloosa: University of Alabama Press, 1992.
Deverell, William. *A Companion to the American West.* Malden, MA: Blackwell, 2004.
———. "The Neglected Twin: California Democrats and the Progressive Bandwagon." In *California Progressivism Revisited,* edited by William Deverell and Tom Sittion, 72–99. Berkeley: University of California Press, 1994.
———. *Railroad Crossing: Californians and the Railroad.* Berkeley: University of California Press, 1994.
———. *Whitewashed Adobe: The Rise of Los Angeles and the Remaking of Its Mexican Past.* Berkeley: University of California Press, 2005.
Deverell, William, and Greg Hise, eds. *A Companion to Los Angeles.* Malden, MA: Wiley-Blackwell, 2010.
Domosh, Mona. *American Commodities in an Age of Empire.* New York: Routledge, 2006.
Drinot, Paulo, and Alan Knight, eds. *The Great Depression in Latin America.* Durham, NC: Duke University Press, 2014.
Driver, Felix, and David Gilbert, eds. *Imperial Cities: Landscape, Display, and Identity.* Manchester, UK: Manchester University Press, 1999.
Dwyer, John J. *The Agrarian Dispute: The Expropriation of American-Owned Land in Postrevolutionary Mexico.* Durham, NC: Duke University, 2008.
Edwards, Rebecca. *New Spirits: Americans in the Gilded Age, 1865–1905.* New York: Oxford University Press, 2006.
Elizondo, Carlos. *The Concept of Property of the 1917 Mexican Constitution.* México, DF: Centro de Investigación y Docencia Económicas, 1993.
Ely, James W. *Guardian of Every Other Right: A Constitutional History of Property Rights.* Cary, NC: Oxford University Press, 2007.
Erie, Steven P. *Globalizing L.A.: Trade, Infrastructure, and Regional Development.* Stanford: Stanford University Press, 2004.

Estrada, William. *The Los Angeles Plaza: Sacred and Contested Space*. Austin: University of Texas Press, 2008.

Ethington, Philip J. "Ab Urbis Condita: Regional Regimes since 13,000 before Present." In *A Companion to Los Angeles*, edited by William Deverell and Greg Hise, 177–215. Malden, MA: Wiley-Blackwell, 2010.

———. "Global Spaces of Los Angeles, 1920s–1930s." In *The Spaces of the Modern City: Imaginaries, Politics, and Everyday Life*, edited by Gyan Prakash and Kevin M. Kruse, 58–98. Princeton, NJ: Princeton University Press, 2008.

Fabian, Ann. *Card Sharps and Bucket Shops: Gambling in Nineteenth-Century America*. New York: Routledge, 1999.

Fingal, Sara. "Your House Es Mi Casa: American Homebuyers in the Baja California Borderlands." *Western Historical Quarterly* 49, no. 1 (2017): 17–41.

Fink, Leon. *The Long Gilded Age: American Capitalism and the Lessons of a New World Order*. Philadelphia: University of Pennsylvania Press, 2014.

Fogelson, Robert M. *The Fragmented Metropolis: Los Angeles, 1850–1930*. Berkeley: University of California Press, 1967.

Foley, Neil. *The White Scourge: Mexicans, Blacks, and Poor Whites in Texas Cotton Culture*. Berkeley: University of California Press, 1997.

Frazer, Chris. *Bandit Nation: A History of Outlaws and Cultural Struggle in Mexico, 1810–1920*. Lincoln: University of Nebraska Press, 2006.

Fulwider, Benjamin. "Driving the Nation: Road Transportation and the Postrevolutionary Mexican State, 1925–1960." PhD diss., Georgetown University, 2009.

Garcia, Matt Garcia. *A World of Its Own: Race, Labor, and Citrus in the Making of Greater Los Angeles, 1900–1970*. Chapel Hill: University of North Carolina Press, 2001.

Gardner, Lloyd. "Woodrow Wilson and the Mexican Revolution." In *Woodrow Wilson and a Revolutionary World, 1913–1921*, edited by Arthur S. Link. Chapel Hill: University of North Carolina Press, 1982.

Gibbon, Thomas E. *Mexico under Carranza: A Lawyer's Indictment of the Crowning Infamy of Four Hundred Years of Misrule*. New York: Doubleday, Page, 1919.

Gilly, Adolfo. *The Mexican Revolution*. New York: New Press, 2005.

González, Jerry. *In Search of the Mexican Beverly Hills: Latino Suburbanization in Postwar Los Angeles*. Newark, NJ: Rutgers University Press, 2018.

González, Juan. *Reclaiming Gotham: Bill De Blasio and the Movement to End America's Tale of Two Cities*. New York: New Press, 2017.

Gottlieb, Robert, and Irene Wolt. *Thinking Big: The Story of the Los Angeles Times, Its Publishers, and Their Influence on Southern California*. New York: G. P. Putnam's Sons, 1977.

Grandin, Greg. *Empire's Workshop: Latin America, the United States, and the Rise of the New Imperialism*. New York: Henry Holt, 2013.

Gray, Paul Bryan. "Judge Ignacio Sepúlveda: A Life in Los Angeles and Mexico City, 1842–1916." *Southern California Quarterly* 95, no. 2 (2013): 141–87.

Greenberg, Amy. *Manifest Manhood and the Antebellum American Empire*. Cambridge: Cambridge University Press, 2005.

Griswold del Castillo, Richard. *The Los Angeles Barrio, 1850–1890: A Social History*. Berkeley: University of California Press, 1982.

Gutiérrez, David G. *Walls and Mirrors: Mexican Americans, Mexican Immigrants, and the Politics of Ethnicity*. Berkeley: University of California Press, 1995.

Haber, Stephen, Armando Razo, and Noel Maurer. *The Politics of Property Rights: Political Instability, Credible Commitments, and Economic Growth in Mexico, 1876–1929*. Cambridge: Cambridge University Press, 2003.

Hall, Linda B., and Don M. Coerver. *Revolution on the Border: The United States and Mexico, 1910–1920*. Albuquerque: University of New Mexico Press, 1988.

Hämäläinen, Pekka, and Samuel Truett. "On Borderlands." *Journal of American History* 98, no. 2 (2011): 338–61.

Hanrahan, Gene Z., ed. *The Bad Yankee: American Entrepreneurs and Financiers in Mexico*, vol. 2. Chapel Hill, NC: Documentary Publications, 1985.

Hart, John Mason. *Empire and Revolution: The Americans in Mexico since the Civil War*. Berkeley: University of California Press, 2002.

———. *Revolutionary Mexico: The Coming and Process of the Mexican Revolution*. Berkeley: University of California Press, 1997.

———. "Social Unrest, Nationalism, and American Capital in the Mexican Countryside, 1876–1920." In *Rural Revolt in Mexico: U.S. Intervention and the Domain of Subaltern Politics*, edited by Daniel Nugent, 72–88. Durham, NC: Duke University Press, 1998.

Hartig, Anthea. "'A Most Advantageous Spot on the Map': Promotion and Popular Culture." In *A Companion to Los Angeles*, edited by William Deverell and Greg Hise, 289–312. Malden, MA: Wiley-Blackwell, 2010.

Hendricks, William Oral. "Guillermo Andrade and Land Development on the Mexican Colorado River Delta, 1874–1905." PhD diss., University of Southern California, 1966.

Hernández, Kelly Lytle. *City of Inmates: Conquest, Rebellion, and the Rise of Human Caging in Los Angeles, 1771–1965*. Chapel Hill: University of North Carolina Press, 2017.

———. *Migra! A History of the U.S. Border Patrol*. Berkeley: University of California Press, 2010.

Herzog, Lawrence A. "Global Tijuana: The Seven Ecologies of the Border." In *Postborder City: Cultural Spaces of Bajalta California*, edited by Michael Dear and Gustavo Leclerc, 119–42. New York: Routledge, 2003.

Hise, Greg. *Magnetic Los Angeles: Planning the Twentieth-Century Metropolis*. Baltimore: Johns Hopkins University Press, 1999.

Hobsbawm, Eric. *Bandits*. New York: Delacorte Press, 1969.

Hoganson, Kristin. *Consumers' Imperium: The Global Production of American Domesticity, 1865–1920*. Chapel Hill: University of North Carolina Press, 2007.

———. *Fighting for American Manhood: How Gender Politics Provoked the Spanish-American and Philippine-American Wars*. New Haven, CT: Yale University Press, 2000.

Horsman, Reginald. *Race and Manifest Destiny: The Origins of American Racial Anglo-Saxonism*. Cambridge, MA: Harvard University Press, 1981.

Hutchinson, William Henry. *Oil, Land, and Politics: The California Career of Thomas Robert Bard.* Norman: University of Oklahoma Press, 1965.

Igler, David. *The Great Ocean: Pacific Worlds from Captain Cook to the Gold Rush.* Oxford: Oxford University Press, 2013.

Immerman, Richard H. *Empire for Liberty: A History of American Imperialism from Benjamin Franklin to Paul Wolfowitz.* Princeton, NJ: Princeton University Press, 2012.

Immerwahr, Daniel. "The Greater United States: Territory and Empire in U.S. History." *Diplomatic History* 40, no. 3 (2016): 373–91.

Instituto Mexicano del Transporte. *Historia de las Juntas Locales de Caminos, 1933–1980.* Mexico City: Instituto Mexicano del Transporte, Secretaría de Comunicaciones y Transportes, 1980.

Irvin, Teresa Williams. *Let the Tail Go with the Hide: The Story of Ben F. Williams.* Bloomington, IN: Unlimited Publishing, 2001.

Jaher, Frederic Cople. *The Urban Establishment: Upper Strata in Boston, New York, Charleston, Chicago, and Los Angeles.* Urbana: University of Illinois Press, 1982.

Johnson, Benjamin H. *Revolution in Texas: How a Forgotten Rebellion and Its Bloody Suppression Turned Mexicans into Americans.* New Haven, CT: Yale University Press, 2003.

Johnson, Benjamin H., and Andrew R. Graybill, eds. *Bridging National Borders in North America: Transnational and Comparative Histories.* Durham, NC: Duke University Press, 2010.

Joseph, Gilbert M., and Jürgen Buchenau. *Mexico's Once and Future Revolution: Social Upheaval and the Challenge of Rule since the Late Nineteenth Century.* Durham, NC: Duke University Press, 2013.

Joseph, Gilbert M., and Daniel Nugent, eds. *Everyday Forms of State Formation: Revolution and the Negotiation of Rule in Modern Mexico.* Durham, NC: Duke University Press, 1994.

Kaplan, Amy, and Donald E. Pease. *Cultures of United States Imperialism.* Durham, NC: Duke University Press, 1994.

Karibo, Holly. *Sin City North: Sex, Drugs, and Citizenship in the Detroit-Windsor Borderland.* Chapel Hill: University of North Carolina Press, 2015.

Katz, Friedrich. *The Life and Times of Pancho Villa.* Stanford: Stanford University Press, 1998.

———. "Pancho Villa and the Attack on Columbus, New Mexico." *American Historical Review* 83, no. 1 (1978): 101–30.

———, ed. *Riot, Rebellion, and Revolution: Rural Social Conflict in Mexico.* Princeton, NJ: Princeton University Press, 2014.

———. *The Secret War in Mexico: Europe, the United States, and the Mexican Revolution.* Chicago: University of Chicago Press, 1984.

Kerig, Dorothy. "Yankee Enclave: The Colorado River Land Company and Mexican Agrarian Reform in Baja California, 1902–1944." PhD diss., University of California, Irvine, 1988.

Knight, Alan. "The Character and Consequences of the Great Depression in Mexico." In *The Great Depression in Latin America*, edited by Paulo Drinot and Alan Knight, 213–45. Durham, NC: Duke University Press, 2014.
———. *The Mexican Revolution*. 2 vols. Lincoln: University of Nebraska Press, 1986.
———. "The United States and the Mexican Peasantry, circa 1880–1940." In *Rural Revolt in Mexico: U.S. Intervention and the Domain of Subaltern Politics*, edited by Daniel Nugent, 25–63. Durham, NC: Duke University Press, 1998.
———. *U.S.-Mexico Relations: An Interpretation*. San Diego: Center for U.S.-Mexican Studies, 1987.
Kramer, Paul. *The Blood of Government: Race, Empire, the United States, and the Philippines*. Chapel Hill: University of North Carolina Press, 2006.
———. "Power and Connection: Imperial Histories of the United States in the World." *American Historical Review* 116, no. 5 (2011): 1348–91.
———. "Race, Empire, and Transnational Identity." In *Colonial Crucible: Empire in the Making of the Modern American State*, edited by Alfred W. McCoy and Francisco A. Scarano, 199–219. Madison: University of Wisconsin Press, 2009.
Kropp, Phoebe. *California Vieja: Culture and Memory in a Modern American Place*. Berkeley: University of California Press, 2006.
Kun, Josh. "Tijuana and the Borders of Race." In *A Companion to Los Angeles*, edited by William Deverell and Greg Hise, 313–26. Malden, MA: Wiley-Blackwell, 2010.
La Botz, Dan. *Edward L. Doheny: Petroleum, Power, and Politics in the United States and Mexico*. New York: Praeger, 1991.
LaFeber, Walter. *The American Search for Opportunity, 1865–1913*. Vol. 2 of *The Cambridge History of American Foreign Relations*, edited by Warren I. Cohen. New York: Cambridge University Press, 1993.
———. *The New Empire: An Interpretation of American Expansion, 1860–1898*. Ithaca, NY: Cornell University Press, 1963.
Lavín, José Domingo. *Petróleo: Pasado, presente y future de una industria Mexicana*. Mexico City: EDIAPASA, 1950.
León-Portilla, Miguel, and David Piñera Ramírez. *Baja California: Historia breve*. México, DF: El Colegio de México, Fondo de Cultura Económica, 2010.
Levy, Jonathan. *Freaks of Fortune: The Emerging World of Capitalism and Risk in America*. Cambridge, MA: Harvard University Press, 2012.
Lewis, Daniel. *Iron Horse Imperialism: The Southern Pacific of Mexico, 1880–1951*. Tucson: University of Arizona Press, 2007.
Lewthwaite, Stephanie. *Race, Place, and Reform in Mexican Los Angeles: A Transnational Perspective, 1890–1940*. Tucson: University of Arizona Press, 2009.
Limerick, Patricia. *Legacy of Conquest: The Unbroken Past of the American West*. New York: W. W. Norton, 1987.
Link, Arthur S., ed. *Woodrow Wilson and a Revolutionary World, 1913–1921*. Chapel Hill: University of North Carolina Press, 1982.
Lipman, Jan. *Guantánamo: A Working-Class History between Empire and Revolution*. Berkeley: University of California Press, 2008.

Lou, Dennis W. "Fall Committee: An Investigation of Mexican Affairs." PhD diss., Indiana University, 1963.

Love, Eric T. L. *Race over Empire: Racism and U.S. Imperialism, 1865–1900*. Chapel Hill: University of North Carolina Press, 2004.

Lummis, Charles. *Awakening of a Nation*. New York: Harper and Brothers, 1898.

MacLachlan, Colin M. *Anarchism and the Mexican Revolution: The Political Trials of Ricardo Flores Magón in the United States*. Berkeley: University of California Press, 1991.

Maggor, Noam. *Brahmin Capitalism: Frontiers of Wealth and Populism in America's First Gilded Age*. Cambridge, MA: Harvard University Press, 2017.

Marcuse, Peter, and Ronald van Kempen, eds. *Globalizing Cities: A New Spatial Order?* Malden, MA: Blackwell, 2000.

Martínez, María Elena. *Genealogical Fictions: Limpieza de Sangre, Religion, and Gender in Colonial Mexico*. Stanford: Stanford University Press, 2008.

Martínez, Pablo. *Historia de Baja California*. Mexico: Editorial Baja California, 1960.

Maurer, Noel. *The Empire Trap: The Rise and Fall of U.S. Intervention to Protect American Property Overseas, 1893–2013*. Princeton, NJ: Princeton University Press, 2013.

McCoy, Alfred W., and Francisco A. Scarano, eds. *Colonial Crucible: Empire in the Making of the Modern American State*. Madison: University of Wisconsin Press, 2009.

McCrossen, Alexis, ed. *Land of Necessity: Consumer Culture in the United States–Mexico Borderlands*. Durham, NC: Duke University Press, 2009.

McWilliams, Carey. *Southern California: An Island on the Land*. Salt Lake City: Peregrine Smith Books, 1973.

Meinig, Donald W. "American Wests: Preface to a Geographical Interpretation." *Annals of the Association of American Geographers* 62 (1972): 159–84.

Menéndez, Gabriel Antoni. *Doheny el Cruel: Espisodios de la sangrienta lucha por el petróleo mexicano*. Mexico City: Ediciones Bolsa Mexicana del Libro, 1958.

Merrill, Dennis. *Negotiating Paradise: U.S. Tourism and Empire in Twentieth-Century Latin America*. Chapel Hill: University of North Carolina Press, 2009.

Meyer, Lorenzo. *Mexico and the United States in the Oil Controversy, 1917–1942*. Austin: University of Texas Press, 1977.

Miller, Roberta Balstad. *City and Hinterland: A Case Study of Urban Growth and Regional Development*. Westport, CT: Greenwood Press, 1979.

Moehring, Eugene P. *Urbanism and Empire in the Far West, 1840–1890*. Reno: University of Nevada Press, 2004.

Molina, Natalia. *Fit to Be Citizens? Public Health and Race in Los Angeles, 1879–1939*. Berkeley: University of California Press, 2006.

Monroy, Douglas. *The Borders Within: Encounters between Mexico and the U.S.* Tucson: University of Arizona Press, 2008.

———. *Rebirth: Mexican Los Angeles from the Great Migration to the Great Depression*. Berkeley: University of California Press, 1999.

Naylor, Elaine. *Frontier Boosters: Port Townsend and the Culture of Development in the American West*. Montreal: McGill-Queen's University Press, 2014.

Needham, Andrew. *Power Lines: Phoenix and the Making of the Modern Southwest*. Princeton, NJ: Princeton University Press, 2016.

Niemeyer, E. V., Jr. *Revolution at Querétaro: The Mexican Constitutional Convention of 1916–1917*. Austin: University of Texas Press, 1974.

Ninkovich, Frank. *The United States and Imperialism*. Malden, MA: Blackwell, 2001.

Norton, Marcy. "Tasting Empire: Chocolate and the European Internalization of Mesoamerican Aesthetics." *American Historical Review* 111, no. 3 (2006): 660–91.

Nugent, Daniel, ed. *Rural Revolt in Mexico and U.S. Intervention*. San Diego: Center for U.S.-Mexican Studies, University of California, San Diego, 1988.

———, ed. *Rural Revolt in Mexico: U.S. Intervention and the Domain of Subaltern Politics*. Durham, NC: Duke University Press, 1998.

Painter, Nell Irvin. *Standing at Armageddon: The United States, 1877–1919*. New York: W. W. Norton, 1987.

Perry, Louis B., and Richard S. Perry. *A History of the Los Angeles Labor Movement, 1911–1941*. Berkeley: University of California Press, 1963.

Pisano, Donald. "The Squatter and Natural Law in Nineteenth-Century America." In *Agricultural History* 81 (Fall 2007): 443–63.

Pitt, Leonard. *The Decline of the Californios: A Social History of the Spanish-Speaking Californians, 1846–1890*. Berkeley: University of California Press, 1966.

Pletcher, David M. *Rails, Mines, and Progress: Seven American Promoters in Mexico, 1867–1911*. Ithaca, NY: Cornell University Press, 1958.

Pomeranz, Kenneth, and Steven Topic. *The World that Trade Created: Society, Culture, and the World Economy*. Armonk, NY: M. E. Sharpe, 1999.

Prakash, Gyan, and Kevin M. Kruse, eds. *The Spaces of the Modern City: Imaginaries, Politics, and Everyday Life*. Princeton, NJ: Princeton University Press, 2008.

Pubols, Louise. "Born Global: From Pueblo to Statehood." In *A Companion to Los Angeles*, edited by William Deverell and Greg Hise, 20–39. Malden, MA: Wiley-Blackwell, 2010.

Raat, William Dirk. "The Diplomacy of Suppression: Los Revoltosos, Mexico, and the United States, 1906–1911." *Hispanic American Historical Review* 56, no. 4 (1976): 529–50.

Renda, Mary. *Taking Haiti: Military Occupation and the Culture of U.S. Imperialism*. Chapel Hill: University of North Carolina Press, 2001.

Rocco, Raymond A. "Latino Los Angeles: Reframing Boundaries/Borders." In *The City: Los Angeles and Urban Theory at the End of the Twentieth Century*, edited by Allen J. Scott and Edward W. Soja, 365–89. Berkeley: University of California Press, 1996.

Romo, Ricardo. "Work and Restlessness: Occupational and Spatial Mobility among Mexicanos in Los Angeles." *Pacific Historical Review* 46, no. 2 (1977): 157–80.

Rosenberg, Emily S. *Spreading the American Dream: American Economic and Cultural Expansion, 1890–1945*. New York: Hill and Wang, 1982.
———, ed. *A World Connecting, 1870–1945*. Cambridge, MA: Belknap Press of Harvard University Press, 2012.
Ruiz, Jason. *Americans in the Treasure House: Travel to Porfirian Mexico and the Cultural Politics of Empire*. Austin: University of Texas Press, 2014.
Ruíz, Ramón. *The Great Rebellion: Mexico, 1905–1924*. New York: W. W. Norton, 1980.
Russell, Thomas Herbert. *Mexico in Peace and War*. Chicago: Reilly and Britton Syndicate, 1914.
Sabin, Paul. "Home and Abroad: The Two 'Wests' of Twentieth-Century United States History." *Pacific Historical Review* 66, no. 3 (1997): 305–35.
Samaniego, Marco Antonio. *Nacionalismo y revolución: Los acontecimientos de 1911 en Baja California*. Tijuana, Mexico: Universidad Autónoma de Baja California, 2008.
Sánchez, George J. *Becoming Mexican American: Ethnicity, Culture, and Identity in Chicano Los Angeles, 1900–1954*. New York: Oxford University Press, 1993.
Sandos, James A. *Rebelión en la frontera: El anarquismo y el Plan de San Diego, 1904–1923*. Ciudad Victoria, Tamaulipas, Mexico: Gobierno del Estado de Tamaulipas, 2010.
Santiago, Myrna. *The Ecology of Oil: Environment, Labor, and the Mexican Revolution, 1900–1928*. Cambridge: Cambridge University Press, 2006.
———. "Rejecting Progress in Paradise: Huastecs, the Environment, and the Oil Industry in Veracruz, Mexico, 1900–1935." *Environmental History* 3, no. 2 (1998): 169–88.
Sassen, Saskia. *The Global City: New York, London, Tokyo*. Princeton, NJ: Princeton University Press, 1991.
Saxton, Alexander. *The Indispensable Enemy: Labor and the Anti-Chinese Movement in California*. Berkeley: University of California Press, 1975.
Schell, William, Jr. *Integral Outsiders: The American Colony in Mexico City, 1876–1911*. Wilmington, DE: Scholarly Resources, 2001.
Schoultz, Lars. *Beneath the United States: A History of U.S. Policy toward Latin America*. Cambridge, MA: Harvard University Press, 1998.
Scott, Allen J., ed. *Global City-Regions: Trends, Theory, Policy*. Oxford: Oxford University Press, 2001.
Scott, Allen J., John Agnew, Edward W. Soja, and Michael Storper. "Global City-Regions." In *Global City-Regions: Trends, Theory, Policy*, edited by Allen J. Scott, 11–30. Oxford: Oxford University Press, 2001.
Scott, Allen J., and Edward W. Soja, eds. *The City: Los Angeles and Urban Theory at the End of the Twentieth Century*. Berkeley: University of California Press, 1996.
Self, Robert. "City Lights: Urban History in the West." In *A Companion to the American West*, edited by William Deverell, 412–41. Malden, MA: Blackwell, 2004.
Sitton, Tom, and William Deverell, eds. *Metropolis in the Making: Los Angeles in the 1920s*. Berkeley: University of California Press, 2001.
Slootjes, Danielle. "Local 'Potentes' in the Roman Empire: A New Approach to the Concept of Local Elites." *Latomus* 68, no. 2 (2009): 416–32.

Smith, Neil. *American Empire: Roosevelt's Geographer and the Prelude to Globalization*. Berkeley: University of California Press, 2004.
——. *Uneven Development: Nature, Capital, and the Production of Space*. Athens: University of Georgia Press, 1984.
Starr, Kevin. *Endangered Dreams: The Great Depression in California*. New York: Oxford University Press, 1996.
——. *Material Dreams: Southern California through the 1920s*. New York: Oxford University Press, 1990.
Stern, Alexandra Minna. *Eugenic Nation: Faults and Frontiers of Better Breeding in Modern America*. Berkeley: University of California Press, 2005.
Stevens, Errol Wayne Stevens. "Two Radicals and Their Los Angeles: Harrison Gray Otis and Job Harriman." *California History* 84, no. 3 (2009): 44–70.
St. John, Rachel. *Line in the Sand: A History of the Western U.S.-Mexico Border*. Princeton, NJ: Princeton University Press, 2011.
Storper, Michael. *The Regional World: Territorial Development in a Global Economy*. New York: Guilford Press, 1997.
Stout, Joseph A., Jr. *Border Conflict: Villistas, Carrancistas, and the Punitive Expedition, 1915–1920*. Fort Worth: Texas Christian University Press, 1999.
Tannenbaum, Frank. *The Mexican Agrarian Revolution*. Washington, DC: Brookings Institution, 1968.
Tatum, Donn B., Jr. "General William S. Rosecrans and the Rancho Sausal Redondo." *Southern California Quarterly* 51, no. 4 (1969): 275–312.
Taylor, Frank, and Earl Welty. *Black Bonanza*. New York: McGraw Hill, 1958.
Taylor, William B. *Drinking, Homicide, and Rebellion in Colonial Mexican Villages*. Stanford: Stanford University Press, 1979.
Torres-Rouff, David. *Before L.A.: Race, Space, and Municipal Power in Los Angeles, 1781–1894*. New Haven, CT: Yale University Press, 2013.
Trachtenberg, Alan. *The Incorporation of America: Culture and Society in the Gilded Age*. New York: Hill and Wang, 1982.
Trubowitz, Peter. *Defining the National Interest: Conflict and Change in American Foreign Policy*. Chicago: University of Chicago Press, 1998.
Truett, Samuel. *Fugitive Landscapes: The Forgotten History of the U.S.-Mexico Borderlands*. New Haven, CT: Yale University Press, 2006.
Truett, Samuel, and Elliott Young, eds. *Continental Crossroads: Remapping U.S.-Mexico Borderlands History*. Durham, NC: Duke University Press, 2004.
U.S. House of Representatives. *Hearings before the Committee on Immigration and Naturalization, Western Hemisphere Immigration*, 71st Congress, 2nd Session. Washington, DC, 1930.
U.S. Senate. *Preliminary Report and Hearings of the Committee on Foreign Relations*, 66th Congress, 1st Session, Document No. 185. Washington, DC, 1920.
Valdés-Ugalde, Francisco. "Janus and the Northern Colossus: Perceptions of the United States in the Building of the Mexican Nation." *Journal of American History* 86 (1999): 568–600.
Vallejo, Jody. *Barrios to Burbs: The Making of the Mexican American Middle Class*. Stanford: Stanford University Press, 2012.

Vanderwood, Paul J. *Satan's Playground: Mobsters and Movie Stars at America's Greatest Gaming Resort.* Durham, NC: Duke University Press, 2010.

Vanderwood, Paul J., and Frank N. Samponaro. *Border Fury: A Picture Postcard Record of Mexico's Revolution and U.S. War Preparedness, 1910–1917.* Albuquerque: University of New Mexico Press, 1988.

Vaughn, Mary Kay. "Cultural Approaches to Peasant Politics in the Mexican Revolution." *Hispanic American Historical Review* 79 (1999): 269–305.

Veeser, Cyrus. *A World Safe for Capitalism: Dollar Diplomacy and America's Rise to Global Power.* New York: Columbia University Press, 2005.

Wallerstein, Immanuel. *The Capitalist-World Economy: Essays.* Cambridge: Cambridge University Press, 1979.

———. *World Systems Analysis: An Introduction.* Durham, NC: Duke University Press, 2004.

Waters, Wendy. "Re-mapping the Nation: Road Building as State Formation in Post-Revolutionary Mexico, 1925–1940." PhD diss., University of Arizona, 1999.

Wexler, Laura. *Tender Violence: Domestic Visions in an Age of U.S. Imperialism.* Chapel Hill: University of North Carolina Press, 2000.

White, Richard. *"It's Your Misfortune and None of My Own": A New History of the American West.* Norman: University of Oklahoma Press, 1991.

Wiebe, Robert H. *The Search for Order, 1877–1920.* New York: Hill and Wang, 1967.

Wild, Mark. "If You Ain't Got That Do-Re-Mi: The Los Angeles Border Patrol and White Migration in Depression Era California." *Southern California Quarterly* 83, no. 3 (2001): 317–34.

———. *Street Meeting: Multiethnic Neighborhoods in Early Twentieth-Century Los Angeles.* Berkeley: University of California Press, 2005.

Williams, William Appleman. *The Tragedy of American Diplomacy.* New York: W. W. Norton, 1959.

Womack, John. *Zapata and the Mexican Revolution.* New York: Vintage Books, 1970.

Woolsey, L. H. "The Settlement of Claims between the United States and Mexico." *American Journal of International Law* 30, no. 1 (1936): 99–102.

Worster, Donald. *Rivers of Empire: Water, Aridity, and the Growth of the American West.* Oxford: Oxford University Press, 1992.

Index

Page numbers in *italics* indicate figures. Page numbers in *italics*, followed by "*m*," refer to maps. Page numbers in *italics*, followed by "*t*," refer to tables.

Acaponeta, 67, 77, 154, 156, 266
Agrarian Claims Commission, 169, 171–72
agraristas: demands of, 142, 144–45, 147, 150; encroachment by, 153, 154; land redistribution and, 157, 158, 160–62, 165–66, 168–69, 170, 173, 174, 244–45n1; organization of, 149–50; U.S.-Mexican Claims Commissions and, 170
agriculture, 30, 45, 64, 143, 157, 192, 210; citrus crops, 21, 28–29; cotton demand, 21, 48, 99–100, 162; nonwhite labor force, 61–62, 115; Quimichis Colony and, 66–67, *89*
Agua Prieta Plan (1920), 244n76
air travel, 202
Alaska, 23, 179
All Year Club (Los Angeles), 198
American Club (Mexico City), 41
American empire. *See* empire
American West, 182, 192, 226n8; capitalist development of, 13, 23, 31, 32, 33; racialized labor and, 49–52, 54, 61; status of investor class in, 229n28; territorial expansion, 10, 11, 12, 31, 228n20, 229n25; urban boosterism, 5–6, 9–10
anarchists, 83, 103, 114
Anderson, Ora, 40
Andrade, Guillermo, 24, 37, 38, 53, 55; as first Mexican consul to Los Angeles, 44–45, 46, 47

Anglo-Americans, 5–6, 48, 49–50, 56; takeover of California by, 26–29, 37, 234n5
anti-Americanism, 109
Applegate, Moray, 95, 142, 154–55, 156, 157, 159–60
Arías, Vicente, 93–94
Article 27 (Mexican Constitution), 115–18, 125, 127; land reform and, 142, 144, 155, 156, 157, 159, 161, 162; U.S. oil producers and, 138, 140, 144, 164
Asian workers, 61, 99–100, 147, 162
Automobile Club of Southern California, 19, 176, 179, 182, 185–93, *187*, 202; map of route of, *177*
automobiles, 180, 182, 186, 201
Avila, Antonio Ygnacio, 33
Avilés, Balthazar, 98

Baja California, 19, 41, 179, 184, 195, 196; California trade with, 100; economic development and, 147–48, 162, 164, 167, 168; investment properties, 21–22, 22, 37, 52–53, 97–98, 100, 123, 174; postrevolutionary period, 147, 161, 166, 167, 168–69, 246n34, 248n75, 249n88; pro-business governors of, 163; revolutionary factions and, 84–86, 97, 98–99, 138; two districts of, 245n15. *See also* Colorado River Land Company; Quimichis Colony; San Isidro Ranch Company

banana investors, 118
bandits, 90, 93–94
banking interests, 31, 35, 163–64
Banning, Phineas, 40
Bard, Richard (son), 154, 157, 158, 159, 160
Bard, Thomas, 19, 63–65, 72, 75, 90, 93; on costs of Mexican Revolution, 92, 174–75; racialized labor system and, 63, 64–65, 67, 68; U.S. Senate seat of, 65; wealth of, 64, 173–77. *See also* Quimichis Colony
Barra, Francisco León de la, 86
Beverly Hills, 19, 70, 205
Blanco Vigil, Cayetano, 182–83, 202, 203, 204
Board of Trade (Los Angeles), 38–39, 42
boosters, 5–6, 9, 10, 16, 39, 230n37; definitions of, 228n22
borderlands, 18, 197; cross-border tourism and, 180, 183, 186–87, 201, 231n48; dynamics of, 203–4; International Pacific Highway and, 19, 180–81, 185–204; investments in, 10, 14, 15, 23–24, 30–31, 52–53, 182; investor losses in, 143–44; Los Angeles ties with, 6–7, 9, 16, 20, 26, 30–31, 39, 46–47, 51, 59, 86, 151–52, 182, 229n28; Mexican migrants and, 209–10; Mexican reordering of power in, 147–54, 188; studies of, 230–31n42; transborder networks, 40–42, 46; U.S. imperial expansion and, 7–8, 30; World War II defenses and, 209; Zimmermann telegram and, 127; *zona prohibida*, 151, 246n35. *See also* Baja California
Border Patrol, U.S., 211
Bradbury, Lewis, 1–3, 5, 7, 30–31, 38
Bradbury Building, 1, 19, 31; interior of, 2, 205
Bradbury mine, 3
Bucareli Treaty (1923), 140, 164, 178
Butler, E. C., 58

Calexico, 100, 195
California Development Company, 41
California-Mexico Land and Cattle Company, 48
California territory: land system, 68; mission system, 187–88
Californios (*gente de razón*), 25–26; elites, 49–50, 63–65, 67, 68, 72; intermarriage with, 50; transfer of wealth from, 26
Calles, Plutarco Elías, 161, 168
Camarillo family, 63–64
Camp, John, 138–39
Canfield, Charles, 69, 70
Cantú, Esteban, 105, 109, 138; CRLC investors and, 97, 98, 99, 101; dictatorial policies of, 147–48, 149; pro-business successors of, 163
capitalism: American expansion of, 9, 13–16, 23, 26, 30–33, 64, 65, 119, 121, 204, 207; Golden Age of, 227n14; international corporate, 112–13; international highway project and, 179; Los Angeles investors and, 7–8, 11, 174, 227n14, 228–29n24; Mexican revolutionary rejection of, 17, 78–79, 93, 94, 112, 114, 115, 120, 170; racial undertones of, 51, 61, 62, 64, 67, 119–20, 121, 127
Cárdenas, Lázaro, 140, 143, 144, 190, 201, 251n37; land redistribution and, 152, 158, 168, 169, 170
Carr, Harry, 184, 195–96
Carranza, Venustiano: American property owners and, 132, 133, 137–38, 155, 241–42n17; consolidation of Mexican federal government by, 102; Constitution of 1917 and, 116; Gibbon's indictment of, 134–36, 137–38; militant unionism and, 103; Obregón's successful coup against, 101, 138, 139–40, 244n76; ouster of Victoriano Huerta by, 120–21, 238n21; Quimichis

270 Index

property and, 94–95, 97, 98, 105; U.S. recognition of, 106, 120; Villa and, 84, 88, 89–90, 95, 105, 106–7, 238n21
Castillo-Muñoz, Veronica, 156
Catedral Metropolitana de la Asunción de María (Mexico City), 205–6
Catholicism, 69, 70–71
cattle ranching, 21, 30
Cave, John, 95
Cerro Azul No. 4 (oil well), 70
Chamber of Commerce, Los Angeles, 13, 21–22, 39, 42–44, 46, 61, 123; investment in Mexican railroad, 166–67; seaport traffic statistics, 180
Chandler, Harry, 19, *165*, 205, 206; background of, 54, 122; Calexico canal project and, 100; claims complaints and settlements and, 171–72; congressional testimony on racialized labor and, 48, 49, 50, 62; on CRLC as civilizing influence, 169, 171–72; Gibbon partnership with, 111, 122, 123, 125–26, 134; influence and wealth of, 48–49, 54–55, 65, 173–74, 210; International Pacific Highway and, 151, 181, 184, 192, *193*; Mexican Constitution and, 116, 117; Mexican consulate and, 46; Mexican investments and, 65, 68, 174, 181; Mexican presidents and, 97, 160–61, 162, 163, 164–70, 178; Mexican Revolution and, 85, 96, 97–98, 99, 105, 109, 178; Otis family ties with, 6, 45, 48, 54; postrevolutionary Mexican connections of, 160–70, 176, 178, 183; promotion of regional growth by, 53, 58–59; San Isidro Ranch and, 41, 146, 151. *See also* Colorado River Land Company
Chester Place (Los Angeles), 70, 71
Chickamauga, Battle of (1863), 32
Chinese workers, 61, 99–100, 147, 162
citrus crops, 21, 28–29

city-empire, 5–6, 8–9, 12, 22, 60, 81, 127–28, 140, 206, 207–9, 210
Claims Commissions. *See* Agrarian Claims Commission; U.S.-Mexican Claims Commissions
Código Agrario (Agrarian Code), 158
Colina, Rafael de la, 201
Colorado Land Commission, 169–70, 249n88
Colorado River Land Company, 22, 41, 51, 55–60, *59*, 68, 75, 113, 128; Chandler's defense of, 169, 171–72; Claims Commission settlement and, 171–72; founding members of, 123; Gibbon and, 123, 125, 130; investment strategies of, 60; irrigation issues and, 65; land losses of, 168, 169, 249n88; lobbying campaign and, 128; lucrative economics of, 99–110; Mexican Article 27 and, 117; Mexican elite and, 62, 109, 161; Mexican Revolution and, 80, 81, 85, 96, 97–99, 101, 107, 109, 208; postrevolutionary status of, 161–63, *163*, 164, 166, 167–70; property tract leasing by, 99, *163*; property transfers and, 145; purchase and scope of, 52–53
Columbus (New Mexico), 105–6, 120
Comisión Permanente for the Carretera Internacional del Pacifico, 182, 198
Constitution of 1917. *See* Mexican Constitution of 1917
Coolidge, Calvin, 178
copper mining, 21, 30, 45–46
corporations, 96, 112–13, 210, 227n14
Cortina, Eduardo, 151–52
cotton, 21, 48, 99–100, 162
Crabb, Henry A., 27
Cuba, 14, 54, 79, 111, 117; U.S. interventions in, 65, 118, 121, 124, 125, 130, 132, 135, 139
Cuéllar, José María, 189

Index 271

Dato, Frederico, 138–39
Davis, Margaret Leslie, 69
Debs, Eugene V., 85
Delpar, Helen, 198
del Valle family, 63–64
Democratic Party, 111, 122
Depression of 1930s, 191, 192, 196, 197–98, 201
Deverell, William, 26–27, 122
Díaz, Porfirio, 7, 12, 14, 15–16, 63, 234n52; administration policies of, 57–58, 62, 67, 114, 115, 118, 156, 158; flight to France of, 118; Los Angeles Consulate and, 44, 45; Los Angeles investors' relationships with, 24, 31, 46, 51, 52, 54, 79, 81, 83–84, 86, 97, 108–9, 130, 133, 140, 161, 170; Mexican oil production and, 71–73; Mexican Revolution and, 34, 82, 83, 84, 86, 88–89, 96, 97, 102; Otis friendship with, 52–54, 56, 57–58, 60; racial background of, 56; resistance to regime of, 82, 83, 115; Sepúlveda and, 41
diplomacy, 23–24, 33–34, 171–72, 178; hard- vs. soft-power and, 179; hemispheric friendship rhetoric and, 35, 198, 208; International Pacific Highway and, 195–96; postrevolutionary Mexico and, 143–44; U.S. recognition of Mexico, 164
Doheny, Edward L., 63, 68–74, 75, 86, 113–41; background of, 69; business alliances of, 97, 101; challenge to Mexican Constitution by, 116, 117, 142; Fall Committee hearings and, 132–33; lobbying campaign of, 113–14, 119–22, 127–37, 143, 178; Los Angeles home of, 71, 72, 82; Mexican local oligarchy and, 102–3, 104, 105; Mexican revolutionary factions and, 99, 109, 118–19, 241–42n17; NAPARM and, 127–28, 243n47; oil riches of, 6, 19, 173, 205 (see also Mexican Petroleum Company); Pélaez relationship with, 102–4; Teapot Dome scandal and, 132, 173; union organizers and, 243n63; U.S. occupation of Veracruz and, 120
Doheny, Edward L., Jr., 132
"dollar diplomacy," 136
Dominican Republic, U.S. intervention in, 51, 79, 112, 118, 120, 136
Dow Jones & Company, 119
Duarte rancho, 2
Dunn, W. C., 77, 78, 89–90, 92–94, 108
Dwyer, John, 144, 168

East, Earnest, 184, 188
economic depression. See Depression of 1930s
Edwards, William, 146
ejido lands, 158, 168, 169, 243n63
Elías, Francisco, 186, 188–89, 192, 194
elites, 11–12, 14, 76, 174, 181, 228–29n24
El Pueblo de Nuestra Señora La Reina de Los Angeles de Porciuncula. See Los Angeles
empire, 1, 7–12, 32–47, 209–13; American continental expansion and, 9–11, 12, 29, 30, 31–33, 35–39, 51, 61, 65, 75, 228n20; borderlands and, 7–8, 22, 30–32, 209; building of, 2, 10, 23–26, 69, 111–41, 117–18n16, 228n23; capitalism and, 11, 35, 61, 96, 228n21; definitions of, 228nn17; economics of, 10, 24, 81, 206–7; expansionism and, 7–10, 22, 25, 30–32, 35; free trade and, 11, 13, 19, 180, 202, 204; Gibbon propaganda campaign and, 123–30; global interventions and, 80–81, 95, 112–13, 116–21, 124, 132, 141, 145, 178; Good Neighbor Policy and, 159, 178, 182, 204, 209; ideology and, 13, 35–36; "informal," 11–12, 16, 31–47, 54, 80–81, 111, 112, 205, 207,

227–28n16; labor force and, 60–61; language of, 5–6; literature on, 229n25; Los Angeles as, 5–13, 22–25, 38–40, 46–47, 52, 53, 60, 72, 76, 81, 86, 93, 100, 105, 127–28, 140, 169, 181, 206, 207–9, 210; Manifest Destiny and, 25, 35–36; Mexican challenge to, 78–79, 86, 92, 93, 94, 96, 142–43, 170–71; Mexican diplomatic relations and, 178; Monroe Doctrine and, 35, 36, 80; new type of, 178, 179, 209, 210; racialization and, 12, 13–14, 15, 24, 36, 48, 51, 53–54, 56, 63, 69, 113, 119–20, 121, 124, 132–33, 235nn9,11; regional economies and, 11, 137–41; resistance to, 79–80; as revolution trigger, 109; Roosevelt Corollary and, 80, 112; "soft power" tools of, 179; tourist sites and, 188; urban dimensions of, 22, 227n13
Escuela Primeria Cuauhtémoc, 147
Espinosa, Martín, 88, 155–56
Ethington, Philip J., 229n28
expansionism. *See* empire

Fall, Albert Bacon, 131–34
farmers. *See* agriculture
Flores Magón, Ricardo and Enrique, 8, 82–86; arrest and imprisonment of, 85, 86, 98, 114; return from prison of, 105–6; revolt (1911) of, 97, 98
foreign investments, 46, 109–10, 111, 209, 210, 228n21; campaign for U.S. interventions and, 116–18 (*see also* NAPARM); impact in Mexico of, 67, 80, 130–31; Mexican Constitution and, 116–17; Mexican postrevolutionary restrictions on, 151, 166, 208; Mexican Revolution and, 78, 80, 87, 114, 132; middle-class Americans and, 65–66; in nineteenth-century Mexico, 33–35, 46; Obregón promotion of, 163, 166; racialized labor force and, 61–76; U.S. government policy and, 112, 118. *See also* empire; land; Los Angeles investor class
free trade, 11, 12, 13, 18, 19, 20, 46–47, 179, 180, 202, 204, 211. *See also* globalization
Fulwider, Benjamin, 202

Gallardo, Leopoldo, 190
Gibbon, Thomas, 59, 111–14, 122–41, 142; background of, 122; challenge to Mexican Constitution by, 116, 117; economic worldview of, 111, 112, 134–35; eulogy for, 122–23; imperialism and, 123–25, 127, 130–31, 132, 134–37, 139, 140, 143, 178; lobbying campaign of, 113–14 (*see also* NAPARM); *Mexico under Carranza* (Gibbon), 134–36; political network of, 125
Gilded Age, 7, 8, 11, 14, 28, 227n14
Gilly, Adolfo, 87
globalization, 13, 19, 22, 51, 179, 202, 204, 206, 207–9, 212, 213
Godínez, José Santos, 156
Goldman, Emma, 83
Gómez, Filiberto, 182, 183, 184, 192, 193, 193, 194–95, 196–97, 199, 246n34
Gonzalez, Juan, 213
Good Neighbor Policy, 159, 178, 182, 204, 209
Good Roads movement, 179
Grandin, Greg, 206
Grant, Ulysses S., 34
Greene, William, 102
Griffith, Griffith J., 3–5, 7, 30–31, 38
Griffith Park, 3–4, 4, 19, 31, 205
Guadalajara, 186, 200
Guadalupe Hidalgo, Treaty of (1848), 26
Guinn, James Miller, 122
Gulf of Mexico, 70, 100

hacienda system, 67, 87–88
Haiti, 117, 118, 120, 136

Hale, George Ellery, 4
Hanna, Phil Townsend, 187–88
Hanson, Don Ole, 195
Harding, Warren G., 132, 138, 140, 164
"hard power," 179
Harriman, Job, 83
Hart, John Mason, 206
Hawaii, 54, 79, 117, 145
Hearst, Phoebe, 41
Hearst, William Randolph, 41
hemispheric friendships, 18, 35, 176, 178, 179, 181, 183, 198, 208
Hernández, Kelly Lytle, 197
Hernández, Pablo, 159
Hidalgo, Guido, 90
highways. *See* International Pacific Highway; roads and highways
hinterlands, 14, 174, 175, 203, 208; "informal" empire and, 47; International Pacific Highway and, 180–81, 182, 197; Los Angeles investments in, 15, 18, 20, 22, 28–30, 38, 39–42, 43, 51, 54–55, 61, 62, 67; Mexican Revolution's impact on, 16, 17, 76, 78, 86–96, 106, 113, 115, 140–43, 152–55; racial ideology and, 48, 50
Honduras, 118
Hoover, Herbert, 178, 184, 196
House Committee on Immigration and Naturalization, U.S., 48, 49
Huasteca oil region, 68, 70–75, 102–4, 243n63
Huerta, Adolfo de la, 84, 101, 102, 139
Huerta, Victoriano, 88, 97, 118–19, 120, 238n21, 241n17
Huntington, Collis, 36–37

immigrants, 28, 61, 99–100, 147, 162, 196; late twentieth-century, 210, 211–12. *See also* Asian workers; Mexican migrants
imperial systems. *See* empire
Imperial Valley, 59, 65, 99, 168

Incorporation of America, The (Trachtenberg), 227n14
indigenous peoples, 25, 26, 103, 119, 124; as labor source, 27, 50, 58, 61, 66, 67, 68, 76; land claims and, 14, 62, 72, 73, 82, 154, 155–56. *See also* mestizos
industrialization, 227n14
"informal" empire, 11–12, 16, 33–47, 111, 112, 170; definition of, 227–28n16; Rosecrans ideology and, 35–36, 47, 54, 63, 207
Interior Department, U.S., 132
International Conference of American States, 184
International Monetary Fund, 209
International Pacific Highway, 13, 19, 176–204, 208–9, 246n34; changing roles of, 201–3; completion of (1957), 203; Depression of 1930s effect on, 197–98; hemispheric friendship rhetoric and, 198; inception of (1929), 180, 203; length of, 179; Los Angeles meeting on, 190–98, *193*; Mexican entry point, 201; Mexican regional tensions and, 199–200; Mexican tourism and, 185–87, *187*; Nogales entry point, 201, 202; opening of first section, 200–201; promoters of, 151, 181–84, 186–87, *193*; route of, *177m*, 184, 188, 189; tourist sites and, 188, 194, 198; traveler issues and, 191–92
International Workers of the World, 85
investments. *See* foreign investments; Los Angeles investor class (*specific types*)
irrigation, 21, 41, 65, 130, 165–66, 167

Jalisco, 186, 189, 199
Japanese workers, 61, 99–100
Johnson, Andrew, 31
Jonathan Club, 146
Juárez, Benito, 34

Katz, Friedrich, 15, 115
Keller, Henry Workman, 19, 41, 146, 149, 163, 206; background of, 181–82; International Highway project and, 151, 181–82, 183, 191, 192, 193, 202, 203, 246n34; wealth of, 173–74
Kerckhoff, William G., 146
Kerig, Dorothy, 162
Kissinger, Henry, 204, 210
Knight, Alan, 52
Knox, Philander, 92
Kramer, Paul, 227–28nn13,16,17, 228n20

labor, 48–76; acts of resistance by, 76, 80, 230n33 (*see also* strikes); empire building and, 60–61; industrial hierarchy of, 74; Merchants and Manufacturers Association and, 13, 21–22, 39, 46, 57, 61, 123, 141; Mexican constitutional reforms and, 116; oil industry and, 74–75, 103, 133, 243n63; open shop, 61, 69 (*see also* unions); racialized system of, 14, 16–17, 28–29, 30, 48–51, 57–62, 64, 66–69, 73–76, 99, 103, 115. *See also* Mexican workers
LaFeber, Walter, 81, 109, 112, 227nn14,16
land, 142–75; Agrarian Claims Commission, 169, 171–72; Bard purchases of, 63–64; definitions of private property debates and, 144; *ejido*, 158, 168, 169, 243n63; empire and, 10; hacienda system and, 67, 87–88; indigenous displacement from, 62, 72, 73, 82–83, 154, 155–56; Mexican Cession (1848), 246n35; Mexican Constitution and, 142, 144, 155, 156, 157, 159, 161, 162; Mexican expropriations of, 104, 115–18, 120, 141–45, 152–59, 161–62, 166–69, 172, 173, 178, 208, 244–45n1; Mexican local organizers and, 144–45, 243n63 (see also *agraristas*); Mexican privatization of, 14–15, 62, 67–68, 72–73, 114; redistribution of, 144–45; speculation in, 21; squatters and, 33, 149–50, 162; Teapot Dome Scandal and, 132; transnational investment properties, 55; U.S.-Mexican Claims Commissions, 144, 170–72, 178, 249n91; *zona prohibida*, 151, 246n35
Land Claims Act (1851), 33
Lane, Franklin K., 111, 116, 122, 125, 126
Latin America, 8, 31, 79, 96; Good Neighbor Policy, 159, 178, 182, 204, 209; U.S. interventions in, 80–81, 112–13, 118, 120, 178, 179. *See also* Monroe Doctrine (*specific countries*)
League of Nations, 137
Lee, T. F., 130–31
Lerdo de Tejada, Sebastián, 234n52
Liliuokalani, Queen of Hawaii, 145
Limantour, José Yves, 70, 71
lobbying, 112–13, 127–28
Looking Backward (Bellamy), 1
Los Angeles: Anglo-American arrivals in, 22–29, 54, 63, 122–23; as city-empire, 5–6, 8–9, 12, 22, 60, 81, 127–28, 140, 206, 207–9, 210 (*see also* Los Angeles investor class); Board of Trade, 38–39, 42; boosterism, 5–6, 11–12, 13, 16, 20, 21–22, 25, 38–39, 42–44, 46, 47; cross-border networks, 46–47 (*see also* borderlands; hinterlands); deep-water port, 20, 39, 44, 122, 123, 180, 206; early history of, 6–7, 10, 23, 25–27, 183; elites (*see* Los Angeles investor class); first gated community of, 70; Flores Magón brothers and, 82, 83, 85, 86; founding (1781) of, 25; global connections of, 20, 207–11, 229n28; growth of, 9, 65, 180–81, 206, 210–11; historical presences in, 205–14; iconic landmarks of, 1, 3–4, 4, 19, 31, 205; in late twentieth century, 205–7; as majority white, 27, 28, 174, 230n37,

Index 275

Los Angeles (cont.)
234n5; Mexican affinities of, 136–37, 182, 205; Mexican and Mexican American population, 27–28, 29, 40–42, 50, 61, 65, 210, 212–13, 230n39, 254n18; Mexican consulate in, 42–45, 46–49, 53; Mexican Revolution and, 17–18, 78, 79, 80–110, 113–14, 142, 207–8; population, 27, 28, 29, 38, 180; postrevolutionary Mexico and, 16, 144–48, 176–213; racial rhetoric and, 14, 17, 47, 48–59, 113–14, 230n37; railroads 28, 36–37, 44, 234n5; regional strategies of, 59–60; tourism, 19, 28, 30, 179, 180, 183, 194, 198, 205; transnational highway (*see* International Pacific Highway)

Los Angeles investor class, 1–35, 79, 86, 111, 122–23, 171, 174, 181, 205, 228–29n24; characteristics of, 11–12; commercial empire of, 5–13, 21–25, 31–49, 51–55, 60, 65–76, 81, 86, 93, 100, 105, 127–28, 140, 169, 181, 206, 207–9, 210, 215–23; companies incorporated to conduct business in Mexico (1886–1931), 215–23; configuration of power of, 143; late nineteenth-century wealth of, 3–35; lobby for protection of, 116–20, 123–24, 127–28, 134–37; Mexican Revolution-related losses of, 98–99, 109, 112, 115, 118–19, 123, 126, 130, 143; Mexican-sourced wealth of, 1, 2, 3, 5–9, 11, 12, 14, 15, 19–22, 24, 28, 30–31, 32, 35, 39–40, 41, 46–47, 51–53, 55–56, 58–60, 62, 65–66, 75–76, 81, 108–9, 111, 112, 130–31, 136–37, 164, 173, 178–79, 205, 206, 207, 234nn57,58; networks of business and political ties, 7, 29–30, 40–44, 46–47, 52, 75, 97, 118, 123; oligarchy of, 62, 85, 105, 106, 113–18, 124–25, 131; postrevolution shifting economic priorities of, 180; racialized rhetoric and, 113; regional strategies of, 59–60; Rosecrans ideology and, 36–37; San Isidro Ranch members, 145–47; Senate Fall Committee hearings and, 132–33; U.S. government relations and, 112–13

Los Angeles Suburban Homes Company, 48

Los Angeles Terminal Railway Company, 122

Los Angeles Times, 5, 6, 12, 30, 39, 45, 167, 182, 204, 210, 211; on arrest of Flores Magón brothers, 84, 85; bombing of building of, 230n33; editorials praising Díaz, 56, 57–58; Gibbon eulogy, 122; imperial expansion promotion, 54; on International Pacific Highway, 184, 200, 202; Kissinger statement, 204, 210; Mexican correspondent, 56, 57, 58, 60; on Mexican revolutionary threat, 105–7; Obregón portrayals in, 167, 168; Otis-Chandler ownership of, 6, 12, 19, 53, 211; urban development promotion, 21

Lummis, Charles, 56, 57, 60
Lyttle, Herman, 158

Madero, Francisco, 84, 85, 86, 102, 241n17; Huerta coup against, 88, 97, 101, 238n21; Los Angeles investor ties with, 97, 118–19

Magonistas. *See* Flores Magón, Ricardo and Enrique

Manifest Destiny, 25, 35–36
masculinity, 146–47
Maurer, Noel, 112, 136
Maximilian I, Emperor of Mexico, 40
Mazatlán, 37, 89, 92, 93
Mejía, Marcelino Magaña y, 165–66, 248n75
Menédez, Miguel Angel, 184

Merchants and Manufacturers Association, 13, 21–22, 39, 42, 46, 57, 61, 123, 141
mestizos, 119, 124, 234n5; Díaz ancestry, 56; displacement of, 62, 82; as labor force, 27, 50, 58, 66, 67, 68, 76
Mexicali, 55, 65, 85, 100, 162, 164, 168–69
Mexican Americans, 14, 16, 40–42, 197, 204; in Los Angeles, 27–28, 29t, 50, 61, 65, 210, 212–13, 230n39, 254n18; Mexican Revolution and, 83; racialization of, 29, 54, 64; sale of land by, 64; transborder networks of, 40–42; vigilante campaigns against, 26
Mexican-American War, 11, 17–18, 25, 32, 35; consequences of, 25–26, 27, 246n35
Mexican Automobile Association, 182–83
Mexican Central Railroad strike, 57–58
Mexican Colonization and Industrial Company, 37
Mexican Constitution of 1917, 109, 114, 125, 126, 127, 142; antiforeign provisions of, 115–18, 130; effects of, 140; land reform and (*see* Article 27)
mexicanidad, 182, 183, 188, 189–90
Mexican migrants, 48, 54, 61, 64, 83, 209–10, 211; International Pacific Highway use by, 197; repatriation and, 191–92. *See also* Mexican workers
Mexican Outlook (NAPARM publication), 129, 130
Mexican Petroleum Company, 51–52, 62–63, 68–75, 101–4, 117, 118–19, 205; Doheny sale of assets of, 173; founding of, 70; lobbying campaign, 128, 132–33, 138; Mexican elite and, 109; Mexican Revolution impact on, 80, 81, 96, 102, 107, 109, 208
Mexican Problem, The (Barron), 119–20, 121

Mexican Revolution: Carranza and, 101, 138, 139–40, 241–42n17, 244n76; consequences of (1920–40), 143–45; constitutionalists and, 88 (*see also* Constitution of 1917); Díaz flight and, 118; economic nationalism and, 90, 113–14; factional conflict and, 84, 88, 95, 97, 98, 102, 105, 136, 238n21; Flores Magón brothers and, 82–84, 97; heaviest fighting areas, 87; Huerta and, 88, 97, 100, 101, 120, 238n21, 241n17; impact on Los Angeles investors, 16, 17–18, 76–110, 112–15, 118–20, 123, 126, 128, 130, 140–43, 152–60, 172–75, 207–8; local political power and, 142; looting and, 89–90; Madero and, 84–85, 86, 88, 97; nationalistic rhetoric of, 104, 109; oil industry boom during, 101–2, 103, 241–42n17; Pershing Expedition (*see subhead* U.S. Punitive Expedition); roots of, 6–7, 8, 9, 14–15, 62, 78–80, 82–84; as social revolution, 114–15; U.S. armed intervention advocates, 17, 81, 85, 92, 107–22, 127, 128–41, 143, 155, 164, 178; U.S. lessons learned from, 178–79; U.S.-Mexico Special Claims Commissions, 170–72, 249n91; U.S. Punitive Expedition, 120–21, 125, 127, 136; U.S. Veracruz occupation, 102, 120; violence of, 77, 107; Zimmermann telegram, 127. *See also* Mexico, postrevolutionary
Mexicans, 14, 40, 63, 147, 196–97, 204; elites, 49, 50, 51, 52–55, 56; in Los Angeles, 27–28, 50, 61, 65, 210, 212–13, 230n39, 254n18; racialization of, 54
Mexican workers, 16, 54, 55, 67–68, 80, 83, 84, 87–88, *88*, 114, 121, 135, 136, 144–45, 158, 192, 196, 197, 210; Californian justification for, 62,

Index   277

Mexican workers (cont.) 64–65, 192, 207; Chandler characterization of, 48–49; crossing of U.S. border by, 197; hierarchy of race and class and, 73–75; revolt of, 80; Southern Californian definition of, 51

Mexico: coastlines, 27, 183–84, 189, 190, 203, 246n35; consulate in Los Angeles, 42–45, 46–47, 53; oil region, 6, 19, 68, 70–75, 101–4, 119, 144, 243n63; Porfiriato, 12, 31, 52, 57–58, 67, 234n52; railroads, 34, 35, 65, 67, 71; Rosecrans ambassadorship to, 23–24, 33–34; ties with Southern California, 9, 18–19, 28–29, 30, 60 (*see also* Los Angeles investor class); transborder networks, 38–42 (*see also* borderlands); U.S. imperialism and, 124, 205; U.S. influence in, 151, 234n52; wealth extracted from, 19; white aristocracy, 49, 50; *zona prohibida* (prohibited zone), 151, 246n35. *See also* borderlands: hinterlands

Mexico, postrevolutionary, 143–213; borderlands importance to, 143; Bucareli Treaty (1923), 140; Depression (1930s) effects on, 201; foreign investments and, 151, 166, 179, 208, 209–10; NAFTA effects on, 204, 210; presidents, 143–44, 158; road building, 13, 19, 182, 188, 190, 199, 202–3 (*see also* International Pacific Highway); tourism, 181, 182–83, 185–88, 189, 194, 195–96, 198, 200, 201, 202, 204; U.S. Claims Commission, 170–72, 178; U.S. Good Neighbor Policy, 159, 178, 182, 204, 209; U.S. official recognition of, 164; U.S. relations, 143–45, 164, 170–72, 176, 178–79, 195–96, 204, 208; World War II and, 201–2

Miller, John, 31–32

mining, 3, 5, 21, 30, 31, 32, 45, 91, 118, 182, 210

Mixed Agrarian Commission, 169, 171
Molina, Natalia, 49
Monroe Doctrine, 35, 36, 93, 178; Roosevelt Corollary, 80, 112, 118
Morrow, Dwight, 178
motion picture industry, 180

NAFTA (North American Free Trade Agreement), 204, 210–12
NAPARM (National Association for the Protection of American Rights in Mexico), 117–18, 127, 128–30, 164, 196, 243n47; policies and goals of, 129–31, 132, 136, 137, 139
National Agrarian Commission, 156
National Bank of Commerce, 89
National Commission of Tourism, 186, 192
native population. *See* indigenous peoples
nativism, 192, 212
Nayarit, 66, 67, 95, 96, 106, 192; anti-Americanism and, 93; Godínez as governor of, 156; International Pacific Highway and, 199–200; land claims and, 154, 156, 158, 168; revolutionary activity and, 82, 86, 87, 88. *See also* Quimichis Colony
Nemer, C. Modesto, 138
neocolonialism, 35
neoliberalism, 207
New Left historians, 227n16, 228n21
New Mexico, 105, 106, 120–21, 131–32
"new presidency," 81
Nicaragua, 80, 118
Nogales, 185, 192, 200, 201, 202
nonwhite populations: as labor source, 61–63, 115; racial hierarchy ranking of, 61–62, 76; U.S. paternalism and, 113; various forms of, 49. *See also* Mexicans; Mexican migrants; Mexican workers
North American Free Trade Agreement, 204, 210–12

Obregón, Álvaro, 165; Chandler friendship with, 98, 161, 162–63, 164, 165, 166–68, 170, 178; coup against Carranza (1920) and, 101, 139–40, 244n76; factional revolutionary action and, 88, 97, 98; foreign oil producers and, 103, 104, 138, 140; land expropriation and, 143, 156, 161–62, 166; U.S. official recognition of, 140, 164–65, 167

Occidental College, 19

oil resources, 30, 82, 119, 120, 121; Carranza policies and, 241–42n17; Huasteca region and, 68, 70–75, 102–4, 243n63; importance in global market of, 101; labor and, 74–75, 103, 133, 243n63; Los Angeles wealth and, 6, 19, 173, 180, 205, 206; Mexican Article 27 and, 138, 140, 144, 164; Mexican nationalization of, 173; Southern California and, 64, 69–70; U.S. Senate committee hearings, 132–33; world's largest oil well and, 70. *See also* Mexican Petroleum Company

Olvera Street renovation, 205

open shop, 61, 69

organized labor. *See* strikes; unions

Ortiz Rubio, Pascual, 192, 195, 196, 198, 201

Osborne, Henry Z., 107

Otis, Harrison Gray, 12, 44, 46, 52–59, *55*, 68, 85, 86; anti-unionism of, 58, 61, 120; background of, 53–54; Chandler family ties with, 6, 45, 48, 54; Colorado River Land Company, 41, 51, 59, 65, 80, 96; Díaz friendship with, 52–54, 58, 60; empire and, 53–54, 65, 180, 207; Gibbon investment partnership with, 111, 123; labor force and, 60, 75; Madero ties with, 97

Otis, Marian (Mrs. Harry Chandler), 54

Pacific Ocean, 176, 179, 181; coastline, 18–19, 27, 183–84, 189, 190, 203 (*see also* International Pacific Highway); Los Angeles port, 20, 39, 44, 122, 123, 180, 206; U.S. trade, 100

Panama, 54

Panama Canal, 20, 80, 180

Pan-American Highway, 184

Partido Liberal Mexicano, 83–84, 85

Partido Nacional Revolucionario, 182

Pasadena, 65–66, 82, 89

Pastor, Luis, 192

Pastora Perez, María (Mrs. Moray Applegate), 154

paternalism, 151, 169, 174

Pelaecistas, 102–3, 105

Peláez Gorrochótegui, Manuel, 102–3, 104, 109

Pennsylvania Railroad, 34

peons. *See* Mexican workers

Pershing, John J., 120–21, 125, 127, 136

petroleum. *See* oil resources

Philippines, 14, 51, 79; U.S. control of, 12, 53, 95, 111, 117, 121, 124, 130, 135, 139, 154, 235n9

Platt Amendment, 121

Plunkett, Hugh, 132

Porfiriato (1876–1911). *See* Díaz, Porfirio

prohibited zone, 151, 246n35

property rights, 17, 57, 110, 127, 141; Cantú disregard for, 147–48; Chandler concessions and, 167; Mexican Constitution and, 115–18, 130, 144–45; Mexican reform laws and, 156–57; Quimichis Colony and, 155–60; revolutionaries and, 89–90, 94, 108, 112, 114–15, 118; San Isidro Ranch and, 145–54; U.S. government protection of, 118; U.S. investors and, 141, 143, 181; U.S.-Mexican Claims Commission and, 171–72. *See also* land

Proposition 187, 212

Index 279

Pubols, Louise, 25
Puerto Rico, 54, 111, 117, 124
Pullman Strike (1894), 230n33
Punitive Expedition, 120–21, 125, 127, 136

Quimichis Colony, 51–52, 62–68, 75, 78; agricultural richness of, 66–67, 88; Applegate management of, 142, 154–55; Claims Commission settlement and, 172; founding of (1910), 62–63, 65; investors in, 66–68, 173; Mexican elite and, 109; Mexican property expropriation and, 154–59, 162, 208; murder of Windham and, 77–78, 93–95, 105, 106, 107–8, 109, 142, 154, 237n1; revolutionary impact on, 80, 81, 82, 86, 87–91, 92–96, 106, 108, 109, 125, 154–57

racial identity: capitalism and, 119–20, 121, 132; as color-based hierarchy, 49–50, 60, 73–74; control of colonized peoples and, 12 (*see also* empire); division of labor and, 49–52, 73–75 (*see also* labor); hierarchy of, 49, 61–62, 65, 73–75, 115, 127, 230n37; Los Angeles development and, 13, 14, 16, 17, 25, 26, 28, 29, 41, 47, 48–76, 113–14, 115, 122, 123–24, 174, 197, 230n37, 234n5; Manifest Destiny and, 25; Mexican elite and, 49, 50, 51, 52–55, 56; Southern California and, 14, 49–50, 61–63, 68, 89, 132. *See also* mestizos; whiteness
railroads, 20, 22, 28, 31, 34, 36–37, 44, 45, 122, 123, 202, 234n5; Los Angeles investors in, 166–67; Mexico and, 34, 35, 57–58, 65, 67, 71, 82, 164, 166–67, 168; petroleum fuel and, 69, 71; strikes, 57–58, 230n33; transcontinental, 28
ranches, 21, 30, 87
Rancho Ojai, 64
Rancho San Pedro, 63

Rancho Santa Clara, 63
Rancho Sausal Redondo, 33, 38
Rancho Simi, 63
Rawles, Joseph, 65–66
real estate, 31, 32, 33, 37, 54, 63, 173; Los Angeles boom in, 28
Regeneración (newspaper), 82, 83, 106
repatriations, 192, 196, 197
roads and highways, 100, 147, 151, 202–3, 208. *See also* International Pacific Highway
Robinson, Henry M., 200
Rodríguez, Abelardo, 161
Romero, Abelino, 153–54
Romero, Matías, 31
Roosevelt, Franklin D., 178
Roosevelt, Theodore, 112, 118
Roosevelt Corollary, 80, 118; statement of, 112
Rosecrans, William, 12, 23–24, 32, 33–38, 39, 40, 44; informal empire ideology and, 35–36, 47, 54, 63, 207; labor force and, 60; "Manifest Destiny, the Monroe Doctrine, and Our Relations with Mexico," 35–36; venture capitalism and, 65
Rosenberg, Emily, 13
Rouaix, Pastor, 115
Ruiz, Jason, 56

Sabin, Paul, 228n20
St. John's Seminary, 205
Sainz, José, 159
Sánchez-Albarrán, Ramón, 157, 158
sanctuary city, 212
San Diego, 20, 98, 145–47, 183, 195, 209
San Domingo Improvement Company, 112
San Felipe indigenous community, 156
San Francisco, 9, 20, 26, 27, 28, 123, 207; labor unions, 39; mining projects, 32
San Isidro Ranch Company, 41, 145–54, 173; borderlands location of, 151–52;

Cantú's occupation of property of, 148–49; Claims Commission monetary settlement with, 171–72; founders of, 181; "friends of Mexico" self-designation, 151; Mexican challenges to, 149–50, 152, 162
San Pedro, Los Angeles, and Salt Lake Railway, 122
Santa Barbara County, 63–65
Santa Fe and Mexican Central Railroad, 37
Santa Fe Railway, 69
Santiago, Myrna, 73–74, 103, 243n63
Sassen, Saskia, 227n15
Scott, Allen J., 227n15
Scott, Thomas A., 63, 64
Self, Robert, 9–10
Senate, U.S., 65; Fall Committee hearings, 131, 132–34
Sepúlveda, Ignacio, 24, 38, 40–42, 46, 47, 53
Seward, William H., 24, 40
Shepherd, C. J., 43
Sherman, Moses, 99
Sinaloa, 3, 87, 88, 89, 192
Siqueiros, David Alfaro, 205
Smith, Neil, 11, 226n8
Snyder, Meredith, 45, 46
"soft power," 179
Sonora, 27, 32, 87, 182, 186, 188, 192
Southern California: agricultural productivity, 28–29, 61–62, 64, 192, 210; Anglo-American extralegal killings in, 26–27; Anglo-American investors in, 30, 59–60, 67, 71, 172; Anglo-American takeover of, 26–27, 33, 37, 54, 63–65, 72, 126; elite transplants to, 11–12, 16, 49–50; International Pacific Highway and, 189, 190; labor union suppression and, 39, 75; Mexican cooperation and, 183–84; Mexican labor force and, 48, 51, 61–62, 64–65, 75, 115; Mexico's west coast and, 18–19 (see also International Pacific Highway); oil resources of, 64, 69–70; Pacific trade and, 100; racialized systems and, 14, 49–50, 61–63, 68, 89, 132; Spanish romanticized past and, 183, 186–88, 195–96, 201; tourism promotion, 180, 201; transfer of wealth, 26. See also borderlands; hinterlands; Los Angeles
Southern Pacific Railroad, 28, 36–37, 45, 88, 168, 189
Spanish-American War, 12, 20, 53, 112, 154
Spanish language, 30
Spanish missions, 183, 187–88
Spanish romanticized colonial past, 28, 182–83, 186–88, 195–96, 201, 204
Special Claims Commission, 144, 170–71, 172, 249n91
squatters, 33, 149–50, 162
Starr, Kevin, 1
State Department, U.S., 136, 171
Stearns, Abel, 27
Sterling, Christine, 205
stock options, 234nn57,58
Storper, Michael, 227n15
strikes, 103, 104, 114, 116; railroad, 57–58, 230n33
Symon, Robert, 37

Taft, William Howard, 81, 108, 113, 118, 120
Tampico oil fields, 70, 71, 133
Teapot Dome Scandal, 132, 173
Tecuala Indians, 155–56
Tijuana, 85, 180, 183, 185, 195, 196
tourism, 19, 28, 30, 179–89, *187*, 191, 200–205; airplane, 202; automobile, 180, 201; cross-border, 180, 181, 183, 186–87, 195–96, 198, 199, 201, 231n48
travel. *See* International Pacific Highway; tourism
Trevino, Manuel Perez, 168

Index   281

trucking, 202–3, 206
Trump, Donald, 212

unions, 13, 122, 141, 168; Díaz policies and, 57–58; Mexican oil workers and, 103, 104, 243n63; Mexican Revolution and, 85; open-shop system vs., 61, 69; suppression of, 39, 75; violence and, 230n33. *See also* strikes
Union Station (Los Angeles), 122
University of Southern California, 19, 70, 205
U.S. imperialism. *See* empire
U.S.-Mexican Commission for Wartime Cooperation, 209
U.S.-Mexico border. *See* borderlands
U.S.-Mexican Claims Commissions, 170–72, 178, 249n91
U.S.-Mexican General Claims Commission, 171, 249
U.S.-Mexican Special Claims Commission, 144, 170, 172

Valentine, William L., 146
Ventura County, 63, 64–65, 66
venture capitalists, 34, 65, 130
Veracruz, 70, 74, 97, 99; militant oil workers, 103; U.S. occupation (1914) of, 102, 120
Versailles Treaty (1919), 137
Villa, Francisco "Pancho," 8, 94; Article 27 and, 116; Los Angeles and, 105; Pershing's Punitive Expedition against, 120–21, 125, 127, 136; raid on New Mexico by, 105, 106, 120–21; revolutionary factions and, 84, 88, 95, 97, 98, 102, 238n21
Villaseñor, Alejandro, 192
Vizcaíno, José Zuloaga, 157

Walker, William, 26–27
Wall Street Journal, 119
Wells Fargo, 41
West, U.S. *See* American West
whiteness, 26–29, 37, 49–50; capitalism and, 120, 127; as Los Angeles majority, 27, 28, 174, 230n37, 234n5; masculinity and, 146, 147; property ownership and, 120; redefinitions of, 51, 56
Williams, William Appleman, 227n16
Wilson, Henry Lane, 120
Wilson, Woodrow, 113, 116, 131, 155; Latin American interventions and, 118; Mexican intervention lobby and, 124, 125, 126, 132, 136, 138–39, 141, 178; Mexican policies and, 108, 122, 151, 164, 238n21; Pershing expedition and, 127; Veracruz occupation and, 102, 120
Winder, William, 37
Windham, William S., 67, 78, 82, 86, 90–94; background of, 89; killing of, 77–78, 93–95, 105, 106, 107–8, 109, 142, 154, 237n1; restrictive policies of, 90–91. *See also* Quimichis Colony
workers. *See* labor; Mexican workers; unions
World War I, 127, 131, 136, 155
World War II, 179, 201–2, 209, 210

xenophobia, 192, 213

Zapata, Emiliano, 8, 84, 95, 97, 102, 116, 238n21; Punitive Expedition against, 120–21, 125, 127, 136
Zimmermann telegram, 127
zona prohibida (prohibited zone), 151, 246n35

www.ingramcontent.com/pod-product-compliance
Lightning Source LLC
Chambersburg PA
CBHW021653230426
43668CB00008B/613